Nationalism, Anti-Semitism,
and Fascism in France

Nationalism, Anti-Semitism, and Fascism in France

MICHEL WINOCK

Translated by
Jane Marie Todd

Stanford University Press
Stanford, California
1998

Stanford University Press
Stanford, California
© 1998 by the Board of Trustees of the
Leland Stanford Junior University

Originally published as *Nationalisme,
antisémitisme et fascisme en France*
in 1982 by Editions du Seuil.

Printed in the United States of America

Assistance for the translation was provided by the
French Ministry of Culture.

CIP data appear at the back of the book

Contents

Tables

Introduction

THIS BOOK, which might also have been called "The National Ego and Its Ills," addresses three principal themes. First, there is the theme of *nationalism*—or rather, nationalism*s*, since the word can be defined in several ways. I have emphasized the two types known to France: open nationalism, stemming from the optimistic philosophy of the Enlightenment and from memories of the Revolution (Michelet's nationalism, but also General de Gaulle's), and closed nationalism, based on a pessimistic vision of historical evolution, the prevailing idea of decadence, and an obsession with protecting, strengthening, and immunizing collective identity against all agents of corruption, true or supposed, that threaten it.

Second, I have attempted to delve into that closed nationalism by means of the imaginary order it has constructed for itself. Politics is constructed less on reason than on myths and mythologies. What camp could claim to escape them? Might not the illusion of political rationalism be the ultimate myth? Nevertheless, the demonology and hysteria of the far right have gone beyond ordinary fictions: it is in the throes of a permanent *anti-Semitic* frenzy. On this theme, I have reprinted studies that were part of my *Edouard Drumont et Cie* (Seuil, 1982), complementing them with new approaches to the problem.[1]

In addition, I felt it necessary to deal with two other categories of France's political history: *Bonapartism* and *fascism*, which are in league with nationalism, and which have attracted new interest recently among historiographers.

In a final section, these three themes are illustrated through particular case histories of politicians and writers who, in one way or another, have marked the history of French nationalism with its variations and contradictions.

PART ONE

French Nationalism

CHAPTER 1

Open Nationalism and Closed Nationalism

IMMEDIATELY following the legislative elections of 1902, which were won by the Bloc des Gauches (Bloc of leftist parties), Charles Péguy wrote in *Les Cahiers de la Quinzaine*:

The elections have proved that the nationalist impulse is much more solid, much more intense, much more unified, much more outspoken than expected. The particular quarrels between the principal anti-Semites and the principal nationalists cannot conceal the danger of anti-Semitism and nationalism from us. On the contrary, if the nationalist parties, poorly led by rival leaders, have nonetheless obtained these results, who cannot see that these parties must have solid support and solid majorities behind them? Movements so far-reaching, so profound, so lasting, are not fabricated through stratagems or artifice.[1]

That word *nationalist*, used here by a writer who was himself called a "nationalist" some ten years later, was of recent coinage. Dictionaries indicate it first appeared in 1798, but throughout the nineteenth century, it was only a learned and forgotten word, which Littré overlooked in his great dictionary compiled during the Second Empire. It was only in the last ten years of that century that the adjective—and the corresponding noun—came to designate a political tendency placed clearly on the right, and even the far right. It appears that the introduction of the word can be attributed to an article by Maurice Barrès in *Le Figaro* in 1892.[2]

In French, moreover, the words "nationalism" and "nationalist" are ambiguous. The same term is used to characterize two different historical movements, which sometimes followed each other, sometimes appeared simultaneously. First, there is the nationalism of peoples who aspire to create a sovereign nation-state—this movement is sometimes also called *nationalitaire*—which in Europe resulted in the treaties that ended World War I and completed the destruction of the great empires. In the twentieth century, that *nationalitaire* movement, which I shall henceforth call "nationalist," was primarily conducted by colonized peoples; the result was access to independence by Third World states. In addition, the same word, "nationalism," has been used, especially since the Dreyfus affair, to label the diverse doctrines that, in an already constituted state, subordinate everything to the exclusive interests of the nation, that is, the nation-state: to its force, its power, and its greatness.

In principle, France could have experienced only the second kind of nationalism, since its unity and sovereignty were achieved long ago. But the reality is not so simple, since one might say that France and the French Revolution directly or indirectly contributed to the nationalist movement that stirred up and reconstructed Europe throughout the twentieth century. At the end of the eighteenth century, nationalism merged with the democratic impulse. When the soldiers of Valmy shouted "Long live the nation!" in September 1792, as the first Republic was about to be founded, that cry not only asserted patriotic enthusiasm in the face of foreign armies, it also asserted the liberty and equality of a sovereign people. To the Europe of dynasties, it opposed the Europe of nations; to the Europe of monarchs, the Europe of citizens.

Hence, France experienced a nationalism before the fact, a nationalism on the left, republican, based on popular sovereignty and calling upon enslaved nations to deliver themselves from their chains. That nationalism has its own history. But it would be wrong to imagine that between this nationalism of "patriots" and the nationalism of "nationalists" (those who adopted the word—Barrès, Déroulède, Maurras, and so many others), a watertight partition existed that isolated one from the other. Between these two movements, we find passageways, convergences, even compromises.

Republican Nationalism

It all began with the French Revolution. The Declaration of the Rights of Man and of the Citizen declared: "The principle of all sovereignty resides essentially in the nation. No body, no individual can exercise authority that does not expressly emanate from it" (article 3). With these words, the Constituent Assembly displaced the source of legitimacy from the hereditary monarch to the French people as a whole: the ancien régime monarchy, and later, monarchy as a whole, was abolished. Laws were to be the expression of "the general will." Logically, that national sovereignty implied the idea of national independence. What was a nation? Not the random collection of populations under the scepter of a dynasty that, at the mercy of wars and matrimonial strategies, varied in its dimensions and composition. No, the nation was itself the result of a general will. Hence, the feast of the Federation on 14 July 1790 posited the principle of the French people's voluntary membership in the national community. That included those who, according to the old law, had depended on foreign sovereigns: the pope for residents of Avignon (Comtat Venaissin was reunited with France in 1791); the German sovereign princes (*Landesfürsten*) for the Alsatians. On 28 October 1790, Merlin de Douai, standing before the National Assembly, replied to dynastic Europe, which was protesting these national principles:

Today, when kings are generally acknowledged to be only the representatives and mandatories of the nations for which they were once considered owners and masters, what is the significance to the people of Alsace, what is the significance to the French people, of the agreements that, in despotic times, were designed to unite the former with the latter? *The Alsatian people have been joined to the French people because they willed it so.*[3]

That will anticipated the upheavals in the political map of Europe: the freedom of peoples to decide for themselves was the revolutionary idea that was to redraw every border. The nationalist movement, which was to spread like wildfire across the continent in 1848, was the first to merge the principles of nationality and democracy. The nationalism of republican France was universal in its vocation: "The God of nations has spoken through France," Michelet proclaimed.

The members of the Constituent Assembly still gave an abstract, legal definition to "the nation." But throughout the nineteenth century, poets and historians, of whom Michelet was undoubtedly the most prominent, endowed the principle of the French nation with an affective content and transfigured that nation's history into a destiny, infusing the cult of patriotism with the mythology of a chosen people.

No one was more successful than Michelet in combining love of France—carnal love of the French land, spiritual love of a French "soul"—and the universal love of humanity. He writes in *Le peuple* (The people):

This nation has two great strengths that I see in no other nation. It has both principle and legend, the most generous and the most humane conception, and at the same time the most continuous tradition.

That tradition makes the history of France the history of humanity. In it the moral ideal of the world is perpetuated in diverse forms. . . . The patron saint of France, whoever that may be, belongs to all nations, he is adopted, blessed, and mourned by the human race.

The matrix of universal revolution, a "living fraternity," France is a "religion." Other nations have their legends as well, but they are only "special legends," whereas "the national legend of France is a path of immense, uninterrupted light, a veritable Milky Way, and the world has always had its eyes on it."[4]

From the beginning, republican nationalism declared peace on earth, but it stood, weapons in hand, ready to confront tyrants. The revolutionary love of the human race was in no way confused with pacifism: the homeland in danger, the levy en masse, the soldiers of Year II (celebrated by Victor Hugo), the very words of *La Marseillaise*, were so many memories and martial words that became attached to the memory of revolution, feeding both the popular imagination and the doctrines of the French left.

The Paris Commune, which rose up against the government of "country bumpkins" (*ruraux*) in March 1871, was largely the result of the frustrated patriotism felt by the republicans and revolutionaries of the capital, during and after the siege of Paris. At the time, it was the far left— Jacobin, Blanquist, even socialist—that displayed "nationalism" against a government believed to have failed in its mission of national defense. The struggle of the Commune against "Versailles" was in large measure a substitute war; the civil war was a stunted version of the national war.[5]

For some twenty years, the 1871 defeat and the amputation of Alsace and Lorraine from the rest of France fed a spirit of revenge against Germany, an endemic fever of patriotism, which was not missing from the accomplishments of the founders of the Third Republic. Léon Gambetta, who had distinguished himself during the Franco-Prussian War through his tireless energy in leading the provinces to rise up against the invader, became, once the peace agreement was signed, the leader of a republican party that, in place after place, in speech after speech, reaffirmed the patriotic imperative and contributed its share to the national legend. Gambetta exclaimed in Thonon on 29 September 1872:

There is not only that glorious France, that revolutionary France, that emancipatory France, pioneer of the human race, that France of a marvelous activity and, as they say, that France, mother to the universal ideas of the world; there is another France I love no less, another France that is even more dear to me. That is the wretched France, the defeated and humiliated France.[6]

Called upon to reconstruct that defeated France, the founders of the new Republic sought to consolidate the nation. Their achievements in schooling in particular assured a truly nationalist pedagogy: history, geography, ethics and civic instruction, and general science were all supposed to contribute toward steeling the national soul by maintaining the memory of the lost provinces, fostering the use of the French language at the expense of "dialects" and "patois" (a project adapted from the Revolution and Abbé Grégoire), and encouraging the worship of national heroes. For a time, there was even some thought of preparing for a children's war: in

1882, three ministers (of war, of public education, and of the interior) signed a decree aimed at expanding school battalions, following an experiment that had taken place two years earlier in the fifth arrondissement of Paris. The army and the schools were to work together for a few years, organizing young people by class into regiments. That attempt proved a failure at the end of ten years or so, but we see that the idea of mobilizing children predated totalitarian regimes: it was conceived under a parliamentary republic.

The preparation for war—albeit a defensive war—had as its aim both the conditioning of the mind and the training of the body. It was Léon Gambetta's friend Paul Déroulède who, in 1882, founded the Ligue des Patriotes (League of patriots) for—in his expression—the "preparation of avenging forces." The league claimed to be apolitical and entirely oriented toward moral and physical conditioning in the interest of revenge. A gymnastic society, a rifle society, and a reserve army, the Ligue des Patriotes was to be to the army what the Ligue de l'Enseignement (Teaching league) was to the schools: an inspiration, an ally, an instrument of propaganda. Nonetheless, in 1886, the declared apoliticism of the league was scrapped: Déroulède entered the political arena. This was a moment of rupture: Boulangism announced a new nationalism of opposition, a nationalism on the right. The blue line of the Vosges was no longer its only horizon: the National Assembly and the Elysée were becoming the ultimate stakes.

Conservative Nationalism

Paul Déroulède made the turning point explicit when his actions became political acts of opposition. In a speech read at a meeting on 23 May 1901, the founder of the Ligue des Patriotes explained:

In Buzenval in 1886, amid red flags criminally unfurled over the graves of our soldiers, in the presence and with the approval of certain deputies, I understood for the first time the state of anarchy into which we had fallen; and I declared for the first time that before liberating Alsace and Lorraine, we would have to liberate France.[7]

Here we have a glimpse of the moment of transition from one form of nationalism to another. Was the presence of red flags at a military ceremony (in commemoration of a battle from the previous war) the reason, the pretext, or the trigger? In any case, Déroulède accurately set forth the new hierarchy of duties: domestic matters first, revenge on the foreigner later! The parliamentary regime was the enemy! The next year, the beginnings of Boulangism offered Paul Déroulède the political solution he was seeking: a plebiscitary republic to replace the parliamentary one.

Nonetheless, Boulangism should not be portrayed as a mere fit of nationalist fever. For three years (1887–89), as the movement developed toward its acme—the legislative by-election in Paris in January 1889—then declined and collapsed, Boulangism was a groundswell of opinion of rich complexity, in which Déroulède's "patriots," Radicals wishing to put an end to the Opportunist republic, socialists dreaming of a social revolution, Bonapartists, and monarchists vying with one another in their schemes to restore the monarchy, all competed with one another. In short, that groundswell of opinion, from the far left to the far right, fed on all the discontents of the moment, crystallized in a general on horseback and a laconic platform—dissolution, revision, constituent assembly—vague enough to allow each clan its own hopes and to authorize each group's calculations. Boulanger offered a potpourri in which each found something to its liking—up to and including the antecedents of fascism.[8]

For our concerns, there is no doubt that this heteroclite movement was the crucible for a new nationalism, which adopted the term only a dozen years later and was moved by a fundamental imperative: a change in regime, the investment of power in one individual directly supported by the national will. The very failure of Boulangism had the effect of fixing the nationalist movement on the right.[9] After 1889, the hope for a restoration of the monarchy collapsed; in 1892, the pope advised French Catholics to rally behind the Republic. The nationalist movement found itself strengthened and clarified by its clientele on the right: a truly "nationalist" doctrine (from that time on, in fact, the term "nationalist" became widespread, thanks to theorists of the new school) was elaborated and diffused, with the Dreyfus affair as its paroxysm. "Doctrine" is an overstatement. It would be better to speak of a set of doctrines, to which various thinkers brought their contributions; they did not find a shared political solution, however, even though the adversary—the parliamentary republic—was common to them all. That anti-Dreyfusard nationalism regrouped thinkers coming out of the Revolution and those stemming from the counterrevolution, but did not merge them completely.

The Dreyfus Moment

Paul Déroulède belonged to the former group. Recovering its enthusiasm during the Dreyfus affair, the Ligue des Patriotes mobilized a large faction of the republican clientele, particularly in Paris. The resolutely "putschist" attitude of its leader Déroulède earned him exile.[10] Although hostile toward the "parliamentary farce," he said he was opposed to a dictatorship and recommended a plebiscitary and populist republic, in which the head of state, emancipated from "the oppressive tutelage of the two Chambers," would be "the first representative of the people." Within the league's sphere of influence, we again find a certain number of ex-revolutionaries, the old far left, either from the ranks of the Blanquists or under the influence of Rochefort. Rochefort's editorials in *L'Intransigeant* brought people of the lower classes, from Paris especially, to the nationalist cause. They were openly anticlericals, sansculottes, and the oldest of them could have participated in the gunplay during the Commune.

Another element was the anti-Semitic component. In reality, the whole of the nationalist movement was steeped in anti-Semitism: from Déroulède to Maurras, from Rochefort to Barrès, everyone denounced the "Jewish invasion." Yet it is still necessary to identify the agencies and structures that were properly anti-Semitic. In terms of newspapers, these were Edouard Drumont's *La Libre Parole* and the various Parisian and regional editions of *La Croix*, published by the Assumptionist Fathers. For the rest, let us simply mention the Ligue Anti-Sémitique (Anti-Semitic league), launched by Drumont, led by the Marquis de Morès until his death, and finally taken over by Jules Guérin, who transformed it into the "Grand Occident of France"—a derisive name targeting Freemasonry, which was generally assimilated to "Jewry" (*juiverie*).[11] The mythology of the anti-Semites called upon the Jew, as a stand-in for the external enemy, to represent the necessary enemy within, in opposition to whom national cohesion was easier to secure.

During the Dreyfus affair, nationalism also attracted to its cause a goodly portion of well-placed individuals, the arts and letters establishment, as the success of the Ligue de la Patrie Française (League of the French nation) attests. This last league drew as much from the society registry as the two leagues mentioned earlier—Déroulède's and Guérin's—recruited from the popular strata. It was created in late 1898, in protest against Dreyfusard intellectuals: members of the Académie Française (François Coppée, Jules Le Maître, Paul Bourget, and some twenty others), members of the Institut, and artists in fashion (Degas, Renoir, Caran d'Ache, Forain, and so on), petitioned on behalf of the army. But the Ligue de la Patrie Française, too high society and conservative to be dangerous, did not survive the Dreyfus affair.[12]

Nevertheless, one of the most illustrious members of the Ligue de la Patrie Française, Maurice Barrès, came forward as one of the "brains" behind conservative nationalism (the other was Charles Maurras). Barrès, who did not have a systematic mind, offered nationalism a theory of poetry. His novels (*Colette Baudoche*, *Les déracinés*, and so on) and his notebooks amounted to a survey of nationalism. A good number of the ideas of his era are found in his works, but they are treated by a sensitive soul, an aesthete who was expert in decking them in colorful language.[13]

Barrès's syncretism (which, to be precise, integrates the 1789 Revolution into a nationalist vision) is generally contrasted to Maurras's sectarian monarchism. At its root, however, Barrès's nationalism is antithetical to republican nationalism. The latter is based on the concept of a nation as the product of a general will, while Barrès's notion is founded in a categorical absence of will: "Nationalism," wrote Barrès, "is the acceptance of determinism."[14] The paradox is that Barrès and so many other conservative nationalists, imbued with anti-Germanism, challenged the French definition of the nation in favor of the German, in which the unconscious submerges the will or consent. In addition, Barrès was led to contradict himself on the matter. It was not his theoretical rigor that assured him the profound influence he exerted on several generations (of writers especially), but rather his sense for the turn of phrase, the metaphor, the evocation. With Barrès, nationalism lost its revolutionary abstraction. An anti-intellectual, he based his passion for the national ego on worship of the land and the dead and sang hymns of praise to rootedness. He challenged the universal dimension, broad horizons, and reduced nationalism to a patch of meadowland. His was a cry of distress emerging from the heart of decadence, in honor of a France threatened with decomposition. The call for "energy," reiterated from one book to the next, became tinged with the colors of twilight, haunted by the workings of death: "My feeling for death, these worms crawling in my cadaver, such is my entire secret life."[15]

Boulangism, the first wave of nationalism, washed up Barrès the romantic; the second wave, that of anti-Dreyfusism, gave French nationalism its doctrinaire positivist, Charles Maurras. He denounced the Dreyfus affair as a foreign plot whose aim was to dissolve the national community with its two guarantors: the army and the Church. Radically pessimistic about human nature in accordance with the counterrevolutionary tradition, he did not believe social cohesion possible except through solid institutional frameworks: the family, professional guilds, the Catholic Church, a unified state. At first, Maurras was republican, without religious faith, and he made the nation his sole priority. From nationalism, he inferred the political solution, discovered at last: the restoration of the monarchy. This was to be a rational royalism, without affective or metaphysical content: "I leave to others," he said, "the old divine right, the solemn foolishness of unintelligent courtiers of the past."[16]

The Maurrassian philosophy elaborated during the Dreyfus affair and in its aftermath marked a break in the history of nationalism. In a sense, that philosophy was its culmination: as much by the force of its logical constructions as by the efficacy of its demolitions, Maurras endowed nationalism with an unprecedented theoretical rigor. Moreover, in his teachings, Maurras set in place a remarkable and far-reaching pedagogical and political framework: the Ligue d'Action Française (League of French action, 1905), the Institut d'Action Française (Institute of French action, 1905), the transformation of the *Revue de l'Action Française* (1899) into a weekly newspaper called *L'Action Française* (1908), the policing organization known as the Camelots du Roi (Hawkers to the king), and so on, in short, an influence extending to several successive generations. At the same time, Maurras's intellectual hegemony over the nationalist current had the effect of drying up nationalism. Maurras's philosophy, it seems, was an exclusive philosophy. The writer who wanted to hear only factual arguments ("to submit to the facts") resolutely eliminated from French patrimony and national wealth everything foreign to his own classicism: the Revolution and all that followed, Protestants, Jews, Freemasons, "wogs" (*métèques*) (the so-called Four Confederated States). Maurras rebuilt France with a hatchet, in accordance with his desires, preferring the abstraction of his system to the concrete realities of his time, and introducing a spirit of orthodoxy and a sectarianism into nationalism that would add to its divisions and contribute to its powerlessness.

In any case, in the first years of the twentieth century, a conservative nationalism assumed its final shape: anti-Dreyfusism was its springboard and unifying principle. Even though the advocates of anti-Dreyfusism were united once more in their nationalism, it was a nationalism that differed profoundly from republican nationalism, child of a young nation, expansive and missionary in impulse, marked by the faith in progress and the fraternity of peoples. Conversely, conservative nationalism, invariably pessimistic, played the great aria of decadence in a chapel of rest shaped like the French Hexagon. France was threatened with death, undermined from within by its parliamentary institutions, by economic and social upheaval ("the Jew's hand" in it was always denounced), the degradation of the old society, the ruin of the family, de-Christianization. All these tendencies blended together, and this mortuary nationalism called for a resurrection: the restoration of state authority, the strengthening of the army, the protection of the old ways, the dissolution of divisive factors. In varying dosages, xenophobia, anti-Semitism, and antiparliamentarianism were dispensed in the manner appropriate to each of the publics targeted. In addition to the spasms of a defeated France—the France that deep down had never accepted the republican regime stemming from the Revolution— let us not forget the fits of anger of a disappointed France, of a people that lent an ear to their new public orators, all the more so in that they had received nothing from the overly bourgeois Republic in which they had placed so much hope. The conjunction between the defeated France and the disappointed France gives meaning to Péguy's words cited above: yes, nationalism had become a profound movement, a mass movement.

The Sacred Union

Nevertheless, that opposition between two forms of nationalism, on the right and on the left, began to weaken when the Reich of Wilhelm II, conducting an aggressive weltpolitik in 1905, took shape as a danger no longer theoretical but rather concrete, immediate, and deadly, during the kaiser's trip to Tangier. That year, French nationalism entered a new phase: republican and conservative forces converged, culminating in the "Sacred Union" of August 1914. Beginning in 1905 and thereafter, nationalists became as obsessed with international relations as they had been with internal affairs in the first years of the century; foreign affairs became the decisive factor in a national passion whose tone had changed.

To illustrate this movement of convergence, let us recall the case of Péguy. Of course, Charles Péguy, for reasons related to the contradictions for which he was criticized, is representative only of himself. And yet, his attitude and his evolution attest to a change in mentality over which he did not have the monopoly, though he expressed it better than others. Péguy had been a militant Dreyfusard, a socialist, a secular republican. Between 1905 and 1914, without ever denying his Dreyfusism or his republicanism, he took positions that were more and more hostile to the Socialist party and at the same time manifested his new Catholic faith. Was Péguy becoming a nationalist? No, he had always been one. But beginning in 1905, his republican nationalism found itself in contradiction with the ideas and practices of his own political community—that of French socialism. Jaurès's parliamentary socialism—an alliance of socialism and Combism—and the deterioration of Dreyfusism into politicking had already turned Péguy against his socialist friends. But the Tangier crisis aggravated his critique and completed his break.

On 31 March 1905, Wilhelm II of Germany, during his brief and theatrical visit to Tangier, questioned the recent Franco-British accord regarding Morocco and declared: "It is to the sultan of Morocco, an independent sovereign, that I make my visit, and I hope that under his supreme sovereignty, a free Morocco will be opened for peaceful competition with all nations, with no monopoly of any kind." The reaction provoked by this Germanic challenge to France, the crisis that followed (Delcassé's resignation from the Quai d'Orsay and the Algeciras compromise of 1906, which, even as it confirmed the independence of the sharifian empire, also recognized special rights for France in Morocco), triggered the fear of imminent war. "It was a revelation," said Péguy. On 19 June 1905, Clemenceau, another Dreyfusard, wrote in *L'Aurore*: "To be or not to be, that is the question raised for us for the second time since the Hundred Years' War by an implacable will for supremacy. We owe it to our mothers, our fathers, and our children to use every means possible to save the treasure of French life, which we received from those who preceded us and for which we must account to those who will follow."[17] The mark of a prescience regarding a mortal threat to France can be found in every party and in every political community; as can its corollary, the desire for a stronger nation.

Gradually, Péguy distanced himself from the left, especially the socialist left. Gustave Hervé was making news within its antimilitarist circles; Jaurès was using it judiciously. To Hervé's *Leur patrie* (Their nation), Péguy opposed *Notre patrie* (Our nation), a book in which he revived the expression "revolutionary nationalism." He was still defending that line in 1913, even though, in an attack on Jaurès—whom he called, among other things, a "voluminous fatso"—he asserted:

In a republic during times of war, there is only the policy of the National Convention. I am for the policy of the National Convention, against the policy of the Bordeaux Assembly, I am for the Parisians against the country bumpkins, I am for the Commune of Paris, for both Communes, against peace, I am for the Commune and against capitulation, I am for the policy of Proudhon and the policy of Blanqui and against the awful little Thiers.[18]

Nevertheless, Péguy's republican nationalism, expressed here in all its purity, is elsewhere slightly altered by "the atmosphere of the time." The author of *Le mystère de la charité de Jeanne d'Arc* (The mystery of Joan of Arc's charity) had recently returned to the Catholic faith, like numerous intellectuals of that period, when scientistic rationalism was increasingly losing ground. Bergson's influence is an illustration of this: the return in force of intuition, the vogue for a certain anti–intellectualism, went hand in hand with the spiritualist renewal. Let us also mention the renewed interest in military service ("service" in the strong sense of the word). In 1913, Ernest Psichari's novel *L'appel des armes* (The call to arms) best symbolized that rediscovery of "military greatness" by a new generation of bourgeois. The desire for "revenge," the will to fight, is made explicit in Péguy's correspondence. In January 1912, he wrote to a friend: "I spent a very agreeable night. I dreamed all night that we were mobilizing." And to another friend: "Glory would consist in entering Weimar at the head of a good infantry platoon." A few days later, to Alexandre Millerand, the new minister of war, he wrote: "If only we might have under you the war that, since 1905, has been our only thought; and not only have it, but make it."[19]

This was "the atmosphere of the time," as I said, because beginning in 1911 and the Agadir affair, the tension in Franco-German relations began to rise. The idea of an unavoidable war spread. Pacifist tendencies were now in the minority. In 1913, the left majority in the Chamber could not prevent the election of Poincaré, a republican on the right, to the presidency of the Republic; on 7 August of the same year, the law requiring three years of military service was passed. In the spring, the Radicals and Socialists carried the elections, but to no avail: they were unable to make the three-year law their shared platform. Since 1905, the drama in international relations had certainly contributed toward changing people's minds, and Péguy is only one illustrious example of this. In 1911, Henri Massis and Alfred de Tarde, under the shared pseudonym "Agathon," published a book entitled *Une enquête sur les jeunes gens d'aujourd'hui* (A survey of today's young people), which revealed the tendencies of the "new wave," and which was confirmed by a series of analogous surveys published by *Le Temps, Le Gaulois, La Revue Hebdomadaire,* and *La Revue des Français.* Later, Henri Dartigue produced a synthesis of these surveys in his book *De l'état d'esprit de la jeunesse française avant la guerre* (On the state of mind of French young people before the war)—a state of mind to which Roger Martin du Gard's *Jean Barois* also attests. That new generation seemed to have acquired an inclination for action; it questioned intellectual anarchy, aspired to order, discipline; asked for moral instruction from art; was active in sports, praised adventure; went to mass; and also participated in the cult of the nation.

In the years preceding the war, France was won over by a diffuse nationalism. Was it the revenge of nationalism on the right, which had been defeated by the Dreyfus affair? Yes and no. Yes, inasmuch as the themes of that nationalism had been diffused through newspapers and books, and its influence can be discerned in the tastes of the time. But no, because as both Péguy and Clemenceau attest, the election of Poincaré as president and the passing of the three-year law were also signs of republican nationalism, which had been awakened by the external danger. This was soon demonstrated when the French entered the war on 3 August 1914. In 1917, Barrès's *Les diverses familles spirituelles de la France* (The various spiritual communities of France) endorsed the reconciliation of enemies against a multifaceted "barbarism." "The genius of France," he wrote, "was dozing on a pillow of vipers. It seemed about to perish, snuffed out by the disgusting coils of civil war. But the bells sounded the tocsin, and now the sleeping nation is awakening in an outburst of love. Catholics, Protestants, Israelites, Socialists, traditionalists, have suddenly set aside their grievances." Exclusion made way for communion.

The episode of the "Sacred Union" is well known and there is no reason to linger on it, except perhaps on one point, a reason for astonishment. How could the Socialists—whose leader was assassinated on 31 July 1914—and the trade unionists of the Confédération Générale du Travail

(CGT, General confederation of workers), both of whom had "declared war on war," who had promised a general strike should mobilization occur, how could these militants, these revolutionaries, have stood side by side with their "class enemies" in the defense of the nation, and this within a few days, a few hours? And how, in spite of the duration of the war, could the French workers' movement have lent its support to national defense until 1918?

Let us pass over the events of July 1914, the powerlessness of the Socialist Internationale to implement an efficient means for preventing war, and let us turn to the key matter: if French socialists participated in the Sacred Union or supported it, it was because revolutionary and republican nationalism was still stirring in their hearts, even after it had been repressed, denounced as class ideology, attacked in all the organs and congresses of the socialist and unionist movement. Let us note some precursory signs. Upon his last release from prison in 1912, Gustave Hervé, champion of antipatriotism, moved toward the position of a "national socialism." That same year, on 16 December, the CGT launched a twenty-four-hour strike with the aim of "organizing the resistance to war." It was a bitter failure. Even in the speeches of those who agitated the most ardently for peace—Jaurès, Vaillant, Allemane, and so many others—there were traces not only of patriotic love but also of a true national pride. The socialists had good reasons for wanting to defend their homeland: in their view, France was still the sanctuary of the Revolution. In the face of an autocratic and aggressive Germany, the defense of national territory became a sacred duty. It was only in 1914 that the socialists reached that conclusion, but Jacobinism was always an element of their doctrine. The various socialist groups were opposed to standing armies and to the bellicosity of the nationalists, but even those who had defiantly declared themselves "antipatriots" for the most part rallied behind the declaration of the antimilitarist deputy Avez: "They say we are 'without a country' because we see no borders between peoples . . . ; nevertheless, if French territory were to be invaded, we would be the first to defend the country that saw the birth of the principles of the Revolution, the progress of civilization."[20] In *L'armée nouvelle* (The new army, 1911), Jaurès challenged Marx and Engels's claim that "the workers have no country," declaring: "A country is not grounded solely in economic categories, it is not enclosed within the narrow framework of class property. It has far more organic depth and far loftier ideals. Its roots grasp the very foundation of human life and, we might say, the physiology of man."[21] In 1905, at the first alarm, the Russian anarchist Kropotkin expressed in plain language the profound thinking of French socialism, whose internationalism was well suited to national pride: "If France were to be invaded by the Germans, I would regret one thing; I would regret that because I am sixty years old, I would probably not have the strength to take up the rifle to defend it. . . . Not as a soldier of the bourgeoisie, of course, but as soldier of the Revolution. . . . Another defeat for France would be a misfortune for civilization."[22]

Decline and Contradictions

After the victory, nationalist exaltation progressively lost its reason for existence. The uncompromising Jacobinism of Clemenceau, who became premier in 1917, complemented the nationalism of the moderate republican Poincaré, president of the Republic from 1913 to 1920. In the years following the war, French nationalism remained on the alert: Germany must pay, Germany must make reparations, because Germany had provoked the world war. Raymond Poincaré, premier once again, supported by a sky blue Chamber that intended to see its treaties enforced, did not hesitate to send occupying forces to the Ruhrgebiet in 1923 to bring the German government to repentance—despite the opposition of the former British and American allies. But beginning in 1924, first the Cartel des Gauches (Cartel of leftist parties), then the foreign policy of Aristide Briand, put an end to the earlier intransigent attitude. The era of collective security had begun; peace became a universal ideal, which every nation-state was obliged to serve as best it could. In 1926, Germany was admitted to the League of Nations, and two years later, the representatives of fifteen states signed the Briand-Kellogg pact in Paris, solemnly proclaiming the universal renunciation of war. People took to imagining that humanity had entered the time of eternal peace, until the economic crisis and the political upheavals that followed elicited new nationalist aggressiveness: in Japan, in Italy, and in Germany. The invasion of Manchuria by the Japanese in 1931 put an end to the illusion: in the 1930s, a new world conflict threatened, finally erupting in 1939.

Throughout these dramatic years, there was a decline in French nationalism and its diverse components. The collective passion for revenge no longer had any reason for existence: the departments of Alsace and Lorraine had been reintegrated into France. The nation had no other territorial claims, and victors are always peace-loving. In addition, the French had suffered so much during the Great War that nationalism was perceptibly weakened by a new current of thought developing on both the right and the left: pacifism. It was an immediate, almost biological feeling that was soon to serve the ideological cause of antagonistic camps.

On 24 November 1924, the Médaille Militaire was conferred on one of those anonymous soldiers, bravest among the brave; he was representative of the heroic rank and file who had been able to resist the Germanic tide. His name was Louis-Ferdinand Destouches, and he had joined up in 1912 at the age of eighteen. Sergeant of a regiment of cuirassiers, gravely wounded in the right arm and head during a mission in western Flanders, he had been cited by the army. But that was not the last to be heard from Destouches. Like many of his fellow veterans, he had waged war in a nationalist state of mind but returned home radically pacifist.[23] In 1932, this same Destouches, who had become a doctor in the meantime, published a book under a pseudonym that would make him famous—"Céline." His first novel was a bombshell in the literary market of the time: *Voyage au bout de la nuit* (Journey to the end of night). Its hero, Bardamu, caught up in the great carnage of 1914–18, crudely expressed the visceral pacifism that was now shared by so many French people: "When they talked to me about France, I for one irresistibly thought of my guts."

What made Céline's pacifism particularly interesting and representative is that it elicited praise from both the left and the right. The press on the far left, still antimilitarist, made *Voyage* a success; it was awarded the Prix Renaudot. Henri Barbusse's communist journal *Le Monde* was the first to defend the sulfurous book. On the right, in *Candide*, Léon Daudet of Action Française also vibrantly expressed his highest praise for the newly revealed talent. That convergence shows to what extent the atmosphere of the 1930s was different from that preceding the first world war. Nevertheless, five years later, when he published his furious anti-Semitic pamphlet, *Bagatelles pour un massacre* (Bagatelles for a massacre), the "anarchist" Céline resolutely placed himself on the far right and completed his seduction of it.[24]

In that literary example, it is important to observe the new conjunction between pacifism and anti-Semitism, which was to be victorious in the discourse of conservative nationalism between 1935 and 1939. As during the Dreyfus affair, nationalism—from *L'Action Française* to *Gringoire*, from Brasillach to Drieu La Rochelle—turned resolutely inward. The crisis of the 1930s gave nationalists the opportunity to resume their indictment of the parliamentary regime, against socialism—which they did not hesitate to link to communism—and in a general way the indictment of the decadence afflicting France. At a time when it was necessary to strengthen the social state—either by restoring the monarchy or by installing a fascist dictatorship—the left, the Front Populaire, and the Jews wanted to lead the anemic country into a new suicidal conflict, in the name of "antifascism." That war, said all the organs of conservative nationalism, was a "Jewish" war, an ideological war desired by the Jews to overthrow Hitler. Hence, whereas before 1914 the Jews were accused by anti-Semites of "betraying" France in favor of Germany, they were now guilty of preventing good relations between France and Germany and of preparing for a new war. For the time being, conservative nationalism, in remaining anti-Semitic, toned down its anti-Germanism and discovered a new vocation for peace. "Today's young people" were no longer those of yesteryear: if they still paraded in front of the statue of Joan of Arc, it was more to display their strength to "the internal enemy"—the socialist, the communist, the "wog," the Freemason, the "yid"—than to fend off a new German invasion.

During that debacle of conservative nationalism in the face of the Hitler danger, one might have hoped for a compensatory republican nationalism put to good use, a determination to proclaim the nation and democracy in danger, threatened by the Nazi conquerors. In fact, the old flame of Jacobin ardor was rekindled here and there against the coalition of foreign courts and the "emigrants from Koblenz." Beginning in 1935, the Communist party, so antimilitarist until then, also rallied behind a vigorous policy of national defense in response to Stalin's invitation and opened its pantheon to all the republican heroes distinguished on the battlefield. Among them, Joan of Arc, perhaps in spite of herself, stood next to the ragtag army of Year II. Maurice Thorez exalted the reconciliation of the red flag and the tricolor flag: precedents were not lacking. But despite that communist burst of energy and a few other similar reversals, pacifism—with all its nuances—was still dominant on the left at the time of the Munich pact.[25] Thus, on the eve of World War II, the French people's state of mind had changed perceptibly in comparison to the patriotic fervor of 1914.

National Revolution and the Free French Forces

At the time of the Munich accord, a French colonel wrote to his "dear, sweet little wife": "German money and Italian currency have flooded the French press as a whole lately, especially what is called the 'national' press (*Le Jour, Gringoire, Le Journal, Le Matin*, and so on), to persuade our people of the necessity of giving up and to terrorize them with the image of war." Then, after the capitulation on 1 October 1938: "Here, then, is détente, and the French people, like starlings, emit cries of joy, while the German troops triumphantly enter the territory of a state [Czechoslovakia] we ourselves built, whose borders we protected, and which was our ally. We are gradually adopting the habit of retreat and humiliation, to the point that it is becoming second nature to us. We shall drain the cup to the dregs."[26] The lucidity of Colonel de Gaulle—for it was he—demonstrates that not all the contemporaries of Agathon (de Gaulle, a graduate of the Saint-Cyr military academy, was twenty-one years old in 1911) were resigned to submission. Less than two years later, the Gaullist adventure was under way.

The years 1940–44 completely transformed the history of French nationalism. While the old Jacobin nationalism may have inspired a portion of the Resistance within France—but without establishing unanimity on the left, whose full-scale pacifism impelled a certain number of representatives to rally behind Vichy, and even to collaborate with the occupier—conservative nationalism was singing its swan song. Within the logic of anti-Dreyfusism and Munich nationalism, that song proclaimed, "Internal affairs first!" Changing the regime was the first priority. Marshal Pétain's National Revolution voluntarily isolated itself from the world at war, wishing to reconstruct institutions and French society in accordance with the principles of the antirepublican, antiparliamentary, and anti-Semitic tradition. That meant not only accepting defeat—while the British ally continued its struggle alone—but above all, collaborating at the state level with Hitler's Germany. It also meant fighting an ideological and military battle against those French people who, in order to continue the fight, were organizing in the Resistance and in the Free French forces. Here was a paradoxical nationalism if ever there was one, the nationalism of a people brought up to hate Germany and now clearly preferring Hitler's new European order to the reestablishment of the republic: "If the Anglo-Americans were to win," said Maurras as late as 1944, "that would mean the return of the Freemasons, the Jews, and all the political staff eliminated in 1940."[27]

But not all the nationalists of Agathon's generation reached the impasse of National Revolution, since one of them, Charles de Gaulle, came to incarnate the spirit of free France. His intellectual training, but also the circumstances placed de Gaulle "above parties." His nationalism, as Jean Touchard has said, was "a syncretic nationalism, a mixed nationalism that incorporated every era and every form of French nationalism into a single synthesis."[28] Every form, no doubt, including that of conservative republican nationalism—but not every content. In particular, de Gaulle had neither the xenophobia nor the anti-Semitism of Barrès and Maurras; in this respect, his nationalism was closer to Péguy's.

All my life, I formed a certain idea of France. Sentiment as well as reason inspire that idea in me. The affective part of me naturally imagines France as the princess of fairy tales or the Madonna of wall frescoes, dedicated to a preeminent and exceptional destiny. I instinctively have the impression that Providence created her for complete success or exemplary misfortune. Should mediocrity mark her actions, however, I have the sensation of an absurd anomaly, imputable to the faults of the French people, not to the genius of the nation. But in addition, the positive side of my mind convinces me that France is not really herself except

when she is in the first rank. . . . In short, in my view, France cannot be France
without greatness.

That extraordinary excerpt, which opens the *Mémoires de guerre* (War
memoirs), shows very well that de Gaulle belonged to the generation of
"1914–18." His nationalism, both syncretic and refined, would be the last
to hold power without wearing a mask. But in an odd paradox, in the two
high points of his career, the nationalist de Gaulle counted other nationalists among the adversaries relentlessly seeking to destroy him. The first of
these adversaries were part of the so-called National Revolution and the
Collaboration. Like them, though not on the same foundations, de Gaulle
had in mind the replacement of the parliamentary republic with a more
authoritarian, and especially, a more effective regime. But unlike them
(and this followed logically from his nationalism), he felt it necessary to
deal with the most pressing issue first: the military victory over an enemy
engaged in a world war. The reform of institutions could come later. For
that, he had to wait until 1958, had to make several blunders, cross his
"desert," and be favored as much by circumstances as by the network of
his faithful. At least, in contrast to the Maurrassians, but with a good dose
of that "organizing empiricism" extolled by Maurras, he succeeded at his
design in stages, without putting the cart before the horse.

The Algerian war brought him back to power and soon led him to a
new confrontation with other nationalists—those who confused the cause
of the French nation with the French presence in Algeria, to be maintained whatever the cost. It is as if, to complete decolonization, France
needed the most indisputable of nationalists as its leader. The power of
national values and the symbols attached to colonization had to be transferred to another venture: the recovery of the nation, of its currency, of
diplomacy. Within a few years, the operation was a success. Far from
weakening the nation's position in the world, Algerian independence allowed Gaullian France to command new respect for the tricolor flag on
every continent. More than that, returning to its sources, Gaullian nationalism made itself the champion of national independence throughout the
world, even in Quebec, against the two "superpowers." Whatever we
might think of that foreign policy, of its results—perhaps more symbolic
than concrete—we must admit that the France of the 1960s, finally at
peace, in full economic expansion, making the American "protector" pay
dearly, experienced a national pride—on the right and on the left—unlike anything it had known for a very long time. But General de Gaulle's
nationalism was obsolete; the words he used no longer sounded right to
the new generations; once he left, none of his successors at the Elysée
Palace dared replicate his discourse. It is as if the only mission of the gen-

eral's nationalism was to return France to its own time, through the use of archaic language.

Metamorphoses

It is legitimate to wonder whether nationalism still has a future in France today. As a feeling, there is no doubt it does. A poll of the Société Française d'Enquêtes et de Sondages (SOFRES, French society of surveys and polls), published by *L'Expansion* in May 1983, showed that the national symbols—*La Marseillaise*, the 14 July, the tricolor flag—"retained the same value" for 70 percent of the persons queried. In addition, the economic changes and their social consequences largely contributed toward awakening the old demons of conservative nationalism, including xenophobia and racism, which despite the euphemisms, are nonetheless a contemporary reality.

Nevertheless, French nationalism seems less and less like a serious political project. Neo-Gaullists themselves have become "Europeans." That is because the French space—territorial space, demographic potential, economic power—appears too weak in relation to the American, Soviet, or Chinese spaces. Thus French nationalism finds itself threatened from above by the integration of France into a group that transcends it. The structures already exist—the European Community, NATO, and so on. That transnational structure offers several exemplary models, two in particular. First, there is the West, the "free world," which is defined by a certain number of shared values, expressed in the institutions of liberal democracies. The second, more limited case, is that of a unified Europe, at least liberal Europe. It is noteworthy that conservative nationalism has a tendency today to broaden its horizon to European dimensions. The new right, fundamentally hostile toward the "West," ferociously anti-American, exalts a European nationalism whose origins it locates, no longer in the Latin, Mediterranean, and classical world of Action Française, but in the Indo-European myth.[29] The European springboard was already praised by the Barrésian Drieu La Rochelle and by a few other nationalists converted to the new order of the 1940s.

At the same time, French nationalism is challenged from below, that is, by demands from independence movements, of which Brittany, Corsica, the Basque region, and even the dubious Occitan region are theaters to varying degrees. Perhaps we ought to entertain the idea that the territorial enlargement of "nationalist" feelings dialectically favors regionalist eruptions. In the *Expansion* poll cited above, 43 percent of French people surveyed considered the autonomist movements "a serious threat to the unity of France." Dedicated to expansion on one side, to separation on the other, traditional nationalism appears today devoid of political prospects—even though the consciousness of being French resists the homogenizing of ways of life and culture from Vienna to San Francisco.

Open Nationalism, Closed Nationalism

In an effort to move beyond the inevitable distinction between right and left, republican nationalism and conservative nationalism, we might observe that France has been the theater of two sorts of nationalism, which have sometimes been expressed within the same political current, by the same speakers or writers: circumstances were the deciding factor. It seems to me that France has known an open nationalism and a closed nationalism. Open nationalism is that of a nation permeated by a civilizing mission, admiring itself for its virtues and its heroes, easily forgetting its faults, but generous, hospitable, in solidarity with other nations being formed, defender of the oppressed, hoisting the flag of freedom and independence for all peoples of the world. We find the spirit and enthusiasm of that nationalism even in the colonialist enterprise. According to Jaurès, an adversary of imperialism, French colonization was not perverse in itself: it contributed to civilization, it was a stage of human progress, provided one had the conviction of one's duty. The trace of that conviction can be found in the nationalism of certain officers intent on defending French Algeria whatever the cost. Things are not so simple, however, and here as elsewhere we must guard against too facile dichotomies. It would be easy to oppose a republican Michelet and an antimodern, reactionary Michelet; Resistance fighters were able to read Barrès, an inspiration to fascist writers, as a lesson in the energy necessary for the antifascist struggle; during the same period, some drew a Pétainist and reactionary lesson from Péguy, others encouragement against Pétainism. In addition, militants of the National Revolution and those of the maquis worshiped the same heroes: Joan of Arc is a good example. The traditionalist corpus and the Jacobin corpus have sometimes produced that open nationalism conjointly. Yet it is a form of nationalism, and not simply patriotism: the latter can be defined as the natural attachment to the land of one's fathers (etymologically), while the former makes of one's own nation a supreme value, in exchange for a legendary past more or less remote from historical realities. Nationalism, yes. But open to other peoples, to other races, to other nations, and not clinging to "France alone."

Another form of nationalism (that of "France for the French") re-emerges periodically, at times of great crisis: economic crisis, institutional crisis, intellectual and moral crisis. Boulangism, the Dreyfus affair, the crises of the 1930s, decolonization, economic depression: our history reverberates with these periods and dramatic events during which a closed nationalism has appeared in successive incarnations as a remedy. It is a closed, frightened, exclusivist nationalism that defines the nation by eliminating the intruders—Jews, immigrants, revolutionaries; a collective paranoia, feeding on obsessions about decadence and conspiracy; a focus on the French essence, each time reinvented at the whim of fashion and scientific discoveries, varying the proportion of Gallic and Germanic influence, the contribution of the North and the Mediterranean, the songs of bards and the poetry of the troubadours. That nationalism is like Père Grandet's passion for gold: it is a treasure to be protected against the countless others who covet it. Instead of representing the nation, that nationalism is nothing but the expression of a clan resolved to put an end to democratic institutions and to purge France of everything that makes for its diversity, its richness. The successive expressions of that paranoid nationalism can be read as resistance to the successive manifestations of modernity: fear of freedom, fear of urban civilization, fear of confronting the Other in all its forms.

Since its dawning in Valmy, French nationalism has continued to convey the best and the worst. When Ernest Lavisse taught that "France is the most just, the most free, the most humane of nations," it was possible to doubt the result of that imaginary competition between nations, but at least that flattering illusion was an obligation: pride could become the servant of virtue. But when the ideal France became simply a humanity contracting, hardening, shrinking to a niggardly and jealous ego, the nationalism that defended its chimerical genealogy and "purity" became one of those French passions from which our contemporary history has emerged bruised—if it has emerged at all.

It is to be feared that the state of crisis in which we have lived since the middle of the 1970s may recreate the conditions for a new nationalist outburst. The open nationalism of General de Gaulle—of the 1960s—is giving way to the sinister incantations of closed nationalism. The demographic decline of France and Europe, the constraints on the employment market as a result of economic changes, the end of the great movements of secularization and urbanization that began in the middle of the nineteenth century, are so many factors producing anxiety in a population affected by unemployment (or fear of unemployment), devoid of protective structures (the village community, the Church, the patriarchal family), and badly in need of a collective enterprise.

The great debacle under way among leftist utopian ideals has added to the psychological insecurity. Fear of the future again runs the risk of favoring the eloquent orators of political oversimplification and the prophets of gloom. The temptation for many is to denounce as agents of evil everything coming from *elsewhere*: to desire the return to national sources as the only chance for salvation. Of course, the question of "national" identity is raised: French, European, Western . . . ? But whatever the response, those who wish at all cost to preserve it, protect it, immunize it, are participating in the same defensive attitude, in spite of the aggressiveness of their vocabulary. As in the past, the political class—professional politicians—are accused of treason: whether liberal, socialist, or communist, politicians are suspected of plotting the dissolution of the national ego in the universal mingling of peoples and civilizations. The expression of that obsession, as Jean-Marie Le Pen and Jean Cau attest,[30] attracts too many people for us to be able to neglect it. As the century comes to an end, it is the sign of civilization's new discontents. Only the historian of the future will be able to measure its scope, but the historian of today can recall its antecedents and grasp its causality through comparison. For lack of something better, that may already contribute toward elucidating a troubling phenomenon.

Nationalism proposes simplistic solutions to sometimes real problems. After all, it is contemporary reality that makes defining our collective identity and our cultural community—the place of the French and of Europeans in a world of increasing demographic imbalance, the security of citizens and its corollary, mutual confidence among residents of a single country—preeminent questions. The responses of nationalism are caricatural and dangerous; they run the risk of being more dangerous than caricatural if other communities, liberal or democratic, remain deaf to the confusion to which they bear witness or powerless to respond to it.

CHAPTER 2

The Return of National Populism

LA FRANCE EST DE RETOUR (France is back): what are we to make of that title of a book by Jean-Marie Le Pen? In conversation, people speak of "fascism"; in certain proclamations, of "totalitarianism"; newspapers are more prudent, wrapping Le Pen's wares in the vague term "far right." The man himself declares he is the spokesman for the "populist," "social and national" right. For once, his definition may be the most accurate. To put it briefly, let us call it a "national populism."[1] An old story.

The phenomenon appeared a century ago, between two well-known political crises, Boulangism and the Dreyfus affair (1887–1900). In those years, a new right took shape, challenging the official representatives of the Conservative party, making inroads into the following on the far left, and troubling the established political game by mobilizing the "masses" around a few slogans that were drummed into them. That new current was "populist." It contrasted the people—their common sense and decency—to a political class corrupted and made soft by parliamentary pleasures. In response to the disorder and the "crooks," the people had to be given back their voice. Like Le Pen, who today recommends "broadening the right of referendum," Drumont, Rochefort, and the Boulangists challenged their equivalent of the "Gang of Four" with the vox populi. Maurice Barrès, the most distinguished interpreter of the trend, elaborated the theory of "the instinct of the meek" against the "logic" of intellectuals. That right asserted it was "social," offering its protection to all the "little guys" against all the "fat cats." Its public was primarily, but not exclusively, the old middle strata of artisans and tradespeople threatened by factories and department stores. The new right was able to rally the members of every profession uneasy about changes in the economic structure of the country. The Depression, the source of unemployment, which lasted until the last years of the century, was able to win it the sympathy of the unemployed, and the secular policy of the regime assured the adherence of numerous Catholics.

Finally, the new right was "national," sanctifying the national community and showing contempt for all others. When Le Pen recites his eternal credo for us—"I love my daughters more than my nieces, my nieces more than the neighbor girls, the neighbor girls more than strangers, and strangers more than enemies"—he is repeating the anthem of a fierce national ego, prey to mass psychosis, walled in against the universe. This is the exact opposite of Michelet, who made France "the moral ideal of the world," and of Montesquieu, an opponent of Le Pen before the fact, who wrote: "If I had known something useful for my family that was not so for my nation, I would have sought to forget it; if I had known something useful for my country that would have been prejudicial for Europe, or which would have been useful to Europe but prejudicial for the human race, I would have rejected it as a crime." Against the humanist tradition, national populism erects tribal egotism into a spiritual and political ideal. The obsession about "race," the phobia about intermixing, the hatred of foreigners, are the usual expressions of that regression to the stage of closed society.

A Discourse in Three Moments

Populist orators are the contemporaries of mass society: national daily newspapers and public freedoms compete to make public opinion a key actor in political life. Professional politicians must reckon with the editorialists and gossip columnists of populist papers—La Croix, L'Intransigeant, La Libre Parole, among others—who rouse their readers with a few simple ideas, not demonstrated but endlessly repeated. With repetition, they obtain an effective contagion effect. The important thing is to find the shocking turn of phrase. As a backer of populism, Rochefort, a former opponent of the Empire, a former deportee to New Caledonia, was a past master at it: France as a whole repeated his plays on words, his bawdy jokes, his gibes. The cruder they were, the more on target. The violent image, the inflammatory turn of phrase attracted more adherents than closely reasoned argument. National populism pioneered a technique of political propaganda that Gustave Le Bon, observer of the Boulangist movement and author of Psychologie des foules (The crowd: A study of the popular mind, 1895), found striking: "Assertion pure and simple, disconnected from all reasoning and all proof, represents a sure means for instilling an idea in the popular mind. . . . In the end, the thing represented becomes encrusted in those deep regions of the unconscious where the motives of our actions develop." And his pupil Le Pen echoes: "Politics is the art of saying and repeating things incessantly until they are understood and assimilated."

What "things"? There are three principal assertions, which make up a system:

1. *We are in a state of decadence.* Le Pen's books and harangues are punctuated with the word "decadence," just as Maurice Barrès was once obsessed with the "twilight of the West." Drumont's dirges also seized on every sign of decrepitude. "Never has France been in a more critical situation," he wrote in *La France juive* (Jewish France) in 1886. And, in an earlier book, *Mon vieux Paris* (My old Paris): "A memory of vanished civilizations haunts you at every instant in this colossal Paris." He goes on to excoriate on the increasing immorality, criminality, corruption, and exploitation of vice, expressing the "overwhelming feeling that society is falling apart," a tragic impression of degeneration. The medical metaphor instilled fear. Like his master Jules Soury, Barrès used pathological images to account for the political ill: "Yes," he wrote in *L'appel au soldat* (The call to the soldier), "Boulanger meant that parliamentarianism poisons the mind, like alcoholism, lead poisoning, syphilis, and that every French person is becoming intoxicated on the verbosity and vacuity of that regime." In the 1930s, no one spoke better of the "crushing fact" of decadence than Drieu, a disciple of Barrès. It was a necrosis undermining the country: "There is a virulent syphilis in France," he wrote in *Gilles*. Similarly, for Le Pen, the fear of AIDS—a fear he sought to exacerbate with his overblown words—came just at the right time in his crusade: a virus was eating away at the social fabric.

2. *The guilty parties are known.* The lugubrious depiction of decadence, inspired by facts that are sometimes averred, sometimes overstated, sometimes made up, and always detached from their context, then combined and exaggerated to dramatic effect, requires that the guilty parties be named. The craftiness of the populist magician is to fix all the responsibility on a few precise heads; to vent the anguish he has fostered in his audience on a minority of maleficent agents, in opposition to whom he can knit together a new and greater union among members of the community. Far from analyzing change—experienced as a nightmare—in terms of its complex causes, the demagogue uses a facile "diabolical causality." During Boulanger's time, the target was primarily the political class, made up of incompetents and betrayers of the trust. But a more "profound" interpretation of decline, which developed and took root in the 1890s, was already under way: "the Jewish invasion." Edouard Drumont, its most famous vulgarizer, thanks to his best-sellers and his daily newspaper, revealed the mystery of this painful shift from blessed times to times of

trouble with an expression of great moment: "Everything comes from the Jew; everything comes back to the Jew." The rest was secondary, subsidiary, and dependent on that central causality, according to which a plot by the sons of Zion was aiming to destroy Christian France.

In the 1930s, with the crisis at hand, Drumont's old cry—"France for the French"—was repeated in unison by a myriad of small, relatively organized groups and by vehement publications that converged in their xenophobic and anti-Semitic hatred. In 1931, Pierre Amidieu du Clos set the tone in the Chamber of Deputies: "We are not suffering from a crisis of national unemployment, but from a crisis of foreign invasion." As one of the most relentless instigators, Henri Béraud assured the success of the weekly *Gringoire*. "Average Frenchman," he wrote in 1937, "admire to your heart's content the beautiful gift the universe has given you, admire the Levantine rags, the filth of the ghettoes, the vermin of the Carpathians, and the Macedonian terrorists." The accession of Léon Blum to the post of premier set off the interpreters of diabolical causality: "The Jew ruins better," wrote Laurent Viguier. "And just as the victor imposes burdens on the vanquished to make his defeat heavier to bear, the Jew has imposed his 'social' law on us to sap all productive activity and prevent any enthusiasm toward work" (*Les Juifs à travers Léon Blum*; The Jews through Léon Blum).

For things to be obvious to the mob, the complex must be reduced to the elementary. To cite once more the author of *L'appel au soldat*: "The popular imagination simplifies the conditions of the real world." In Le Pen's national populism, the Maghrebi immigrant has taken the place of the Jew, though heavy hints tend to demonstrate that the latter is not always exonerated. "Everything comes from immigration; everything comes back to immigration." Unemployment? "Two and a half million unemployed are two and a half million immigrants too many." Criminality? The weekly newspaper of the National Front publishes a regular column on the misdeeds of the "invaders." The demographic crisis? Foreigners are contributing to it by occupying public housing in the place of French people, who are thus discouraged from having children because of a lack of lodging. The imbalance in trade? The exportation of currency to immigrants' countries of origin is the cause. And so on. Hence it follows that French "natives" have "the right of legitimate defense" against "the surge of Asian and African populations." Threatened with "submersion," we must react.

3. *Fortunately, behold the Savior.* Barrès, who is a decidedly good guide, writes of Boulanger: "What does his platform matter, they have faith in his person. Better than any text, his presence touches hearts, excites them. They want to return him to power because they are confident that in

every circumstance he will feel the same way as the nation." A providential man must lead us out of decadence the way Moses led his people out of Egypt. All forms of populism find the political solution by choosing a man already chosen by the gods, whose mission will be to purge the state of its exploitative servants and give the voice back to the people. After Boulanger's defeat in 1889, the populist movement was unable to find a replacement for him: that was one of the weaknesses of anti-Dreyfusism, torn between several leagues and coteries, with Déroulède, Drumont, Rochefort, Jules Guérin, or some other general all incapable of asserting themselves. In the 1930s, with a fresh outbreak of national populism, the war among leaders and the competition between leagues increased. In 1935, Jean Renaud of Solidarité Française (French solidarity) demanded a president of the Republic "like Salazar." The same year, Gustave Hervé, ex-champion of socialist antimilitarism, who had moved on to "national socialism," found something better: *It's Pétain we need* ("If, just between us, Boulanger was a fake, Pétain is no fake, he is pure and modest glory"). The military defeat of 1940 did the trick. And in fact, Pétain embraced the program of old populism that had been revived in the 1930s: the *statut des Juifs* (statute on Jews), the war against Freemasons, the adjournment of Parliament sine die, the reconciliation of classes in the *Charte du travail* (work charter). It was all there, except the voice returned to the people. Sometimes—another exemplary case—populist demands, playing the role of the sorcerer's apprentice, have favored the coming to power of an unexpected or uncontrollable savior. Poujade prepared the way for de Gaulle, whose every action turned out to be the opposite of Poujadist hopes: strengthening industrial and commercial concentration, bringing an end to French Algeria.

What today marks Le Pen as the providential leader for his compatriots has to do with several notable traits he glories in. First, his nationality. He boasts of his Breton origins, and for good reason, since in the beginning was the Celt, the Frenchman of granite, much tougher than the French people made of sedimentary rock, those who accumulated in the far west of Europe as a result of successive waves of conquest. And Le Pen even combines the two formulations of the *nationalitaire* principle. Jean-Marie is French by dint of the long chain of his ancestors, which terminates in his blond (?) mane and blue eyes. But Le Pen is also French because he deserves and wishes to be so: his enlistment as a paratrooper in Indochina and Algeria attests to this. A pureblood in the German manner and a volunteer in the French: you can't do better than that. To these certificates of membership, he adds virility. Nothing makes him happier than to pose in combat gear: combat uniform, the red beret of the paratrooper, boxing gloves. He poses in front of Dobermans, standing as the "strong silent type" à la John Wayne. His homophobia completes the picture of the su-permale. Always braving misfortune, rising again to meet all adversity, "alone against all," he pursues his mission. The corollary of virility is will. "The multitude still listens to the man gifted with a strong will," writes Le Bon. In Le Pen, that will manifests itself as the absence of doubt, the absence of negative moods and of intellectual scruples: in word and deed, he demonstrates the need for the victory sign. He is a man of the mob, a man from the mob, from the masses. He is the opposite of a political in-sider raised in the seraglio and educated at the Ecole Nationale d'Aminis-tration; nor is he a bourgeois gone astray. He does not represent the peo-ple, he *is* the people par excellence. Finally, like all demagogues, he is a born orator: without his verve, there would be no Le Pen. He captivates with his turns of phrase, where inaccuracy is equaled only by bad taste; flatters old people with Pétainist and Maurrassian slogans ("Life is not neutral," "France first"); amuses the gallery by turning insults on their head ("I am the vile brute who climbs and climbs . . . "). But he also captivates with his gift for drama and suggestion. All his art consists in in-stilling fear (we are threatened, invaded, contaminated) and reassuring in the same breath ("I am your 'rampart'"). That is how he wishes to appear, this man who intends to reestablish work, family, nation, capital punish-ment, and the Latin mass.

On the Proper Use of a Demagogue

For nearly twenty years, whatever his talents on the stage, Le Pen had the ear of only tiny minorities of unyielding revanchists. The following he has suddenly acquired demonstrates the rise of confusion, shared by many: the employment crisis, the feeling of insecurity, the apparent powerlessness of government leaders on the left and right, anxiety about the future. We hear less talk about another ill: that which has taken root in our political culture. The period we are passing through, in fact, is not troubled only by the birth of a postindustrial society, which has provoked a chain reaction of disruptions and, because of them, profound worry. At the same time, we are experiencing a crisis in our political representations: a crisis of the nation-state, destined to merge with a larger European unity; a crisis of national memory, as attested in the historical revision of the Revolution, our myth of origin; a crisis of populist frameworks, with the erosion of unions and of the Communist party; a crisis of socialist ideology, after the Mauroy experiment and the Fabius counterexperiment; the powerlessness of the Gaullist "rallying." On what shared beliefs are we going to base the new citizenship? In this difficult period of transition, none of our old po-litical communities have known how to address head on and in depth the problem of immigration, and that problem accounts for Le Pen's entire following.

For nearly a century, France was able to welcome and integrate millions of foreigners. Several institutions cooperated in this venture: schools in the first place, with a secondary role for military service, enterprise, the workers' movement. A progressivist ideology with its roots in republican optimism lay behind that enterprise: rallying behind the nation of human rights, secular democracy, the nation about which Michelet said, "It is truly more than a nation, it is a living fraternity," was a matter of course. Within two generations, an immigrant became a citizen. Were these all just myths? Yes, undoubtedly, but living, active, creative myths! Yet the left, in power at the time of the rise of the National Front, allowed itself to be intimidated by the ideology of difference. And the right that replaced it does not seem better armed against its inhibiting power. In the name of difference, the ideologues of the New Right have preached "everyone go home," and Le Pen defends himself against charges of racism: he speaks of his respect for "the identity" of others. In the name of difference, a certain leftist tendency has conceived the idea of a "multicultural" group, the dream of a polyphony in which each person would sing in his or her own way for the happiness of all. While some settle the problem through exclusion, others do so by denying national community. The two positions, though not perfectly symmetrical, both attest to the same lack of confidence in the values (Judeo-Christian, republican, secular) that formed this country and in our capacity to transmit them. By apparently contradictory means, both arrive at the same disaster: segregation—de jure or de facto. Will the socialist left and the liberal right, placing themselves above partisan disputes, be able to ward off that threat and implement a policy of appropriate integration, but without fear or neurosis? That would entail both means (for schooling especially) and principles (a single set of rights, a single law for all). Such is the challenge that the return of national populism has issued to us in spite of itself. That is more important to consider than Le Pen's effect on the next presidential election.

CHAPTER 3

French Anti-Americanism

THE COMMON prejudices and stereotypes regarding foreign nations are shared by all people. The French are no exception to the rule. Hence we have long been obsessed by two nations: first, England, the age-old rival from Joan of Arc to Mers el-Kébir; then Germany, the hereditary enemy from Napoleon to Hitler. Since World War II, however, the old European nations have largely lost their unyielding nature. The tendency toward unifying Europe is becoming a necessity, the contrasts are less sharp, a cultural common market is becoming a reality. As a result, the passionate Anglophobia and anti-Germanism of the past are now considered signs of senility.

In contrast, anti-Americanism is apparently faring well, if we are to judge by the French press of recent years. After Minister of Culture Jack Lang, speaking in Mexico City in July 1982, made a kind of declaration of war against "American cultural imperialism," the press—with *Le Nouvel Observateur* and *Le Monde* in the lead—seized on that lovely subject for summer debate and gave free rein to the sharpest and most varied sentiments. Nevertheless, it was clear they could not hold forth about the United States as about any other country. The *other*, the American, even when despised, is not invoked the way the *Angliche* or *Boche* once was. The American is not radically different from us, but is part of us, our bad side to be repressed. It was easy not to "gulp down" the old hereditary enemy, because its ethnic difference leaped out. The exteriority of the threat fostered unambiguous hatred. But as for America, composed of every fragment of the world, the rough draft of a planetary civilization, we fear it because it is within us, because there is a high probability it represents our own future.

Of course, there is also a specifically political anti-Americanism, but it is fairly recent. As a "mass" feeling, it did not truly emerge in leftist public opinion until the Cold War. Yet for a long time, and in all political communities, French citizens sensed, not from the United States (with which they were never at war) but from American society and mores, the threatening figure of anti-France.

We must go back at least to the beginning of the nineteenth century. We have at our disposal a first guide: the thesis of René Rémond—whose study ends, unfortunately for us, in 1852.[1] Nonetheless, it deals with a key period, when a reversal of the positive American myth into a negative myth occurred. Let us emphasize that it was a "myth," inasmuch as American society was quite unknown in an age when the navy consisted of sailing ships: if "the American entity was at the heart of a permanent debate," it was less as a result of information possessed about it than of prejudices and conflicting ideas proper to France.

Prior to the first measures taken by the independent United States, French people applauded the simplicity of American life: according to Rousseau, a natural world was being built on the other side of the Atlantic. That was not the view of Bonald and the traditionalist and extremist school, which stormed against the abstraction of the United States's construction, where nature counted for nothing, and vituperated against a combination of boredom, conformism, and utilitarianism in American society, which was explained as the absence of history and tradition, among other things. The aristocratic spirit of the extremists denounced nascent America as the height of bourgeoisism, a place where hierarchy was sustained only by money.

That criticism, by far a minority view under the Restoration, gained ground under the July monarchy; by about 1834–35, in fact, the reversal in public opinion was complete. La Fayette's death in 1834 is a good reference point, as René Rémond tells us: "With him gone, and ceasing to block people's vision," everyone's eyes were opened. In particular, criticism from the left began to reinforce the criticism from the right. The break with the past in 1789–93 had already weakened the "American dream" in France. The French Revolution, writes François Furet, "now incarnated, it and it alone, liberty and equality, the great beginning of the emancipation of men. There was no place in Jacobin thought for two pilot nations."[2]

The new socialist school of the 1830s denounced America and the principle of antiegalitarian individualism that lay at the foundation of its social life. Thus Buchez, a socialist with a touch of Christianity, wrote: "It is egotism solidly organized, it is evil regularized and systematized, in a word, it is the materialism of human destiny." The theme of American materialism, launched by the right and taken up by the left, continued to make news. "Brute instincts," "carnal appetites," "pecuniary passions": this was far from the pastorale first imagined. Above all, democratic and republican criticism did not fail to assail the poor treatment to which Indians and blacks were subjected: "That gang of slaveholders," wrote Dr. Cerise, "speaks of fraternity and equality and makes a shameful traffic in human flesh."

Beginning in 1830, visits to America became less rare. Travel accounts slowly altered the lithograph of the past. And then, with the election of President Jackson, American political mores proved to be extremely undesirable. Those most favorable toward the United States—Stendhal, for example—confessed their repugnance for the vulgarity, utilitarianism, and religious bigotry of a people "who have no opera," "no fancy or imagination." In the footsteps of other French commentators, Tocqueville in particular, Stendhal was frightened by the "tyranny of public opinion," which had replaced traditional forms of despotism, but with even more constraints.

The criticism, coming first from conservative quarters, thus spread to liberal and democratic ranks. Regarding the United States, each faction denounced a bugaboo composed of its own aversions and defined itself in opposition to it. For some, it was the misdeeds of equality, for others intolerant conformism or slavery, but all agreed in judging Americans a coarse people, insensitive to the life of the mind, trapped within the most insipid bourgeois utility: "The American of the United States," writes Comtesse Merlin, " . . . understands neither the beautiful luxury of the arts nor the universal enthusiasm of chivalrous devotion; his life is an eternal geometry class."

There was Tocqueville, of course, to whom we owe the most perspicacious analysis of American society. But people found in Tocqueville only what they were looking for: his desire for objective interpretation—to overcome his aristocratic prejudices—was rarely a lesson for anyone else. The United States was not interesting in itself; images of it served as proofs and illustrations for contradictory discourses.

Apart from the purely political aspects, which as yet carried little weight, cultural divergences became obvious. René Rémond, in the conclusion of his study, proposes to formulate these in geographical terms: "North versus South." On one hand, a northern civilization, "daughter of Protestant England," a commercial society, "the reign of an enterprising bourgeoisie, a republican government, freedom of the press, widespread education." That civilization was admired by the eighteenth century; Americanophilia took up where Anglophilia left off. In contrast, "the Latin and Catholic, rural, aristocratic or liberal Frenchman discovered he was closer to the civilizations of the South." French public opinion redefined its specificity—by taking a stand against the danger of Americanization.

Under the Second Empire, liberals and republicans, under Bonaparte's sway, acquired a new taste for America's public mores and freedoms. The abolitionist campaign, the war of secession, the victory of the North, and the elimination of slavery earned the United States the sympathy of French liberals once more. Nevertheless, it was American society, as it existed or as it was imagined, that provided the opportunity for the most contradictory commentaries. Literature, and especially theater, got hold of it and presented caricatures of Americans that are destined to survive. These stereotypes, at least for the years 1861–1917, are familiar to us through the work of Simon Jeune, who devoted a book to them.[3] The Yankee businessman earned the lion's share of attention on the stage. Bold, energetic, "king of copper or salted pork," that braying ass, often a crackpot, offered a spectacle to be laughed at for his lack of culture and savoir-faire: "The philistine knows nothing of Western manners, lacks delicacy and taste, proclaims his disdain for the fine arts. Finally, his habit of wishing to calculate everything in dollars, his predilection for ballyhoo," his naïveté, his admiration for everything excessive, ostentatious, and gaudy, made him an entertainer in spite of himself.

Among these theatrical creations, let us mention in particular those of Labiche and Sardou. Within twenty years, Labiche produced and reproduced the same stereotype three times; the first incarnation was named William Track in *Les deux merles blancs* (The two white blackbirds). Simon Jeune describes him this way: "He is brutal, tyrannical, breaks furniture in fits of jealousy, as well as vases, statuettes, fans—ready to replace them immediately. He has the need to strike: he needs some nigger at his beck and call for relief. . . . He is a noisy puppet on a string." The vaudeville American was launched; he was to be a great success. But people were not satisfied with laughing at a grotesque. Going beyond farce, commentators placed satire within a struggle for civilization. Hence in January 1861, relating the success of Victorien Sardou's *Femmes fortes* (Strong women), Paul de Saint-Victor wrote: "We cannot applaud too much that arrow, shot from far off at the American monster, which, spewing smoke, advances toward us. His horrific breath has already frozen our minds and tarnished our morals." It was thus a matter of defending "the good old French traditions," as Jeune writes.

The industrial boom in the United States in the late nineteenth century, the key place it occupied in a good number of enterprises, forced the admiration of many. Thus Taine's *Graindorge* illustrates the constant presence of counterpoint in our literature.[4] All the same, notes Simon Jeune, even in works tinged with Americanophilia, the American "provoked a smile or elicited laughter." This feeling of superiority, which manifested itself in the attitude of French authors and translated the self-satisfaction of popular prejudice, was to undergo a slight shift in the twentieth century. In this regard, as in many other areas, World War I was the beginning of a new phase.

The intervention of American forces in World War I in 1917, the decisive role they played, and the role assumed by President Wilson in the peace settlement imposed a new image of the United States: it became an indisputable world power. Despite France's gratitude toward its ally, the question of war debts poisoned relations between the two nations. France wanted to link the debt it had contracted toward the American treasury to the payment of reparations from Germany, which the Treaty of Versailles had granted it: Americans energetically rejected this proposal, in that they had not ratified said treaty. They hobbled together a system of triangular reimbursement, until the economic crisis put an end to German reparations, and European debtors to the United States stopped their reimbursements. That was in 1932. America, offended by that "dishonest" Europe, found reason to reinforce its isolationism.

Nonetheless, during the years of prosperity, the dynamism of the American economy, its productivity, and the methods of Taylor and Ford fascinated a good number of French people concerned with entering their own country in the race for profit. As witness to that admiration, consider Hyacinthe Dubreuil's *Standards*, published in 1929, whose subtitle was "Comment un ouvrier français a vu le travail américain" (How a French worker viewed American work). Dubreuil was not one traveler among others. He actually earned his own way—he was a mechanic—going from one factory to another over a period of fifteen months, at the end of which he gave a largely positive assessment of the work methods of American industry: "The scientific organization of work," he said, "is the indispensable tool of true socialism." But apart from the fact that such "mass production" worried small-time employers in France, American industrialism appeared to certain observers as the culmination of the materialist civilization already stigmatized in the preceding century. Behind the admiration, the old fear of America reemerged, first in the moderate form of studies such as André Siegfried's, and then, with the surging economic crisis, in the form of multiple converging attacks, the intention of which was to defend French civilization, threatened with bankruptcy.

In 1927, Siegfried published a remarkable analysis entitled *Les Etats-Unis d'aujourd'hui* (The United States of today),[5] in which he warned his contemporaries that "the American people are creating a completely original society": they had entered a "new age of humanity." What had they done? They had created the consumer society. Obviously, Siegfried did not use that expression, which appeared only later; he said that Americans had converted luxury "into general consumption." To that effect, the finality of their efforts was a goal of production: this was "a society of profit, almost a theocracy of profit." And he went on to admire American efficiency and the enormity of the material progress that stemmed from it: all workers had their own homes, their own bathtubs, their own automobiles . . . something French people could only dream of during those years. But, Siegfried tells us, watch out: "There is an almost tragic price to be paid, that of millions of men reduced to automated work." The diagnosis was clear: the standardization of industry led to the standardization of the individual. What comforts existed in that country, but what conformity as well! And there we have it: lack of art, lack of refinement, lack of individual spirit; the loss of craftsmanship signaled the end of the unique product. Born of individualism, American society had become a mass society.

The Wall Street crash and the world crisis brought criticism of the United States to a paroxysm. In the early 1930s, news reports and essays proliferated, attacking the nation of Ford and Taylor, the source of every ill afflicting France. The financial success of Georges Duhamel's *Scènes de la vie future* (Scenes from future life) is significant.[6] Like Siegfried, but in more categorical terms and without the nuances, Duhamel denounced the new civilization being created on the other side of the Atlantic, a civilization threatening the European continent. In America, the future member of the Académie Française saw the need to preserve France's own future: "At this moment in the debate, let every Westerner loyally denounce everything American in his home, in his clothing, in his soul."

Duhamel's pamphlet spared nothing: not cinema ("a diversion of helots, a pastime of illiterates"), records ("canned music"), sullen drunkenness (in France, drunks were happy), the too lovely legs of ladies ("obviously mass-produced"), the invasion of advertising, the omnipresence of the automobile, jazz (there was no music in the United States except "nigger monochords"), elevators, the horrible promiscuity of all races of the world ("all peoples elbow to elbow"), the excessive interest in sports, food ("nothing seems healthy, natural"), the uniformity of taste (the inevitable harangue about French cheeses, all "good, healthful, strong, substantial, amusing"). All of which led this traveler to praise the threatened charms of lovely French civilization: "Will you disappear one day, the little bistros at home, the low little rooms, warm and smoky, where three old fellows, shoulder to shoulder around a tiny iron table, wolf down beef bourgignon, tell one another stories, and laugh—oh God!—laugh as they play the piccolo?"

In 1931, two angry young men, Robert Aron and Arnaud Dandieu, assessing the danger to French civilization, denounced the "American cancer,"[7] in other words, "the supremacy of industry and banking over the

entire life of the era." In that pamphlet, characteristic of the antiproduc-
tivist current, we again find the same opposition between "sentimental
and local traditions of long date," which are defended "as healthy and real
entities," and what the United States represented: "an artificial and morbid organism." These two authors saw Americans as "nomads," "uprooted
people . . . subject only to the barbarous imperative of production and
pointless speculation." A barbarian from the West ("Wherever the American passes, the grass does not grow back"), the Yankee had undertaken the
colonization and subjugation of Europe.

The image of America was now well rooted in people's minds. In that
Malthusian France, which explained the crisis in terms of overproduction,
at a time when the majority of its residents lacked the elementary means
for a decent life, the New York skyscraper represented the threatening
erection of modernism, contrasted to the agreeable medieval bell towers.
Every banality already mentioned flourished, in "great literature"
(Bernanos to Céline) as in comic strips (*Tintin en Amérique*, published in
1931, is one of the best illustrations), with more or less talent, more or less
sagacity.

Translations of American literary works fed that critical current in the
1930s. It was only in 1930 that Sinclair Lewis's *Babbitt* was translated into
French, winning the Nobel Prize the same year. In addition to the works
of John Dos Passos, William Faulkner, and Erskine Caldwell, who painted
American society with an often ruthless coarseness, Paul Nizan published
his translation of Theodore Dreiser's *Tragic America* (Rieder, "Europe" collection, 1933). In that well-documented essay, the American novelist
mounted an assault on American capitalism, the jungle of social Darwinism, the ferocity of the trusts and the crushing of the majority by an un-
scrupulous minority. In the grip of the economic crisis, France expected
no more solutions from an America that had dazzled it during the years of
prosperity: the main lessons of the time were coming from Italy, from
Germany, or from the USSR. The thesis of American liberalism was gut-
ted. The successful watchwords of the decade—"corporatism" or "the
planned economy"—were drawn from models that challenged that of the
United States, which the Great Depression was reducing to nothing.

The Roosevelt presidency and the New Deal provoked a tremor of in-
comprehension in France. There was such a fetish about currency that the
Keynesian policy of the new president and the free-floating dollar caused
a scandal. In *Le Temps* of 6 July 1933, Edmond Giscard d'Estaing went so
far as to assimilate the devaluation of the dollar to "the most audacious
negation of Western spiritual values." And when Roosevelt was triumphantly reelected in 1934, Father Gaston Jèze believed he was justified in
asserting, in *La Dépêche du Midi*: "The American experiment is completely

bankrupt" (4 December 1934).[8] Moreover, the tenuous character of trade and diplomatic relations between the two countries made America seem very distant to the French.

Everything changed with World War II and the years that followed. The Vichy regime and collaborationist literature developed a marked hostility toward the United States. Lampoonists in particular took up the theme of "Jewish America" (the title of a 1941 work by Pierre-Antoine Cousteau), which Roger Lambelin had already elaborated with distinction in the early 1920s.[9] The role played by the United States in the defeat of the Axis powers, the relative decline of the United Kingdom and of France, the new danger of Soviet expansionism: within a few years, the Americans moved from isolationism to all-out intervention. On the ruins of the great antifascist alliance, they became the champions of the "free world," confronting a Stalinist empire that was pushing back its borders "to within two Tour de France relays," in General de Gaulle's expression.

There was nothing more logical than that accession of the American republic to Western leadership: nature, demography, and industrial capacity all contributed toward it. But that novelty, brutally imposed by the war, elicited resistance in France and created the various forms of political anti-Americanism. To give an account of them, I shall use a typology borrowed from Jean-Baptiste Duroselle.[10] He identifies four particularly clear cases, two on the left—the Communist party and the neutralist current—and two on the right—Gaullism and the colonialist faction.

The new American hegemony elicited French opposition in various configurations. First, that hegemony reduced France to a power of the second rank. French nationalism rejected that idea; at the very least, it wanted to delay and limit its effects. That was the historic role of General de Gaulle, to incarnate nationalist resistance to American supremacy. Although I cannot summarize the history of Gaullism here, I might mention that the large share of energy expended by de Gaulle to defend what he called "the greatness of France" came at the expense of the powerful ally on the other side of the Atlantic. For the nationalist de Gaulle, the USSR logically appeared less dangerous, since at least for the immediate future, France was not in danger of becoming dependent upon it. Conversely, almost all the gestures of national affirmation made to the West implied a defiance of America: resituating France among the ranks of the great powers in spite of Roosevelt, recognizing the People's Republic of China, withdrawing from NATO, building a national nuclear arms force, and so on. Throughout his life, de Gaulle defended a certain idea of France against American patronage. The general, whose nationalism was not that of "France alone," jousted throughout the world on behalf of national entities and against imperial powers. Having lost its own empire, nationalist France—represented by the returned general—exalted nation-states against empires, from Mexico City to Phnom Penh.

What de Gaulle, in his passion to "safeguard our national personality," expressed in refined language, a number of his faithful said with less restraint: "For a country such as France," wrote the journalist Philippe de Saint-Robert in 1967, "the only positive policy consists of humbling the White House."[11] In the nationalist vision, the USSR seemed to be a "heretical" power no doubt, but also an "objective" ally; Richelieu had felt the same way about Protestant powers in his struggle against the very Catholic House of Hapsburg in Austria. Saint-Robert was not afraid to assert: "The evolution of Russia toward an armed and organized pacifism, which has much in common with the French imperative for national independence, seems . . . like an effect of the more notorious successes of the regime, which has all the same allowed . . . the progressive transformation of a Spartan and isolated society into a productive society, then a consumer society, masterfully assuming world responsibilities." Given that premise, his conclusion is no surprise: "It is possible that the day will come when the world danger will be Chinese; but it is certain that today it is American."

The anti-Americanism of the colonialist right had points in common with Gaullist anti-Americanism, in the sense that it was also based on nationalist convictions. But whereas de Gaulle grasped the ineluctability of decolonization and attempted to make that necessity the basis for a new national power, the colonialist right clung to the immediate defense and *manu militari* of a French presence abroad that was increasingly in dispute. Thus we come to the second exemplary case: decolonization. The United States was in favor of it, based on an "anticolonialist" ideology. More concretely, its primary preoccupation was to maintain its policy of containment against the USSR. It knew to what extent movements of national independence could favor the advance of communism: the case of China was not forgotten. Where these nationalist movements were already infiltrated by communist forces, as in Indochina, the Americans lent their cooperation to the old colonial powers. Elsewhere, where communism still counted for little, they encouraged independence. Except in the case of a direct confrontation between East and West, they considered wars of decolonization so many causes weakening the Western camp. From the beginning of the Cold War, the entire American strategy had been governed by that formidable struggle with the USSR.

Paradoxically, the colonialist right relentlessly opposed decolonization in the very name of the Western defense against communism. What it did not know was that the old colonial nations were no longer masters of that world strategy. Washington was making the decisions. The Algerian war, and especially the Suez Canal affair in 1956, were the privileged moments in that colonialist anti-Americanism. On 2 July 1957, Senator John F. Kennedy defended the idea that the Algerian war was no longer a problem for the French alone; he criticized the Republican Eisenhower administration for being too favorable toward France and challenged it to seek a solution that would recognize the independent personality of Algeria. The future president of the United States was treated to the tenacious resentment of the supporters of French Algeria.

In relation to other eras, the phenomenon of anti-Americanism took on new scope during the Cold War, because of the circumstances surrounding the high-pitched ideological conflict. Nevertheless, there was more continuity than novelty in the actual content of anti-American attacks.

The antagonism between East and West mobilized progressive communist militants and other leftist intellectuals on the political front, but the arguments in favor of that particular battle were drawn from a stock of preexisting grievances. These were piled up against what constituted—or would constitute—the foundation of American civilization, which was portrayed as an anticulture, that is, a French anticulture, an intrinsic anti-France, an antihumanism.

Before elaborating on that observation, let us recall the importance of the 1947 break. The anti-Americanism of the Communists was forcefully asserted at the congress of the Parti Communiste Français (PCF, French Communist party) in Strasbourg in late June 1947. It was the very beginning of the Cold War. The previous month, communist ministers had been dismissed from the Ramadier government. In his lengthy report, Maurice Thorez sharply criticized "American expansionism," drawing much of his support from Lenin's words: "The omnipotence of financial capital belonging to monopolies, the search for outlets to receive the flood of commodities, the exportation of capital, the military buildup, are truly the characteristics of imperialism as Lenin defined them." The word had been uttered. The entire interpretation of international policy now had to pass through the grid of the Leninist theory of imperialism.

Two camps faced off. Two worlds, two universes, confronted each other. On one hand, "an aggressive and decadent world wallowing in contradictions"; on the other, the coalition of true democracies under the leadership of the USSR, "rampart of world peace."[12] For of the two blocs, one wanted peace, while the other was preparing for war.

That brutal and crude opposition between the two blocs, the two systems, was picked up as a leitmotif by journalists, communist intellectuals, and a good share of "fellow travelers." One of the latter, Claude Aveline, gave the clearest illustration of it in *Les Lettres Françaises* (French letters):

On one hand, capitalism: a system, a society, a civilization with a capitalist base. On the other, socialism: a system, a society with a socialist base. That alternative has become more concrete with each passing day, between two blocs that are becoming more openly enemies with each passing day. There is no possibility of agreement, the diplomats themselves hardly imagine claiming it any longer. One of the two blocs has to disappear. The world must choose. . . . In the battle between the two blocs, the *engagés* writers of whom I am thinking, and of whom I am part, have deliberately opted for socialism. We believe it is fate, and a desirable fate. We do not believe improvement of the capitalist system possible. We do not believe that capitalist society can miraculously become more humane and more just. We are persuaded that civilization with a capitalist base is bankrupt and fraudulent. It cannot recover, except in appearance and with ever more cynical and two-faced deceptions. And in the end, it will sweep away its architects, because it has already cost too much, and because it continues to cost its victims.[13]

During the Cold War years, the PCF formulated and repeated the slogan of "the struggle for peace," which by definition implied solidarity with the USSR and postulated anti-Americanism. The underpinnings of the latter were simple. The defense of the USSR in every domain, and in particular, the defense of its foreign policy, became the touchstone of "proletarian internationalism." The imperative forced upon Western communist parties was to use all the "formal liberties" of liberal democracies to conduct a campaign against everything that threatened the interests of the USSR, which were indistinguishable from those of world peace. The United States and NATO were the first targets. Hence the national and regional communist press orchestrated the protest against the presence of American troops in France following the creation of NATO. François Jarraud has studied the case of Americans in Châteauroux between 1951 and 1967.[14] "In 1952," he writes, "*La Marseillaise* became involved in a violent anti-American campaign, massively hammering away at a few themes on a daily basis." In particular, the American was an "immoral individual," "the occupation was worsening the material conditions of existence," it was a "danger for the city," a "danger on the highway," and so on. From then on, the walls of French cities were painted with the command, "US, go home!" France did not want to experience another occupation.

This last theme was launched in the Communist press even before the creation of NATO; on 28 October 1948, Pierre Daix signed an article in *Les Lettres Françaises* entitled "France, pays occupé" (France, an occupied country). It concerned the invasion of movie theaters by American films following the Blum-Byrnes accords of 1945–46:

Just as the French people paid homage to Leni Riefenstahl under the Occupation, today, with the same base instinct, *Le Film Français* has devoted a special dithyrambic issue to pay homage to the honorable Joseph M. Schenk, general manager of production at Twentieth Century Fox. . . . Night always mounts its assault on the world from the West. But this is a starless night, with the oppressiveness of a new Middle Ages without faith to sustain it, without hope of life beyond the grave. A night without chinks, a night of inquisition, of ruin, of obscurantism, of ultimate and total degradation. A night that finds within itself its own end. That night is beginning to invade us. It is only a desperate operation, the vain effort to protect the last lairs of a bygone past from the victorious offensive of light. We have only to hold fast, to resist, beginning today.[15]

The neutralist intellectuals, not to be confused with the communist intellectuals, expressed themselves in *Le Monde*, *L'Observateur* (which became *France Observateur*), *Esprit*, and *Les Temps Modernes*, developing theses on the United States that were more nuanced, but whose intent was generally harsh. At the risk of oversimplifying, let me attempt to convey the state of mind of that intelligentsia between 1947 and 1956 with two quotations from Simone de Beauvoir's *Les mandarins* (The mandarins). Henri, one of the novel's main characters, says: "I suspect that everything is not perfect in the USSR, it would be surprising if everything were. But in the end, they are the ones on the right path." And Anne, the heroine, echoes with this reflection: "America now means the atomic bomb, the threat of war, nascent fascism."[16]

The America of the 1950s left itself open to the sharpest criticism. The McCarthyist hysteria, the "witch hunt" it unleashed, the Big Stick diplomacy of Dulles, everything fostered the accusation that it was a bellicose state, blinded by its anticommunism and dragged into imperialism by its trusts. During the Rosenberg trial, Jean-Paul Sartre declared frankly: "Do not be surprised if we shout from one end of Europe to the other: 'Careful, America is rabid!' Let us cut all ties that attach us to it; if not, we will be bitten in turn and become rabid ourselves."[17]

Nevertheless, as noted above, the discourse of anti-Americanism is not simply political; it is not homologous with the discourse of anti-Sovietism, which under the same historical circumstances of the Cold War, was also given free rein. In fact, the latter remained within the political and ideological sphere: with respect to the USSR, criticism focused on the Marxist-Leninist foundations of the system, the new Stalinist autocracy, the terrorist regime. Russian culture was not at issue. Only the state superstructure was called into question, and it could be ascribed to an accident of history. By contrast, in anti-American discourse, the very essence of the United States, the substance of its culture, its entire history, were witnesses for the prosecution.

During his conflict with Hubert Beuve-Méry, when both were on the staff at *Le Monde*, René Courtin gave an account of the neutralist attitude of the editor, using moral arguments: "He is not Stalinist, and has no sympathy for the Russian regime. But he has an even stronger hatred of American civilization. Russia is still better than the United States. Russia is odious but it is not totally despicable. It is poor, it has the sense of disinterested effort, of anonymous and communitarian work. Thus it would pass the acid test."[18] Is René Courtin's judgment extreme? In any case, it made obvious the motivating force of an anti-American sensibility, illustrated in many earlier and contemporary writings, which lay behind a political choice.

France Against the Robots

Hence we find ourselves at the intersection between two forms of anti-Americanism, the political and the cultural. French intellectuals—communist, progressivist, or neutralist—of the 1950s attacked not only the diplomacy of the Department of State and the fascist trappings of McCarthyite America; more profoundly, they also rejected a cultural model, which they assimilated to mass culture. Despite their declared inclination in favor of the lower classes, intellectuals were learned people, the depositories of high culture—which still held sway in France. The authority of Left Bank writers, the prestige of the Ecole Normale, the *agrégation* put to social use, the importance of *littérature engagée*, and the intellectual following in political life generally were so many French realities unknown in the United States, which in any case did not offer a comparable status to its writers and professors. Above all, since the aftermath of World War I, the United States had been developing traits characteristic of a mass culture as we know it today, in which advertising, most radio (and then television) programming, comic strips, and Hollywood movies forcefully challenged intellectual powers.

Anti-American criticism—behind its purely historical aspect—has increasingly asserted itself as an enterprise of "resistance" (see above, Pierre Daix) to the colonization of our mores and culture by big business; it continues to do so to this day. In their political campaigns, communist intellectuals and their fellow travelers began to make better use of the weapons of cultural criticism as the products and by-products of American mass culture multiplied, especially after the implementation of the Marshall Plan. The Blum-Byrnes accords of 28 May 1946 liquidated France's war debts toward the United States; in return, Americans severely bent the rules of protectionism. In that way, American films were able to make massive inroads into French movie theaters. We know the rest: the banality of *Reader's Digest*, Coca-Cola, the comics, blue jeans, and so on. Admirers of Soviet socialism found only too much evidence of Yankee imperialism, and in their diatribes, they possessed allies on all sides: the colonization of France was in progress; Marx and Racine were fighting the same battle!

In "A un ami américain" (To an American friend), Vladimir Pozner writes:

Already, your myths are surging through France. I find these old acquaintances once more on our screens, in the display windows of our bookstores, on the racks of newspaper kiosks, and even in official speeches. I recognize the tool kit, which has already proved useful and which no one even took the trouble to conceal: films, best-sellers, magazines, digests, comic books, color photos of pinup girls. And long live American democracy! And long live the American paradise in technicolor! Have you read *Amber*? Have you seen *Gilda*? Did you know that a million copies of the French edition of *Readers' Digest* have been printed? Buy one today! My dear, yesterday I drank an extraordinary Coca-Cola, and that's all there is to say about that.[19]

Thus, twenty years after Duhamel's tiring stay in the land of Rockefeller, in 1948, one of his fellow workers, Armand Salacrou, brought back notes from a recent trip to the United States, expressing the permanence of a transpolitical repulsion: "Go into the first bar you come across on your first day in New York," he writes,

the bartenders serve you the same way that the workers in Charlie Chaplin's *Modern Times* tightened bolts. . . . Day by day you move deeper into an organized solitude, and you feel these creatures are overwhelmed by the impossibility of getting out. By chance, I attended the eighteen hundredth performance of *Oklahoma*. . . . During the intermission, I suggested to the friend accompanying me that we go to the theater bar. (I was thinking of the charming bustle of the Saint-Georges bar, of the little café at the Théâtre Montparnasse, where the proprietor tells jokes . . .). My friend and I arrived at the end of a line. . . . Standing one behind the other, we advanced slowly, and finally I stood before a faucet of iced water; above it was an automatic paper cup dispenser, you might say. You pull off a cup. You drink fast. You throw the wet implement, already flattened by your fingers, into a new and improved basket, and the next person in line is already pulling off the cup, which is also standing in line in its automatic dispenser. I shall never forget that encounter with a slow line of mute men and a line of paper cups in front of a faucet of cold water.[20]

This is a key and highly symbolic scene, which reveals the fundamental opposition between a civilization of human beings and a civilization of androids, between bistro civilization (red wine and conviviality) and bar civilization (potable water, paper cups, anonymity). Duhamel depicted the gloomy and clandestine alcoholism of Americans during Prohibition; after the war, Salacrou saw only water drinkers. No matter, the same solitude haunts that robotic, sanitized, and conformist people, on which the almighty dollar imposes its law.

The counterpart of that predominance of the assembly line is the scarcity of cultural models: reproduction has replaced invention. In 1948, statistics in hand, Pierre Abraham demonstrated that the number of titles published in France is greater than the number published in the United States:

That means that the United States is a standardized, rationalized country, admirably launched on the path of automation, which does not feel the need to distract the public by giving them the choice of too many titles. . . .

On the whole, a Bible, an arithmetic book, crib notes on engineering, a brief account of business law, five aviation novels for children, ten spicy novels for the ladies, and twenty works of anti-Soviet propaganda for potential draftees every year ought to be enough to calm all desire for reading, don't you think?

That also means we are tired of the incessant din about Yankee superiority.

A country as large as Europe that is not capable of publishing more than half the number of the titles we bring out, in this little pocket handkerchief of a country (torn and mended) between the Channel and the Mediterranean! That's what they want to offer as our ideal, our model, the one leading the parade? Come on![21]

Also in *Les Lettres Françaises*, Henri Malherbe, who received the Prix Goncourt in 1917, judged the American novel this way: "A commodity mass-produced by wily industrialists, with the mechanical extravagance that goes into the construction of automobiles over there."[22]

Mass-produced commodities, mass-produced culture, mass-produced sentiments: in every domain, identical products are reproduced. Even human beings seem to come from the same mold: the prototype of the pinup girl had the effect of molding a new feminine species, and the communist press mobilized against it: "A battle in which we have something of our own to say: pinup girls versus Filles de France." *L'Avant-Garde*, a newspaper for communist youth, warns its readers against "the glorification of the pinup": "The pinup, that is, the American-style woman, the painted doll whose goal is love, a rich husband, a great deal of pleasure without the slightest effort."[23]

Yet all these considerations, all these brief sketches, all these cookie-cutter judgments, with their exaggerations and their share of truth, were used by communist literature for partisan ends but were not invented by it: they already existed, continued to prosper among the most various writers, including those least suspect of colluding with the Soviet camp. Among a thousand examples, let us take that of François Mauriac. Unlike Georges Bernanos, Mauriac was not a herald of old France, a maniacal misoneist, or a political adversary of the United States. He can serve to represent the received ideas about America current in the literary establishment. Here is his view in 1959, but his judgment seems to be invariable, long established, and definitive:

In the end, my sympathy goes out to the leader of a great people, which I certainly admire; but that people, in many aspects of their genius, are more foreign than any other. I have never visited them. . . . What would be the point? They have done much more than visit us: they have transformed us. The rhythm of our daily lives has fallen into step with their own. Their music orchestrates our days with millions of records. Thousands of films, on every screen in Paris and the provinces, impose their ideas on every subject upon us: a certain stereotype of woman, the interchangeable star that Brigitte Bardot or Pascale des Batignolles or whoever has become, but above all the worship, the idolatry of technology, of every sort of technology invented by man and to which man has become enslaved, the folly of speed, the giddiness that affects all the sheep in the West, a flurry from which none of us escapes: excess in all things, which is the one thing in the world that is least consistent with our genius.[24]

Such is the worry expressed by French elites of every political stripe: the French genius, the French essence, the culture and civilization of an old country shining for the world, are threatened with deterioration, even disintegration, with annihilation by the invasion (the "occupation") of American standards. Criticism by these elites—politics aside—is directed at both material productions and productions of the mind, at mores as well as mentalities.

We might wonder whether that anti-Americanism is not an elite attitude—that of literary elites in particular. In fact, the results of polls taken in France between 1952 and 1957 show that the image of the United States was clearly positive—even among Communist voters.[25] The American way of life may have horrified bourgeois intellectuals, but it fascinated a society that aspired toward the improvement of its standard of living, a society that was tasting the first fruits of growth.

Apart from political factors, the reservation or hostility of intellectual elites toward the American model has had two principal causes: first, the appearance of a mass culture that called into question the position of intellectuals in French society; and second, the resolutely antimodernist, anti-industrial, antitechnological current—best expressed in Georges Bernanos's *La France contre les robots* (France against the robots).

In both cases, the figure of America assumes an allegorical aspect. Those who go to the United States apparently do so only to confirm their prejudices; most of them, like François Mauriac, do not bother to go at all, since, under American influence, French culture has already undergone a transformation, the equivalent of a falsification. In every case, America offers itself less as a reality of flesh and blood than as a repulsive myth: the future of French civilization (or of civilization generally, for many) lies solely in uttering a global "no" to that anticulture and antihumanism symbolized by the United States.

In the 1960s, anti-Americanism became all the stronger in that it combined the anti-imperialism of the far left and radical left, which reached its height with the Vietnam War; Gaullist nationalism, which became a missionary on every continent; and the first criticisms of something that was becoming a reality in France and was baptized "consumer society." That wave subsided in the 1970s. Several events contributed toward that drop: the death of de Gaulle and then Pompidou; the end of the Vietnam War and the withdrawal of American troops (1973–75); the election of President Carter; the collapse of Soviet legitimacy under Solzhenitsyn's influence (the translation of the first volume of *The Gulag Archipelago* appeared in 1974). In addition, a number of French people were struck, sometimes seduced, by the dynamism and inventiveness of the protest movements made in USA. For some, California, the site of all sorts of social experiments, became a new promised land. A single example will suffice to make that evolution concrete. Within an interval of eleven years, *Esprit* published two special issues devoted to the United States. In March 1959, under the general title "L'homme standard" (The standard man)—already suggestive—an indictment was made of what would be called a "quiet totalitarianism." According to one of the editors, "in the postwar United States, without internment camps, without rigged trials, without totalitarian terrorism, an entire nation became fixed in conformism" (Sidney Lens).[26] In October 1970, the same journal published an issue on "Les Etats-Unis en révolution" (The United States in revolution), which contains, among other things, the advance proofs of Edgar Morin's *Journal de Californie* (California journal), one of the first manifestoes of "pro-American" revisionism by the intelligentsia. Those behind the times were still looking toward Beijing, while the fires of cultural revolution were burning in the Far West.

If intellectual circles thus evolved perceptibly in their representation of America, with the help of the changing face of the world and charter flights, anti-Americanism nevertheless remained a constant in the ideological marketplace. The election of Reagan and his proclaimed determination against the USSR revived Cold War anti-Americanism. The monetary policy of the White House was another subject for conflict between France and the United States. But above all, the fear of Americanization, at a time when blue jeans, rock and roll, and fast food were wreaking havoc in the country, called for new responses. These came from Gaullists "on the left," socialists and other personalities fairly favorable toward the new majority, which in 1981 launched a committee for the defense of "national identity." Another Gaullist on the left, Michel Jobert, minister of foreign trade, gave the most vigorous expression of France's indignation at President Reagan's monetary policy. Finally, Jack Lang became the herald of our cultural identity.

Nevertheless, the most chemically pure anti-Americanism is today found in the publications of the New Right, where it is clear that the ideology of "roots" and anti-Americanism are correlative notions. Defining itself as European, anti-Christian, and antiegalitarian, the New Right attacks America as the heart of a soulless "Western civilization," which is not the civilization of our old Europe.[27]

In the March-April 1982 issue of *Eléments*, Alain de Benoist returns at length to the objectives of the current he has led. In his view, the enemy is egalitarianism, which engenders decadence. But today, egalitarianism has taken on two apparently opposing aspects: that of American liberalism and that of Soviet Communism. But the fundamentals of politics consist in knowing how to designate the "main enemy." Alain de Benoist tells us he would prefer not to have to choose, that in his view Europe must assert itself against both empires. Nonetheless, if we are compelled to take sides whatever the cost, then we must not hesitate: "The choice must be the camp that, in practice, is objectively the least favorable toward universalism, toward egalitarianism, and toward cosmopolitanism. . . . The main enemy for us will thus be bourgeois liberalism and the American Western Atlantic, for which European social democracy is only one of the most dangerous stand-ins." In opposition to the society that made individualism a fundamental value, the ideology of the New Right opts for one that prefers "peoples and cultures" to individuals. If dictatorships "bruise" individuals, and "often under abominable conditions," they at least have the advantage of not annihilating peoples. While the West founders in "communism," "it is in the East that positive notions such as the conception of the war of existence, the desire for conquest, the sense of effort, discipline, and so on, are maintained with more force—sometimes with a pathological force."

Benoist also explains that as Europeans, we are the natural adversaries of sea power, of "American thalassocracy." All in all, if he truly had to choose—and may his Olympian gods forbid it—he would have less difficulty resigning himself to the idea of one day wearing "the cap of the Red army" than "to living on hamburgers in Brooklyn." It is clear that the French far right should no longer be confused with the "defense of the West." The reshuffling of ideological cards is clearly never-ending.

For two centuries, America has continually occupied our collective unconscious. Stereotypes have permeated our everyday language in an ambiguous manner. On one hand, the incarnations of the American model have stirred the imagination of French people, first, as the land of simplicity, equality, a paradigm of the natural, and then, as a laboratory for the future industrial world, nation of efficiency and cutting-edge technology, a youthful society capable of adapting to anything. The United States has continued to fascinate the old "Gallo-Roman" country, entrenched in its caste hierarchies and historical baggage.[28] America has always represented the place where everything was possible, where a poor émigré had a chance to transform himself into a brilliant intellectual or a rich businessman. But simultaneously, in the French imagination, American society has been the concentrated realization of all the threats burdening national identity.

First, the French have asserted their superiority through the laughter and scorn they display toward what has seemed to them a sort of anticivilization. Vulgarity, conformity, and naïveté were the marks of a society with no aristocracy, no culture, no finesse. On this subject, Gustave de Beaumont, Tocqueville's companion, said, "To have elegance in taste, one must first have it in mores." But American mores lay themselves open to every sort of mockery; they retained a certain incorrigible savagery. Then, when American industry took off in such a formidable manner, that anticivilization became the specter of France's own future. America was despised less for what it was than for the collapse of what had made French civilization what it was—a civilization of peasants and notables. The French values of moderation, balance, good taste, and the gold standard seemed to be threatened by Yankee excess, the headlong rush toward the future, mass civilization. The left and the right competed with each other in their anathema. One side denounced capitalist turpitude, racial segregation, the infernal logic of the technological infrastructure, the horrors of savage liberalism. The other criticized an artificial society without traditions and without history, cosmopolitan intermixing within cities, the neglect of natural hierarchies. All dissolved in curses against the worship of numbers, the reign of the dollar, and mass pseudo-culture.

In modern-day America, essayists, journalists, and politicians all find fodder for their own themes once again. But if America represents a single idea or a single image, it is no doubt that of industrial and urban civilization, which spurs us on and worries us. Beyond political disputes, America stands as the caricature of a painful transformation: the loss of the old pastoral, agricultural civilization, where the France of days gone by sank the chief roots of its identity. America is painful for us in that it does not lead us to dream about our past but forces us to be lucid about the scenes of our future life. Duhamel, despite the mediocrity of his pamphlet, found the right expression.

In addition, the American challenge is not simply a mental picture. By virtue of its economic, military, and political power, the United States carries within itself the threat of a uniformization of the Western world—and beyond. The English language, transformed into "American," runs the risk of becoming the new koine of an "Atlantic" civilization, shaped by the North American's way of thinking. Many scientists have already abandoned their native language and publish their research in English, the new Latin of technology. It is undoubtedly the duty of nations and learned bodies to respond in a coherent manner to that challenge. But in that policy, protectionism will never be more than an adjuvant to be handled with care; demonstrations of anti-Americanism will be little more than an outburst of powerless spite. The important thing is to know whether French people, whether Europeans, at a time when the use of satellites has nearly obliterated the last fortifications of national boundaries, will have the ambition and the resources to assert their identity and their particularity in positive terms, by means of their own genius, in a technologically shared civilization. That is what is at stake as we approach the end of this century.

PART TWO

The Nationalist Imagination
and Anti-Semitism

IN LATE JANUARY 1910, Paris was floundering. The swelling Seine had overrun its banks. In the areas bordering the river, people soon had to borrow makeshift boats or rafts. Edouard Drumont, a publicist who had become famous over the course of a twenty-five-year unbridled anti-Semitic campaign, had to flee his apartment in the seventh arrondissement when the water soaked his carpets.

Who was responsible? After all, in every catastrophe, even a "natural" one, the guilty party must be sought out. Drumont set to it as always. There was no railroad accident, bloody riot, or public calamity for which he did not track down and find the responsible party. To tell the truth, that boulevard Sherlock Holmes never varied in his conclusions. Without fail, he fired back proof of the repeated offense: it was the Jew, again the Jew, always the Jew.

He sometimes needed a good dose of imagination. The scoundrel always had plenty to spare. All the same, where could the sons of David be found in the waves flooding Paris? Elementary, my dear Watson, Drumont tells us. If water overflows, it is because it was not held back upstream. And upstream of Paris there had been some recent deforestation; in the companies responsible for it, might there be some cousins of the Rothschilds? Hence "the furious deforestation carried out by the Jews was indisputably the principal cause of the flood."

Like his contemporary Léo Taxil, we might attribute what he calls Drumont's "Jewmania" to mental illness, except that Drumont had hundreds of thousands of readers; he was elected deputy in Algiers in 1899; he had countless admirers and disciples. Was he paranoid? That hardly matters: he was read, celebrated, taken seriously. Pierre Boutang, not the least significant of our nationalist writers, believed him an excellent writer. He is therefore someone who deserves attention. His hysteria stirred people up.

The following passage on the high water in Paris deserves to be cited as a sample of the paralogical approach common in Drumont and his friends: "Cutting down the forests of France to bare stumps, which has been pointed out on all sides, was nothing but a new 'sign of the end,' to be added to all the other symptoms of decomposition that we have had the occasion to observe for twenty or thirty years."

Decomposition, degeneration, decadence: the first great wave of modern anti-Semitism inaugurated by *La France juive*, published by Drumont in 1886, developed within the sinister fissures of a society that was coming apart. At least, that was the view of anti-Semites, since the reality was hardly compatible with their dark tales and their air of catastrophe. At the very moment when so many French people imagined they were at the "apogee" of civilization or at a radiant stage in the "irreversible march of progress," it seems that many others felt a deep sense of anxiety, dazed by that electric and republican *fin de siècle*. In the guise of a news item, the text on the charity bazaar fire—which must be read as a sort of true fable—elicits the apocalyptic shivers actively sought out by a part of French society. Anti-Semitism was one of the "responses" to the supposed decadence that conservative or nationalist writers believed they saw overwhelming France.

The same news item allows us to catch a glimpse of another factor accounting for the diffusion anti-Semitism enjoyed: the misleading simplifications of "diabolical causality." Drumont, who was one of the most popular vulgarizers, has a privileged place in this study. His writings were the first synthesis—or, more accurately, the first conglutination—of modern anti-Semitism in the French language, bringing together the anti-Jewish inheritance of the Christian tradition, the Judeophobic anticapitalism of the populist and socialist strata, and finally, the racist theses of the new anthropological science. Drumont seized on anything that could feed his obsession, regardless of the contradictions. He appealed to religion even as he broke the priests' sabers in two; he fraternized with the socialists, but only to better slash the red flag to tatters; he took pride in his scientific arguments and vocabulary ("microbe," "analysis," "malady"), but as a believer in the devil and his horns, he knew how to decree the "bankruptcy of science" when necessary. Was Drumont simplistic? Of course. But he was one of the very first to understand that in the era of triumphant journalism, where public opinion was becoming an issue, political propaganda targeting the "masses" did not use syllogisms, but rather unwarranted assumptions, crude effects, and sentimentalism.

In the nationalist movement, which filled the end of the nineteenth century with its clamor, Jews had a role to play. Through an effect of repulsion, they revealed national identity to itself. To be French, people were told at the time, meant above all not being Jewish. Simultaneously, as I will attempt to show in the chapters that follow, two powerful and antagonistic myths took shape: the myth of Joan of Arc, the positive heroine, and the myth of the Jewish archetype, its negation. During this same period, the time of the Dreyfus affair, when nationalism clearly took its place on the right, anti-Semitism stopped appearing officially within leftist ranks. The story of the relation between the left and the Jews, which has had its ups and downs, is the subject of another chapter.

All in all, rampant, diffuse, vulgar anti-Semitism, which has affected nearly all French political communities, in the end became a doctrine located within the ranks of nationalism—closed nationalism, "the nationalism of nationalists," in Raoul Girardet's expression. The chapter entitled "The Dreyfus Affairs" is intended to show the reproducibility of the model. In 1989, in an interview with *Présent*, Jean-Marie Le Pen was still speaking of the "Jewish internationale": anti-Semitism's influence within the far right is still a reality, or more precisely, it is one of the most solid elements by which to identify the far right.

CHAPTER 4

A Foretaste of Apocalypse:
The Charity Bazaar Fire

ON 4 MAY 1897, at about four-thirty in the afternoon, a young Paul Morand, accompanied by his grandmother, who had come to pick him up after school as she did every day, was returning home along Rue Marignan. Passing by Rue Jean-Goujon, the future writer was witness to one of the most famous "catastrophic" events of the century: the charity bazaar fire.

The charity bazaar had been founded in 1885 by members of Catholic high society. Its president was Baron de Mackau, its secretary Baron Robert Oppenheim, and the organization committee was similarly composed of authentic representatives of the aristocracy. Every spring, the bazaar brought together a certain number of charitable organizations (The Little Sisters of the Assumption, the free schools of the Saint-Louis-en-l'Isle parish, the Catholic circle of workers, organizations for children and for the blind young women of Saint-Paul, and so on), each possessing a counter, where patronesses busied themselves offering various objects the committee had collected to generous passersby. That pious and philanthropic demonstration was also one of the most important dates on the society calendar, "one of the most elegant and aristocratic places to meet," said *L'Eclair*, adding: "Under the cover of charity, many things were permitted that on any other occasion would have been prohibited by the social code. In exchange for a handful of louis, the young and lovely Baronne de Z—— let her admirers plant a kiss on her cheek. 'It's for my poor,' she said, blushing with happiness."[1]

That year, the bazaar had been set up in a vacant lot on Rue Jean-Goujon. In an area eighty meters long and twenty meters wide, an old Paris street had been reconstructed with a medieval decor. Each counter had a picturesque sign—*The Silver Penny, The White Pelican, The Golden*

Lion, and so on. In one corner of the bazaar stood a novelty that was expected to be a great success: a movie projector. To get to the projection room, customers inserted fifty centimes into a turnstile. Everything was covered by an enormous awning, which made the heat from the sunny days even more suffocating.

It is understandable that the unusual and illustrious site, the concentration of so many pretty women, and finally, the catastrophe that crashed down on that cardboard Middle Ages could have inspired one of Paul Morand's short stories—"Bazar de la Charité" (Charity bazaar)—where we read the most gripping descriptions of the disaster within the fictional plot of the story:

Clovis turned around quickly and saw a flame rising up from the rostrum. It coiled around the projector, which in an instantaneous crackle, began to melt, along with all its film. It was too late to find safety or to flee, for the fire had already opened its yawning mouth toward the sky and its claws made their way through the crowd.

The awning over the bazaar swelled with hot air like a Montgolfier, made the ropes crackle, stretched tight a vast banner speckled with yellow, then with red, and finally with black, which perforated before ripping. The lifted heads, blinded by the sun, did not see that the canvas ceiling was burning; it was only when it had given way to the rush of air that it sagged under its own weight and collapsed on those in attendance.

Before they understood that they were going to be roasted, before they had looked around for a way out, the fire had already poured down on their shoulders. Ruches and festoons, straw from the big hats, muslin from dresses, taffeta from flounces, silk from parasols, veils, ribbons, and feathers, organdy and percale, all the light, wispy fabrics dressing up the bodies of women happy to abandon themselves to an early summer, lit up like a bonfire and blazed in the warm air, which was permeated by exquisite perfumes and ambergris lotions.

That memorable fire is valuable to the historian, and not only for its anecdotal and literary interest. It, along with other exemplary news events, acted as a catalyst, and the reaction it provoked in the society of the time reveals profound realities about that era, brutally stripped bare. Newspapers—especially daily newspapers—which were then at their apogee, reigning without peer over the other media, amplified the "reaction" to such an extent that it was heard in the smallest village. Linotype turned a murmur into a din. The fire was no longer confined to one neighborhood of Paris; the whole country was set ablaze. The newspaper spread the horrors of the charnel house, relating day after day the most intimate and appalling details. Dread and then commiseration soon gave way to conflicting commentary; the sacred union in the face of death was abolished, conflicting interpretations erupted on graves that were barely closed. The event became ideological fodder; rescuers had pulled baronesses from the fire only to hand them over to doctrinaires.

Macabre Rescuers

The fire on Rue Jean-Goujon triggered an excitement in the press that was to last almost the entire month of May, while on the site of the disaster, now the site of a pilgrimage, street peddlers sold gawkers freshly minted lamentations:

> L'or affluait au millieu des sourires,
> De jolis doigts le faisant ruisseler,
> Quand tout à coup virbre un cri de délire:
> Dans le Bazar le feu vient d'éclater.

> Gold flowed amid smiles,
> Trickling through pretty fingers,
> When all of a sudden a hysterical cry rang out:
> Fire had just erupted in the bazaar.

As *L'Eclair* put it, in the matter of poetry, "haste is a poor counselor."

If the bazaar fire provoked a flood of more or less rhyming commentaries, it was certainly because of its scope and brutality. All the same, as we will show, the other great tragedies—mining disasters, for example—were not the occasion for such emotion. The news item resonated as it did because of the social status and sex of the victims. Almost all were from the aristocracy or the haute bourgeoisie, and the overwhelming majority were women: "Once again," wrote Drumont, "death chose the most charming and the most noble heads. Nothing was lacking, not even an archduchess, sister of the empress of Austria." The violent contrast between the "smart outfits," the "shining faces," the "creatures happy to be alive," and the "horrifying catastrophe" became a cliché among all the journalists, and then a theme for political and metaphysical reflection.

The unexpected juxtaposition of beauty (an assembly of worldly, refined women) and (sudden, random) death was all the more fascinating in that this was one of the great themes of romanticism, illustrated throughout the nineteenth century. In the last twenty years of the century, moreover, as Mario Praz has demonstrated, that theme took on all the trappings of "decadentism." All of Gustave Moreau's paintings, which addressed the theme of "the fatality of evil and death, incarnated in feminine beauty"; the etchings of Félicien Rops, for whom evil was personified in woman; and the literary writings of Huysmans, Barbey, Villiers de l'Isle-Adam, Jean Lorrain, Marcel Schwob, and the young Barrès vied with one another to combine "flowers and torments." Barrès wrote in his *Cahiers*: "In

these imagined torments, there is something somber and strangely voluptuous that humanity will savor with delight for centuries."

The *fin de siècle* was in fact sadistic. Its literature and its art delighted in
spectacles of horror, frenzied scenes, descriptions of rare perversions, a
fondness for sacrilege:

> Le meurtre, le viol, le vol, le parricide
> Passent dans mon esprit comme un farouche éclair

> Murder, rape, theft, patricide
> Pass through my mind like a fierce bolt of lightning

said Maurice Rollinat, that second-rate Baudelaire. And René Vivien
added: "Je savoure le goût violent de la mort" (I savor the violent taste of
death). It is clear that deep ties existed between the newspaper accounts
of the bazaar fire and that "decadent" literature. The self-satisfaction with
which the newspapers of the time described not only the tragedy but also
and especially its consequences attests to an obvious propensity toward
sadism: the transfer of the more or less charred cadavers from Rue Jean-
Goujon to the Palais de l'Industrie, where they were displayed for identification by their families; the meticulous description of the remains; the
sorting of lost objects; the scenes of lamentation. Moreover, in this century
where the objective, scientific, statistical mind had the upper hand, the
journalist's unhealthy curiosity was masked under the cold pretensions of
legal medicine, which only added to the grotesque horror of the articles.

Thus *Le Soleil* of 6 May provides this list of bones found: "2 skull fragments, 2 rib fragments, 1 fragment of a long bone, 1 posterior process of a
vertebra, 1 skin fragment, and 3 bundles of hair." On 12 May, *Liberté* announced that "the sum total of various objects discovered in sorting has
risen to 427," and later explained that "this morning, twenty-eight one-
horse garbage wagons and thirty-one two-horse garbage wagons trans-
ported ninety cubic meters of ashes, dust, and debris to the dump, gates
Brancion to Bagnolet." That was a relatively harmless assessment compared to the horrible descriptions the public was fed in the days following
the tragedy. Journalists described young women and nude girls, "devo-
tional medals" around their necks; entirely nude cadavers, "except for an
ankle boot and a bracelet"; abominable mutilations almost unbearable to
look at; decapitated bodies; scalped heads; intestines spilling out, held in
place by the remains of a skirt; "incomplete" debris, "carbonized hands,
formless remains." Although they said, "You get dizzy, your heart fails
you," they continued the lugubrious description, down to the most horrid
details: "A little girl—barely four or five years old—in her nudity displayed her still rosy flesh"; "The tortoise-shell comb Mlle Rosine Morado

was wearing in her hair melted from the heat, and today is part of the scalp of the unfortunate girl, whose suffering is horrendous."

The scenes of identification of the bodies were narrated with a precision that seems strange to our eyes. We are told how dentists, called upon to help, examined the jaws of their presumed patients; how surgeons looked for traces of the most intimate operations; how families fought over remains. "They rushed to the cadavers, turned over scraps of fabric with feverish hands, examined the jewels lying on the dead. . . . Clenched jaws refused all examination. A scalpel had to be used. The cheeks were slit with a wide gash. The molars appeared and with them the tell-tale fillings." In addition to the inventory, more detailed every day, of hair, tibias, and even "kilograms of intestines" found, we are also surprised by the astonishing meticulousness with which they itemized feminine underthings. These things allowed families to identify their dead: garter buttons, scraps of camisole, pieces of petticoats—"silk, with bluish-gray stripes on a white background [which] indicates a certain wealth," a black silk petticoat, a lace slip, and a thousand other elements of the most macabre fetishism.

The third day after the fire, six victims were still unidentified. The newspapers unscrupulously gave "the most compete information [as it was taken] at the dictation of Dr. Socquet." We are spared nothing, as the police description of "cadaver no. 5" attests:

A woman measuring about 1.6 meters, healthy, old and pearly stretch marks on the abdomen proving maternity. Some hair on the legs. Corns on the second and fourth toes of the right foot. Wore garters above the knee. On her: the remains of pantaloons with hemstitched scalloping and six tucks. A scrap of undershirt with a wide hem made of fine linen. Two elastic garters without buckles, the seams of one of them done in large stitches with black thread. A worn ankle boot with pointed toe, medium heel, sole 22 centimeters long.

This morbid, necrophilic, fetishistic press coverage, making claims to science and love of the human race so as to better savor the carnage, unwittingly promoted the assimilation of woman to hell—like all the dark romanticism of the time. "Love and voluptuousness, pain and love call to one another in our imagination," said Barrès in *Du sang, de la volupté et de la mort* (On blood, voluptuousness, and death).

The War Between the Sexes

The attraction/repulsion to the opposite sex was expressed in ambivalent attitudes toward the victims. After they had been stripped bare, had their intestines whipped about, and been reduced to the most funereal of nomenclatures, they were lent assistance. Within a few hours, the rumor spread that all the men present at the time of the fire, thinking only of their own escape, had taken every possible measure to get out of the flames, not hesitating to knock people over, trample them, force their way through, at the expense of the women abandoned in the fire.

On 16 May 1897, the deaths were tallied. One hundred and twenty-one persons perished during or after the fire. Of 116 identified, 110 were female and only 6 male. That disproportion fed the rumor that the men present had behaved like brutes.

"It is now an unfortunately confirmed fact," wrote *La Libre Parole* of 16 May 1897, "that in the charity bazaar catastrophe, men displayed the most deplorable attitude. There is no doubt that some of them, with their fists and blows of their canes, forced their way through groups of panic-stricken women." From then on, anecdotes trickled in about what *L'Intransigeant* called the "acts of ferocity committed at the charity bazaar by high society *franc-fileurs*."[2] *L'Eclair* found the right expression: this was "a women's Agincourt." Eyewitness accounts were collected: "The women able to escape the flames, having recovered from their daze, are now beginning to speak; they attest to the cowardice of the men and to their brutality." We are told that "the hats of ecclesiastics" were found on the site of the disaster; their owners did not bother to come reclaim them. Reporters said that a young man who had brought two lady friends to the bazaar slipped away at the right moment, then, having calmly returned to his circle, declared aloud: "At this moment, the little women of Paris are frying" (*Gil Blas*). A footman recounted that a woman friend of his mistress had her elbow dislocated after being hit by a gentleman's cane, that another man bit a young woman's ear, that the unfortunate women being treated at the hospital continually cried out in their delirium: "Look, there's more men about to trample me." Soon, people were talking of nothing but the pusillanimity of the men present, of their cynicism and ferocity. According to police reports unknown to the newspapers, "certain individuals assert that Duc d'Alençon used his cane and even his stiletto to push aside those who blocked his way. The story is being repeated and we believe we should record it without further confirmation."

The legend of the "Gardenias" took root. Several newspapers mocked and berated the elegant youths, flowers in their lapels, who had failed in all their duties. Handbills were distributed in the street to gibe at the "royal runaways," "the baron of Getaway," "the art and manner of pulling your feet out of the fire without getting roasted," "the knights of Cowardice."

Women, Be Women

Once that attitude of cowardice had been denounced, a few commentators attempted to seek its cause in "the changing mores." In *Le Soleil*,

Furetière was sorry that "the worship of woman" was weakening—but he made women themselves responsible for it: "At the first women's congress, I protested forcefully against the revolutionary inclinations of some of the women leaders who found men's courtesy toward women insulting." As a result, he said, there was too much familiarity between young men and girls: "Walking, riding horses, riding bicycles together, the promiscuity of a life of camaraderie," portended a future of competition in the employment market, even though it was only proper to spare women "work contrary to their nature or which might interfere with their providential mission, motherhood."

In *Le Temps*, in the meantime, it was claimed that the war between the sexes threatened to spread to all of society. At the Ecole des Beaux-Arts, where women had very recently been admitted to certain classes, male students raised a great racket against the "second sex," requiring police intervention. A good part of the press defended the students: a woman architect, can you imagine?

The moral of the fable was that women should remain women so that men would remain chivalrous. But what did it mean to remain a woman? It probably meant resembling the portrait drawn by M. de Kerohant at *Le Soleil*: "Yes, in all classes of society, woman knows how to be heroic because she has heart. Her head is often flighty—a scatterbrain—but her heart is good." And it is the heart that inspires the spirit of sacrifice, suggests acts of devotion and abnegation. Victor Hugo wrote one of his most beautiful lines on the subject: "Quand tout se fait petit, femmes, vous restez grandes" (When everything is becoming small, women, you remain great). The debate on the value of women and the cowardice of men was cut short, however. After all, the men in question were not just anyone, they were men of "the upper crust" (*de la haute*), as they said at the time. That is why a few newspapers set to demolishing the rumor. *Le Gaulois* undertook a broad survey of the men and women who survived the fire and established the misleading, or in any case exaggerated, nature of the rumor. There may have been a few bad moves in the panic, but they were the exception.

Then the matter became social and political, the war between the sexes giving way to the class struggle: "Well, then," wrote *Le National*, "the blood of these victims cries out and wants to be avenged. If Parisians had their hands on the distinguished and select personalities who not only let go of the women they were flirting with a minute before but detesably sacrificed them to escape from the furnace, if Parisians had their hands on them, they would make quick work of applying the lynch law to them." The article was entitled "Les muscadins impunis" (The unpunished dandies).

Since the ladies of the bazaar took back their first declarations and asserted the perfectly dignified conduct of the men present, Henri Rochefort declared in *L'Intransigeant*: "These ladies know that the individuals with whom they associate and whom they marry to their daughters are the most cowardly, the most abject, and the must despicable men imaginable; but, in the interest of religion and aristocracy, they will continue all the same to pretend they believe in their respectability."

Class Struggle

The "cowardice of the little gentlemen," as *La Patrie* put it, was less an expression of the weaknesses of the male sex than of the irreversible decline of the old ruling classes. The republican press was happy to contrast that inertia with the bravery and temerity of the children of the people, represented by the generous rescuers, those fleeting figures on the front page who attracted populist fervor for several weeks.

In the days immediately following the disaster, the press had recorded a few discordant voices contradicting the fine unanimity in commiseration to which editorialists devoted their purple prose. "Mourning for the rich!" was heard here and there, before the charred debris. In an influential article entitled "Esprit de classe" (Class spirit), Clemenceau denounced the way the state and the Church had exploited the "awful disaster for class interests and class spirit." He deplored the fact that people were less moved by victims of the firedamp explosion than by the bazaar victims, as if for the latter "there [was] a criminal twist of fate, while for the former, there [was] nothing extraordinary, eliciting no more than two days of commonplace laments and noisy alms." He ended with the antagonistic images of fleeing dandies and rescuers from the lower classes:

Look at those young men from high society who strike panic-stricken women with their canes and boots, who slip away like cowards from the peril. Look at those servants to the rescue. Look at those workers who happen to be passing by, heroically risking their lives: the plumber Piquet, who saved twenty human beings and returned to his shop covered with burns without saying a word. Meditate on that if you can, last representatives of the degenerate castes and bourgeois ruling parties of class spirit. (19 May 1897)

For several days, the republican dailies tried to top one another with populist hagiography. They depicted the rescuers: the plumber Piquet, returning to his shop after pulling twenty women from the fire "without noticing that his face was scarred with terrible burns"; the coachman Eugène Georges, "the hero who went into the inferno on Rue Jean-Goujon at least ten times, probably more"; the cook Gaumery at Hôtel du Palais who, after pulling the bars off a window overlooking the vacant lot that separated the hotel from the bazaar buildings, helped dozens of women get through that unhoped-for exit; the coachman Vast; the groom Trosch; the cesspit worker Dhuy. *Le Jour* intended to celebrate "the generous valor of the children of the people," organizing a "rescuers' banquet" in their honor.

"And it was the people, the anonymous people, who in the person of these chance brave souls, revealed—through the heroism of a few obscure, unknown, and ignored passersby among them—that they are the possessors of the principle of action and life."

On 20 May, the rescuers' banquet took place in the Salle du Gymnase on Rue Huyghens. A reporter from *Le Jour* commented that "it was one of the most brilliant." Music, speeches, toasts: there was no objection on principle. All the same, the comments of a few of the orators attracted the wrath of the rightist press, which attacked the "free-thinking louts," the "filthy Communards" who had taken the floor and tried "to insult God and the priests."

Le Soir, which expressed the view of the ruling classes, castigated the press campaign, which

on the pretext of glorifying the little people, [covered] with mud those who did not have the luck to be born plumbers. It is to be hoped that the vain and ill-considered polemics unleashed on the subject of a catastrophe that did not entail political and social inferences will be definitively closed. On all sides—the lower classes, the bourgeoisie, and the aristocracy—people have done their duty. An oligarchy of courage is no more tolerable than the political oligarchy and, in order to raise the ration of praise falling to the cesspit workers, you do not have the right to take any away from the sons of crusaders" (22 May 1897).

Nonetheless, the class conflict was again given free rein at a session of the Chamber at the end of May. The words of Albert de Mun, Catholic deputy, provoked the hostility of the far left, which reminded him of his past as a "Versaillais" against the Commune: "You have insulted our cadavers," the old Communard Pascal Grousset cried.

La Petite République commented: "The Comte de Mun, 'that supplier of machine guns,' too easily forgets that it is the sons of the Communards he once had massacred who are now the only ones capable of saving the wives and daughters of all his aristocratic gang from danger" (30 May 1897).

The Exterminating Angel

In the debate following the fire, the class conflict, though manifest, was not as sharp as the metaphysical conflict. Or rather, in large measure, the class struggle was expressed through the religious question. On the eve of the Dreyfus affair, which was to lead to, among other things, the separation of Church and state, France was still profoundly divided between Catholics, who generally embraced the values of the ancien régime, and freethinkers, who were solidly behind the "republican contingent." Since 1879, that is, since MacMahon had left the presidency, the Republic had been progressively secularized, to the great displeasure of the "clerical contingent." Secularization, the great sin of France—"the eldest daughter of the Church"—was vilified by Reverend Father Ollivier, a Dominican, at the commemorative ceremony of Notre Dame. Félix Faure, the president of the Republic, and members of the Méline government were in attendance.

Father Ollivier seized the opportunity—too good to pass up, in fact—to reassert the Catholic vocation of France. If God had allowed that dreadful fire, it was because he wanted to warn the people of that country. He wanted "to give a terrible lesson to the pridefulness of this century, when man talks endlessly of his victory over God." And the Dominican, alluding to the immediate cause of the disaster, attributed to the explosion of a projector light, went on to speak ironically of "the achievements of science, so vain when not linked" to the science of God. The scientistic century was being punished: "The flame he claims to have wrested from your hands like Prometheus of old, you have made into the instrument of your reprisal."

In the presence of the atheist and Freemason representatives of the Third Republic, the impetuous Dominican denounced the profound cause of the disaster: "France deserved this punishment for having again abandoned its traditions. Instead of marching at the head of Christian civilization, it has consented to follow as a servant or slave doctrines as foreign to its genius as to its baptism." France had taken the wrong road, the road of apostasy, and "the exterminating angel has passed."

This theme of a sacrifice of innocents to regenerate sinful France was to inspire inexhaustible glosses and moralizing writings, by writers who made every effort to set the sermon of Father Ollivier to alexandrines. Let us cite, for example, *L'incendie du Bazar de la Charité* (The charity bazaar fire), a mystery play in two scenes, written by the canon L. M. Dubois, and published by the Librairie Salésienne in 1899.

In this piece of doggerel, destined for "boarding houses with a distinguished clientele," the good canon made every effort to demonstrate, in the gleam of the fire, that France must return repentant to the faith of its fathers. After a few evanescent dialogues, "the angel of expiation" gives the moral of the story:

Ah maintenant de deuil votre coeur s'emplisse;
Recueillez tout le sang versé dans un calice.
Le Seigneur a fauché sa divine moisson,
Dans un monde incroyant, il a pris sa rançon.

And now with grief let your heart be filled;
Collect in a chalice all the blood spilled.
The Lord has mowed down his divine harvest,
In an unbelieving world, he has exacted the cost.

The same idea was also expressed in *La Croix*, the newspaper of the Assumptionists, in the aftermath of the catastrophe—a catastrophe so sudden, so extraordinary, that no one could "mistake [its] providential design." Alluding to the sacrifice of Joan of Arc, which is celebrated in May, *La Croix* wrote: "There is no remission without the shedding of blood, and if the foundation of the Church was sealed with the blood of three million chosen martyrs, coming to form a procession to the Crucified, why should the reestablishment of a more Christian life in our France not be announced by this pyre, where lilies of purity blended with roses of charity?" (7 May 1897).

It goes without saying that the republican, radical, and socialist press vehemently rejected that Catholic interpretation of divine punishment and necessary sacrifice aimed at the re-Christianization of France. Father Ollivier's sermon, delivered in the presence of the highest authorities of the state, elicited vengeful replies. At the rescuers' banquet, a singer expressed secular indignation—in octosyllables:

De quel limon sont donc pétris
Les tonsurés au coeur de pierre
Qui verraient flamber tout Paris
Sans une larme à leur paupière?

Tribuns d'Eglise, ivres de fiel
Et de rancune apostolique,
Qui prennent à témoin le ciel
Des crimes de la République?

What sort of clay are they molded from,
These tonsured men with heart of stone,
Who could see all Paris go up in flames
Without a tear upon their lash?

Church tribunes, drunk on gall
And on apostolic spite,
Who take heaven as their witness
For the Republic's crimes?

The far left was not satisfied to attack "the ignoble Father Ollivier" (H. Rochefort), "that priest preaching from the throne of the wanderer of Judea" (Clemenceau) in the press. Where the clerical press saw the sign of divine intervention, the republicans were delighted with that proof of God's nonexistence. Since the catastrophe had erupted immediately after the benediction and departure of the papal nuncio on a Catholic site devoted to a work of charity, it was easy to indulge in commentaries "on the illogical, unspeakable conduct of *that* God, conduct that would be criminal if such a mythical being actually existed" (*La Lanterne*, 6 May 1897). Hence the obligatory commentary from *Le Radical*: "The day that the spirit of science, of calculation, of certainty, and of prophylaxis has clearly and in practical terms taken the place of all our fanciful, imaginative preoccupations and our ridiculous faith, on that day we will have exercised dominion over nature and carried out our missions as men" (12 May 1897). The chairman of the Chamber, Henri Brisson, at the session of 18 May, challenged "the conception of a god who, not content to have struck down our country twenty-six years ago, would have again taken a hundred generous women as hostages for our crimes [prolonged and repeated applause] and would pursue France with his wrath until he has forced it to reestablish unity and obedience [new and lively applause]."

The conflict became political because of the presence of the president of the Republic, the Freemason Félix Faure, at the Notre Dame ceremony: "What a beautiful spectacle, these atheists, these hypocritical Freemasons praying for noble ladies who could not pronounce their names without making the sign of the cross" (Clemenceau). That spectacle was no more to the taste of the far right. Paul de Cassagnac's newspaper, *L'Autorité*, recalled that the Republic "robbed the monasteries . . . chased the Church and God out of schools and hospitals." But the far left especially was indignant about the holy water Félix Faure had received without flinching. In the Chamber, the Méline government had to justify itself to the champions of secularism, who reminded him that Father Ollivier, who belonged to the order of Dominicans—a dissolved order—had already raised a scandal during MacMahon's time by declaring from his pulpit at Notre-Dame-de-Lorette, "Republicans are like cheese: the more there are of them, the more they stink."

"A Beginning of Justice"

We should note, however, that in the Catholic camp, a few independent individuals registered their dissent. Hence there were allusions in the provincial press to the refusal of the Catholic ruling classes to loyally follow the recommendations of Leo XIII regarding social policy. A completely different but more thunderous reaction came from Léon Bloy. He was a writer, poor to the point of abjection, an incantatory visionary, theological fundamentalist, destroyer of the bourgeoisie. He bellowed like a prophet, vituperating against a Catholicism that had fallen into sinister mediocrity. He could not read the tragedy of Rue Jean-Goujon as anything but an unknown truth about the Catholic hierarchy. It was a punishment, in fact—God's punishment for the Church's scandalous compromise with money:

My dear André, I hope I am not scandalizing you by telling you that upon reading the first news of that dreadful event, I had the clear and delicious sensation of an immense weight being lifted from my heart. The small number of victims, it is true, limited my joy. Finally, I said to myself all the same, finally, FINALLY! Now is a beginning of justice.

That word "bazaar" tacked onto that of CHARITY! The terrible and burning Name of God reduced to the status of modifier for that obscene word!!!

In that bazaar, then, signs borrowed from seedy bars, from bordellos—AT THE SPINNING SOW, for example; priests and nuns moving about those narrow aristocratic pathways and dragging poor innocent creatures with them!

And the papal nuncio coming to bless all that!

Two searing pages follow on the glory of the avenging Holy Ghost:

As long as the papal nuncio had not given his benediction to the lovely clothes, the delicate and voluptuous carcasses covered by these lovely clothes could not have assumed the black and horrible form of their souls. Until that moment, there was no danger.

But the benediction, the Benediction, unspeakable sacrilege from one who represented the vicar of Jesus Christ, and hence Jesus Christ himself, was what it always becomes, that is, FIRE, which is the howling, roving binnacle of the Holy Ghost.

Then, immediately, FIRE was unleashed, and EVERYTHING RETURNED TO ORDER.

Fin de Siècle

Since the *fin de siècle* has become fixed in our minds through the Dreyfus affair, we may have too much of a tendency to imagine the psychology of that society of 1900 as being more rational than it was. Between those who stood up for justice before anything else and those who battled for order and the nation above all, we imagine an opposition between two rationally defensible theses. And in fact, the exchange of arguments between the Dreyfusard left and the anti-Dreyfusard right, from which Maurras later deduced his monarchist system on empirical grounds, often appealed to reason, despite the passions involved.

Nevertheless, the triumph of reason was far from obvious, in spite of the "progress of science," the achievements of public education, and the progressive secularization of the state. We might mention at least two phenomena of the time that attest to the profound resistance to that conquest of reason: first, the rise of occult sciences, black magic, Satanism; and second—but psychologically linked to the first—the extraordinary development of anti-Semitism beginning in the 1880s.

The most serious newspapers spread the rumor that the charity bazaar fire had been predicted a year before it occurred by Mlle Couédon, a famous seer, in the salons of Mme de Maille. Before a large audience, she was reported to have declared, after invoking "the angel Gabriel":

> Près des Champs Elysées,
> Je vois un endroit pas élevé
> Qui n'est pas pour la piété
> Mais qui en est approché
> Dans un but de charité
> Qui n'est pas la vérité . . .
> Je vois le feu s'élever
> Et les gens hurler . . .
> Des chairs grillées,
> Des corps calcinés.
> J'en vois comme par pelletées.

> Near the Champs-Elysées
> I see a place not too elevated
> Which is not for piety
> But which is approached
> In the aim of charity
> Which is not the truth . . .
> I see fire rising up
> And people screaming . . .
> Flesh roasted,
> Charred bodies.
> I see them as if in shovelfuls.

People who listened to her were supposedly spared. In fact, *Le Gaulois* of 15 May 1897 reported that "none of the guests of that evening, all more or less assiduous in charity sales, perished or were even harmed in the horrible catastrophe of last 4 May."

Another story of presentiment was repeated by all the newspapers as a "singular phenomenon." The morning of the disaster, Sister Marie-Madeleine from the Orphanage for Blind Youth told her friends: "You will not see me again; I will be brought back burned alive." The nun did in fact die in the fire that afternoon.

At that *fin de siècle*, people proved to be curious about the occult sciences and all phenomena of parapsychology. Penny novels, elite literature, and newspapers alike recounted numerous tales of bewitchment, black masses, and ritual murder. It was within this context that Drumont wrote his most hysterical anti-Semitic arguments.

There is no apparent reason why anti-Semitism should have manifested itself in this episode. Those liable for the fire were not Jewish, and since the Rothschild mansion was actually contiguous to the bazaar lot, many women were brought to the stables of the famous Jewish baron and saved. However, in examining the press file, knowing the anti-Semitic obsession at the end of the century, I expected to find one of those manifestations as stormy as they were common. As it happens, it occurred when I was no longer expecting it. To compensate for the losses caused by the fire, *Le Figaro* took the initiative of organizing a fund. It was a success from the first day. But then, an anonymous donor sent in a million francs in one lump sum to advance the charity bazaar the exact amount of the proceeds from the previous year's sale. After a few days of uncertainty, *Le Figaro* thought it could reveal that the exceptional gift had come from Baronne Hirsh— that is, from a Jew. She immediately denied it. There was an outcry. On 19 May, Paul de Cassagnac wrote an article for *L'Autorité* entitled "Trop, trop de Juifs" (Too too many Jews). The Jews, he said, are not more generous than Christians; they are simply richer. But since it was known that the money in question was of Christian origin, *Le Figaro*'s attitude was odious, because it wished to "exalt the Jews and suppress the merit of Catholics." Drumont's *La Libre Parole*, French monitor of anti-Semitism, following its usual inclinations, could not waste such a godsend. When the provenance of the famous gift was made public—Mme Lebaudy, a Catholic—*La Libre Parole* glorified the ostentatious charity of high Jewry, transforming the columns of *Le Figaro* into a Golgotha almanac,[3] and ripping apart "that cynical plutocracy of gold" ("Les deux charités," *La Libre Parole*, 19 May 1897).

In the months that followed, anti-Semitism, which broke in successive waves and found the legal proof of its fantasies in Captain Dreyfus's conviction, expressed in its own pathological manner the deep anxiety of a society that was trembling at its foundations. The Drumont doctrine, sustained by the leagues, a powerful press, and often the crème de la crème of the ruling classes, allowed the French petty bourgeoisie to find reassurance in the face of transformations affecting the old rural civilization. Anti-Semitism made its appearance as a reaction to the fear inspired by modernity. Industrialization, urbanization—and, on equal footing—the secularization of French society, the wave of anarchy, and the progress of the workers' movement provoked a deep and lasting uneasiness in many strata of society. In this respect, Drumont's books—with all their hallucinations, obsessions, and phobias—are revealing inasmuch as they found an extraordinary following.

The nineteenth century ended in a climate of confusion and uncertainty—witness the wave of literary decadentism, rich in catastrophes and permeated with the idea of decline. "To dissimulate the state of decadence we have reached would be the height of insanity. Religion, mores, justice, everything is decaying. . . . Society is disintegrating under the corrosive action of a decadent civilization," wrote *Le Décadent* as early as 1886.

The charity bazaar fire was interpreted as a precursory sign. Of what? Opinions diverged on that matter. But in opposition to a small minority of freethinkers who explained the disaster as a matter of chance, and chance as a matter of calculated probabilities, most contemporaries rejected the reasoning of primary school instructors. Secret laws governed the world. The Catholics recalled their credo even as they interpreted this divine sign in diverse ways, as we have seen. But whether Catholic or not, the French people had the impression they were living under the threat of fate. The Catholic Bloy proclaimed at the time: "Be prepared . . . prepare yourselves for many other catastrophes next to which the infamous bazaar will seem benign. The end of the century is near and I know that the world is threatened as never before."

A less prophetic observer, Henry Céard, wrote at the same time, in May 1897: "With our heads in the sand, we refuse to be persuaded that at every hour, [life] threatens us, and even as I write this the day is full of perils and fear." Under the threat of this frightening *tomorrow*, all sought reassurance in their own manner, in the name of science, in the name of occult practices, in the name of faith, in the name of various chimera. And very often, politics itself was only one area among others to which contemporary Westerners transferred their obsession with death, disguising it all the while.

The history of anxiety is an enormous subject for the historian.

CHAPTER 5

Eternal Decadence

THE DISCOURSE of "decadence" is once more in the air. The word, drummed into us by the leader of the National Front in each of his shows, has acquired a new validation as a result of Julien Freund's scholarly work recently devoted to it.[1] We have entered a new phase, perhaps a long and painful era of abasement; we are rushing toward the abyss. France is decomposing. National identity is becoming blurred. There are no more ideals, no colonies; spelling is deteriorating. Corruption is spreading. Criminality is growing. Young people are being ruined by drugs and irreligion, thus accelerating the end of the world. Society has entered a state of advanced anomie, which is translated into more robust terms: "Everything is going to hell!"

It is an old tune, which the French have heard since the Revolution. We have had two hundred years of uninterrupted "decadence," despite occasional appearances to the contrary: that is one of the most firmly rooted convictions of reactionaries, a conviction diffused in cycles, especially in times of economic recession, political uncertainty, or social unrest. It is a refrain as old as the world, already hummed by the Greeks and Romans, and it has regained favor among the public, like an old buried horror coming to the surface of civilization. In France, Barrès became its cantor at the end of the last century; Drieu La Rochelle, his avowed disciple, made it his anthem in the 1930s; Pétain and his bishops made it the principle of the "Great Collapse" (*Grande Culbute*) of 1940. In his turn, Jean-Marie Le Pen, record shop owner of Trinité-sur-Mer, who knows a successful song when he hears it, sings the refrain onstage. As in previous cases, the only choice remaining after a diagnosis of decadence is between Restoration and Apocalypse.

***

Decadence is not a scientific concept, but a vague notion with rich connotations. In inventorying them, we shall better grasp the content and ideological function of this everyday term, which is used carelessly in this instance. Without claiming to be exhaustive, I offer a few correlatives that have constantly appeared with the theme of decadence:

1. Hatred of the present. In his *Dictionnaire des idées reçues* (Dictionary of received ideas), Flaubert already observed this tendency. We read in the article "Epoque (la nôtre)" (Age [our own]): "Thunder against it.—Complain it is not poetic.—Call it an age of transition, of decadence." The philosophy of decadence, in a Dantesque approach, takes on the task of cataloguing all living signs of the Fall, even when they are contradictory. An inability to live in the here and now lies at the root of everything. A hundred years ago, Edouard Drumont launched his complaint: "Never has France been in a more critical situation."[2] What is intolerable about the present is that it is open to all possibilities; it is dangerous, like an intersection without stoplights or traffic cops.

2. Nostalgia for a golden age. The present is odious in that it is one stage in the degradation of an original model privileged as a blessed time, a paradise lost that has been assaulted by modernity. The representation of history varies depending on the author: one grieves for the time of cathedrals, another for the beauty and order of the age of Louis XIV, another even for the Napoleonic age. The important thing is to understand that the old harmony between man and nature, between man and the divine, or between man and man, has been shattered. "I dream incessantly," says one of the characters in Drieu's *Gilles*, "of the value of gold, of primitive value before any deterioration."[3]

3. Praise of immobility. "What do I like about the past?" asks Barrès. "Its sadness, its silence, and especially its fixity. I am troubled by movement."[4] Decadence is often just a synonym for "change." Maurras wages war on romanticism, an aesthetics of instability, and praises classicism as an absolute standard: order, measure, symmetry, discipline, alignment.[5] Even for Plato, the golden age was already that of a perfect political state, that is, a definitively immobile political state. Change is evil. Roots are good. "For my part," declares François Brigneau, "I love France and a certain France, an agricultural, familial, artisanal France; I do not love the France of cities."[6] That leads to the abundant exploitation of the forest metaphor in the literature of decadence. The tree is a metaphor for fixity, for remaining in one place over time; it is figure of authenticity, of genealogy. The tree is a symbol for sedentary genius, in contrast to the evil spell of Jewish-style nomadism. To beech or not to beech: "What this beech tree says will always be said again, in one form or another, forever."[7]

4. Anti-individualism. For most thinkers of decadence, what has been lost is an organic world with a *head*, accepted hierarchies, men in solidarity with one another out of need (and not by choice, as Rousseau's *Social Contract* would have it). From that perspective, liberalism is much more despicable for many people than socialism, since it leads to the disintegration of the state and the ruin of society, where collectivist revolutions take root. Bonald, one of the master thinkers of counterrevolution, wanted to put the individual back in its place once and for all: "Man exists only for society and society forms him only for itself."[8]

5. Apologia for a society of elites. Decadence comes from the weakening or the end of the old elites. "France as it has been constructed by universal suffrage," writes Renan, "has become profoundly materialistic; the noble concerns of the France of yesteryear, patriotism, enthusiasm for the beautiful, love of glory, have disappeared with the noble classes, which once represented the soul of France. Judgment and the management of things have been transferred to the masses; and the masses are listless, crude, dominated by the most superficial self-interest."[9] For Julius Evola, one of the most systematic theorists of decadence, universal history is subject to the law of caste regression: after the priestly caste, the warrior caste, and the bourgeoisie, the servant classes have now seized power. François Brigneau is less speculative, simply declaring: "I have a kind of horror of the plebs."[10] The reign of the plebs, the reign of public assistance, the reign of laziness!

6. Nostalgia for the sacred. The thinkers of decadence are not necessarily Christian. Some of them denounce Christianity as a doctrine of dissolution (see, for example, the anti-Christian interpretations of the "fall" of the Roman Empire), but the loss of the sacred, the end to taboos, the despiritualization of man and society, are denounced as so many scourges. Materialism has taken hold of people's minds. Bonald tells us that is because "religion is the reasoning faculty of every society." And Louis Veuillot adds: "O decadence of a people without God! Decadence without remedy and without hope."[11] And Péguy echoes: "That awful penury of the sacred is without a doubt the deepest mark of the modern world."[12]

7. The fear of genetic degradation and demographic collapse. The philosophy of decadence feeds on the anxiety elicited by a deterioration in the group, the race, the national collectivity through the increase in individuals deemed inferior. Gobineau and Vacher de Lapouge formulated these phobias in the nineteenth century with respect to interracial marriages, which necessarily resulted in the worst physical and moral abominations. Maurice Bardèche blamed "the anarchical freedom of democracies" for having opened society "on all sides to every deluge, every miasma, every fetid wind, with no sea wall against decadence." He depicts Western man as a poor soul abandoned defenseless on a steppe:

Monsters make their nest on that steppe, rats, toads, snakes, turn it into a sewer. That swarm has the right to grow, like any other nettle or weed. Freedom means the importation of anything whatever. All the filth other peoples want to get rid of also has the right to settle on the steppe without delay, to make noise, to make law, and to mix negroid dreams, the stench of witchcraft, cannibal nightmares with our blood. . . . The appearance of an adulterous race within a nation is the modern form of genocide, and democracies systematically favor it.[13]

The present-day fear of "Arab submersion" is accompanied by an apprehension about European depopulation through "demographic collapse." Jean Cau writes: "We have the impression that the Western womb has dried up, its ovaries shriveled and its belly barren."[14]

8. *The censure of moral values.* Almost all the literature on decadence rails against sexual license (see the cliché on "the Romans of decadent times"). In fact, that license contributes to genetic degradation. In the past, it was syphilis ("Everything is but syphilis," the hero of *A rebours* [Against the grain][15] imagines, and Drieu writes: "There is a virulent syphilis in France");[16] today, it is AIDS. Bad morals lead to putrefaction and death. There is only one solution, writes the far right newspaper *Présent*: marital fidelity. In the same way, Renan praised "chaste peoples" and maintained that the French made love too often.[17] Jean Jaélic, in *La Droite, cette inconnue* (The unknown Right) arrived at this clinical conclusion: "We could almost define the republic as the rejection of a profound sexual discipline"[18] (an apothegm no doubt dedicated to Louis XIV!). Particular mention must be made of homosexuality, whose visibility, real or imaginary, is a sure sign of decadence. In 1955, Jean-Marie Le Pen gathered the overwhelming evidence together in a single phrase: "France is governed by pederasts: Sartre, Camus, Mauriac."[19] The writer, the intellectual, even the mere college graduate belong in effect to maleficent categories.

9. *Anti-intellectualism.* "France is afflicted," declared Pierre Poujade in the middle of the 1950s, "by an overproduction of people with degrees, economists, philosophers, Polytechnique graduates, and other dreamers who have lost contact with the real world."[20] The prophet of decadence privileges instinct, habit, prejudice, reflexes conditioned by generations of human beings who have lived on the same land, at the expense of reason, a pretentious reason led astray by schoolmasters and intellectuals. "Intelligence!" said Barrès, "What a little thing on the surface of our beings!"[21] During the same period, Gustave Le Bon uttered this lament: "The schools today form malcontents and anarchists and prepare for decadent times among Latin peoples."[22]

Here is Le Pen's updated version: "I am sure we grant excessive importance to the university, to schooling. . . . Culture is not the exclusive goal, life is the goal."[23]

These nine correlatives are not exhaustive; we find them to a greater or lesser extent among thinkers and vulgarizers of decadence. They form the body of antimodernism and of antidemocratism. Various interpretations, not mutually exclusive, may be advanced.

First, there is the Marxist-style explanation, based on class struggle. Within that perspective, the discourse of decadence is the discourse of the defeated. It entails an inversion of signs: what is progress for the people, the masses, former slaves, is decadence for the aristocracy and its clientele. Hence, from the masters's perspective, the end of slave society is experienced as decadence. Similarly, for small businessmen and artisans, the construction of department stores and strip malls has the effect not only of ruining them but of handing victory over to the mediocrity of mass-produced goods. It is self-evident that for the landed aristocracy defeated in 1830, bourgeois France, whose history truly began under Louis-Philippe, was the beginning of the end.

Second, there is a historical explanation, emphasizing the observable variations in intensity in the discourse of decadence. It is perceptible in times of trouble, inaudible in times of prosperity. When crisis speaks, it speaks in Decadentese. It is remarkable that at a time when France was about to lose its colonial empire, in the early 1960s, everyone spoke of progress, growth, "greatness." These were not just pretexts for General de Gaulle; the economic boom, the restoration of state power, international détente, the conquest of space all favored sales of Teilhard de Chardin's books rather than those of Maurice Barrès.

Third, if we open the angle of the historical viewer a bit wider, we can also put forward the notion of the great change Karl Popper called the end of closed society. The relatively brutal shift from tribal, rural, and patriarchal society to urban, industrial, and liberal society provoked a series of fears, which can be summed up in the primary one, "the fear of freedom."[24] The indeterminateness of historical change and of individuals' futures has replaced the determinism of closed society, the reproduction over generations of practices and customs, simple faith. Life is no longer repetition, but risk. Solitude, anxiety, and fatigue are often the high price to be paid for it. Once upon a time, everyone was where he or she belonged.

Fourth, a more anthropological interpretation would assimilate the discourse of decadence to the discourse of a person facing death. As individuals grow old, they have a tendency to overestimate the happy days of their childhood. There is always a drawback to being born, as Cioran says, but it gets worse with age. The selective work of memory tends to obliterate the negative aspects of the early years. The nostalgia for a protected world acts to derail the intellect: one moves from one's own life to the history of society. It is only rarely that old people experiencing a decline of their own strength do not imagine they are experiencing the decay of their country. Mircea Eliade writes: "Significantly, one may observe a certain continuity, across the ages and across many cultures, of human behavior with respect to time." To be cured of the effects of time, one must "go back in time," return to "the beginning of the world."[25]

However we envision that etiology, the discourse on decadence is never innocent. It is in step with individual and collective behavior. It can justify contempt for the world, a fatalism leading to nonparticipation, to withdrawal into mysticism: such was the case for René Guénon in *La crise du monde moderne* (The crisis of the modern world, 1927). It can favor an aesthetic attitude: the "Decadents" presented themselves as a rare essence, a residual species from the golden age who, far from the masses, were allowed every eccentricity. But not everyone is Huysmans, and those who cannot create a Des Esseintes must be content to rail against television, soccer, or rock and roll. There are even more pernicious uses of decadence: the term assumes its definitive force in appeals for monocephalous power. Since there is "decadence," we must put an end to its supposed causes, which are reiterated, confirmed, and verified: foreigners, Arabs, Jews, general laxity, and by degrees, political freedom. We must prepare for the "conservative revolution," the return to "values," and the cult of a providential leader.

Every month, Abbé Georges de Nantes sends the message of traditionalism, *La Contre-Réforme catholique* (The Catholic Counter-reformation) to his faithful. In issue 241 of March 1988, we read:

Now, I tell you: will you have the courage to pray that in the next "debacle," a new Philippe Pétain will be given us—"*divine surprise*"!—who, knowing what awaits him afterwards! will be capable of "giving the gift of his person to France, to attenuate unhappiness"? For I am persuaded that in his incommensurable love for us, the good Lord will have us endure the same punishments as in 1940–44, so that this time, we, a lying and murderous people, will be forced to repent and truly return to Him, instead of condemning our saviors to death, or to life in prison!

Q.E.D.

CHAPTER 6

Diabolical Causality

THERE IS ALWAYS an explanation for human misfortune. At least, human beings always need an explanation. If they are unable to find it, they invent it. Plots, the secret work of conspirators, conspiracy: in the end, one always finds a trace of them in the causes of defeats, epidemics, or decadence.

The conspiracy theory, writes Karl Popper, is the view that everything in society, including things that by general rule people do not like, such as war, unemployment, poverty, penury, come about as the direct result of the designs of certain powerful individuals and groups. The inspector directing the investigation wonders who has benefited from the crime: that is how the detective novel explanation of history proceeds. Once the plot has been uncovered, the enemy named, and light shed, anxiety subsides and energy is mobilized. "Diabolical causality" (the title of a book by Léon Poliakov)[1] makes "the origin of persecution" (the book's subtitle) comprehensible.

There are vast numbers of conspiracies, either occasional or lasting. Hence, seeking to understand—but without too much effort—the causes of the uprising of the Paris Commune in 1871, a certain number of publicists "revealed" the sole cause, the primary cause responsible for all the evil: the activity of the Workers' Internationale. According to some, the Internationale, created in 1864, had several hundreds of thousands of members—statistics without any relation to the very modest reality.[2] Their activity was overestimated; in short, there was hysteria. But the hysteria was not gratuitous: apart from the fact that it saved people the trouble of reflecting on the profound causes of the Communalist movement, the misdeeds of the government of national defense, and the errors of the Conservative Assembly in Versailles, it also justified the repression and ban of the Internationale in France.

History has known a variety of "demons" and "scapegoats," including, perhaps surprisingly, the Jesuits. In the early seventeenth century, the idea spread that the aim of the famous Society of Jesus was no more nor less than the assurance of "universal domination." The origin of this rapidly leaked secret was a counterfeit document fabricated in 1613 by a former Polish novice who had been dismissed. The text went through more than three hundred editions under the title *Monita secreta societatis Jesu.* In 1762, under Louis XV, the Jesuits were banished from France. In the nineteenth century, Edgar Quinet, Eugène Sue, and Jules Michelet adopted and developed the themes of Jesuitophobia better than anyone else. In particular, the reverend fathers were accused of wanting "to naturalize in France the anti-French genius of Austrian Spain, of which Jesuitism is the true expression."[3]

The Freemasons also had their hour of glory. Their "underground" rites and anti-Catholicism were an invitation to those faithful to Rome, especially the Jesuits, to denounce their machinations. Drumont, for example, explained that Freemasonry was "entirely devoted to Germany," which allowed him to explain Jules Ferry's "treason." "Freemasonry told Ferry: 'If France is to rise again, it will need the union of all its sons. You will provoke a dreadful and unimaginable religious war.' And Ferry replied: 'I will obey.'"[4]

Freemasonry was in league with the devil because it took up the Enlightenment torch against Catholic dogma. "Since the temptation," Eugen Weber explains,

Satan has always symbolized power, the idea that the world and the self could be dominated by thought, reason, speculation, invention, and will, independent of God, his will, and his authority. Incapable of imagining knowledge as a personal acquisition, the men of the Middle Ages, often encouraged by the Church, attributed knowledge to diabolical intervention. Like Dr. Faustus, Roger Bacon and Pope Sylvester II supposedly signed pacts with the devil, and it was to the devil that Pope Gregory XVI attributed the invention of the steam engine.[5]

The greatest conspiracy in history, carried out on a global scale, nonetheless remains the fantastical Jewish conspiracy, as it was imagined in the nineteenth century. In the end, Hitler decided to "radically extirpate it."[6] At least an honorable mention in this competition of the imagination may be bestowed on Urbain Gohier, who explains in *La terreur juive* (The Jewish terror):

Although dispersed across the surface of the earth, the 12 million Jews compose the only homogeneous, and the most resolutely nationalist, nation. In the modern world, their dispersion does not prevent a narrow community of interests, an extraordinary discipline in the acquisition of universal domination. Watchwords launched by the heads of the Jewish nation in whatever part of the world they find themselves are transmitted, heard, and obeyed immediately in every country; and countless obscure and irresistible forces immediately prepare for the desired effect, the triumph or ruin of a government, an institution, an enterprise, or a man.

We learn a bit later that the mysteries of that formidable organization have been plumbed, through the very opportune discovery of *The Protocols of the Elders of Zion*, which was in fact invented by the czarist police, and whose shady history Norman Cohn has since recounted for us.[7]

With the aid of Marxism, one might have hoped that historical materialism would put an end to that detective novel interpretation of history. Not so! Poliakov assures us that Marx, in his articles for the *New York Daily Tribune*, written during the Crimean war to pay the rent, "denounced the Jews and the Jesuits as the chief evildoers assailing the Old World." More profoundly, Marx revealed other causes, the true causes behind those generally advanced, those that betrayed "class interest, the de facto primary cause acting like a hand in the shadows—which is the cardinal principle of all demonology."[8] Again for Poliakov, Marx demonized the bourgeoisie and simultaneously maintained the old "diabolical causality" in new forms. In its 1936 French version, this gave rise to the myth of the "two hundred families."

Conspiracy continues to fare well. Should a coup d'état occur in Africa or South America, the hand of the CIA or the KGB is immediately denounced as a sufficient cause. "American imperialism" wraps its tentacles around the globe, and spy films have taught us to beware of the omnipresent Soviet agent. Even nations are not immune to the practice: in 1981, Moscow denounced foreign dealings in Poland. How could anyone imagine that Polish workers could have risen up on their own against their Socialist government? German conservatives once explained the defeat of their empire as a "dagger in the back," inflicted on their army by the Social Democrats. The enumeration of such supposed machinations would be endless: without any fuss, they explain the twilight of the West, the contradictions of the Third World, the failure of socialist regimes.

Totalitarianism is rooted in simple ideas. The twentieth century is teeming with them. Men, women, and children by the millions have created them and have paid the price. That is because it is not easy to admit the complexity of history, the multiple causes behind every social or political phenomenon, universal relativity.

Before many others, French nationalists understood the public demand for *simplification*. An action cannot be grounded in too subtle or too nuanced an analysis of the living context; in contrast, it becomes a rallying cry if it is based on a univocal causality and a mythological system of representation that allows people to bypass the rational approach. Undoubtedly, every political act implies this basic assumption. The choice of a reasonable policy itself more or less requires theatricality, symbolic expression, and justifications that are not addressed to the intellect alone. In France at the end of the nineteenth century, the nationalist school—and herein lies its modernity—knew how to capture people's attention through methods that later became commonplace. At the beginning of the "mass" era, it often had better success than its socialist rival in providing a fictional *why* for the misfortunes of the world. The heterogeneity of reality discourages political passion. Some will say that "everything can be explained," "everything is simple," "everything is becoming clear," provided we break through the surface of lies coming from politicians-profiteers and their hired hands. The nationalists claimed they were raising the curtain and removing the masks. In their ardor to demystify, they became the mystifiers.

CHAPTER 7

Edouard Drumont and 'La France juive'

MODERN ANTI-SEMITISM developed in Europe in the last third of the nineteenth century. Germany and Austria were the first to set the tone. Following the stock market crash in 1873, which extended from Vienna to Germany, a certain number of Jewish patronyms were found to be involved in the debacle, and an initial campaign was launched, in which Pastor Adolf Stöcker was to play a preponderant role. More distinguished individuals supported anti-Semitism in scholarly writings: Treitschke, Konstantin Franz, Paul de Lagarde. The most relentless of authors, Eugène Dühring, gave a systematic account of the grievances against Jews in a book published in 1880: *The Jewish Question, A Question of Race, Mores, and Culture.*[1]

Somewhat later in the 1880s, the French people came to know a first great wave of anti-Semitism in their own country. As in Austria and Germany, a financial event seems to have been the starting signal, in this case the crash of the Union Générale, a Catholic bank that supposedly fell victim to the "Jewish" bank.[2] In addition, in accordance with the encyclical *Humanum genus* of April 1884 condemning Freemasonry, the Catholic daily *La Croix* increasingly combined attacks on Jews and Freemasons. In 1885, the Jews were almost completely forgotten, but in 1886, the Assumptionist newspaper published a long series written by Admiral Gicquel des Touches, former minister of the Duc de Broglie, on what would become known as "the Jewish invasion." Was this a coincidence? A few weeks earlier, an obscure publicist—Edouard Drumont—had published a thick book at his own expense. After gathering dust in crates for some time, it began to sell astonishingly well. The book was *La France juive.*

In mid-April 1886, Drumont's book was published in two volumes totaling twelve hundred pages with the publishers Marpon and Flammarion. The author was a virtually unknown journalist of forty-four, though he had already published a few books, including one on Paris. He was a contributor to *Le Monde*, a Catholic daily with limited circulation, and had written for various newspapers since the Second Empire, without attracting any attention to himself.

At first, his new book was met with general indifference. *La France juive* was not the first to be devoted to the Jewish question in France, but even the most notable among the earlier ones had been failures. Nonetheless, Drumont's book soon became the first best-seller on anti-Semitism in France.

That success was primarily limited to the first two years of sale, 1886 and 1887. A 145th edition is listed for 1887 in the catalog of the Bibliothèque Nationale. Ten years later, the Dreyfus affair contributed toward relaunching the title, and in 1914 it attained its 200th edition. Obviously, it would be useful to know how many books were printed for each edition. Unfortunately for our curiosity, there was no rule governing the matter. However, the many previous editions would certainly have encouraged the editor not to fix the number of volumes ordered from the printer too low. A range of one thousand to five thousand seems plausible. If we adopt the lowest hypothesis, then about 150,000 copies were sold in one year: a considerable number, if we recall that the first edition was produced at the author's expense, and at a time when books sold considerably fewer copies than they do today. That is not all. In 1887, an illustrated edition of *La France juive* was published. On that occasion, the editor had posters displayed depicting Drumont as a knight departing to fight the new Saracens, bankers and stockbrokers. In addition, in 1888 a popular version was published in a single volume with Victor Palmé and by 1890, that edition was in its tenth printing. Victor Palmé directed the Société Générale de Librairie Catholique, located at 76 Rue des Saints-Pères in Paris; he also had a branch or subsidiary in Brussels (the Société Belge de Librairie) and in Geneva, which assured the diffusion of *La France juive* to neighboring francophone countries.

What about editions after 1914? Drumont died in 1917, and the atmosphere of the Sacred Union attenuated the anti-Semitic passion in France at that time. This was an era when Barrès, who had developed the theory of "uprooted peoples," praised the Israelites as among the authentic "spiritual families" composing France. In the 1930s, however, Drumont's theses were again picked up and endlessly repeated by the press and literature on the far right, which was enjoying a resurgence. One final edition of the book appeared in 1941; for all intents and purposes, Drumont's way of thinking was dominant at the time. Exhibits were devoted to him; his life and his battles were once more discussed. Finally, after World War II, Jean-Jacques Pauvert, setting aside all taboos, published excerpts from *La France juive* in a Drumontesque anthology edited and annotated by Emmanuel Beau de Loménie: *Edouard Drumont ou l'anticapitalisme national* (Edouard Drumont, or national anticapitalism, 1966). The editor minimizes the interest of *La France juive*, in which Drumont defined "too unilateral a thesis," only to better extol what followed. As it happens, in *La fin d'un monde* (The end of a world), supposedly Drumont's masterpiece, we read a good summary of his constant hysteria:

> The strength of the Jews lies in the fact that they no longer proceed as in the past, through isolated misdeeds; they have founded a system in which everything holds together, a system that embraces the country as a whole, that is equipped with all the organs necessary to function. They have strengthened the points by which they might have been taken, have silently modified laws that troubled them, or have obtained warrants that paralyze the implementation of those laws. They have made the press the servant of capital, so that it is unable to speak.

In short, the clearest merit to be found in Beau de Loménie is his propagation of the euphemism "national anticapitalism," which allows people to practice a quiet anti-Semitism. In any case, that demonstrates Drumont's continuing influence, at least within a certain political community.

Can the great success of Drumont's best-known book be explained in a rational manner? We might at least attempt to list factors relating to the historical moment, as well as more remote and more profound factors.

The launching of the book benefited in great part from the new situation of the press. The 1881 law, technological improvements, the abundance of newspapers, and the growth of the reading public were so many new conditions that worked to the advantage of Drumont's book. Hence, it was an article in *Le Figaro*, published on 19 April 1886, that first elicited curiosity. Its author, Francis Magnard, was fairly critical, mentioning Drumont's "childish credulity" and obsessions, but in the end his judgment of *La France juive* was based on extenuating circumstances: it had been provoked by a republican regime engaged in persecuting Catholic milieus. Three days later, Father de Pascal published a dithyrambic review in *La Croix*, though he expressed a few similar reservations. A large proportion of the press followed, even including *La Revue Socialiste*, which in December 1886 published an article by Benoît Malon, certainly critical, but whose length validated the book's importance. The article was entitled "La question juive" (The Jewish question).

In addition, the press's interest was sustained by various incidents resulting from the publication of the book, in the first place the duel between Drumont and Arthur Meyer. Meyer, an assimilated and converted Jew, editor of *Le Gaulois*, the daily monitor of good society, provoked Drumont to settle their quarrel man to man, a quarrel started by the accusations of an author lacking the most elementary subtlety. This duel between two men of the press took an unusual turn: twice, and in violation of all the rules, Meyer, fighting hand to hand with Drumont, pushed away his adversary's sword with his left hand, and finally pierced his thigh. A trial followed, and Arthur Meyer was eventually fined two hundred francs. The tragicomedy put Drumont—unknown the day before—and his vengeful book in the spotlight.

In a general way, the press, far from killing books and bookstores, was to serve the publishing industry and trade. This is demonstrated by the diffusion of lengthy novels in serial form in the dailies of the time. It was because there was now a free press, with numerous newspapers competing with one another, that *La France juive*, like so many other books, could take off.

That, however, was only incidental. The success of Drumont's book had more profound causes. On this matter, let us distinguish between the two ends of the chain: the transmitter of the message and the receiver. Drumont, taken for an indisputable writer by his disciples, had a lively style, a sense for the shocking formulation, and the art of crediting gossip, approximation, and generalizations as so much serious information, of posing as a historian and social analyst. What did he say that his predecessors had not? Nothing very new. But he combined every form of anti-Semitism; he knew how to unify into a single historical perspective—by turns social, religious, and political—the three principal sources of anti-Jewish passions: first, Christian anti-Judaism; second, popular anticapitalism; and third, modern racism.

Christian Anti-Judaism

We are indebted to Pierre Pierrard's *Juifs et Catholiques français* (French Jews and Catholics),[3] for having shed light on Drumont's sources: "Drumont," he writes, "contributed a great deal to the scandal of assimilating Catholicism and anti-Semitism." Pierrard begins his study with the French Revolution, but it has long been known that the "Christian roots of anti-Semitism" go back to the anti-Judaism of certain Fathers of the Church.[4] In the eyes of numerous Catholic and counterrevolutionary authors, the new element, during and after the revolutionary period, was the supposed responsibility of the Jews for the fall of the ancien régime. The Revolution that emancipated the Jews could not fail to have been the work of Jews. Such was the sophism that triumphed in a series of works, whose lesson was summed up by Drumont: "The only one who benefited from the Revolution was the Jew. Everything comes from the Jew. Everything comes back to the Jew."

That "occultist" history, which aims to explain all social and political phenomena as a Jewish plot, began with Abbé Augustin de Barruel, for whom 1789 was the final result "of the conspiracy of secret societies." As the author of that thesis, which is the argument of his *Mémoire pour servir à l'histoire du jacobinisme* (Essay on the history of Jacobinism), in 1806 Barruel received a letter from a man named Simonini, who pointed out the true guilty parties behind the Freemasons and the fanatic perpetrators of revolution: the Jews. The fact that anti-Christian societies were organized and maintained by those who, by the fact of their religion, were respected by Christian society, was a defensible hypothesis. But Simonini went further: he revealed that the Jews "were promising themselves that they would be masters of the world in less than a century." The wild imaginings of that so-called Piedmont captain had no immediate effect; but his letter was published in Paris in 1878, then reproduced in numerous anti-Semitic works.[5]

All the same, such ravings ought to be counted among the sources of *The Protocols of the Elders of Zion*, a historical fake that Maurras as well as Hitler used to advantage. Without reaching the same heights, numerous authors who were opposed to the Revolution, such as Bonald, combined their antiliberalism with "Christian" anti-Judaism. It appears that under the Second Empire, such literature was abundant: Pierre Pierrard gives a list of pious novels with suggestive titles and mentions the *Mémoires d'un ange gardien* (Memoirs of a guardian angel, 1862), which had a lasting following. The book depicts a little boy "horrified by the cruelty of the Jews, Jesus' tormentors." Pierrard also cites more "serious" works, especially one by Gougenot des Mousseaux, which appeared under the title *Le Juif, le Judaïsme et la Judaïsation des peuples chrétiens* (The Jew, Judaism, and the Judaization of Christian peoples)—which went unnoticed at first, but was destined to become, in the words of Norman Cohn, "the Bible of modern anti-Semitism." According to that imaginative author, the Kabbala recommended the worship of Satan, and the aim of Kabbalist Jews was nothing less than the reign of the anti-Christ. In the struggle that pit the Church against Freemasonry at the time, Gougenot des Mousseaux's book provided weapons against Jews and Masons simultaneously—henceforth a classic combination. Pius IX congratulated its author. At a time when medieval Christianity seemed to be on a path toward disintegration, when the temporal power of the popes was about to be reduced to its most simple territorial expression, when new ideas called Roman dogmatism into question, numerous Catholic authors were tempted to denounce any number of conspiracies—in which Freemasonry orchestrated its designs in the company of Jews—as being at the origin of these many dangers. As an example, the "Roman question" elicited the fable that the plot against the papacy had been directed by a certain "Piccolo Tigre," a Jewish

Freemason. Monseigneur Gaston de Ségur, son of the famous countess, wrote a book on the matter, *Les Francs-maçons* (The Freemasons, 1867), which went through thirty-six editions in five years.

The war of 1870–71, the taking of Rome by Italian patriots, the Commune, and the advent of the Third Republic again provided pretexts for anti-Jewish literature. While the *Civiltà cattolica* of Roman Jesuits heaped "all the crimes of the earth upon the heads of the *Hebrews*," in France the schooling laws of the Freemason Jules Ferry lent credit to the dogma of the "Judeo-Masonic plot." In the proliferation of clerical publications that repeated and illustrated this theme, let us note the birth in 1884 of *La Franc-maçonnerie démasquée* (Freemasonry unmasked), a monthly Catholic review that lasted until 1924. One of its editors wrote in 1885, that is, one year before Drumont's book appeared but one year after the encyclical *Humanum genus*: "The Jew is a man of the [Masonic] lodge, because for him, his lodge is essentially the means to success." We catch a glimpse of the double equation: Republic = Freemasonry = Jewry. For its part, *La Croix*, which became a daily in 1883, undertook an ardent campaign the next year against the lodges. Imperceptibly, as we are told by Pierre Sorlin, who has written the history of the newspaper, "it came to link the Jew and the Mason."[6]

Medieval Judeophobia was thus revived almost a century after the French Revolution. The Jew, emancipated by revolutionary law, was now considered by Christian anti-Semites to be the hidden inspiration for 1789, the animating force behind Freemasonry, the instigator of secular laws, the persecutor of Congregationists, the promoter of anticlericalism, the relentless enemy of Christian religion and civilization. In Gougenot des Mousseaux's formulation, the Jew was "the chief engineer of revolutions."

That "religious" anti-Semitism was already coming into contact with nationalism in a few authors, who were quick to assimilate France and Christianity. Louis Veuillot is representative of those Catholics-and-Frenchmen-forever. For example, in November 1870 he wrote in *L'Univers*:

I, a Catholic Christian of France, as old in France as the oaks and rooted like them, I am constituted, deconstituted, reconstituted, governed, ruled, pruned by vagabonds in mind and morals. Renegades or foreigners, they have neither my faith, nor my prayers, nor my memories, nor my expectations. I am subjugated to the heretic, the Jew, the atheist, and to a composite of all these types, which is close to resembling the beast.[7]

These few examples suffice to show that on the eve of the publication of *La France juive*, the Catholic public could have been in a receptive state. "Everywhere," said Drumont, "you find the Jew trying to destroy, directly or indirectly, our religions. Divorce is a Jewish invention, the Jew Naquet made divorce become our law. Our beautiful funeral ceremonies irritate

the Jews: an engineer by the name of Salomon heads a society for crema-
tion, which he would like to make obligatory. It is a Jew, Camille Sée,
who is organizing high schools for girls, in a way that will exclude all religious teaching."[8]

On several occasions, Drumont protested his respect for other religions,
including Judaism, declaring his intention not to attack Jews on that score.
Nonetheless, old medieval anti-Judaism still inspired him, even though he
modernized it:

> The Jews hate Christ in 1886 as they hated him in the time of Tiberius Augustus;
> they heap the same humiliation on him. Whipping the crucifix on Good Friday,
> profaning the Host, soiling holy images: such was the great joy of the Jew during
> the Middle Ages, such is his great joy today. Once he attacked the bodies of chil-
> dren; today, it is their soul he targets with atheistic teachings. Once he bled, now
> he poisons: which is better?[9]

For Drumont, a nonconformist Catholic posing as the defender of
Christian values, the link was established between ritual murders, of
which Jews had been accused since the Middle Ages, and the passage of
secular laws: "What they worship in the ghetto is not the God of Moses; it
is the horrible Phoenician Molech, who needs children and virgins as human sacrifices."

"Economic" Anti-Semitism

The theme of anticapitalism was also central to Drumont's vision. "Honest
and laborious France" had fallen under Jewish oppression in several stages
since the Revolution of 1789. The emancipation allowed Jews, who were
limited to the role of usurers in the ghetto, to take over the entire financial apparatus of the country—as attested by the recent episode of the
crash of the Union Générale or, on the same continuum, the colossal fortune acquired by the Rothschilds.

Even today, the name "Rothschild" evokes the relics of popular anti-
Semitism, a sometimes naive expression of a class struggle that could find
no better expression. Numerous authors who embraced the Revolution or
who numbered among the pioneers of socialism in France often confused
Jews and capitalists in their reprobation, and contrasted the productive
lower classes to "Jewish finance." Michelet, Fourier, and Proudhon among
others fed modern anti-Semitism with their diatribes. But through semantic slippage, the term "Jew" was often used by these writers as a synonym for "usurer," without explicit reference to the racial or religious origin of those they condemned. It was sometimes a different matter, however. Although Proudhon, for example, defined the Jew as *the antiproducer,*

thus implying that any middleman, whatever his origin, was a "Jew," he also indulged in petitioning for the abolition of synagogues, among other desirable measures.[10] All the same, none of these authors treated the question in depth. It was Toussenel's *Juifs rois de l'époque* (The Jews, kings of the age, 1845) that was Drumont's "leftist source"; Drumont referred to it as "an immortal masterpiece."

In fact, Toussenel's work is filled with the same ambiguity observed in his master Fourier and in other anti-Jewish socialists. On one hand, he completely and reciprocally assimilates the Jew and the financier, to the point of condemning Protestant and Catholic speculators as "Jews"; on the other hand, he sometimes makes it clear that the Jews he is speaking of are descendants of the biblical people. Hence, in the introduction to his notorious book, Toussenel asserts: "Like the people, I call by the despised name 'Jew' any trafficker in currencies, any unproductive parasite living on the substance and work of others. Jew, usurer, and trafficker are synonymous for me." He is inconsistent, however, and later explains that the Jew is indissociable from the Bible.

I do not know the great things the Jewish people did, having never read their history except in a book that is all about adultery and incest, butchery and savage wars; where every revered name is soiled by infamy; where every great fortune invariably begins with fraud or treason; where the kings who are called saints have men murdered so they can steal their wives; where the women who are called saints get into bed with enemy generals in order to cut off their heads.

And further on: "As for those who ruthlessly put to death all the prophets inspired by the Holy Ghost, who crucified the Redeemer of men and insulted him on the cross, I do not call that people the people of God."

There we have it: for Toussenel, the Jews are not just any usurers, but are really and truly those that the ancient Catholic liturgy for Good Friday named the *perfidi*, and who for years were called "deicides." But no, that would be too clear! Toussenel adds: "Whoever says 'Jew,' says 'Protestant,' mark my words." Thus the Englishman, the Dutchman, and the Genevan are all similarly "Jews," and Toussenel's book, a violent polemic against triumphant plutocracy under the July monarchy, is not exactly the book of an anti-Semite. As Léon Poliakov remarks: "There are many chapters in *Juifs rois de l'époque* where the Jews are not in question at all. In reality, Toussenel's real goal was to denounce the reign of money." Nonetheless, by means of his ambiguities and certain of his formulations ("Power to the strong! Death to parasitism! War on the Jews! That is the motto of the new revolution!"), Toussenel became one of the foster fathers of the anti-Semites, so much so that Drumont defined his "only ambition" as to be able to prove himself worthy of that prestigious "prophet."

Within this current, we can overlook Marx's contemptuous evaluations of the Jews: still largely unknown in France at the time Drumont's book was published, they could not have influenced him. But that reminder for the record of "Jewish anti-Semitism" (Poliakov) gives us a sense of the extent of anti-Jewish sentiments from one end to the other of the socialist community. The development of financial capitalism could only reinforce that tendency: it was easy to contrast the worker's poverty—forgetting the vast majority of the Jewish people—to what was called the shameful wealth of the Jew Rothschild. The theme was endlessly revived and illustrated with a thousand details, so that as a result of selection (speaking only of Jewish, or strictly speaking, "Jewified" finance) and accumulation, anti-Semites inculcated in their readers the conviction that the entire banking apparatus was in the hands of Jews—and moreover, in the hands of the "Frankfurt Jew," the German Jew. The Jew made possible and completed Bismarck's handiwork.

Racism and Occultism

A last element, which also swelled the confluence of Christian anti-Judaism and "economic" anti-Semitism, must also be taken into account. This was the favor enjoyed by racist theses in the second half of the nineteenth century, theses that claimed to be fundamentally scientific, and which Drumont used as a further ingredient to enrich his synthesis.

Ready to seize on anything that fell into his hands to discredit the Jewish community, he did not fail to use to his own account theories of the time that opposed "Aryans" and "Semites" on the biological as well as the historical plane. In *La France juive*, again without giving his sources, he alludes to at least three authors: Taine, Gellion-Danglar (*Les Sémites et le Sémitisme* [The Semites and Semitism], 1882), and especially Renan, whose *Histoire générale et système comparé des langues sémitiques* (General history and comparative system of Semitic languages) was obviously an influence. These authors, and others he does not cite, led him to consider the Aryan/Semite dichotomy as one of the keys to universal history. He appropriated Renan's idea that "the Semitic race, compared to the Indo-European race, forever represents an inferior composition of human nature."[11] The result was the battle between the Angel and the Beast, which summed up the history of humanity: "From the earliest days of history, we see the Aryan in a struggle with the Semite";[12] "The Trojan war was a race war, Aryans versus Semites; the invasion of Spain and the South of France by the Saracens was also a race war, as was the heroic revenge of the crusades, whose superb effort lasted three centuries."[13] "What is a true revolution composed of? It always has a racial question at its foundation."[14]

At the time of the Dreyfus affair, Dreyfus's guilt seemed perfectly obvious. It could be deduced from "his race," as Barrès said, and Drumont was of the same opinion: "It is a question of race, and all the metaphysical arguments have nothing to do with it."[15]

Millennial characteristics in the form of fixed stereotypes, still "observable" in our societies, were attached to these two ethnic poles. The antagonism between them was self-perpetuating, and their origins were lost in the mists of time. To put it succinctly, the Aryan was the man of the ideal, of transcendence; the Semite was the man of reality, practicality, matter. The former had his natural milieu in the forest; the refuge of the latter was the desert.

Men of the forest, "the sons of heaven eternally concerned with higher aspirations," had nothing in common with "the predators from the sands of Arabia," the eternal wanderers concerned only with "present life." "The Semite is money-grubbing, greedy, scheming, subtle, wily; the Aryan is enthusiastic, heroic, chivalrous, disinterested, frank, and trusting to the point of naïveté."[16]

The physiognomy of Jews was only too identifiable, and their physiology displayed features of its own. "The principal signs by which the Jew can be recognized remain: that infamous hooked nose, blinking eyes, clenched teeth, protruding ears, square fingernails, flat feet, round knees, ankles turned out in an extraordinary manner, the soft and clammy hands of a hypocrite and traitor. Often enough, he has one arm shorter than the other" (34). "He smells bad" (104); "he is susceptible to all maladies indicating corruption of the blood"(103). But "in accordance with a phenomenon observed a thousand times during the Middle Ages and asserted anew during the cholera outbreak, the Jew seems to enjoy a particular immunity to epidemics. It seems there is a sort of permanent plague inside him, which protects him from the ordinary plague" (104).

We could continue with that ludicrous anthology for some time, but let us confine ourselves to Drumont himself by way of conclusion. He explains very scientifically: "Truly, these people do not have a brain shaped like our own; their evolution is different from ours, and everything coming from them is uncommon and bizarre."[17]

The racism characteristic of the second half of the nineteenth century embraced science—anthropology, biology, and linguistics. Drumont's book, on the other hand (but is this really contradictory?), even while diffusing science's "discoveries," was also steeped in the *fin de siècle* climate, which found new glamour in other, occult sciences. "Between 1885 and 1890," writes Victor-Emile Michelet, an expert on the matter, "two movements of thought, similar in their tendencies if not in their reference points, were launched to overturn the deleterious beliefs in fashion at the time, namely, scientific materialism and its stand-in, literary naturalism. These two parallel movements [were] Symbolism and Occultism."[18] In 1884 *Le vice suprême* (The supreme vice), the first novel by Sâr Péladan, was published and caused a sensation: "It exploded like a bomb," Victor-Emile Michelet tells us, "above the swampy naturalist literature of the time and spread the exciting vapor of the occult world outward." As Papus, a pseudonym used by Dr. Encausse, said in his *Occultisme contemporain* (Contemporary occultism, 1887): "Science rests on no true foundation." Another science had to be found: the science of the hidden, reserved for initiates. A superior knowledge of things had to be pitted against reigning rationalism, metaphysics against physics, alchemy against chemistry, the affirmation of the correspondences between man and the universe against the negation of God. That return in force of occultism was accompanied by a public fervor for everything having to do with spiritualism, Satanism, all the strange and sulfurous practices whose vogue is superbly illustrated in Huysmans's novel *Là-bas* (Over there).

But on this matter, Drumont maintained an ambivalent attitude. On one hand, he condemned "witchcraft" as the work of the Kabbalists, the Talmudists, the Jews par excellence, who for centuries had kept alive "abominable mysteries" in their ghettos. On the other hand, he had a hard time resisting their fascination. If he happened to attend a seance, it was—he tells us—only "by chance."[19] Conversely, he declared clearly: "I admit to believing, to a certain extent of course, in chiromancy, which Dumas called 'the grammar of societies to come'; I believe in it, not as in fortune telling, but as in a science."[20] Above all, he believed in diabolical evil spells: "Note that barely a hundred years ago the Demon was freed from all surveillance, and already suicides have increased tenfold, madhouses are full, everyone is talking about the 'great neurosis.' All the Scandinavian Jotums, all the Cabiri of Africa, all the thaumaturges, all the concocters of philters, all the haruspices of imperial Rome or Alexandria are unleashed upon Paris."[21] Drumont was himself a pioneer, a discoverer, someone who decrypted the Jewish Evil behind official social science. "The truth is that we are surrounded by mystery, that we are living in mystery,"[22] he said; at least he, Drumont, could plumb the mystery of our decadence. He knew. He had found the explanation. He knew the secret.

In his readings of popular novels, Drumont also cultivated that attraction for the secret, the hidden, the underground, which fed all his anti-Semitism. "I have always had a weakness, I do not hide it, for those exceptionally organized oddities that transport us to a world of ideas different from the world we live in, which sometimes lift the veil on the future to reveal unexpected horizons."[23] And he added, more explicitly: "Imagine what our sons will think when they observe that the imaginary adventures of Rocambole are nothing compared to what we have actually seen happening since the Jews have been the masters in our country."[24]

Drumont unwittingly identified the level of his own writings, the category of the fantastic (*rocambolesque*), for which Ponson du Terrail earned his opulent notoriety. His books belong in some way to the category of the serial novel, in which invariably maleficent Jews played the role of the villain and the popular soul living in thatched cottages required that he be punished.

Thus *La France juive* linked the ancient and modern forms of anti-Semitism, the religious and the profane, science and the wisdom of nations, the rational and the irrational: that anti-Semitism was made up of *everything* and had a response to *everything*. It was a simple idea by virtue of its univocal nature, supported by a profusion of illustrations presented as so many proofs.

The Sociology of Reception, or Anti-Semitism as Doctrine

All these scattered, even contradictory influences prove that the time was ripe for anti-Semitism as a political doctrine; the years prior to *La France juive* had created the conditions for its birth. The ideological and political triumph of the republicans confirmed the Catholic public in its conviction that there was a perverse alliance between Jews, Freemasons, and republicans. Simultaneously, the crash of the Catholic Union Générale, for which the Jewish bank was held responsible, fueled "economic" anti-Semitism, which was lent further support by a long period of crisis and unemployment that followed. Was this not the occasion to bring the Catholic people and the working people together under the same banner? First glimpsed under Boulangism, this beginning of a reconciliation between the popular classes and Catholic conservatives and against the Opportunist Republic was now in Drumont's hands; in his writings, he was to establish its guiding principle for the future. That principle was anti-Semitism.

Drumont, by blending together all anti-Jewish, Judeophobic, and anti-Semitic elements expressed before him, was able to elevate the Jewish myth to the height of an ideology and a political method. His oeuvre represented "a crossroads in the history of anti-Semitism, the meeting of two currents, the Catholic and the socialist" (Pierrard). In fact, with fundamentally reactionary positions, filled to overflowing with monarchist sympathies, Drumont (out of naive sincerity more than Machiavellianism, no doubt) attempted to bring down the republican regime with the complicity of revolutionary socialist troops. That unnatural alliance he was hoping for apparently had some chance of success at the time: anti-Semitism, to be precise, would secure it. Drumont displayed a social sentimentalism, a "vague socialism," which became increasingly pronounced with each book, though he never abandoned his anti-Semitism for all that. Hence, after the rifle fire that occurred in Fourmies during the demonstration of 1 May 1891, he published a shattering book. So as not to weaken the tradition of counterrevolutionary historiography, according to which every event is the result of a conspiracy, it bore the significant title *Le secret de Fourmies* (The secret of Fourmies). What was the "secret" of Fourmies, then? It was, Drumont revealed, that the prefect and subprefects of the department of Nord, hence the responsible parties for the rifle fire of 1 May, were—have you guessed yet?—Jews.

Just as remarkable was the vision of the Paris Commune elaborated little by little by Drumont. Opposed to the Paris revolution during the seventy-two days of its existence, he proved increasingly "understanding" toward the Communards over the course of his writing career. The aim of that belated sympathy was to use the memory of the Commune and the popular classes associated with it against the bad Republic, which, owing to the Freemasons, the Jews, and the Opportunists, had asserted its power as much against the socialist Republic as against the restored monarchy. He wrote: "The officers dragged through the mud by Jewish newspapers for going to mass have told me, 'At the next Commune, count on us. We will never again lay our hands on our workers, and, even if their hands are black with gunpowder, we will take no notice. We now know whom we must strike; we know the true fomenters of civil war'" (*La France juive devant l'opinion*). The productiveness of such a cordial understanding between the French army and the revolutionary people is obvious. They now had a common enemy: it was the Jewish, capitalist, and anti-Catholic Republic. In *La fin d'un monde*, Drumont took to glorifying the honesty of Communard workers; if there was a "ferocity" in the ranks of the Commune, it was entirely bourgeois in origin. "The School of Brothers, where most of the workers were raised, produced fewer instigators of butchery than the university." The purpose of such a mordant assertion is clear, the dreamt-of union between Catholics and workers against the freethinking, Jewish, and bourgeois Republic. The reader certainly has the right to know the "secret" of the Commune. Why did so many French people do battle against so many other French people? Once more, as you may have guessed, it was because of the double game of Jewish bankers: "In Versailles, they made a display of feelings of indignation; in Paris, they subsidized the insurrection to satisfy their hatred toward the priests and, at the same time, to complicate the political situation so that their financial contest would pay off better."

We could cite other examples: how Drumont spoke of Jules Guesde, the sympathy he displayed toward the Blanquists, how he went so far as to shower praise on Tridon's *Molochisme Juif* (Jewish Molechism), whose anti-Catholic thesis was the exact opposite of his own, how he justified anarchist attacks. Therein lay his cunning novelty: to stir up popular forces against the achievements of the French Revolution (custom-made by the Jew), even though these popular forces still embraced it.

In that undertaking, Drumont was not always understood by his following. Discerning conservatives were quickly frightened off by the social turn his anti-Semitism was taking: his Jewish anticapitalism was in danger of striking the bastions of Catholic capitalism on the rebound. They were eventually able to get something out of the Semitic bugaboo during the Dreyfus affair, all the while laughing at Drumont's socialistic daydreams. "Such circles, in effect," says M. Beau de Loménie with reference to the business class, "had very little inclination for the early Drumont's anti-Semitism, which targeted economic and social reforms and ran the risk of dangerously threatening their privileges. But they were now ready to welcome the new anti-Semitism, oriented toward the struggle against antimilitarist, anticlerical, and Marxian Semitism."

The fact that numerous conservatives were seduced by "a thesis that tended to hold the Jews alone responsible for all our ills" was astonishing only to an innocent like Drumont, or like his biographer. In fact, this was the true political function of anti-Semitism: as soon as indigent mobs—small businessmen and artisans victimized by the economic evolution—exploited workers, and peasants forced to leave the countryside were shown that the Jew was responsible for all their ills, social conservatives had an inestimable weapon. Deriving strength from their control of the press, they orchestrated the developing myth for their own use. Class conflicts vanished: there was now nothing but a minority of Jewish profiteers crushing the vast majority of their Aryan and Catholic victims.

But if, as Bebel said, anti-Semitism is "the socialism of imbeciles," it might also on occasion prove to be an excellent political formula capable of reconciling opposites, linking extremes, and stirring up the masses in an affective and irrational manner as a means of seizing power. However inconsistent it may have been, Drumont's anti-Semitism can be considered the sincere attempt of a bourgeois man, revolted by the social effects of the capitalist boom, to unite the little people and old France against the modern world.[25] Ideologically, we know that the undertaking had repercussions: from Maurice Barrès to Drieu La Rochelle, the theme of decadence, combined with misoneism, had anti-Semitism as its common denominator. But above all, in addition to a literary sensibility, Drumont invented a mode of action. In establishing anti-Semitism as a system of universal explanation, he made the Jew the negative pole of nationalist movements: it was in relation to the Jew, against the Jew, that nationalists defined their French or German identity. They were proud to belong to a community and to know clearly who the adversary was who threatened its unity and life. As Maurras said: "Everything seems impossible, or horribly difficult, without that providence of anti-Semitism. Through it, everything fits together, everything is smoothed over and simplified. If I were not anti-Semitic out of patriotic desire, I would be so out of a sheer sense of opportunism."[26] That protean myth of anti-Semitism was an intermediary that allowed people to dream of uniting anticapitalist forces with the capitalists themselves, of uniting Catholics with atheists, small businessmen with shareholders in monopolies, workers with employers. Although it is an exaggeration to depict Drumont as a proto-Nazi, it is not too much to say that his experience and his ideas were among the French sources of national socialism.

From Theory to Practice

In his study of fascism, the German philosopher and historian Ernst Nolte placed Drumont next to La Tour du Pin and Barrès[27] under the banner of "radical conservatism," which appeared as one of the prefigurations of the fascist movement.

Under the conditions of the republic, therefore, radical conservatism tended to take the wind out of the sails of the worker's movement by emphasizing its own battle against the bourgeois world, and by substituting the hate-image of the capitalist with its own hate-image, the Jew. It was by nature rabble-rousing and anti-Semitic. Its very radicalism gives it a more modern look. The consequences of its anti-Semitism harbored a conflict with the old conservative force of which it was a radical offshoot.[28]

And although Drumont, the promoter of the myth, was not a man of action, he did not lack disciples ready to put the most dynamic of his ideas into practice. In particular, there was the odd Marquis de Morès, whom Robert F. Byrnes, his American biographer, has called "the first National Socialist."[29]

The Marquis de Morès, a dashing equestrian, former student at Saint-Cyr, son-in-law of a superrich American, quick to squander a large share of his in-laws' fortune in various ventures in succession (a ranch in North Dakota, a cooperative in New York, a railroad in Tonkin), constant brawler, indefatigable fencer, and tiger hunter in Nepal, in 1888 discovered the explanation for all his disappointments in *La France juive*: the hand of the Jew was involved. At a time of declining Boulangism, he wandered the political countryside with the same audacity and the same lack of foresight he had previously manifested in raising and trading cattle. At least he had one idea, that of the necessary fusion between nationalism and socialism, between the "revolutionary worker" and the "Christian conservative." Impatient and impetuous, Morès proclaimed his voracity for action: "Life has value only in action," and—something Drumont had never imagined—this delinquent marquis, who had once teamed up with hoboes and cattle rustlers in the American West, decided to found an astonishing association, to the indignation of his respectable family. It was called "Morès and his friends," and can be considered a kind of model in a minor key for the storm troopers to come. It included a heteroclite gang of anti-Semites, anarchists, former Boulangists, unemployed workers, men without faith or law, under the orders of the valiant horseman, dressed in a red cowboy shirt and a broad sombrero; with them were reinforcements of La Villette butchers, attracted to the musketeer when he attacked a Jewish firm guilty of selling spoiled meat to the army. With his troop, Morès organized attacks aimed at frightening stock market financiers; organized a vast electoral campaign; shouted that "during the Commune 35,000 men were killed [and] this time, it will be enough if 200 or 300 usurers are killed." He publicly embraced Louise Michel; appealed to the army, asking it to take the side of unemployed workers; got three months in prison with no chance of reprieve for his provocations; and, on being freed, voted for the strikers. He loosed his troops on Jewish demonstrations; wrote programs for universal happiness, stealing from Louis Blanc and Proudhon, all the while swearing his loyal respect for "religion, nation, family, and property"; and soon denounced French socialists in the name of "socialism," claiming they had all sold out to Germany, England, or Jewry. He loudly declared that the new society would have the peasantry, the working class, and the army as its foundation; dreamed of an alliance with the Arabs to thwart English expansion; and in short, raged at every stop and on every occasion, until he committed the error of attacking Clemenceau, whom he accused of being an "English spy." That triggered: first, a withering counterattack by the Radical leader, who condemned the champion of anti-Semitism for being the debtor of notorious Jews; second, a rift with Drumont; and third, Morès's departure for Algeria in late 1893. There he attempted to interest financial backers in his dreams of conquest, did not succeed, then without thinking mounted a suicide expedition toward the South, where he met his death during a battle with the Tuaregs.

At his funeral on 19 July 1896, a reconciled Drumont delivered the eulogy, in which he said, notably:

He wanted all the children of this nation, great once more, to be happy, to have a right to life, not to be condemned to feed a handful of exploiters, parasites, and sharks with their work. That is why he battled Jewry. . . . Like Boulanger, he dreamed of returning the country, which was drowning in the parliamentary muck, to itself, of substituting the healthy activity of life for a regime that gives off an odor of corruption and decomposition, and under which France is suffocating.[30]

In that summary of Morès's life, we catch a glimpse of what has come to be known as "protofascism." Germany was not its only theater. On this matter, Nolte, though perhaps wrong to neglect somewhat the properly German roots of National Socialism, is right to object to William Shirer's *The Rise and Fall of the Third Reich* for considering Germany in isolation and "National Socialism as the inevitable result of German history as a whole."[31] Norman Cohn shows us that when Morès was concluding his feats in France, in Nicholas II's Russia the Black Hundreds were at work, and they had a future as well. They were just as attached to the throne and the altar as Drumont's disciples; these "political adventurers engaged in anti-Semitic agitation and terrorism . . . broadly appealed to extremist demagoguery . . . used common criminals to perpetrate murders and to provoke pogroms [going beyond Morès in that respect]."[32]

A new right was born at the end of the nineteenth century, parallel to the boom in industry and the workers' movement, a far right that remained attached to basic reactionary themes, but attempted to borrow some of its watchwords or traits from rising socialism. It did so by assimilating them to anti-Semitism, the unlocatable site of contradictory aspirations and antagonistic classes. As a personality, Morès also demonstrates the importance of the role played by certain déclassé individuals who had a vitality as unbridled as their demagoguery and who made cunning use of myth.[33] Marx said of "the nephew" Napoleon III, that events and historical figures occur as it were twice, "the first time as tragedy, the second time as farce." In moving from Morès to Hitler, that evolution occurred in reverse: farce preceded tragedy.[34]

Modern anti-Semitism is a complex phenomenon, and its numerous causes—religious, economic, social, psychological—are difficult to hierarchize. My purpose here has been simply to show one of the political functions of the Jewish myth, which appeared as the federating principle of diverse, even contradictory forces, put to the service of the counterrevolution. Drumont, Morès, and their successors failed in their design, even though the end of the nineteenth century seemed to favor the undertaking. Socialist circles and the popular classes were far from being rid of their "economic" anti-Semitism, as we see, for example, in the writings of Lafargue[35] or in issues of *La Revue Socialiste* between 1885 and 1890. The divided and defeated monarchist contingent no longer knew which saint to worship. In addition, beginning in 1882, the economic crisis that struck France provoked a long period of social difficulties. As a universal weapon, anti-Semitism targeted the Republic (Jewish in origin and nature) and defended Catholicism (attacked by Jewish Freemasonry) and the people against capitalism (Jewish usurers, Jewish banking). The Dreyfus affair appears to have been decisive in France, however: in the end, anti-Semitism became fixed on the right, and the socialist movement seems to have purged itself of its last anti-Jewish relics. Action Française, whatever it may have claimed, was never a populist movement; in the years 1936–44, it was Drieu La Rochelle and Doriot who seem to have learned Drumont's lesson, but with no more success than their master. The republican government, which had taken root and been consolidated through a continuous battle with counterrevolutionary forces, seems to have secreted effective counterpoisons. But it is fitting to observe that though the international workers' and socialist movement was able to denounce the illusions of anti-Semitism among the ranks of the working class, other factions of the popular classes were not so well immunized. Without true class organization, without their own ideology, the "middle classes" threatened by economic evolution and the concentration of capital—small business owners, small tradespeople, investors ruined by the collapse of currencies, and so on—were able to find in anti-Semitism a nostalgia for a golden age that had been destroyed by the "Jewish invasion."

Anti-Semitism is not dead in France. Of course, the effects of decolonization, particularly the war in Algeria, and the Arab-Israeli conflict have reshuffled the cards: the French far right on the whole, discovering that the Jews can also be good defenders of "the West" on occasion, has shelved its anti-Semitic passion. But if the far right is now careful in its handling of the Jews, the attentive reader of its weekly newspapers is well aware that "philo-Semitism" is all a matter of opportunism, and that the old myth is always ready to be born again from its warm ashes—as a few "little phrases," wordplays, and other formulations by Jean-Marie Le Pen attest. Since 1984 Le Pen has become a populist leader, capturing a strong minority of the electoral body (see Chapter 2, "The Return of National Populism"). Moreover, the conflict in the Near East has given new life to a certain anti-Semitism on the left, from which "anti-Zionism" is not always exempt.[36] Anti-Semitism on the right can also find new pretexts in the existence and evolution of an Israeli state.

Anti-Semitism is not only a moral and intellectual monstrosity; as an instrument of reactionary policies, it lies beyond notions of right and left, bringing together every form of racism. It is the negation of pluralist society, the morbid exaltation of the national ego, and finally, one of the seeds of totalitarian barbarism.[37]

CHAPTER 8

Joan of Arc and the Jews

JOAN OF ARC did not disappear from history when she was burned at the stake in Rouen. Like several great figures of our national past, she has survived over the centuries, not only thanks to poets and historians, but also, and perhaps especially, because she became symbolic as a historical subject, as one of the things at stake in the partisan war waged by French ideologues, especially since the end of the nineteenth century.

The title of this chapter may seem surprising: what does the history of Joan of Arc have in common with the history of French Jews? Quite simply, French anti-Semites have chosen to reserve a privileged place, a leading role, for the "Bonne Lorraine." The object of a cult of the nation created by moderate republicans, who wanted to use her image as an instrument for consensus in a profoundly divided country, Joan of Arc was finally seized upon—at least in part—by generations of journalists and writers who made every effort to spread the myth of the Jew in France, or later, to naturalize the Nazi hysteria in that country. Joan and the Jews? Let us say rather: Joan against the Jews.

The extolling of Joan of Arc as a national heroine began first on the left, as Michelet's book attests. With the 1871 defeat and the proven failure of efforts to restore the monarchy, a republican deputy, Joseph Fabre, in 1884 defended the idea of a national holiday devoted to Joan. Ten years later, Fabre, now a senator, repeated the idea before the Luxembourg assembly, which approved his plan. The historical circumstances were unique: the moderate republicans had just won the legislative elections of 1893, but the far left was becoming worrisome. Even more than the emotions provoked by anarchist attacks, the massive arrival of fifty socialist representatives to the National Assembly gave pause. As it happened, the moderates, threatened by their left flank, could hope for decisive support on their right, owing to the political attitude of Pope Leo XIII, who recommended that French Catholics "rally" behind the republican regime. From then on, the national celebration in honor of Joan of Arc, for which Fabre became the hard-working propagandist, appeared as one of the seeds of national unity, for which extremists on the left and right had to pay the cost. Premier Charles Dupuy supported Fabre's plan in the Chamber on 8 June 1894: "There will be only one thing standing above us all: patriotism, bearing the name of Joan of Arc." Since the national celebration on 14 July was still repugnant to Catholics because of its revolutionary cachet, a complementary national holiday in honor of Joan of Arc might secure the reconciliation between the center left and the center right of the republic of gentlemen, within the affective universe of symbols. Since Joan the Christian had had the good taste to be condemned by a man of the Church, she was able to please both clericals and anticlericals, who could all identify with some part of her story. The Jews were included within that unanimity: they compared Joan to Deborah, Queen Esther, and Judith. Or so it was proclaimed in 1890 in the Nancy synagogue, at a ceremony in honor of Joan of Arc, whose statue had been offered to the municipality by a certain Osiris. Alphonse de Rothschild made a similar present two years later to the Cluny museum.[1]

Alas! Clerical zeal, spurred on by the far right, and anticlerical zeal, excited by the far left, each tried to raise the biggest ruckus; the worthy centrist plan of fraternization behind the standard of the Maid of Orleans failed, under cross fire from the lodge and the chapel. "Are we going to continue to fight around the statue of Joan of Arc, with blows dealt by crowns and emblems?" asked the editorial writer at *Le Jour* (1 June 1894). For the left, in fact, the woman the Church had just declared Venerable (in a decision of the Sacred Congregation of Rites in January 1894) was no more than an ideological agent in the service of priests and reactionaries.[2]

Since the anniversary of Joan of Arc's death had not yet been voted in as a national holiday by the two assemblies, the clerical and nationalist right seized upon it. The month of May became an annual occasion for a confrontation between nationalists and freethinking republicans. In their enthusiasm, demonstrators on the far right who thronged to the statue of the heroine on Place des Pyramides very quickly associated their fervor for Joan of Arc with hatred of the Jews. Parisian anti-Semites thus found a seasonal site for a pilgrimage. The press and police reports relate these annual scuffles. The slogan "Death to the Jews!" blended with "Long live Joan of Arc!" Demonstrators on the right were not content to chant: equipped with rubber stamps, they printed "Death to the Jews" on walls, even "on the sides of public facilities" (*L'Evénement*, 19 May 1896).

The Dreyfus affair was the final event to structure French nationalism around the "Jewish" myth. The ceremonies of May 1898 in honor of Joan carried the two complementary cries—"Long live Joan of Arc" and "Down with the Jews!"—to new heights. On 8 May, Edouard Drumont was elected deputy in Algiers. The next day the Algiers *Croix* wrote: "On 8 May, the holiday for Joan of Arc, liberator of France, the sun rose radiant in an azure sky, our souls trembled with noble enthusiasm, as on the morning of a battle where the three colors of our flag were to be defended against foreign and cosmopolitan filth" (signed "The Crusader"). Through a process of identification, the anti-Dreyfusards made the lofty figure of Joan into an archetype of French nationalism, the exact opposite of Dreyfus. The liberator of France and the Jewish traitor were henceforth matched like two antagonistic parts of a single machine.

The Thalamas affair in 1904 provides another example of the fusion between the two myths—the positive myth of Joan and the negative myth of the Jew. The consequences of the Dreyfus affair swept Emile Combes into power. The nationalist right railed against General André, minister of the *fiches*. In May, the celebrations for Joan of Arc were the occasion for new incidents. In *L'Action*, Laurent Tailhade called Joan of Arc an "idiot." The nationalist takeover of the heroine provoked insults by anticlericals against the "clerico-military Maid," the "military Mascot," "the clerico-secular idea dangerous to all free thought" (*L'Action*, 23 April 1904). The symbol's place on the right and far right can serve to explain the Thalamas affair, which erupted in November. Originally, it was a minor scandal: a twelfth-grade teacher at the Lycée Condorcet was taken to task by his students for doubting the holiness of the Lorraine maid. But the incident was skillfully exploited by nationalists, to the point of becoming the object of a discussion in the Chamber of Deputies on 1 December 1904. It was an occasion for a few colorful exchanges between the left and the right, during which Jaurès in particular was accused of uttering "the words of an Englishman."

Nationalists and anti-Semites had found a noble cause to defend, against a regime that had handed over "the country to Jews and Freemasons" (*La Libre Parole*, 25 November 1904). On 29 November, Drumont, indulging in his usual objurgations, declared: "They're quite a gang in teaching establishments, in learned societies, in magazines, in academies, all Jews, Protestants, Freemasons, who have given one another a hand up and have succeeded in making people believe they have regenerated, transformed, renewed literature, history, and science."

Over the next few days, *La Libre Parole* embroidered on the regime's complicity with Freemasons and Jews. The equation Thalamas = Freemason = Englishman = Jew inspired an article by Gaston Méry, entitled "De Cauchon à Thalamas" (From Cauchon to Thalamas; 2 December 1904). At a meeting on 5 December, François Coppée was frantically applauded and greeted with the cry: "Down with the Jews!" Drumont's newspaper commented: "It is like a signal, the whole room repeats the cry, a true rallying cry." In the meantime, news circulated of the death of Gabriel Syveton, who had dared slap Combes's minister, General André. At his funeral, the nationalists chanted: "Long live Joan of Arc!" and "Down with Thalamas!" Finally, on 15 December, a large meeting took place in the Salle des Horticulteurs, called by the different leaders of French nationalism "against the insulters of Joan of Arc." It was Dreyfus more than Thalamas who was in the dock. A message from Drumont read from the rostrum, in reference to Joan of Arc, elicited ritual cries: "Long live Drumont!" "Down with the Jews!"

That association between Joan's religion and anti-Semitism did not end with World War I and the Sacred Union. The victory of the Front Populaire and the end of the 1930s were to again combine those cries of love and hate in the publications and the ranks of French nationalism, which were increasingly drawn to the fascist example. They shifted their attention from Dreyfus to Blum. The leader of the Front Populaire was Jewish: that was all that was needed for the far right to see him as the source of the nation's troubles. Anything could provide a pretext for *Je Suis Partout*, for example, to ill use the Socialist leader. On 15 May 1937, Jean-Jacques Brousson had to admit that "M. Léon Blum did not dare suppress the national holiday of Joan of Arc"—which did not prevent him from asserting: "Obviously, the nation's saint is not in favor among the fanatics of the Pasionaria. A virgin who believes in God and country! Oh! If only there had been a demonstration in favor of Judith, who slipped into the tent of Holophernes and politely cut his throat! But a heroine who makes an offer of peace before the battle . . . "

Rebatet jubilantly observed in the same newspaper, on 1 April 1938: "Anti-Semitism is being reborn in France with singular vigor." It would take the Vichy regime to establish it as law. The cult of Joan of Arc was simultaneously one of the ordinary rites of the Pétain regime. France's national saint may have never been so well treated as during the time when the Jews were persecuted in the name of the law. In fact, in an odd paradox, the regime of the "Grande Culbute," as Bernanos called it, made every effort to make the epic of Joan into an allegory of legitimacy. The imposture ended in a climax: the symbol of the Resistance was the object of the most iniquitous of misappropriations by the regime of capitulation. "Although the means differ for Pétain and for Joan, the battle remains identical."[3]

The end of that peculiar undertaking of recuperation was marked by those who, misusing the name of Joan of Arc, enacted the *statut des Juifs*. The Free French forces and the Resistance operating in France found better reasons to seize the heroic shepherdess from the hands of anti-Semites.

The Anti-Jew

Over the course of half a century, the Joan of Arc of anti-Semitic nationalists took root in their writings as a myth of identification, to be opposed to the Jewish myth of repulsion. The qualities, attributes, and emblems associated with Joan were in effect the exact opposite of those the anti-Semite reserved for the Jews. Joan incarnated Frenchness, the quintessence of French civilization, its sublimation, whereas the Jew, whatever his historical incarnations—Dreyfus or Blum—crystallized the elements of rejection in the troubling figure of the Other, the Stranger introduced into the family circle, which he would work relentlessly to destroy. To assess the complementary nature of the two myths, we need only indicate a few correspondences between them in a brief sampling.

The Myth of Joan of Arc	*The Jewish Myth*
I. LAND, ROOTS	I. WANDERING, THE CITY
The peasant "She is a child of the land, daughter of laborers. . . . She was raised as a peasant, as a good peasant of France, vigorous, with solid good sense and bright gay humor."[4]	*The nomad* "They [the Jews] are speculators, usurers, bric-a-brac dealers, official receivers, quibblers, politicians."[21] "It is a race of nomads and Bedouins."[22]
Work, effort "No, Joan does not belong to international capitalists. "Joan belongs to French nationalism in its most realist, most profound sense, in the way it is most attached to the earth. To the humble people of the villages, to their celebrations, their fairies, their work. . . . "Joan does not belong to money, to ideologues, to false defenders of a rotting civilization, since she belongs to eternal youth and creative vivacity."[5] "Joan was a daughter of the true hard-working people."[6]	*Speculation, capitalism* "Immense Jewish fortunes are the fruit of no real labor, of no production."[23] "It is he [the Jew] who has given the international feudalism called capitalism its most inhumane and sprawling form."[24]

Healthy and natural life "She was led to share the simple and strong emotions of that life in the fields. . . .

"A popular environment healthy for soul and body."[7]

"She loved natural things with a passion one does not find again until Jean-Jacques."[8]

The People "She was a child of the people."[9]

"If, as she declared . . . , she did not know 'A from B,' she was in contrast animated by that ardent faith, that active faith that moves mountains."[10]

2. THE NATION

National unity "In the powerful expression of the Marshal, Joan of Arc is . . . the heroine of national unity."[11]

The servant of royalty (By definition)

Against the English "It is clear why the followers of a Jew who dreamed of handing France over to the foreigner [Dreyfus] might

A morbid world "They [the Jews] take pleasure in rubbish and lamentation, like Job on his dung heap."[25]

"He [the Jew] is susceptible to all maladies indicating corruption of the blood."[26]

The Intellectuals "The most frivolous of Jewesses rams the stock market and the Sorbonne down your throat."[27]

2. ANTI-FRANCE

The agent of decomposition "The Jew, who is the antisocial being par excellence, can only be an agent of dissolution; he resumed his eternal role as destroyer; he set fire to the new nation that was made for him, just as he set fire to Jerusalem."[28]

"Every Jew is by necessity a traitor to the country in which he sets up his nomad's tent."[29]

"Israel necessarily betrays, just as the ox chews its cud and the elephant has a trunk."[30]

The profiteer of the Revolution "The Jew confiscated the Revolution for his own profit, and he was the sole beneficiary."[31]

Jews-Englishmen "You know the name we give the enemy that replaced the invading Englishmen of the fifteenth century in our coun-

have borne some resentment toward the young and touching creature who delivered us from England's yoke."[12]

try and that is trying to subjugate us through the corrupting power of gold, just as England wanted to subjugate us through the brutal force of iron. For us, that enemy is called the Jew and the Freemason."[32]

"The English, perhaps even more than in the fifteenth century, want the destruction of France as a united, great, and free nation."[33]

3. SPIRITUALITY

The Catholic saint "The figure of Joan of Arc appears as a black spot in the immaculate blue of triumphant materialism."[13]

3. MATERIALISM

Deicide "The Jew had the Redeemer killed, and since the day that heinous crime was perpetrated, the deicide people, who bear the curse of heaven, have been dispersed across the face of the earth, odious to all, cursed by all."[34]

The supernatural "The nightmare of rationalism and free thinking."[14]

Utilitarianism "The Semite is money-grubbing . . . seeing almost nothing beyond the present life."[35]

Virginity "Gentlemen, have you observed that of all the heroines who appear in the Old Testament, not one was a virgin? Deborah was the wife of Lapidoth. . . . Judith was a widow. Esther had taken the place of Vashti beside Ahasuerus. . . .

"What superiority in Joan of Arc!

"She is a virgin, and this time, the love of the nation is no longer compelled to resort to the artifices of an inferior love."[15]

Prostitution "It was Jewesses who provided the largest contingent of prostitutes in the great capitals."[36]

4. THE SUPERIOR RACE

"The first spurt of Gallic blood."[16]

4. THE INFERIOR RACE

"I am the first to recognize that the Semitic race, compared to the

"We beg the French people not to make the highest symbol of their race into a self-righteous and moralizing heroine."[17]

"A Celt she was, that Joan of Arc who saved the nation."[18]

"She was able to communicate her warlike ardor to the best soldiers of her age."[19]

"Once more, Joan alone had that clear inimitable genius, that of her race, naive beauty."[20]

Indo-European race, forever represents an inferior composition of human nature."[37]

"It has been only in the last few years that people have begun to notice that the Jew is a very particular being, organized in a manner distinct from our own, functioning altogether outside our own functioning, having aptitudes, conceptions, and a mind that differentiate him absolutely from us."[38]

"Wholly without military courage."[39]

"After centuries, the Jews bear on their faces the stigmata of the infamy in their blood."[40]

That *essential* antagonism between Joan of Arc and the Jews inspired an audacious hypothesis that even has a logical tie to the foregoing schema. A haranguer on the right, M. de Kerohant, formulated it in 1894, at a time when the moderate republicans, as we have seen, were attempting to make Joan a symbol of reconciliation. It involved Bishop Cauchon, the burdensome memory of Bishop Cauchon. Don't you see? Good heavens! But, of course, it's that he must have been—Jewish![41]

CHAPTER 9

The Dreyfus Affairs

DURING THE school year 1961–62 (I was in my first job, at the high school in Montpellier), I discovered the persistence of anti-Dreyfusism in certain French families. After devoting a lesson to the Dreyfus affair in the senior class, I was surprised to hear a student dispute the Jewish captain's innocence with unassailable self-assurance. Did he have arguments to present? No, but he *knew*. He knew from his father, who had it from his grandfather, that Dreyfus was a spy in the payment of Germany, no matter what might have been said or written since 1898. An article of faith carved in stone, an inalienable part of the family's cultural inheritance, it was not to be discussed. Twenty years later, André Figueras published *Ce canaille de D . . . reyfus* (That son of a bitch D—reyfus), in which he wrote: "Not all truths ought to be silenced. And especially this one, that Dreyfus was not innocent."[1] We must resign ourselves to the inevitable: for a small minority of French people, the rehabilitation of Dreyfus remains a scandal, the result of a conspiracy, the memorable proof of the decadence that has afflicted France since the advent of democracy. Conversely, in the heat of combat, the last guardians of the Republic do not fail to refer to the famous Affair: "Emile Zola had many enemies," François Mitterrand declared on 10 October 1976 at a ceremony in Medan: "Who were they? And who were Dreyfus's enemies? Look at them: they are not difficult to see. Dreyfus's enemies, Zola's enemies are still here. Their sons and daughters in spirit have a certain eternal form. The society of that era has been able to reproduce itself to our own time."[2]

Let there be no misunderstanding: the Dreyfus affair was unique. In its complexity, it is hardly transposable to later eras. Nonetheless—and both François Mitterrand's words and André Figueras's book attest to this—the Affair has produced a phenomenon of remanence lasting to our own time.

Its hysteresis loop is not yet complete, and almost none of the French political communities escape it. It is not, however, these belated effects that I propose to inventory here, but another phenomenon, one of resonance. It seems to me that during the twentieth century there have been, if not reproductions of the Dreyfus affair, then at the very least a series of correspondences with it, inasmuch as the Affair was a revelation and a catalyst, whose dramatic intensity laid bare a new type of confrontation within French society. In other words, I propose to inquire whether despite its unique character, there may not be a homology between the Dreyfus affair and certain later events—imperfect in the details, but perhaps tenable in substance. To that effect, I must first set out the principles of the new type of conflict revealed by the Dreyfus crisis, before examining its analogies over time.

The Earlier Major Conflicts

The various conflicts that tear apart (and structure) contemporary society are never simple. Every large-scale conflict is a tangle of particular conflicts: every social conflict of some importance is multipolar. The Dreyfus affair lends itself to diverse interpretations. Within its interwoven and confused realities, we need to define the principal contradiction. What is it in relation to other conflicts?

At the risk of simplifying the richness of social relations, let us grant that two types of large-scale conflict pitted French people against one another during the nineteenth century: the struggle surrounding the ancien régime, inherited from 1789; and the class struggle, inherited from the industrial revolution. The historian never observes these two models in their paradigmatic purity. The bourgeois/proletarian polarity (so rare in its pure state) and the Revolution/Restoration polarity vie with one another at the heart of every social confrontation, producing contradictory case histories; the two polarities may combine together or may contradict each other.

In France, the class struggle was waged in the most visible manner in three dramatic episodes. In the words of Benoît Malon, these were the three defeats of the proletariat:[3] the revolt of Lyonnais silk weavers (*canuts*) in 1831; the June Days in 1848; and finally, the Paris Commune in 1871. In this last case, the class consciousness of the Communards is unconfirmed: the most fervent and the most proletarian among them usually fought for the Republic and against the reaction after they had enlisted to serve the nation and to battle the invader. But to assure ourselves of the class nature of the conflict, we need only examine the social composition of the fighters: the majority of the victims of Bloody Week belonged to different corps of manual workers.[4] The Paris Commune, however, far from announcing an increase in class warfare in France, instead ended the cycle. The bourgeois/proletarian face-off now presented itself only in a latent or partial manner—in the case of strikes in particular. Of course, the trade unionism of direct action had as its ambition to maintain the hand-to-hand combat between producers and bosses through the intermediary of the myth of the general strike. But in vain. The antagonism between the "two fundamental classes" was no longer apparent in the Third Republic; it appeared only in diluted form in local conflicts or was integrated into the second type of conflict, which pitted the right against the left. The last attempt at large-scale confrontation on the basis of the class struggle was aborted in late May 1920, with the failure of a series of strikes launched by the CGT, beginning with the general strike of railway workers. Subsequently, both in the victory of the Front Populaire in 1936 and the victory of the left in 1981, it would be wrong to neglect the class dimension, but it would also be ill-advised to privilege it: there were now more than two actors onstage.

The second typical large-style conflict inherited from the nineteenth century was the opposition between the right and the left. That ideological opposition only partially amalgamates the social opposition between the bourgeoisie and the working class, if only because of the importance of the middle classes, who have always been divided between the two political poles. Moreover, the political sphere cannot be reduced to the social sphere. That confrontation has been objectified in the question regarding the form of government; it is a direct descendant of the Revolution and the constitutional uncertainties that arose from it throughout the last century. It took the form of an antagonism between what François Goguel has called the forces of movement and the forces of the established order. In the end, the former identified with the republican contingent, while the latter remained faithful, to varying degrees, to the idea of monarchy and the spirit of restoration. The crisis of 16 May 1877 was the event that did the most to bring about the crystallization of that opposition: the electoral campaign that followed the dissolution of the Chamber pitted two clearly differentiated contingents against each other, one led by Léon Gambetta, the other by Albert de Broglie. For the second time since the passage of the constitutional laws of 1875, citizens voting by universal suffrage pronounced themselves in favor of a republican majority. The republic lost its revolutionary and bellicose connotations; leftist groups as a whole incarnated its legitimacy. Standing opposed to that left, indistinguishable from the republican contingent, was a nostalgic, monarchist (in the broad sense), and clerical right. The Catholic hierarchy had wagered its authority in that campaign to the benefit of conservatives.

From then on, despite its many divisions and lasting disagreements, a leftist tradition took root in France in a lasting manner. It adopted the mission of defending the government and took the principle of union at the hour of danger as a categorical imperative. The "republican defense," the "delegation" of leftists," the "bloc of leftist parties," the slogan "no enemies on the left," were so many methods or watchwords that structured a "leftist" pattern of behavior, reinforced by a memory, a sensibility, an ideology. Leftists stood ready to reassemble when necessary the disparate elements of the republican "contingent." The right had more difficulty constituting itself as a unified force; the repeated failure to restore the monarchy led its architects to seek another principle of identification. Little by little, the right, reinforced by defectors from the left—which was progressively won over by collectivist currents—had a paramount tendency to assert itself in opposition to the left. In successive waves, it brought together spiritual communities that could not identify with republican, anticlerical, and socialist ideologies. In that sense, the dividing line between the left and the right evolved noticeably. Beginning in 1938, when the Radicals broke with the Front Populaire and formed an alliance with the right, a decisive change could be observed: the left was never again what it had been. Even so, a residual radicalism offered the left, victorious in 1981, a stock of republican traditions without which it would have been only a "Marxist" left.

The Dreyfus Conflict

The Dreyfus affair does not fit the mold of these two types of conflict. No doubt the left/right conflict, beginning with the formation of the Waldeck-Rousseau government in 1899, occupied political center stage for several years, but that was a political consequence of the Affair rather than its foundation. Similarly, the class struggle model hardly prevailed on that occasion (though we should grant it its role): the socialists' hesitation to support the Dreyfusard camp left the Affair outside class confrontation. An in-depth analysis of the actors present, however, prevents us from ruling out all class considerations. The sociology of Dreyfusard intellectuals did not take the same form as that of nationalist writers.[5] Nonetheless, in the Dreyfus affair the dividing line was located elsewhere.

A first element alerts us to the novelty: the massive participation in a public affair by those who were henceforth to call themselves "intellectuals."[6] The political class got involved only against its will, pulled in, badgered, summoned to take into account an affair that the vast majority of parliamentarians wanted to confine to the judicial perimeter. The Dreyfus affair was a moral cause first of all: the defense of a man unjustly convicted. Because of the resistance to a new trial mounted by the officers and statesmen concerned, that moral cause became a conflict of ideas, putting two value systems at odds with each other, systems whose substance it is important to recall.

In opposing the efforts of revisionists, the anti-Dreyfusards actually incarnated nationalism, which thus did not coincide with the rightist camp or with a social class. From both the sociological and the political points of view, this was a new right: the list of contributors to the Henry Monument[7] and studies on the composition of the leagues[8] make it clear that a good number of nationalists may have been republicans, even Communards.[9] That new right was not unified, and was able to assume the many faces Zeev Sternhell has set forth under the name "revolutionary right": members of leagues, anti-Semites, strike-breaking unionists, and so on. The new right had its celebrants in journalism and literature: Drumont, Rochefort, Barrès, and a little later, Maurras. Paris was the privileged site for its deployment, not only in street demonstrations, but also in the evolution of elections. Boulanger's electoral victory over the Radical Jacques in January 1899 already marked a shift; in 1900, the municipal elections revealed that Paris had moved toward nationalism. The new right had a dual origin: it was descended from the conservative, ex-monarchist right, but it also included a populist element whose roots were often on the left. If the majority of readers of *La Libre Parole* were "clericals" (which is not certain), the readers of Rochefort's *L'Intransigeant* were in any case not regulars at Sunday mass.

As has often been said, nationalism as it was structured at the end of the nineteenth century was exclusivist. It can be defined first by its phobias: parliamentarianism, German espionage, the foreigner, the Jew. A special mention should be made of anti-Semitism, which was its most solid cement. The denunciation of "the Jewish invasion" succeeded in mobilizing "the bourgeois and the proletariat," "clericals and atheists," "republicans and monarchists." From beginning to end, the Dreyfus affair assumed its dramatic and symbolic dimension only because of the Jewish identity of the accused. Anti-Semitism was used by all nationalists as a form of panlogism, a system of universal explanation that found its principle in the identification of an exogenous causality. More systematically, Barrès and Maurras conceived of the representation of a French entity rooted in a history, a people, and a religion—an entity afflicted with decadence and threatened with entropy by the work of foreigners. Maurras produced his theory of the four confederated states: Protestants and Freemasons—both strangers to the religion of the French people—and "wogs" and Jews— strangers pure and simple, and potential traitors.

One of Barrès's observations suggests what was at the heart of the debate between nationalists and Dreyfusard intellectuals: "To speak of justice when a man condemns another man! Let us be satisfied to speak of social preservation."[10] What is a man, in effect, a mere individual, compared to social cohesion—that is, compared to the totality? From this came the idea that even if Dreyfus were innocent, one would still have to refrain from rehabilitating him: his fate was too minuscule compared to the risks to which the advocates of his cause were exposing the army and the country. The defenders of Major Henry supported a holistic conception of society, irreducible to particulars: it was a totality to be saved by any means, by a counterfeit document if necessary, when "social preservation" required it.

A paranoid nationalism took root at the end of the nineteenth century in one sector of public opinion, in order to regain control of social cohesion, which was threatened by modernity. That modernity, through its two attributes—democracy and industry—compromised custom in favor of individual liberty; where nationalism favored cohesion, modernity fostered dissolution. In the eyes of nationalists, Germany was the enemy, but an opportune enemy. The presence of its aggressive power at the border provided the occasion for intellectual and moral reform. Regaining control meant reaffirming tradition against all the factors undermining national cohesion. That form of nationalism did not stop at the spirit of revenge; more than that, it turned inward, toward the past, toward its sources more than its future. The first to be targeted was the democratic and liberal government—"The Jewish and Masonic Republic." But behind the political project was a spiritual reaction to decadence: the defense of French interests was understood as the defense of a perfected civilization, placed in danger by the new mobility of persons and things.

Nationalism found its direct enemy in the camp of anti-France. Within, a vast conspiracy linked all who supported the existing government. But the Dreyfus affair brought to the fore the privileged adversary of the nationalists: intellectuals. Let there be no misunderstanding about the word. There were obviously intellectuals in both camps. But the renowned writers and members of the Académie Française in the Ligue de la Patrie Française (League of the French nation) did not claim to be "intellectuals"; the word, initially used derisively, applied to those who had cut themselves off from the organic body of France, who were losing their instincts as French people by exercising their reason in defiance of national interests. Intellectuals on the right were only the mouthpieces for the French race, the voice of an eternal France, from which they refused to isolate themselves; true intellectuals had retreated from society and claimed to direct the public on matters of state in the name of intellect.

Two Value Systems

In fact, Dreyfusard intellectuals defended their own interpretation of social cohesion. In their view, what undermined it was injustice toward individuals, a blind *raison d'état*. For them, social cohesion could come about only through an act of voluntary adherence. Society did not transcend individuals except insofar as these individuals were citizens, that is, free.

During Zola's trial, before the politicians involved had entered the fray, two systems pitted values against each other term for term:

Dreyfusism	Anti-Dreyfusism
Truth	Authority
Justice	Order
Reason	Instinct/natural laws
Universalism	Exclusivist nationalism (anti-Semitism, xenophobia)
Human rights (individualism)	Social preservation (holism)

It is undoubtedly in that last dichotomy (individualism/holism) that we catch a glimpse of the ideological conflict. On one side were those who placed the safeguarding of human—individual—rights above all else; on the other, those who privileged social cement over individual interests. Two ethical systems confronted each other, but also two political systems. The ethics of human rights implies a democratic government; the ethics of organic society, a system favoring unity, order, and hierarchy, implies either an authoritarian regime or—a conclusion Maurras drew from his own nationalism—a monarchy, which maintains the cohesion of the totality, under siege by all the deadly influences of the new times.

Two institutions capitalized on the hopes of the anti-Dreyfusards: the Church and the army. Organized around the principles of unity and hierarchy, by their very nature they contributed toward binding the social fabric together. Conversely, the Dreyfusards were tempted to see these two bodies as the relic of a prehistory—that of human reason—which they had to accommodate, but without forgetting to limit its prerogatives. Anticlericalism and antimilitarism (to varying degrees) logically coexisted within Dreyfusism—just as anti-Dreyfusism welcomed the majority of Catholic troops (see the role of *Le Croix* in the Affair) and the whole of the military hierarchy.

As we know, the political outcome of that opposition again assumed the form of a duality between left and right. Thus the original ideological conflict of the Affair was couched in the terms of an old conflict. Everything was decided, or almost, with the 1902 elections and the formation of the Bloc des Gauches. It is nevertheless true that the ideological antagonism, which made the Dreyfus affair a crystallizing moment in a conflict of values that had remained vague until that time, was to find itself reactivated throughout the twentieth century.

Anti-Dreyfusism was varied in its troops, its orators, and its newspapers. In the years that followed the Affair, one political community made every effort to monopolize the nationalist inheritance and its representativeness: Action Française, which came out of the Affair, raised anti-Dreyfusism to the heights of exaltation and theoretical rigor.[11] As the vestal virgin of nationalism, Action Française set to the task of defending to the death its vulgate of the Affair as a myth of origin. The Maurrassian movement was born and grew into an exterminating angel, at the very moment when France was supposedly threatened with decomposition, under the combined action of Jews, Freemasons, intellectuals, and foreigners. To the death, denying all the evidence and arguments contrary to its theory, AF remained the depository of the "national" version of the tragedy: the culpability of the Jews, rehabilitated through the anti-France conspiracy. Although its aim was monopoly, Action Française did not achieve it, since many nationalists remained deaf to Charles Maurras's monarchist inferences. Until World War I, *La Libre Parole* and *L'Intransigeant* remained influential. This was clear in 1908 with the acquittal of Grégori, who had shot at Alfred Dreyfus with a revolver while Zola's ashes were being transferred to the Pantheon. But over the long term and with incomparable consistency, *L'Action Française* remained the newspaper of anti-Dreyfusism, from which it had originated. In the years following Dreyfus's rehabilitation, far from laying down its weapons, it increased the number of symbolic demonstrations: on 29 June 1907, a gold medal was returned to General Mercier in the Salle Wagram; on 4 October 1908 in Nîmes, a meeting was held to protest the inauguration of the monument erected in memory of Bernard Lazare; the daily *Action Française*, created in 1908, persistently attacked the "traitor," earning the newspaper condemnations; lectures on the topic, "The Lessons of the Dreyfus Affair," were delivered throughout the 1920s; in February 1931, the play adapted from the German by Jacques Richepin and entitled *The Dreyfus Affair* caused an uproar that ended in a prolonged suspension of performances. Fifty years later, a disciple of Maurras, André Figueras, was still writing: "The Dreyfus affair was the catalyst that organized anti-France and endowed it with a doctrine and a method."[12]

The continuity of the reference to Dreyfus, however, has only symbolic interest. It is the dual value system, revealed in his trial, that assures the paradigmatic quality of the 1898 conflict. That conflict subsided with, and as a result of, World War I: the Sacred Union seemed to reunite the French community; Dreyfusards and anti-Dreyfusards, antimilitarists and militarists, Jews and anti-Semites now formed a single nation in the face of the external danger. The war might pass for a revenge of anti-Dreyfusism, in that it imposed order and restored the military values of discipline and hierarchy. But old Dreyfusards were able to fight the war on behalf of individual rights, completing the work of the French Revolution by defeating the old regimes of Central Europe. In any case, justifications on each side resulted in a spirit of national defense, where the Dreyfusard conflict was no longer at issue. Only after the war, during the 1920s, did the nationalists once more set out to assault the "Dreyfusard party," responsible for the carnage of 1914–18 because it had led to a weakening in the system of national defense.[13] We must look beyond the postwar period, however, if we want to see the reproduction, mutatis mutandis, of a conflict of the Dreyfusard type. Three incarnations are visible: the political crisis set off by the events of 6 February 1934; Marshal Pétain's National Revolution; and the Algerian war. In these three moments of internecine French struggle, we again find ourselves in the presence of a conflict of values that prevailed over class and party conflicts.

The 1930s

At first glance, the multidimensional crisis of the 1930s seems rather to combine the two "classic" conflicts. The victory of the united left forces in the Rassemblement Populaire (Popular rally) in May 1936 and the wave of strikes in June meant that the interests of the left coincided with those of the proletariat and, therefore, that the interests of rightists corresponded with those of management. But that coincidence of interests was fleeting, lasting only for the duration of the Matignon negotiations and the passage of the social laws that followed—laws passed, moreover, by numerous elected officials on the right. In fact, the class conflict was complicated once more by the importance of the middle classes, which made the proletariat/bourgeoisie duality short-lived and deprived the left of a true class base. The unity of the Front Populaire was due to a political alliance against the renewed danger of the leagues: "antifascism" was a modern version of the old republican defense. But divergences in economic interests and in policy (foreign policy in particular) fairly quickly destroyed the pattern of left versus right.

The revived ideological conflict opposing nationalists and intellectuals between 1934 and 1939 appears to have been more lasting. To be sure, no other scandal comparable to the Dreyfus affair provided a focus for the controversy: it must therefore be grasped in its diffuse state. Fundamentally, it was as if all the necessary conditions existed for another Dreyfus affair—except the trial and the judicial "error."

Encouraged by writers more or less close to Action Française, by Drumont's epigones, and by the admirers of the strong regimes that had been established in Italy and Germany, the nationalism of the leagues gained a new voice and new vigor against a decadent parliamentary regime, against immigrants who were taking jobs away from the French people, and against Jews and intellectuals who were undermining the foundations of national unity. Confronted by the leagues, intellectuals, who had once more mobilized and regrouped into a vigilance committee, denounced fascism and supported the first measures of the Rassemblement Populaire.

France, wrote Jean Renaud, "must fight the enemies within, who are called unionized teachers, shady financiers, communists, cartelists, and politicians. . . . The unity or link is established among them by the lodges, the leading sovereigns of treason and the indisputable dispensers of sinecures. Nothing resists the criminal assault of all the forces of disunion, themselves subject to the occult powers of the Jewish internationale."[14]

Even more than in 1898, the external enemy proved to be less threatening than the enemy within. "Anti-France" was within the walls. In the end, the result was neopacifism on the nationalist right: France could do nothing against Germany as long as it had not reestablished authority in the state and nation. Confronted with Hitler, French nationalism took the side of reactionary defeatism: "A war for justice and right, to install the Republic in an intact Germany, to assure the prosperity of the Jews, to fabricate a mythological Czechoslovakia, to leave the wretched old men of French democracy with their sinecures? Might as well abdicate immediately and spare us two or three million young cadavers."[15]

Throughout the 1930s, the poets of decadence once more repeated the old Barrésian couplets from the time of the Dreyfus affair. In looking closely, moreover, we find, if not the due process of a trial, then at least the choice of a scapegoat, who once more assumed the characteristics of the Jew—in this case, Léon Blum. In this respect, it is not arbitrary to note that the sort of attempted lynching to which Léon Blum was subjected on 13 February 1936 on Boulevard Saint-Germain indeed represented a punishment—capital punishment—that linked Blum to Dreyfus. It is easy to see the differences in the situation of the two men. But in addition to the fact that Léon Blum was a notorious Dreyfusard, the differences collapsed in the eyes of nationalists: once more, France was being "betrayed" by a Jew. That man "is not from around here," Georges Suarez had already declared in *Gringoire* (19 April 1929). In the same newspaper nearly ten years later, Henri Béraud again explained that Blum did not belong to the French nation, to the soil of peasant France:

Blum, I have some land that comes to me from my folks, and I have some that I have paid for out of my savings. If God allows, I will buy more, as much as I can buy. I know the price of an arpent of vineyard, the value of a hectare of wheat. And never, my poor Blum, will either I or my parents blush about this property that we fought for, from father to son, . . . for this land that neither you nor your family have ever known how to cultivate and defend.[16]

The rural tradition was incomprehensible to nomadic "Talmudism": the anti-Blumist, anti-Semitic literature of the years preceding World War II says a great deal about the timelessness of the nationalist mythology dating from Dreyfus's era. After a year of the Blum government, the explanation for all French difficulties once more became luminous: "The Jew Blum did everything to bring about war, and war under the harshest conditions for France: with the minimum amount of gold and the minimum number of allies, since his policy alienated us from Italy, which was our ally in the last war and is now on the side of Germany."[17]

Emerging in response to that new wave of anti-Semitic, xenophobic,[18] and antiparliamentarian nationalism, the Comité de Vigilance des Intellectuels Antifascistes (Vigilance committee of antifascist intellectuals) and the Front Populaire did not last long. Too many contradictions were at work in their ranks. Never since the Dreyfus affair, however, had anyone witnessed such a revival in the battle of ideas. France had been weakened by the lasting effects of World War I, the economic crisis, the failures of the political system, and demographic decline. Once more, the anthem of decadence was being sung, a hymn to "France alone"; and once more, Jews and Freemasons were being denounced as traitors. Once more, intellectuals spoke up and signed their names to protest the reappearance of the old adversary, now called "fascism," which they railed against. Nevertheless, the camp of intellectuals displayed divisions: the quarrel between the pacifists and antipacifists muddled its antifascist resolution. All the same, the war of ideas flared up again between the major newspapers of the nationalist press (*L'Action Française, Gringoire, Je Suis Partout*) and those of intellectuals (*Vigilance, Vendredi*). The name of Alfred Dreyfus was brought into it. On the occasion of Dreyfus's death in July 1935, Charles Maurras noted "the coincidence": "Alfred Dreyfus expired on the 146th anniversary of the taking of the Bastille. . . . The consequences of the Dreyfus affair were not only antimoderate, antiproprietary, antihereditary, and anti-Catholic, they were also and above all antipatriotic and antimilitarist."[19] On 14 July of the same year, the conference for peace and liberty was held in Buffalo Stadium. Victor Basch, president of the Ligue des Droits de l'Homme (League of human rights), recalled the league's battles on Dreyfus's behalf:

"At that very moment," wrote Jean Guéhenno,

they were burying the colonel, "Captain" Dreyfus, in the Montmartre cemetery (and that might lead some to believe that certain men truly have a destiny that governs as it should the vicissitudes of their life, and even the moment of their death, so that their existence is given all its value). Then, suddenly, on its own and in a single movement, the entire crowd filling the immense amphitheater rose and, in a silence that touched the heart, each person thought of the dead man. . . . There was not one of us who, on the brink of tears, did not feel at that movement that he was transmitting a tradition of justice from one generation to the next.[20]

The Anti-Dreyfusards in Power

From the outset, the new regime, created out of the military disaster of May–June 1940, was inspired by the traditionalist and nationalist pool. The exclusionary measures taken against the Freemasons and the Jews, the suppression of normal schools, the exhortation to return to the land, and the "whitewash" policy, as the decisions of the Vichy regime directed against the very memory of the parliamentary republic were called (for example, streets named after Jaurès and Zola were rebaptized with Pétain's name) were so many elements, sometimes legislative, sometimes symbolic, of revenge. More than ever, that desire for revenge turned inward. The quintessence of France, the rural, artisanal, monarchist, and Catholic tradition was continually exalted against all the poisons of decadence that had almost corrupted it. When the Vichy regime expelled Jews from the army, *La France au Travail* supplied this commentary: "We will have no more Dreyfus affairs."[21] For his part, Robert Valléry-Radot explained: "The National Revolution is above all the insurrection of real wealth created by work against fictive wealth in the Jewish manner."[22] In that context, none other than Léon Blum could become the principal defendant in the Riom trial, which opened in February 1942. It was a botched but highly symbolic trial, in the spirit of its organizers. The *Action Française* of 28 January 1942 denounced "all Blum's Jewish, intellectual, and moral vices" and proposed "to erect a stake to burn the Declaration of the Rights of Man and the works of Rousseau, Kant, and Blum."[23] The Parisian press increased in violence: "Daladier was politically and morally a coward," wrote Stéphane Lauzanne in *Le Matin* (11 February 1942). "That bull was only a cow domesticated by England and bridled by the Jews. . . . Léon Blum was the conscious and satanic preparer of defeat, the man who inoculated the virus of laziness into the blood of a people."[24]

Once more, anti-Semitism assured a continuity of behavior: Drumont's *La France juive* was reprinted, and Robert Brasillach praised it as "the ingenious precursor of French national socialism";[25] lectures, ceremonies, and exhibitions were organized, establishing to an even greater extent the

psychological conditions for collaboration in the round-ups and deportations of Jews. "We are beyond salon talk, we have reached the point of
pogroms."[26]

In an odd aberration, the nationalism born of anti-Dreyfusism had led
to a policy of collaboration with the "hereditary enemy" occupying national territory. Thus Maurras supported submission to the exigencies of
Gauleiter Sauckel,[27] because, in his eyes, the victory of Germany was
preferable to "fatal illusions": "If the Anglo-Americans were to win, that
would mean the return of the Freemasons, the Jews, and all the political
staff eliminated in 1940."[28] In 1943, Joseph Darnand, a former leading figure in the Camelots du Roi, became chief of the Milice, which fought relentlessly against "Bolshevism" and the Resistance.

The Resistance and the Free French forces, which railed against the
Vichy regime and the many faces of collaboration, had neither political
nor social unity. Let us note, however, that at first, they too existed outside
political parties and were the result of the acts of individuals. In addition,
despite the diversity of the themes advanced, in many texts we again find
the defense and illustration of Dreyfusard values. The Resistance struggle
was not only patriotic in nature; it described itself as a moral struggle.

"To ask whether one is republican," wrote an anonymous philosopher
in the Resistance,

is to ask whether the notions of right and justice have any meaning; or else, in order to decide between political intuitions that contradict one another and that
may present themselves as equally self-evident, whether there is another method
of choice besides violence and war; or even more simply, it is to ask whether there
is anything ethical in the matter of politics. No, Maurras and his minions openly
reply. Yes, maintain those who expressly call themselves republicans.[29]

The following conclusion to an article entitled "Au-delà de la nation"
(Beyond the nation) appeared in *Libération* in September 1943: "We repeat, the greatest victory of France will not be the victory of armies but
of ideas. May God let us bring the new gospel of the Rights of Peoples
into the world, as in 1789 we brought forth the Rights of Man."[30]

The ideology of the Resistance, however, though partly in the direct
line of Dreyfusard ideology (universalism, human rights, and so on) was
nourished, oddly enough, by a source that had contributed little to Dreyfusism: the Christian democratic current. Thus the Church was divided
by the event and did not form a united bloc: whereas most members of
the hierarchy gave their blessing to the National Revolution, the young
people emerging from the Catholic youth movements and many Christian writers were among the first Resistance fighters. The army, another
privileged institution of the old anti-Dreyfusards, did not escape that di-

vision—though the two shares were unequal. The face-off between the General and the Marshal is the best symbol of that division. The result was that, in the Resistance, anticlericalism and antimilitarism ceased to occupy the place they had had in the Dreyfusard model. Simultaneously, nationalism on the other side was curiously modified by the fascist spirit and national socialist temptations: for the younger anti-Dreyfusards, the time for "France alone" had passed. Darnand as well as the journalists of *Je Suis Partout* took Maurras for an outdated teacher. Nonetheless, the core of the National Revolution and that of the Resistance each contained some of the many ideas that animated the struggle between the anti-Dreyfusards and the Dreyfusards. It is no accident that Charles Maurras, hearing the outcome of his trial in January 1945, and learning he was sentenced to life in prison and the loss of all civil rights, cried out as his final words: "It's Dreyfus's revenge!"

The Army Again in Question

The collapse of the Vichy regime brought on by the defeat of Hitler's Germany culminated in the ruin of the anti-Dreyfusard line. The Nuremberg trials—to mark that phase with a symbolic reference point—put an end to sixty years of anti-Semitism; the founders of the Fourth Republic reconciled the secular and Christian traditions. Apparently, when the world entered the atomic age, France was exorcised of its old demons. However, under that Fourth Republic, and particularly during the last years of the regime (1954–58), the Dreyfusard conflict resurfaced in a new area: decolonization. The principal actors on the metropolitan stage were not so much professional politicians—most of whom could not resolve to imagine decolonization necessary—as members of two opposing and heterogeneous camps, which waged battle in all the forums of public opinion, and sometimes in the street. On one side were the defenders of French Algeria and the army; on the other, intellectuals, reunited in the defense of human rights. Beginning on 6 February 1956, the date of the ill-fated journey of Premier Guy Mollet to Algiers, the policy of colonial repression defended by the Socialist leader received the approval of the overwhelming majority of the Socialist party and of Parliament. Outside Parliament, opposition to the Algerian war was limited to intellectuals who made their protests known either in newspapers ("opinion pieces" in *Le Monde, L'Express, France-Observateur,* and *Témoignage Chrétien,* the "big four of French counterpropaganda," in Jacques Soustelle's expression), in journals (primarily *Esprit* and *Les Temps Modernes*), or in forums specially created for the purposes of that struggle against colonial policy and its methods (*Témoignages et Documents, Vérité-Liberté*). The debate on torture perpetrated by members of the army in Algeria reproduced an exemplary case history that was typically "Dreyfusard."

In January 1955, an article by Claude Bourdet and François Mauriac denounced cases of torture in Algeria. In November of the same year, the specific commitment of intellectuals took the form of an action committee against continuing the war in North Africa. On 5 April 1956, Henri Marrou, professor at the Sorbonne and former companion of Emmanuel Mounier, published an opinion piece in *Le Monde* entitled, "France ma patrie" (France, my nation), which earned him a police search of his home five days later. On that occasion, M. Bourgès-Maunoury, minister of national defense, made fun of the "dear professors"—an expression that would become famous. Throughout 1957, the denunciation of torture was reinforced by all the testimony from soldiers returning from Algeria. In February, there was the publication of the Jean Muller dossier by *Les Cahiers de "Témoignage Chrétien"*; in March, there was the brochure *Les rappelés témoignent* (Returning soldiers testify). In the same month, Pierre-Henri Simon, a Catholic writer of moderate opinions, published his version of Zola's "J'accuse" in the form of a pamphlet, published by Seuil under the title *Contre la torture* (Against torture). A change had clearly occurred since Zola's time, given that in this case, the author was a Christian;[31] moreover, that Christian said he was himself "a child of the university and the Ecole Normale," and his contribution was presented as a moral act on behalf of truth and justice. The epigraph he chose gave the book its universalist stamp; Pierre-Henri Simon borrowed from Montesquieu: "If I had known something useful for my family that was not so for my nation, I would have sought to forget it; if I had known something useful for my country that would have been prejudicial for the human race, I would have rejected it as a crime."

The acts and writings of intellectuals against torture and repression in Algeria multiplied. We need not make a list of them here.[32] Let us simply underscore that in no other period since the Resistance were so many names of literary writers and academics engaged in a public battle; never since the Dreyfus affair had intellectuals constituted a political pressure group to that extent—a *parti*, as it was called in the last years of the nineteenth century. Contrary to the situation in 1899, these intellectuals were not backed up by the political left; to be more exact, it was unfortunately the socialist left that systematically covered up the scandal of torture. It was that left within the government, allied to the rest of the noncommunist left, that placed the army above suspicion.[33] Guy Mollet had replaced Jean Jaurès. All the same, let us point out that one politician, the Radical Pierre Mendès France, attracted the vengeful hatred of the advocates of French Algeria. Mendès France signed the Geneva accords, ending the first war in Indochina with the almost unanimous support of Parliament. But to no avail, he was still considered a "sellout." When the Algerian conflict erupted in November 1954, he declared his conviction that Algeria had to remain French, but again it was no use: Poujadists, senior officers, and extremists in all the smaller groups made him out to be the "traitor." In the eyes of his detractors, his resignation from the Mollet government on 23 May 1956 only confirmed his vocation for "betrayal." Thus, if the Algerian conflict appears to have been purged of all anti-Semitism—if only because of the Franco-Israeli alliance against Nasser during the Suez expedition—there were nonetheless obvious signs of the old passion, in particular in the Poujadist press and papers on the far right, such as *Rivarol*. These signs, however, were kept within legal limits.

By way of illustration, let us mention one demonstration among hundreds of others: that organized by various extremist movements against the abduction of Captain Moureau in southern Morocco by rebel bands. The demonstration took place on Saturday 30 March 1957, in front of the Arch of Triumph and along the Champs-Elysées. There was shouting, overturning and setting fire to vehicles, repeated cries of "Al-gérie-française!" The windows of *L'Express* were broken with paving stones. Signs were brandished bearing inscriptions hostile to Mendès France and Mauriac. "A uniformed paratrooper perched on the shoulders of his comrades pronounced a brief harangue, seeking to denounce a rotting regime served up by cowards." Chairs taken from an outdoor café were thrown at peace officers, while demonstrators repeated: "Shoot Ben Bella!" "Power to the army!" and "The firing squad for Mendès France!"[34]

The *Observer*, cited in *Le Monde*, described the moral situation in early April 1957 as follows: "A number of French people judge that in the face of Algerian rebellion and terrorism ruthless methods are justified. But those whose consciences are now compelling them to protest represent that part of France that has taken the side of people who love human freedom and respect human dignity."

In the opposing camp of French Algeria, we find the various themes of anti-Dreyfusism, with all its nuances and formal variations: the taboo surrounding the army (President René Coty declared in Verdun on 17 June 1956, "Duty is simple and clear. To those who are not kept to military discipline, it commands at least the minimum of civic discipline, which prohibits any act, even any word capable of causing disorder in the souls of the children of the nation whom the Republic calls to arms"); contempt for intellectuals ("exhibitionist in heart and mind"); exaltation of a paranoid nationalism (which included the reactivation of the cult of Joan of Arc); phobia about foreign plots;[35] antiparliamentarianism in all its forms; and so on. No doubt it was not easy to blend together nationalism coming from the far right and Vichy and the nationalism that embraced the memory of the Resistance. But new syntheses took place under these historical circumstances; Georges Bidault, former president of the Conseil National de la Résistance (CNR, National council of the Resistance) became the ally of Jean-Louis Tixier-Vigancour, a former Pétainist. At a meeting held 11 February 1958 by paratrooper deputies Le Pen and Demarquet and the Front National des Combattants (National front of veterans), despite the fact that the name "Mendès" was booed, "the fighters of Verdun and those in the anticommunist struggle [that is, in the LVF]" were united in a single homage from Demarquet. The cards of nationalism were reshuffled, historical memory no longer prohibited a united front against the new symptoms of decadence. Anticommunism took the place of the old anti-Semitism—once so useful in bringing people together—as the cementing element. The withdrawal of the PCF's support for Guy Mollet beginning in autumn 1956, the events of 1956 (the twentieth congress of the Soviet Communist party, the crushing of the Hungarian revolution) favored the isolation of communists and made instrumental anticommunism all the easier. "To abandon" Algeria was not only to renounce imperial greatness and to leave nearly a million Algerian-born French citizens defenseless, it was also, for many officers and political leaders, to abandon the Mediterranean and Africa "to the Soviets."

Intellectuals responded to that idea of decadence by embracing patriotism itself: "Above all, we must cease to associate the words 'decadence' or 'abandonment' with the emancipation of colonized peoples. On the contrary, how can we not see that such emancipation in a sense seals the very success of the mission we set for ourselves and constitutes its justification?"[36] Whether it was the honor of the army or the greatness of the nation that was at stake, analogous arguments were made at sixty years' distance. Once more the ethics of human rights stood opposed to the ethics of organic society; those who defended respect for and emancipation of colonized peoples stood opposed to those who extolled the defense of Algeria, French territory, and the army—possessor of national values—at the expense of all "patriotic counterfeits." All the same, the scenario of the Dreyfus affair was reversed in 1958. It was the neonationalists who were victorious, thanks to the support they received from the French population of Algeria and the army, and thanks to General de Gaulle. This time, the mechanism of "republican defense" seized up, because of the divisions within the left and the very responsibility the majority of Socialists had taken for the revival of nationalism. We know that, in a historical paradox, it took the nationalist Charles de Gaulle to annihilate the effects of colonial neonationalism after four years. It was thus General de Gaulle who had to assume Waldeck-Rousseau's role, to the detriment of the parliamentary regime, which no one seemed to want any longer.

Several conclusions may be drawn from the foregoing:

1. The uniqueness of the Dreyfus affair cannot be minimized. Although I believe I was able observe a few reproductions of its central conflict, these had neither the same scenario (judicial matter + moral crisis + political crisis + victory of the leftist bloc and rehabilitation) nor the same content (there were variations in the role of the army, the Church, and anti-Semitism, among others). In none of these reproductions do we find the same simplicity of the moral conflict. Even in the case of the Algerian war, those who disdained the methods of repression were not defending an innocent party: the Front de Libération Nationale also used violent methods, even against Algerians, methods whose atrocity provided an argument for counterterrorist violence. It is clear (see Table 1) that while it may be legitimate in the historian's eyes to observe "remakes" of the Affair, it is so only in a very imperfect manner. Perhaps a closer analogy would have to be sought in other countries: I am thinking of the Sacco-Vanzetti affair, or the Stalin trials. Case 2 of this table presents only diffuse elements of a new Dreyfus affair; case 3, like the previous one, includes a new upheaval within a much broader conflict; in case 4, there are undoubtedly clearer elements of a case history close to the Dreyfus crisis, with the obligatory changes.

2. Despite these disparities, I felt I needed to elevate the Dreyfus conflict to the level of a historical paradigm that has continued to function as a point of reference to our own time.[37] I situated that conflict in the opposition between "intellectuals" and "nationalists"—new words that emerged during the Dreyfus era.

3. I have not insisted on the sociology of the nationalism that took shape at the end of the last century, but there is one constant in it: the importance of social strata threatened by economic changes. "Little white guys" constituted the typical clientele of the leagues, and we also find them during the 1930s, under Vichy, and at the core of Poujadism. By definition, they were also the majority of the victims of decolonization in Algeria. That socioeconomic center of gravity corresponds to a defensive ideology that expresses itself in a certain number of recurrent or revived phobias and fantasies (anti-Semitism, xenophobia, appeal to a providential man, and so on). From this point of view, the Dreyfus crisis and its later incarnations are the expression of a struggle between the champions of a threatened old society and the champions of a modernity whose aspect varies over time.

4. It seems to me that for the most part, the content of the perma-

Table 1

The Dreyfus Affair and Subsequent Reproductions

	THE INTELLECTUALS	THE NATIONALISTS	THE SCAPEGOAT
Dreyfus Affair	"Manifesto" of Intellectuals, January 1898	Ligue des Patriotes Ligue Antisémitique Ligue de la Patrie Française Birth of Action Française *La Libre Parole* *L'Intransigeant* *La Croix*	Alfred Dreyfus
1930s Crisis (1934–39)	Comité de Vigilance des Intellectuels Antifascistes	Action Française Leagues Fascist-leaning groups Large weeklies (*Gringoire, Je Suis Partout*)	Léon Blum (13 February 1936)
National Revolution and Resistance	No central organization before the Comité National des Ecrivains (CNE)	In power under Vichy regime	Léon Blum (principal defendant in Riom trial)
Algerian War	Comité d'Action des Intellectuels contre la Poursuite de la Guerre en Afrique du Nord Comité de Résistance Spirituelle Manifesto of the 121 (September 1960) *Les Temps Modernes* *Esprit*	Neonationalism regrouping the nationalism of the anti-Dreyfusard tradition (AF, fundamentalist Catholics) and "republican" nationalism (former Resistance members, members of the left and anti-clericals of the "colonial party"); Poujadists	Pierre Mendès France

nence/modernity conflict pits an individualist vision of society against a holistic vision. For the Dreyfusards, a single man has the value of inalienable humanity for the community. In this respect, since the Stalin trials, we can no longer situate the Dreyfusard tradition entirely on the left: with respect to these trials, the communist ethic developed a vision of society that was more totalitarian than even far right nationalism. Conversely, a part of the Dreyfusard sphere of influence is in the direct line of a liberal right that has identified itself particularly with the evolution of the Democratic Alliance. On the other hand, as we saw during the Algerian conflict, a large sector of the left feeds nationalism or acts as a screen for it.

5. In the successive "Dreyfus affairs" I believed I was able to identify, we find a more or less clearly signaled presence of a scapegoat (to use René Girard's term), whose Jewish identity is pointed out: Dreyfus, Blum, Blum again, Mendès France. Anti-Semitism, which has become less acute since 1945 and has been officially banned, nonetheless continues to provide in latent form the scapegoat against whom nationalism intends to reunite the ranks of the nation.[38] In that regard, the observer of the times we are living in will not fail to invoke the case of Simone Veil, and the defamatory literature that has attempted to discredit her since the passage of the 1975 law on "voluntary interruption of pregnancy." That literature says a great deal about the permanence of a current one believed forever dried up "after Auschwitz." In a symmetrical manner, how can we not mention the far right's harassment of Robert Badinter, Garde des Sceaux, since 1981?

If the Dreyfus affair represents a new type of conflict in French society,[39] it seems to me that is in the first place because of the emergence of the two new and heterogeneous forces it provoked and the opposition between them it crystallized. The first was a new clerical establishment, the second, a new right, which took the name of nationalism during that affair. Intellectuals collectively established themselves as guardians of the social philosophy issuing from the Enlightenment; human rights took root as the charter of their universalism. Against these new clerics, who are accused of being at odds with the community, nationalism expresses the desire for social safeguards and a political reaction based on the diagnosis of decadence.

CHAPTER 10

The Left and the Jews

THE TOULOUSE *Dépêche* is a republican newspaper, a leftist daily. In 1895, Jaurès submitted articles to it every week. The previous December, ex-Captain Dreyfus had been condemned to be deported for an act of espionage. It was not yet an affair; it was not yet "the Affair"! On 13 March, attention turned to the declaration of Raymond Gendre, a Radical Socialist deputy from Dordogne, who expressed his opinion on "the Jews." Well then! Deputies on the left were thus obliged to give their "view" on the Jews at that time? But our astonishment increases when we read, beneath the name of the honorable parliamentarian: "I maintain that political and financial Jewry, which is eating away at us, is the greatest social scourge of the day." Who was this Gendre? The *Dictionnaire des parlementaires* (Dictionary of parliamentarians) indicates that Gendre was elected in Sarlat over a conservative candidate; he embraced the "republican ideal." To be precise, in his struggle "for an honest, economical, and popular republic," he denounced the collusion in power between Opportunism (the left center) and "Jewry." What was the comment of *La Dépêche*? There was none. Not a word of objection.

Thus the rejection of anti-Semitism by leftists has not always been an obvious categorical imperative. The right and far right have not always held the monopoly on prejudices of "race." But we cannot remain content with that general observation, which would bring anti-Semitism back down to the level of commonplaces. We must rather seek to know more precisely what the relationship has been in France between the left and the Jewish community since 1789—that is, since the left has existed. In embracing the long term, we may be able to see things more clearly.

Let us first use a telescope to quickly sweep across some two centuries of French history. Three landscapes emerge, one after another, three moments of solidarity between the left and the Jews: the Revolution, the Dreyfus affair, and the fight against Hitler. In the course of these three "crises" of different natures, the left, in affirming and developing its ideas, was led to intervene in what early on came to be called "the Jewish question." All the same, if we exchange our binoculars for a historian's magnifying glass, we must quickly concede that the good relations between the left and the Jews, brightly proclaimed on three occasions, are far from exhausting the problem. The reality has not always been as luminous as the great principles, and the great principles themselves have not been without perverse effects.

The New Era of Liberty

At the beginning of that history, then, stands a glorious monument: the emancipation of the Jews by the Constituent Assembly on 28 September 1791. During the very first weeks of the Assembly in 1789, Abbé Grégoire, one of the most prominent members on the left, attracted his colleagues' attention to the question. In his *Motion en faveur des Juifs* (Motion in favor of the Jews), he asserts:

The Jews are members of the universal family that must establish fraternity among peoples; and the Revolution spreads its majestic cloak over them as over you. Children of the same father, set aside every pretext for hatred of your brothers, who will one day return to the fold; open a refuge to them where they can peacefully rest their heads and dry their tears; and may the Jew, showing tenderness to the Christian in return, finally embrace me as his fellow citizen and his friend.

These generous words were not to the liking of all the deputies. Despite Mirabeau, Clermont-Tonnerre, and Robespierre, who joined with Abbé Grégoire, the right succeeded in delaying the event. Abbé Maury, though proclaiming he was opposed to all "oppression," denied the Jews the status of Frenchmen and, as a result, of citizens. That was also the idea of the Alsatian deputy Reubell, the most relentless adversary of emancipation. Since the beginning of the Revolution, Alsace, where the majority of French Jews were living, had been the scene of actual pogroms as part of the agrarian movement. Reubell introduced an objection into the discussion; it came not from a rightist but from a future Montagnard. There was no unanimity on the left in favor of the Jews. All the same, the decree of 1791 sealed the alliance between the Revolution and the Jews.[1] As Bernard Lazare later wrote, it "liberated all those pariahs from an age-old servitude; it broke all the bonds that the laws had burdened them with; it pulled them out of ghettoes of every kind, in which they had been imprisoned; it turned them from cattle into men."[2]

In addition to the fifty thousand French Jews emancipated by the Revolution, hundreds of thousands of European Jews were emancipated by the armies of the Republic and the Empire. Heinrich Heine has recounted how in Holland, Italy, and Germany, Napoleon's armies entered the cities of Europe to the acclamation of Jews. "France," said Samuel Lévy in a letter to the Constituent Assembly, "France . . . is our Palestine, its mountains our Zion, its rivers our Jordan. . . . Freedom has only one language, and all men know its alphabet. The most servile nation will pray for it, for it has broken the chains of slaves. France is the refuge of the oppressed."

The left kept a touching engraving of this sublime marriage between Revolution and liberty in its family album. All the more so since after the emancipatory wave, the Jews were subjected to a severe backlash. First, in France itself, Napoleon adopted restrictive measures concerning the Jews in 1806. Then, in most European countries, where the counterrevolution seized control after 1815, anti-Jewish legislation was reestablished. A new French revolution, that of 1848, had the glory of signaling a new liberation, which especially benefited Jews in Germany and Austria. At the end of the nineteenth century, only Romania and Russia enforced anti-Jewish laws within their borders.

The counterrevolutionary movement was very quick to denounce that "collusion" between the Jews and the Revolution. In 1806, Bonald wrote: "The Jews cannot be and will never become, whatever efforts they might make, citizens of a Christian country, as long as they have not become Christians themselves." Anti-Semitism on the far right went so far as to denounce the Jews, emancipated by the Revolution, as the secret cause of the Revolution itself.[3] In its own way, that anti-Semitism consolidated the ties between the left and the Jews.

Rothschild Shuffles the Cards

The Revolution was therefore emancipatory, there is no doubt about that. However, through its universalist proclamations and the cult of reason that marked it for some time, the Revolution also brought about a renewal of the "Jewish question." Particularists rebelled against assimilation; in addition, religious particularism was contrary to the new national religion. During the feast of the Federation, provincial deputies vied to produce united professions of faith. There were no longer "Bretons" or "Auvergnats" or "Provençaux," but only French people belonging to a single nation. The next year, during the Assembly debates on active citizenship, Clermont-Tonnerre forthrightly asserted: "To the Jews, as a *nation*, one must refuse everything; but to Jews as *men*, one must grant everything . . . ; there cannot be a nation within the nation." If that precept—

legitimate in itself—is pushed a bit too far, one might find oneself faced with the following alternative: either Jews lose their particularities, assimilate completely (give up the Sabbath, kosher food, and so on), and so become fully French, since they cease to be Jewish; or they keep their customs and laws, and have to be "expelled." Whereas the right (Abbé Maury in particular) said, let us respect the religious convictions of Jews but not make them citizens, the left for its part, in offering citizenship to the Jews, might have ultimately been prohibiting what was not yet called the right to be different.

That hyperassimilationist tendency took a terrorist turn in 1793. The militant atheism of the sansculottes did not wage battle only against the Catholic Church. The Convention had to resist the mandates of populist branches demanding that circumcision and the celebration of the Sabbath be banned; and in certain cities, popular pressure was put on Jewish merchants, forcing them to open their shops on Saturday.

An anti-Judaism on the "left," antireligious in foundation, thus came to complement the age-old Catholic anti-Judaism. In his zeal to "crush infamy," Voltaire had already attacked the Bible and the Jews on many occasions. In his *Dictionnaire philosophique* (Philosophical dictionary), he wrote under the article "Jews": "In them, you will find only an ignorant and barbarous people, which have long combined the most sordid avarice and the most despicable superstition." It was the unyielding character of the Jewish religion that made the Jews survive within nations, while preventing their assimilation. Diderot said it clearly: "The religion of the Jews and that of the peoples among whom they live do not allow Jews to be incorporated into them; the Jews must form a nation apart."[4]

The most irreligious tendencies on the left continued into the nineteenth century, stigmatizing the Jewish religion, guilty in particular for having given birth to Christianity. At the end of the Second Empire, revolutionary students joining Blanquist ranks and calling themselves "Hébertists" were the most relentless in their struggle against God in general and the Jews in particular. Gustave Tridon belonged to that revolutionary environment; his book, *Du molochisme juif*, published posthumously in 1884, earned him Edouard Drumont's praise, despite Tridon's antitheism. The book was a declaration of war against Judeo-Christian monotheism, which Tridon contrasted to classical pagan Greece and modern science.

All the same, antireligious anti-Semitism (targeting "Semitism and its direct descendant, Christianity")[5] occupied the minds of fewer "progressivists" than another form of hostility toward the Jews, older in origin but reinforced by the very progress of the Jews in modern societies after their emancipation had been achieved. The July monarchy was a time of social ascension for a good number of Jewish families, including the Roth-schilds, who took on almost mythological dimensions.

Louis-Philippe was one of the monarchs most favorable toward the Jewish community. On 1 February 1831, the Chamber of Peers approved by a large majority a bill from the Chamber of Deputies, placing the Jewish religion among other denominations supported by the religious budget. As Bernard Lazare said: "It was the definitive collapse of the Christian state."[6] In a manner more visible to public opinion, Jewish names now appeared in the most prominent places. Jews were in the Chamber (Crémieux, notably, was elected in 1842), on the stage (Rachel), on concert bills (Meyerbeer), and especially, in financial affairs, in banking and at the stock market. James de Rothschild, the youngest brother in the famous Frankfurt family, had acquired a position of incontestable power in banking. The colossal fortune the Rothschilds had accumulated was not kept discreet. The newspapers were soon full of its splendors. In 1836, Heinrich Heine depicted the Rothschild mansion on Rue Saint-Florentin in one sentence: "It is the Versailles of the absolute monarchy of money."[7] That ostentatious wealth favored popular anti-Semitism, which easily moved from Rothschild to Jews as a whole, all more or less "Rothschilds." Thus high finance, whose rise was remarkable under the July monarchy, soon became a synonym for "Jewish finance," despite the very Christian names of Casimir Perier, Laffitte, and Schneider.

Also in the 1840s, a "socialist" anti-Semitism was added to anti-Semitism on the left. It was not the deed of the Saint-Simonians, prophets of industrialism; numerous Jews even belonged to that "new Christianity." But other schools more or less lent their voices or pens to it. In "On the Jewish Question" in 1844, Marx wrote, among other things: "Money is the jealous god of Israel, beside which no other god may exist." But there was no need for Marx. Fourier's disciples found several encouraging formulations in the works of their late master, and one disciple, Alphonse Toussenel, developed them in a book published in 1845, *Les Juifs rois de l'époque*. It was a very confused work, which made the term "Jew" a most elastic notion, but which was stuffed full of formulations to delight Drumont, who saw the book as an "immortal masterpiece." "The Jews," we read, "are a nation within the nation, whatever they might do and say, and before long, they will be the conquering and dominating nation here." No doubt by "Jews" Toussenel meant "any trafficker in currencies," and he especially targeted "financial feudalism," but his attacks on the Bible and the fact that he adopted the universal linguistic confusion between "Jew" and "usurer" place him among the anti-Semites; the passages he quotes from Fourier indicate his filiation and the continuity of the phenomenon. Contemporaries of Toussenel, also adversaries of capitalism, illustrate this.

The anti-Semitism of the young Marx in Germany was echoed in the man who was to become his rival and adversary in France, Joseph Proudhon. In his posthumous *Carnets* (Notebooks), published about twenty years earlier, we find judgments that resemble calls for pogroms.

Thus a new hostility was expressed against the social elevation of emancipated Jews, some of whom—though only a few—occupied the most prominent positions. In addition to a counterrevolutionary anti-Judaism, whose continuous traces can be followed throughout the July monarchy and the Second Empire, voices were heard within what might be called the revolutionary and socialist community in the broad sense. In it, an anti-Jewish discourse was given free rein on two registers, which were very often confused: hostility toward the Jewish religion, and hostility toward high finance—that is to say, Jewish banking, with the part being taken for the whole. Conversely, political regimes that were hardly on the left—those of Louis-Philippe and Napoleon III—took up the mantle from the Revolution, which had emancipated the Jews, and proved favorable toward them. The solidarity between the left and the Jews lost its fundamental necessity; not until the Dreyfus affair did it assert itself again within the scandal of national tragedy.

The Drumont Effect

Until the 1880s, there was no real "Jewish question" in France. The first ten years of the Third Republic were completely occupied by the central conflict between monarchists and republicans. Ninety years after their emancipation, a good number of French Jews had abandoned the religion of their forbears. They were on the path toward complete assimilation into the French nation. Alfred Naquet—who had married a Catholic woman—could thus say in a speech to the Chamber in May 1895: "For more than thirty years, I have associated almost exclusively with non-Jews." That total integration of the Jewish community had been theorized by the Jews themselves under the name "Franco-Judaism." Certain authors such as Théodore Reinach went so far as to imagine the extinction of Judaism by means of complete assimilation: "Let emancipation, equality, penetrate everywhere, not only the laws but mores and ideas, and the Jewish feeling will increasingly lose its harshness and will no doubt be completely extinguished in the end."[8] That tendency toward assimilation was arrested by two concomitant facts, however: the immigration movements of Jews from the East and the development of a combative anti-Semitism in France.

In the early 1880s, several factors contributed toward an anti-Semitic current. After the assassination attempt on Alexander II, Russia went through a period of violent repression, during which pogroms were legalized by official anti-Jewish measures. Thousands of Russian Jews came to the West, especially to France. The next year, about a thousand Galicians, fleeing Austria-Hungary after persecutions, sought refuge in Paris. From 1881 to 1939, the composition of the French Jewish community was transformed in several successive waves. In the words of Pierre Vidal-Naquet, these immigrants from eastern Europe exerted a "constant antiassimilationist pressure."[9]

That phenomenon had only just begun in the early 1880s. Other more decisive factors played a role. First, there was the definitive triumph of the republicans over their monarchist and clerical adversaries. In 1883, a weekly appeared with the shameless name *L'Anti-Sémitique* (The Anti-Semitic), bearing an epigraph as clear as its title: "The Jew, now there's the enemy!!!" The newspaper did not have a large readership and it ceased publication in 1884, but it already expressed a good share of the themes that would be developed with resounding success by Drumont in his *La France juive* of 1886. Transformed into a principle of universal explanation, the Jew was accused by Drumont of having destroyed old Christianity, of having set in place the Freemason Republic, starved the proletariat, and secretly directed the destiny of France. The starting signal for the anti-Semitic movement had been given. The creation of Jules Guéridon's Ligue Anti-Sémitique and the launching of *La Libre Parole* and its echo, the Assumptionists' *La Croix*, followed.

What did the left do in the face of that anti-Semitism on the far right? When we read the leftist press of the time, and especially the socialist newspapers of the 1890s, we are struck by how little interest anti-Semitism elicited. Even worse, a certain number of Socialist and Radical personalities were able to advance anti-Jewish opinions, apparently without eliciting any indignation. It was simply a matter of "opinion": one might or might not be anti-Semitic; it did not seem to be of any consequence.

We saw earlier that a Radical deputy could make anti-Jewish declarations in the Toulouse *Dépêche* without attracting any wrath. But what about the socialists? Their theoretical positions were contrary to anti-Semitism in principle. Hence, the Guesdist weekly *Le Socialiste* explained to its readers on 26 July 1892: "Capitalist exploitation will be saved by amusing the workers with the 'yids,' as they say, who have become scapegoats. . . . What respite for contemporary society if, instead of pursuing the struggle between the 'haves' and the 'have-nots,' in order to expropriate the latter, the struggle could be displaced, reduced to one between the 'have foreskin' and 'have not foreskin'!"

The vocabulary of that statement already suggests a certain accommodation of vulgar anti-Semitism. In fact, socialist journalists had no problems of conscience in repeating the popular insults and the well-worn gibes at Jews. The word "Jew" itself, as the dictionaries of the time attest, was generally understood as an insult. That is why a little later, certain Dreyfusards recommended striking "the word 'Jew'" from the language, and keeping the term "Israelite" simply to evoke the faith and the religion.[10] Clearly, Jews were not handled with kid gloves, though not all socialists used the term "yids," which is regularly found in Emile Ponget's anarchist newspaper *Le Père Peinard*.

Skillfully, Drumont and his disciples did their best to flatter socialists and unionists by jumping on the Jews. They were engaged in the same battle against capitalism (necessarily Jewish for Drumont). That sort of complicity is notable during certain public meetings, including those of the Marxists in the Parti Ouvrier (Workers' party);[11] it was even feared by certain observers, such as Anatole Leroy-Beaulieu.

On 27 February 1897, Leroy-Beaulieu, a Catholic and liberal republican, gave a lecture at the Institut Catholique de Paris on the theme of anti-Semitism. Before an audience broadly infiltrated by militant anti-Semites who interrupted him throughout, he demonstrated the intellectual inconsistency of anti-Semitism. One of his arguments is noteworthy from our point of view, however. That defender of liberal society denounced anti-Semitism's anticapitalism and "ingenuous socialism." And he added: "A kind of socialism sui generis, socialism by rights if you like, socialism disguised in vague Christian formulations," *but* "working, whether it wishes to or not, for the benefit of the other socialism, atheist socialism, revolutionary socialism."[12]

Certain socialists perceived that convergence to be useful for their political projects. In the name of "ingenuous socialism," the popular crowds Drumont dragged behind him might be recruited, at least up to a certain point; socialists might take advantage of their dynamism and then lead them to "true" socialism. Astonishing points of contact were the result. In the Chamber debate of 1895 mentioned above, Naquet attracted the attention of his colleagues to what he called "the policy of the *opening*" among certain socialist thinkers: "When anti-Semites have opened the breach, we shall pass through it." And the shorthand minutes of the debate note "shows of agreement on various benches of the far left." The Socialist deputy Rouanet, who was not anti-Semitic, nonetheless clearly said: "That is why I approve of M. Drumont's campaign."

Thus Edouard Drumont did not enjoy too bad a reputation among the socialists, at least until the Dreyfus affair. The very year *La France juive* was published, Benoît Malon devoted an important review to it in his *Revue Socialiste*. Malon, making allowances for "injustices" contained in *La France juive*, nonetheless declared that "this book deserves . . . to be discussed." And even as he observed that capitalism "as a whole," and not Jewish capitalism alone, was culpable, Malon let himself drift into a commentary on "high Jewry" and "the noble Aryan race"—a sign of the time.

In 1890, Albert Regnard, a contributor to the same *Revue Socialiste*, published a work entitled *Aryens et Sémites* (Aryans and Semites). Writing within the same perspective as the Blanquist Tridon, whose views he explicitly embraced, he revived that antimonotheism on the left, combining it with the now widespread "scientific" considerations on racial ideas. And that man on the far left recognized "enormous merit" in Drumont and was grateful to him—regardless of his errors—for having reasserted a "stunning truth." Which truth? The infamy of capitalism? Of course, but more than that: "The reality and excellence of the Aryan race, of that unique family to which humanity owes the marvels of the century of Pericles, the Renaissance, and the Revolution—the three great ages in the history of the world—and which alone is capable of preparing for and bringing about the supreme achievement of social renovation."

That is what a socialist could print several years before the Dreyfus affair. He may not have convinced the majority of his comrades, but he did not elicit any protest either.

As for "races," they were gossiped about, quibbled over, classified. Like everyone else, the Jews themselves accepted that distinction between a "Semitic race" and an "Aryan race." Let us repeat: before Hitler, anti-Semitism was rarely seen as a doctrine of death. For many on the left, anti-Semites were imbeciles; they were not potential executioners.

And What About Jaurès?

Amid that confusion, it is important to observe the behavior of Jaurès. He was an intellectual who did not allow himself to be dominated by passion and knew how to make the doctrinal distinctions required. But we must admit that the "pure," the "clairvoyant" Jaurès, more attached than others to the immortal principles of the Revolution and the Republic, a convert to socialism since 1892 (the year he became one of the stars on the far left in the Chamber), was not visibly vigilant in his antiracism. He was even "somewhat affected," as Madeleine Rebérioux tells us, "by the popular anti-Semitic current, in which he sometimes detected 'a true revolutionary spirit.'"[13]

Of course, on several occasions, Jaurès denied he was anti-Semitic. "I have no prejudice against the Jews," he wrote in 1889. But during the Panama scandal, which Drumont seized upon as a "Jewish" scandal, Jaurès paid more attention to the positions of anti-Semitism. Until the Dreyfus affair, his relations with Drumont were amicable. Drumont could not say enough in praise of that socialist of the soil. He had similarly cordial relations with the Marquis de Rochefort, a former Communard and a former Boulangist, who was increasingly steeped in nationalism and anti-Semitism, and eventually became one of the champions of anti-Dreyfusism.

In April 1895, Jaurès took a short vacation to Algeria. There he discovered the existence of a virulent form of anti-Semitism. Far from condemning it, he gave an account of it in the Toulouse *Dépêche*. In two articles published on 1 and 8 May 1895, he explained that "in the rather restricted form of anti-Semitism a true revolutionary spirit is being propagated in Algeria." And Jaurès turned to his own account the arguments of the anti-Semitic lobby against "Jewish power." Jaurès did not know that the majority of Jews in Algeria, emancipated by the Crémieux decree of 1870, belonged to the lower levels of society: he saw only "Jewish usury," which united "the European" and "the Arab" against it.

Let us summarize. Until 1898, anti-Semitism was perceived by the left as a whole—and particularly by the socialists—as neither opprobrium nor a serious threat. At the international socialist congress in Brussels in 1891, an American Jewish delegate asked for a firm condemnation of anti-Semitism. The congress, not judging discussion "necessary," confined itself to passing a motion that condemned *equally* "anti-Semitic and *philo-Semitic* excitations." That last adjective was added to the initial text at the request of two French delegates, Regnard and Argyriadès.

In the years that followed, nothing interdicted anti-Semitism among the ranks of the left. Jokes about Jews were common currency in every political sector. The anti-Semitic movement, from which socialists kept their distance on the theoretical plane, appeared to many of them to be rich in revolutionary potential. Socialists and anti-Semites found common ground in certain meetings and electoral battles against a common adversary: the Opportunist Republic, the speculators' Republic, the Panama Republic, where the "Jewish" presence was to be stigmatized. Going even further, certain socialists did not hesitate to turn to their own account the racist theories regarding the superiority of "Aryans" over "Semites." To various degrees, as we have seen, there was room for anti-Semitism within the left.

The "Dreyfusard Revolution"

As one point in that history of relations between the left and the Jews, the Dreyfus affair brought to a clear end the semicomplicitous relations between the left and anti-Semites. All the same, that break appears more obvious to us with the hindsight we possess; at the time the choices were made, there was a long period of equivocation. In addition, the first person to stand up forcefully to the new war against the Jews was not a politician. That initiative fell to Emile Zola, even before Bernard Lazare convinced him of Dreyfus's innocence. On 16 May 1896, *Le Figaro* published his article, "Pour les Juifs" (For the Jews), in which Zola expressed his "surprise" and "growing disgust" at the campaign under way against the Jews; he denounced "fanaticism" and appealed for "universal fraternity."

That same Zola, supported by Clemenceau, in launching his "J'accuse" (I accuse) in *L'Aurore* on 13 January 1898, two days after the acquittal of Esterhazy by the war council, triggered what would come to be called the "Dreyfusard revolution." The left was far from unanimous. There was Clemenceau, of course, who entered the fray in October 1897 and wrote article on top of article in favor of a new trial until December 1899; who found the simple but ingenious title—"J'accuse"—given to Zola's letter; and who made the Dreyfusard cause into the ultimate battle of the French Revolution. Apart from him, however, the tendency was rather not to call into question the judicial matter and to preserve the army from all suspicion. On 19 January, after the legal action taken against Zola, a manifesto was published by thirty-two Socialist deputies, who declared themselves above the fray.

The legislative elections were to take place in May 1898. And parliamentary Socialists were sensitive to the penetration of nationalist and anti-Semitic watchwords within the lower classes. Rochefort's popularity was significant in that regard. He, a former Communard, the former escapee from New Caledonia, the "red marquis," remained one of the "idols" of the Parisian people, even though he had become a nationalist (the word had just been invented) and an anti-Semite.

The first center of resistance to nationalism and the first Dreyfusard battalions were located less in Parliament than in the antiparliamentary tendencies of the workers' movement: in the Allemanist group and in the columns of its newspaper *Le Parti Ouvrier* (The Workers' Party), and among the anarchists surrounding Sébastien Faure and *Le Libertaire*. In late 1897, they made their choice and braved Rochefort without ambivalence. On 17 January, after Jules Guérin organized an anti-Semitic meeting in Tivoli-Vauxhall, Faure's anarchists and the Allemanists took the platform by force and dispersed the meeting.

These antiparliamentary groups had perceived the anti-Semitic peril before the Socialist deputies. Following Zola's article, anti-Jewish demonstrations resounded throughout the month of January. In all the large cities, Jewish shop windows were broken, synagogues stormed, individuals assaulted. From Rennes to Grenoble and from Lille to Marseilles, the same slogans reverberated: "Death to the Jews! Death to Zola! Death to Dreyfus!" The paroxysm was reached in Algeria, where beginning on 18

January, a Jew hunt was launched in Algiers. For four days, a crowd spurred on by Max Régis, who suggested they "water the tree of liberty with Jewish blood," broke loose, shattering, devastating, plundering Jewish shops, with Constantine and Oran soon following Algiers's example.

From that point on, Jaurès no longer saw anti-Semitism as part of that rather crude "revolutionary spirit" he had thought he could discern three years earlier in Algeria. In January, he entered the Dreyfusard battle. Esterhazy's trial—which he attended—Zola's accusatory cry, the influence of a few friends such as Lucien Herr and of young students at the Ecole Normale such as Charles Péguy, and holding everything together, anti-Semitic street violence all worked to bring him into the battle after months of hesitation.[14]

Zola's article was the spark. His courage gave others courage. A petition was circulated to review the Dreyfus trial. It was to be the birth certificate of an intellectual left; several thousand signatures were collected. In the lives of most of the signers, something changed. "The Dreyfus affair," wrote Julien Benda, "made me move from intellectualism to intellectual action, from proud and distant thought to thought that goes out into the street."[15]

It was during the Zola trial, between 7 and 25 February 1898, that the Ligue des Droits de l'Homme was founded, on the initiative of Senator Trarieux. On 4 June, during its first general assembly at the headquarters of the Sociétés Savantes (Learned societies), Trarieux traced out its program: "To defend against veiled threats of counterrevolution the fundamental principle of the Declaration of the Rights of Man, on which the equality of the nation has rested for a hundred years." Continuity was once more proclaimed between the Revolution and the Dreyfus affair.

It is noteworthy, however, that many on the left were reluctant Dreyfusards, even after the elections of May 1898, which brought twenty-six nationalists and anti-Semites to the Chamber, with Drumont, elected in Algiers, in the lead. In the socialist camp, the Guesdists were to keep their distance throughout the Affair, justifying their actions by appealing to the class struggle. On 9 July 1899 in Le Socialiste, Paul Lafargue was still sneering at the "bourgeois Dreyfusards who have annoyed us so much with their imprescriptible justice." All the same, in their congress of September 1898, the Guesdists asserted the reactionary character of anti-Semitism—"wretched fraud" and "worker's trap," which "Bebel could rightly call the socialism of imbeciles."

How long that "Truth" took to reach its goal once it was set in motion! Progressively, anti-Semitism became fixed on the far right. What common denominator more effective than anti-Semitism can be imagined between the anticlerical Rochefort and the Assumptionists at La Croix, or between

Drumont and Déroulède? It was the war cry against the Jews, so well suited to sustain populist passions, that united their nationalism and the sacred defense of the army. There was no longer any doubt that anti-Semitism was a weapon of the "reaction." Yes, but . . . Even while battling nationalist demagoguery, many socialists still had great difficulty getting rid of their assumptions about Jews. Once again, Jaurès is a good indicator. He had entered the fray to defend a man and a principle with all the weight of his influence, all the gifts of his mind, and all the fire of his eloquence. And yet, in June 1898 one again catches him declaring, in a speech in Tivoli:

We are well aware that the Jewish race—concentrated, passionate, subtle, always consumed by a kind of fever, a fever for profit when it is not a fever for prophecy, we are well aware that it manipulates the capitalist machinery with particular skill, a machinery of plunder, lies, corruption, extortion. But we say: it is not the race we must crush, but the machinery it uses, and which Christian exploiters use as well.[16]

All the same, by 1899 it seems that the die was cast. The republican people, called upon on several occasions to go out into the streets to defend the regime, now opposed Guérin's leaguists and Rochefort's imprecations. Péguy tells of the large demonstration of 11 November 1899 for the "triumph of the Republic." He tells how "the cheers of acclamation in the name of Dreyfus—a public, violent, provocative acclamation" were "the greatest novelty of the day, the greatest rupture, the greatest breaking of seals in this century."[17] The cry "Long live Dreyfus!" by the Parisian people, who for a decade had been subjected to the propaganda of anti-Semitic hatred, clearly marked a new stage: the left was ridding itself of racial prejudice.

And yet because nothing is ever completely over in history, attacks against the Jews did not totally disappear between the end of the Affair and 1914. The political consequences of the great battle over Dreyfus led to the victory of the Bloc des Gauches and of Combism. In the eyes of the far left, socialism, led by Jaurès, appeared to be wallowing in parliamentary delights. It was a new betrayal of the class struggle! In 1906, the judgment of the Cour de Cassation rehabilitating Dreyfus provoked an article by Robert Louzon in *Le Mouvement Socialiste* entitled "La faillite de dreyfusisme ou le triomphe du parti juif" (The bankruptcy of Dreyfusism or the triumph of the Jewish party), which claimed "that a party exists whose leader is Jewry, owing to their financial power and commercial and intellectual activity."

We know about the backsliding of Georges Sorel, a former Dreyfusard and contributor to the same newspaper, in which he published his *Réflex-*

ions sur la violence (Reflections on violence; 1906) glorifying the CGT. In about 1910, his antiparliamentarianism and the decline of revolutionary unionism pushed him into the outstretched arms of the theorists of Action Française. Although he remained there only for the space of a few years, his evolution indicates at least the vulnerability of a certain far left to the renewed temptations of anti-Semitism. If we needed another, less famous example, we might mention that of Emile Pataud. A stout-hearted fellow, secretary of the electricians' union, he abruptly plunged the city of Paris into darkness in March 1907 by means of a surprise strike. He too was attracted by the militants of Action Française, and by 1911 he had become the chief orator at an anti-Semitic meeting; his electricians' union refused to exclude him despite protests. It was only in 1913 that the CGT succeeded in expelling him, following an assault he launched with his friends against the editors of *La Bataille Syndicaliste*. A snag of anti-Semitism was still attached to union organizations.

In general, however, the Dreyfus affair purged the left of the more or less ordinary anti-Semitism observable in the early 1890s. No doubt the Dreyfus affair did not directly pit anti-Semites and philo-Semites against each other. The stakes of the battle, both moral and political, were more complex. On the moral plane, the Dreyfusards defended the universal cause of truth and justice against the particular cause of *raison d'état*. In that area, not all Dreyfusards were on the left, even though there were more freethinkers than Catholics among them. On the political plane, the issue was to preserve republican institutions, democratic freedoms, against a nationalist movement resolved to put everything on the line. But the Jewish question was raised on both planes. Dreyfus's condemnation and Esterhazy's acquittal did not occur independently of the fact that Dreyfus was Jewish. As for nationalism, whose frenzy and audacitiy made the regime tremble, it had privileged anti-Semitism as one of its federating and mobilizing themes. In response to that far right, which railed against the Jews, the left soon began to wage war against the "priests." Emile Combes was its chief general, and the separation of Church and state its outcome. Never since the crisis of 16 May 1877 had there been such close combat between the left and the right. At the same time, the centrists and other Dreyfusard or Christian democratic Catholics were cornered: anti-anti-Semitism became even more rooted on the left.

The Dreyfusard victory occupies a place of choice within the leftist legend. Emile Zola's funeral in October 1902 stands as one of the noble scenes of republican theater. Anatole France, a freethinker and Dreyfusard, delivered the eulogy of the great writer in the Montmartre cemetery. After recalling what Jules Guesde had called "the greatest revolutionary act of this century"—he was speaking of "J'accuse"—Anatole France ended with this expression of pride: "There is only one country in the world in which these great things could have come about. How admirable is the genius of our nation!"

Blum the Accused

Between 1933 and 1945, a third sequence of events of modern history established closer ties between the left and the Jewish community: the common struggle that pitted them against nazism.

During that period, France experienced a second outbreak of anti-Semitism. World War I, the "solidarity of the trenches," and renewed prosperity had not abolished all anti-Semitic prejudice in the 1920s. At least it was not the subject matter for ordinary editorials, however; it was not even a major factor in the formation of the first instance of French fascism, the Faisceau, though its founder, Georges Valois, had expressed anti-Jewish views before 1914. Wladimir Rabi sees it as a "good-hearted anti-Semitism," compared to that which raged in the 1930s.[18]

That fresh outbreak of racism belonged to a larger context of xenophobia caused by the economic crisis.[19] In December 1931, a deputy even declared to the Chamber: "We are not suffering from a crisis of national unemployment, but from a crisis of foreign invasion." That simplistic explanation expressed a broadly accepted idea. Did not *L'Humanité* recognize the havoc such ideas were wreaking even in communist ranks?[20] The far right recited all the verses of the song Drumont had made fashionable: "France for the French!" All the same, that proclaimed hostility toward the foreigner was given the opportunity to rise to a higher pitch after Hitler came to power in 1933. By the tens of thousands, proscribed persons were coming to France. The Jews, designated victims of the new regime, represented the largest contingent of these. French mutual aid was organized; personalities of every social class and of every conviction offered their support. Camille Chautemps, minister of the interior, made this solemn and reassuring assertion in April 1933, that France would remain "faithful to [its] generous traditions of hospitality." That did not prevent the French government from alerting departments to the "extreme circumspection" they ought to use in allowing "Jews chased out of Germany" to come to France.[21]

That official prudence in the welcome to be reserved for the first victims of nazism was already hardly flattering to the centrist left in power. But what is there to say about the racial hatred that overflowed in the press of the far right, which was very prosperous in those years? The title of Jules Guérin's newspaper—*L'Anti-Juif* (The anti-Jew)—even made a reappearance; this time, the newspaper's director was Louis Darquier de

Pellepoix. As for the late Drumont's *Libre Parole*, it took on new life under the direction of Henri Coston. In a general way, at least until the law enacted on 20 March 1939, which prohibited all racist propaganda in France, there was an anti-Semitic competition in the large, so-called national newspapers such as *L'Ami du Peuple, L'Action Française, Je Suis Partout*, and *Gringoire*, which reverberated in a series of more obscure and more relentless publications.

The electoral victory of the Front Populaire and, a little later, the civil war in Spain were the occasions for new vehemence. For the first time, a son of Israel, Léon Blum, became premier—an event that was denounced in the Chamber itself by Xavier Vallat, as a disgrace inflicted on that old "Gallo-Roman" country. The far right transferred all its hatred onto Blum. Jean-Pierre Maxence summed it up in one sentence: "Every fiber of M. Léon Blum represents the foreigner." Speeches, articles, caricatures, and even books against "the Jew Blum" piled up. In 1938, the work of a certain Laurent Viguier, *Les Juifs à travers Léon Blum* (The Jews through Léon Blum) was published by Editions Baudinière. Its subtitle explained: *Leur incapacité historique de diriger un Etat* (Their historical incapacity to lead a state). In substance, that pamphlet set out the "diagnosis" made on the first page: "Evil comes from the Jew." That is only one example of the rhetoric of violence, the pogrom that was as yet only on paper.

In any case, the Front Populaire was accused by the most virulent of its adversaries, not only of making common cause with the "Jews," but of being the expression of their policies, the next phase in their conquest of world power. Whatever its timidity (notably in its immigration policy),[22] in France the Front Populaire represented the political pole of resistance to nazism and made an effort to safeguard the threatened Jewish communities. However, with the twilight of the Front Populaire in May 1938, the Radicals in power did not hesitate to promulgate decrees targeting immigration, which led Socialists and Communists to add their protests against "those Draconian texts."

The "Final Solution" and Its Consequences

After a first period of uncertainty,[23] World War II took on the aspect of a planetary confrontation between "democracy" and "fascism." In the eyes of Western allies, the precious alliance with the Red army had roughly that sense. The Nuremberg trials in 1945 solemnly confirmed the victory of Good over Evil. The struggle against nazism and the Jewish cause had become confused; they were inseparable; they were equally sacred. The Jew was the exact opposite of the Nazi. Anyone who had struggled against the Nazi had struggled for the Jew. The *collabos*, those who had taken the side of the executioner, officially held the monopoly on anti-Semitism. The Vichy regime, which denied it had been pro-Nazi, was nevertheless the regime of the *statut des Juifs* and the Milice. The France of the Resistance—in its reality and its myth—waved the standard of antiracism. Of course, not everyone on the right had been a collaborator—de Gaulle was the living proof of that—and not everyone on the left had been in the Resistance. But communists and socialists reaped the political benefits of the postwar and post-Vichy period.

The Communist party, which had become the strongest of the leftist parties, was not stingy in its declarations of friendship toward the survivors of Auschwitz and other death camps. Like Soviet diplomacy, the French Communists lent their support to the state of Israel, which had been born in suffering. There were numerous French Jews in "the party of the executed." In May 1948, Florimond Bonte cried out before a crowd that had gathered in the Vélodrome d'Hiver: "To the new Jewish state, born in the midst of the most painful labor and from the heroic struggle of the best sons of Israel, I bring you a warm greeting of welcome from the French Communist party, which is always in solidarity with those who battle for freedom, democracy, and independence." That was no doubt the apogee of solidarity between the left and the Jews.

Anti-Semitism was condemned by the left, even more than it had been after the Dreyfus affair. The horror of the Nazi charnel houses seemed to require that hatred of the Jew be suppressed forever more, in every sector of public opinion. But the left, laying claim to the heritage of the Resistance, found additional reasons to love and protect those who had escaped what would be called the Holocaust.

The Ambiguities of Anti-Zionism

We must acknowledge that that postwar idyll has passed. If today the organizations on the left as a whole remain intransigent in their principles, it is also clear that a dispute between a certain number of them and the Jews has come about.

The crisis began in 1949. At that time, Stalin launched the first of a series of campaigns in the USSR for which the Jews paid the highest cost. First, there was a denunciation of "cosmopolitanism"—a crude camouflage for new purges, to which Soviets "of Jewish origin" were exposed.

That "anticosmopolitanism" was fairly quickly backed up by "anti-Zionism," another way of thinning the ranks of communists in the USSR and in popular democracies, and of keeping Jewish communities subjugated, especially by depriving them of their own modes of expression. The 1952 Slansky trial in Prague is the best-known instance of that new assault. To cite merely two indignities, Lise London, the wife of one of the accused, requested the tribunal impose "the must rigorous" punishment on her husband,[24] and a son asked that his father, who had become his "worst enemy," receive a death sentence.[25]

What, then, were the reactions of the press on the left? *L'Humanité*, devoid of all journalistic curiosity regarding the workings of that rigged trial, willingly subscribed to the official explanations: "It is against their own country and its government of popular democracy that the so-called Jewish nationalists—Zionists—who are spies pure and simple, have placed themselves in the service of the United States, where anti-Semitism rages" (25 November 1952). That set the tone. The theme of a conspiracy, taken up by the Soviet press, flourished anew. But if observers had the bad taste to suspect anti-Semitism in that indictment of an alleged "Zionism," where the majority of Jewish communists were implicated, the Communist party immediately turned the accusation on its head: it's other people who are anti-Semites!

Was that the view of the rest of the left? In fact, writes François Honti in an article for *Le Monde*: "Anti-Zionism is not anti-Semitism." All the same, he tells us, "the chief justice [of the tribunal] did not . . . miss an opportunity to point out Jewish origins as a defect, or at least as an aggravating circumstance, all the while calling Zionism the 'worst enemy of popular democracy'" (29 November 1952). The distinction between anti-Zionism and anti-Semitism was not as obvious in actuality as the Communists asserted. A few days later, *Le Monde* returned to the question. In a much better researched article than the earlier one, Georges Penchenier demonstrated that the communist regimes, "under cover of anti-Zionism," were "really and truly practicing anti-Semitism" (3 December 1952). The same contradictory views were found in the columns of *L'Observateur*, a weekly of the intellectual and neutralist left. While Claude Bourdet denounced "the systematic excitation of anti-Semitic passion" on the occasion of the Prague trial, Gilles Martinet wrote a reassuring counterpoint: "Anti-Zionism should not be confused with anti-Semitism."

The next year the scandal of the "white smock conspiracy" erupted in Moscow. Doctors, Jews for the most part, numbering among the medical authorities of the USSR, had allegedly been hired by Israeli and American organizations to make attempts on the lives of Soviet leaders. Zhdanov's death was supposedly attributable to them. It was a fantastic scenario, but the anti-Semitic nature of the Stalinist attacks did not escape anyone's notice except the Communists'. On 27 January 1953 *L'Humanité* gloriously published a declaration from ten French leading figures of the medical establishment (including a few Jewish communists) to the effect that "putting the band of criminals someplace where they cannot harm the USSR has been a very great service to the cause of peace." Once more, the PCF endorsed the Stalinist aberrations without displaying the shadow of a doubt. Anti-Semitism was impossible in the USSR, because it was *unthinkable*: "The whining about the deserved punishment for a few criminal Zionists in the service of American espionage can only make us forget that, in our country, the main suppliers for Hitler's charnel houses are going free and are preparing to resume service, if they have not already done so." That was François Billoux's conclusion in *L'Humanité* on 18 February 1953.

Alexander Werth, a progressive British journalist who lived in the USSR for several years, wrote in *L'Observateur*: "It is completely obvious that the Soviet authorities are gravely suspicious of the Jews, especially those who proclaim they are Jews before anything else. The suppression of the only Yiddish newspaper in Moscow, the *Einheit*, the liquidation of the Jewish publishing house, of the 'Jewish antifascist committee' and of the Jewish theater are the proof of this" (29 January 1953).

Thus up to that point, only the Communist party seems to have laid itself open to suspicion, through its silences and the justifications it provided for Stalinist anti-Semitism. The series of events that followed was to bring the PCF out of its isolation.

The end of the 1950s and the 1960s were marked by successive and accelerated stages of decolonization. In France, the Algerian war put the left on the spot. Guy Mollet's Socialist government assumed responsibility for the repression of the "Algerian rebels." To reach Colonel Nasser, their principal foreign support, Mollet launched the Suez expeditions in autumn 1956, in an agreement with British conservatives. That military and diplomatic episode was condemned by international opinion as a whole, with Americans and Soviets in the lead. At the very least, the Israeli government, implicated in that dubious affair, was found to be in complicity with the Mollet government. French and Israeli socialists would remain on good terms, for better or worse.

That 1956 war had weighty consequences for the relations between Israel and the rest of the left. The idea people had of the Hebrew state changed abruptly, and the relation between the left and the Jews was troubled by that change.

In addition to the Communists, who condemned the expedition and the behavior of the Ben-Gurion government, a new left, primarily intellectual and defined by its anticolonialist positions, looked at the Jewish state with new eyes. It was no longer the promised land of refuge for the victims of persecutions and the survivors of the camps, but rather an ally of colonialism. As François Furet wrote: "In the new configuration, the Israeli conqueror [takes] the place previously occupied by the Jewish plutocrat during the nineteenth century, in the imagination of the right and the left."[26] It was a difficult dilemma for Jews of the Diaspora: either they must remain in solidarity with Israel, but by assuming *volens nolens* the aspect of the "Jewish colonialist"; or they must refuse to be confused with the Israeli conqueror, but at the price of the community ties that linked them to other Jews.

Less than nine years later, the Six-Day War completed the metamorphosis. The theme of imperialism, succeeding that of anticolonialism, unified the militants and intellectuals of the left, whose anti-Americanism had been aggravated by the Vietnam War. Israel was named as the accomplice—an "objective" accomplice in the best of cases—of American imperialism. The Palestinian cause took the place of the Algerian cause. Anti-Zionism in France took on an unprecedented scope.

There is no inevitable slippery slope leading from anti-Zionism to anti-Semitism; the expression "anti-Zionism" refers to very diverse political attitudes.[27] But beginning in the late 1960s, declared hostility toward Israel was suspect on several occasions of "neo-anti-Semitism."[28]

The Maoists of *La Cause du Peuple* found it necessary to denounce "the imperialist and Zionist plot" (February 1969). For those of *L'Humanité Nouvelle,* "Zionism [is] the spearhead of imperialism in the Middle East" (25 May 1967). For those of *L'Humanité Rouge,* "Zionism is fascism" (4 January 1973). For the Trotskyists of *Rouge,* "the fundamental nature of the Zionist project [is] expansionist, racist, colonialist" (24 August 1973). That leftist press, even as it rejected "the confusion between anti-Zionism and anti-Semitism," denied the state of Israel the right to exist: "The very existence of the state of Israel is the source of the conflict ravaging the Near East. And behind Israel, the American eagle is responsible above all. American imperialism arms that policeman of its economic interests in the region, supports that wholly made-up enclave, and is ready to sustain Israel down to the last drop of Arab oil" (*Rouge,* 12 October 1973).

From *L'Humanité* to *L'Humanité Nouvelle,* from *Rouge* to *L'Humanité Rouge,* a self-evident equation took shape: Israel = American imperialism. The dilemma facing the Jews of the Diaspora has become thornier. If they do not clearly come out in favor of the Palestinian cause, do they not then run the risk of having themselves placed on the bench of the accused by the anti-imperialist left? As for those who, without accepting Israel's political choices with closed eyes, nonetheless wish to defend its contested right to exist, they risk being suspected ipso facto.

The slippage from declared anti-Zionism to de facto anti-Semitism—especially during the Yom Kippur war in 1973—is less noticeable in France than in other countries.[29] All the same, the *structural* analogies between the Zionist/imperialist plot—denounced by both the French Communist party and by numerous leftist groups—and the old universal Jewish plot can be troubling. Is this mere coincidence? For Alain Finkielkraut, "anti-Semitism sometimes changes its name, but never its story."[30]

In any case, the time when the unanimous left and the Jews sang in unison has now ended. Now that the prevailing struggles are against imperialism, the cause of Israel has excited a squabble in the house of the militants. In its many variants, anti-Zionism has collided head on with old solidarities.

By the Beard of Marx and of the Prophets

Can we draw a few conclusions?

1. If we wish to accept the—disputable—idea that political life in France is primarily organized around the poles designated "right" and "left," we must take the philo-Semitic tradition of the latter for an established fact: the emancipatory Revolution, the Dreyfus affair, and the Resistance have punctuated history with an alliance wearing republican colors. The French Jewish community is very conscious of this, if we are to judge by a poll by the IFOP published in *Le Point* on 30 January 1978. It indicates that 56 percent of "practicing" Jews voted on the left. Let us note, however, that electorate's very clear preference for the Socialist party. This should come as no surprise, given the attitude of the Communist party and the USSR toward the problems in the Near East. Nonetheless, there is no such thing as a "Jewish vote." A strong minority gives its votes to the right. Apart from the fact that Jews do not define themselves solely as Jews, but belong to different social classes and have varying ideas and interests just like other French people, we ought to observe that since the July monarchy, a current on the moderate right has sustained a lasting philo-Semitism. Representing a certain liberal bourgeoisie above all, first Orleanist and then republican, it often found itself caught in the cross fire between the left and the far right. A minority of Catholics, liberal republicans especially, have been in that political community traditionally sheltered from anti-Semitic prejudices.[31] There has thus never been an exact coincidence between the left and anti-anti-Semitism.

2. Vigilance in the face of anti-Semitism has not been indestructible on the left. Anti-Jewish prejudices, avowed until the Dreyfus affair, more discreet thereafter, and forbidden after Hitler, have nonetheless always been detectable.[32] In addition, it is clear that, until and including World War II, anti-Semitism was rarely taken for what it is, namely, a danger *in itself*. Here are some examples among others of that repeated deficiency in the analysis.

In 1942, during the massive round-ups, the communist resistance distributed a tract: "A bas l'antisémitisme!" (Down with anti-Semitism!) It proclaimed solidarity between the French people and the Jews, "our brothers": "Counter the barbarous and sadistic measures of the Krauts and the Vichyists by manifesting your sympathy and solidarity toward the persecuted Jews in every circumstance and by lavishing warm affection on their children." Compassion and action, an impeccable combination. But how did this communist tract assess the reasons for that anti-Semitism? In fact, Hitler's racist theses were reduced to mere methods of operation: "Just as in Germany the purpose of anti-Semitic campaigns was to mask the true enemy from the German people—the plutocrats and their Nazi guard dogs—the Hitlerians would now like to unleash hatred of the Jew to make hatred of the Kraut disappear."[33] Already, on 11 November 1938, following *Kristallnacht, L'Humanité* explained to its readers the blatantly false reasons for the racist outbreak invented by the Brownshirts: "Mr. Hitler needed a pretext [the assassination of the Nazi von Rath by a Jew in Paris] to cast the mistakes and errors of his regime onto the heads of the Jews." From the communist point of view, *Mein Kampf* was considered only a smoke screen ideology for the "guard dogs" of German big capital.

If we take that long history into account, it appears that Marxism, embraced by a good part of the left, underestimated the problem of racism by vulgarizing the primacy of the economic over the cultural and by reducing history to one of its plot lines, namely, the class struggle. Just as the Guesdists relegated anti-Semitism to the ranks of an ideological prop of the capitalist reaction, the Comité de Vigilance Antifasciste interpreted nazism as a German variant of fascism, which was only a product of big capital "with its back to the wall." In that "materialist" vision of history—in which bankers and CEOs plot our destinies—cultures, religions, and mentalities look like walk-on parts, ephemeral superstructures and ideological settings destined to evaporate under the radiant heat of triumphant socialism.

L'Humanité clearly expressed the consequences of that simplified representation of the human tragedy, of the Jewish question, during the Six-Day War:

Racial discrimination and anti-Semitism are the deed of the reaction, of the exploiting social classes—and not the deed of one *people* or another as such. . . . The massacres of Auschwitz, of Buchenwald, and so on, were the deed of *fascism*, that is, the most bestial form of capitalism. The solidarity of the victims of racism is thus and ought to be solidarity against fascism, against the social strata it represents. And it embraces the solidarity of all adversaries of fascism, and more generally, of capitalism, which is its "always fertile belly," whether these adversaries are Jews or not. (20 June 1967)

In other words, the upshot of that reasoning in the form of sorites is: anti-Semitism = fascism = reaction = capitalism. Hence anti-Semitism can finally be assimilated to capitalism; to fight against one is to fight against the other. In following that reasoning, it appears that: 1. the USSR, a socialist power, can in no case be accused of anti-Semitism, for that would be a contradiction of terms; 2. anticapitalism can dispense with anti-anti-Semitism, since one is contained within the other; 3. since most Jews, in the name of dual loyalty to their country and to Israel, belong to the imperialist—and therefore the capitalist—camp, they are the true anti-Semites.

The truth is that the Jews have been persecuted for two millennia, not as capitalists or proletarians but as Jews. It follows that the Marxist-Leninist reasoning runs out of steam when faced with anti-Jewish measures taken by "socialist" and not "imperialist" states. We are then faced with a situation where the *unthinkable* nature of the thing spares one the need for any conjectures. There is nothing to do but give up and mouth clichés.

Etiemble wrote the following in 1957, which ought to give us pause for reflection: "If I were to seek today the primary cause of the most serious vices of our society, I would find that class spirit itself undoubtedly commits fewer murders, in any case creates less abjection, than racial prejudice." As long as the left, whether Marxist or simply Marxian, continues to reduce history to its most simple antagonisms—bourgeoisie/proletariat, imperialism/anti-imperialism, Zionism/anti-Zionism—it is to be feared that the uneasiness between the left and the Jews will persist. In their tragic complexity, the Jewish facts are absolutely irreducible to any of the binary terms of those three alternatives. Like other facts, Jewish facts are stubborn, to paraphrase Lenin.

Thus anti-Semitism is a total social fact, irreducible to any unicausal interpretation. Its origins and the reasons for its development are multiple, and I have not attempted to give an inventory of them here. Rather, I felt it was important to insist on two—unequal—kinds of anti-Semitism with reference to several French cases: first, the anti-Semitism that expresses a nostalgia for a *closed society*, in Popper's sense; and second, that which embraces socialist universality.

The first kind of anti-Semitism has been expressed most naturally and most continuously in the counterrevolutionary, traditionalist, and Catholic community. To simplify matters, we might distinguish among three stages in the ideological construction of the counterrevolution; in each of them, the Jew as myth unifies the goals of the reaction.

1. The political revolution of 1789–93 gave rise to a literature protesting it and its distant echoes, a literature that progressively made the Jews,

beneficiaries of the emancipation of 1791, the true agents of the ancien régime's destruction. In the eyes of anti-Semites, the osmosis between the Jews and the Freemasons explained the rest of republican history: the secularization of society, the separation of Church and state, the destruction of the family (the Jew Naquet was the one responsible for the passage of the law reestablishing divorce in 1884), the expulsion of religious communities, and so on. The "Judeo-Masonic plot" relentlessly pursued the destruction of Christianity.

2. Although the industrial revolution in France was not characterized by the brutality with which it occurred in England, the economic transformations in banking, commerce, and industry, which marked the period of expansion of the Second Empire, encountered ways of thinking that were more favorable to the old way of doing things than to accelerated changes. After the 1871 defeat, the bloody scenes of civil war in Paris caused a first dread: the "dangerous classes" were surrounding "decent people." In his report to the National Assembly concerning the 18 March insurrection, parliamentarian Martial Delpit expressed "the great and honest conservative view," saying frankly of revolutionary workers: "We are in the presence of a new barbarian invasion." Because of the insane projects launched by Napoleon, Paris had attracted these barbarians: "Because of railroads, the ease and cheapness of communication, Paris has become the meeting place for all those seeking their fortune, a *domestic California*." Paris became Babylon, a pandemonium of vices, crimes, and incredulity, the endpoint of the most disquieting immigration. Drumont devoted one of his first books to his "Old Paris," henceforth controlled by cosmopolites, where "soon, we natives will be only strangers." For the anti-Semite, the Jew necessarily presided over the urbanist revolution. The rootless Jew, the eternal nomad, prospered in the city. There, he was still the opulent beneficiary of change, through the intermediaries of the bank and the stock market, which he controlled. The economic crises took anti-Semitic furor to its point of greatest violence: the eternal Jew was implicated in the havoc of progress. Counterrevolutionary ideology, haunted by the dream of an old France whose harmony rested on a combination of rustic and Christian virtues, pitted the rural values of our ancestors against the false values of the modern world. The Jew necessarily occupied the place of the antipeasant in that bucolic vision: someone whose fortune rested on the uprooting of peoples and the frenzy of progress.

3. The socialist and communist revolution completed the crystallization of the Jewish myth. Jews were not only capitalists, they were revolutionary subversives as well. Not only did they destroy society from above (as bankers, business people, Freemason politicians), they also undermined its foundations. Rothschild and Marx were waging the same battle for the

demolition of Western society. For anti-Semites, the 1917 Bolshevik revolution appeared to be one of the last incarnations of the "Jewish conspiracy." "Judeo-Marxism" or "Judeo-Bolshevism" became a well-worn theme in the far right press during the 1930s, even though Stalin had undertaken to liquidate Jewish Communists.

These three elements of anti-Semitism supported or complemented one another. They were the fantasmatic expression of milieus that had fallen prey, economically and culturally, to threats. Sometimes these threats were precise: the secular republic, industrial development, the boom in big business, the rise of the workers' movement. Sometimes they were obscure: the fear of an uncertain future deprived of the reassuring limits that had guided society in earlier centuries—one family, one Church, one corporate body, one hierarchy. More profoundly, anti-Semitism was an expression of the fears of certain social strata or certain cultural milieus in the face of change: the acceleration of social movements, geographical mobility, "the end of a world," as Drumont said, a world that was conceived as a time that was almost unmoving. Underlying all Drumont's writings is the painful feeling of what Durkheim called "anomie," the regular decomposition of traditional societies: "As long as the dazzling lily had its roots in the strong earth of traditions and beliefs, it rose majestic and poetic under the sky; today the soil is arid and the lily, already wilted from the impure fumes of the invaders, droops and takes on the yellowish tint of something that is going to die."[34]

What remains of the far right in France has not lost that taste for death and entropy, but it also occupies its mind with the cheerful images of the good old days. As François Brigneau, editorialist of *Minute* in 1978, put it: "I love France and a certain France, an agricultural, familial, artisanal France; but I do not love the France of cities. . . . I am closer to the country of spinners, of washerwomen, the shops of yesteryear. People may have worked there for twelve hours a day, but they sang in the shops; people no longer sing. I am horrified by the cities, workers' housing, mechanization, that is all true."[35]

As a result, anti-Semitism ought to have become fixed on the political right, the reactionary, antiliberal far right. But anti-Semitism also raged on the left, particularly before the Dreyfus affair. No doubt we ought to note from the outset that, in the society of the late nineteenth century (and of today?), there was no internal coherence on the right or the left. The two categories are too reductive to do justice to the complexity of mentalities. In addition, political parties were only in the embryonic stage. The Boulangist crisis, among other things, showed how ideological confusion can find its way into political life. Many feelings shared by the Catholics were also shared by voters on the left. "Diabolical causality" was used by people who did not even believe in the devil. Drumont was popular among the electorate on the left and on the right, at least until 1898.

In addition to the assimilation of Jews and bankers, which has often been done since the July monarchy, other causes fed hostility toward the Jews in certain areas of the left. Because of their religious and legal tradition, reinforced by their situation as a minority, they had consistently been respectful of the state; this certainly made them suspect, especially within libertarian and anarchist currents. The good relations the social elites of the Jewish community maintained with the July monarchy and the Second Empire certainly fed anti-Jewish animosity here and there.

There is another cause, more lasting than the first: the contradiction, at least in appearance, that existed between the universalist project issuing from the Enlightenment and taken up by the republican and socialist ideal, and Jewish specificity; between the secular ideal and the religious foundation of that community. For a time, the left and a good number of French Jews thought they could settle the problem through assimilation. But for Jews, that implied a sacrifice of their identity, disloyalty to their ancestors and to their faith. Therein lay the source of a misunderstanding that could never be truly transcended. Socialist republican universalism encountered the same pitfall as Christian universalism (Catholicism): the irreducibility of Jewish consciousness.

Two opposing forms of ethnocentrism ("culturocentrism" would be a better term) competed to create or to exacerbate anti-Semitism: a singularist or differentialist ethno-culturocentrism and a universalist ethno-culturocentrism.

The first was the deed of counterrevolutionaries. They, as Joseph de Maistre said, did not believe in Man ("There is no *man* in the world. In my lifetime, I have seen Frenchmen, Italians, Russians . . . ; but as for man, I declare I have never met him in my life; if he exists it is certainly unbeknownst to me"). They believed in particular human groupings, in national and religious singularities. For counterrevolutionaries, the Jew existed; he had his attributes, his traditions, his own culture. Some would say: his race. Within that current, anti-Semitism fed an aversion for the modern world and defended a lost social harmony, for which the mythological figure of the emancipated Jew was the perpetual agent of dissolution: the Other, the different, the relentless enemy of the norm, the instigator of mobility, the wanderer, the agent of destruction. For exclusivist ethnocentrism, the Jew was destined for the ghetto or for exile.

The second sort of anti-Semitism was proper to the left. Its universalist ethnocentrism wanted to extend the benefits of French-style Enlightenment to all peoples. In the name of reason or the classless society, it tended toward the negation of the Jewish entity. Within that progressivist perspective, the Jewish community was called upon to dissolve into a human fraternity, and old beliefs and superstitions were destined to be extinguished. In this inclusive ethnocentrism, the Jew was destined to be assimilated or despised.[36]

As we know, many Jews chose the path of assimilation. Going even further, numerous Jewish intellectuals participated in the dream of a revolution announcing a harmonious society and a new humanity. Without nostalgia for a past that had ordinarily mistreated them, many of them participated in the socialist utopia. But although they sacrificed their identity on the altar of revolution, other people assumed the task of reminding them of it. Whether atheists or converts, whether in the movement or against the movement, under the gaze of the anti-Semite they became Jews once more, against their will. "Real socialism," as it was erected in eastern Europe, has proved to be another "closed" society, where the Jews as well as other minorities are still seeking their place.

The acceptance of otherness, of plurality, of difference, is not automatic. When it exists, it tends toward hierarchization and exclusion. The dominant, homogeneous group imposes its norms; the marginal groups must adopt them as the price of their existence. Only the "open society," armed both against counterrevolutionary nostalgia and totalitarian utopias, can offer the chance for a truly pluralist democracy, capable of integrating Jews without forcing them to alienate their own being, their collective memory, their dual solidarity (as French people and as Jews).

The era of decolonization has gradually led us to scale back our "civilizing mission"; our gaze no longer looks down on others; as for civilization, we have discovered there are others besides our own.

To conceive of the universal through differences, to defend one's own right to difference within a universalist perspective: nothing is more difficult than to respond simultaneously to that dual imperative, but that is the condition for a livable society today.

PART THREE

Bonapartism and Fascism

IN AN ARTICLE, "L'ombre des Bonaparte" (The shadow of the Bonapartes), published in the Free French press in 1943, Raymond Aron made a comparison between Bonapartism and Boulangism on one hand, and fascism on the other. In particular, he wrote:

> Bonapartism is . . . at once the *anticipation* and the *French version* of fascism. It is an anticipation because the political instability, national humiliation, and concern for social achievements—combined with a certain indifference toward political achievements—characteristic of the revolution created a plebiscitary situation in the country on various occasions, at the very time of ascendant capitalism. And it is a French version because millions of French people compensated for their customary hostility toward their political leaders with a passionate enthusiasm crystallizing around one person designated by the events. It is also a French version because an authoritarian regime in France inevitably lays claim to the great Revolution, pays verbal tribute to the national will, adopts a leftist vocabulary, professes to address itself to the people as a whole, beyond parties.[1]

In that anti-Gaullist article, Aron intends to warn his fellow citizens against the seduction of a personal power that, far from being counterrevolutionary like Pétain's power, would be based on the popular will. The article is polemical, but not lacking in pertinence. De Gaulle subsequently demonstrated his attachment to democracy on several occasions, but in his institutional preferences, his methods of government, and the very means he used to return to power, there are too many correspondences between Gaullism and Bonapartism for us to reject that kinship without discussion, even if that purported association has angered so many admirers of General de Gaulle. I have thus attempted to follow the continuity and the breaks in the Bonapartist tradition, from the first emperor to Charles de Gaulle.

To say that Bonapartism was an anticipation of fascism is more debatable. No doubt such an analysis has already taken place. Hence, certain Marxists, such as Thalheimer in the 1920s, maintained that fascism displayed the same class peculiarity as Bonapartism: here was a state that enjoyed a certain *autonomy*, because of the *balance* realized within civil society between the bourgeoisie and the proletariat. The dominant classes sacrificed their "political domination" in order to preserve their "economic domination," to the benefit of a "master savior."[2]

Other traits are also comparable: the crisis situations during which Bonaparte and Mussolini took power, the importance of a charismatic leader, contempt for parliamentary institutions, administrative and policing centralization, the state's exuberance, large public works projects, and so on. In hindsight, one might even conclude that fascism had the same function in Italy as the Second Empire in France. Nonetheless, the two phenomena were not contemporary. Bonapartism was a French phenomenon of the nineteenth century; it was one of the modes of transition between absolute monarchy and liberal democracy, constituting a sort of mixed regime—half-monarchical, half-democratic—built on the institutional failure of the Revolution. The question is whether, mutatis mutandis, Gaullism stems from that tradition.

In its Italian realization, fascism too was established on the failure of a disunited and unstable liberal democracy. But it occurred in 1922. Between the two regimes, two major events had taken place: World War I and the Bolshevik revolution. If fascism was a new political category, it was owing to its *totalitarian* finality. Even while performing the functions of Bonapartism—arbitration among parties, organization of a personal dictatorship, unification and centralization, economic initiative on the part of the state, social trends trumpeted by propaganda, police surveillance of the territory or of prominent personalities and so on, fascism also aimed to unify society in accordance with a military model, a state ideology, and finally, an expansionist will. Let us recall one of the most dense definitions of fascism, that offered by Philippe Burrin:

The constitutive elements of fascist ideology are thus integrated into a hierarchical and tendentious structure: this involves forming a national community permanently mobilized around the values of energy, faith, and sacrifice; a community constrained by a totalitarian unity that rules out all allegiances other than an exclusive loyalty to a leader who decides the collective destiny absolutely; and finally, a militarized community, united in an enterprise of domination that is in itself its principle and its goal.[3]

Such a definition allows us to grasp the similarities between fascism and nazism rather than fascism and Bonapartism. France, however, was not completely cleared of charges of constructing a fascist ideology. Even though fascism was only in an outline phase, a certain number of movements and a certain corpus of ideas fed the twentieth-century counterrevolution, even in the view of Mussolini himself (see Chapter 12, "Outlines of a French Fascism"). To conclude that "French fascism" is therefore the most authentic form, for the very good reason that it was never corrupted by power, is to present an untenable paradox; yet that is one of the paradoxes that has established the reputation of Zeev Sternhell.[4] I shall return later to that debate.

I also discuss another debate of sorts: after Sternhell broadly implicated a number of leftist individuals and movements in the elaboration of fascist ideology, odd colloquia began to take place in the 1980s—after the Socialists had returned to power—in which a mixture was cheerfully concocted between socialism and fascism! The history of ideas: what you get out of it depends on what you put in![5]

CHAPTER 11

The Bonapartist Temptation

"THE NAPOLEONIC idea consists of reconstituting French society—turned on its head by fifty years of revolution—and of reconciling order and freedom, the rights of the people and the principles of authority." That is how Louis-Napoleon Bonaparte expressed it in 1840 from his exile in London.[1] Let us retain two key words from his affirmation of what he calls "the Napoleonic idea," and which we shall call "Bonapartism": the people and authority. In 1862, after he had become Napoleon III, the same author published a life of Julius Caesar. That was no accident. The Roman reference was apt not only for the conqueror but also for the man who wanted to establish his absolute order on the basis of the plebeians' consent. The Napoleonic regimes established in France at the beginning and then the middle of the nineteenth century both asserted themselves as strong and personal regimes for the people. Bonapartism was a modern form of Caesarism.

The show of arms at the origin and the end of the Caesarian and Bonapartist regimes might lead us to believe in their fragility, or even their artificiality. In fact, however, Caesarism founded a lasting empire, and the two Napoleonic empires were more stable than the regimes they replaced. If we add to that observation the fact that in the twentieth century two parliamentary republics—in 1940 and in 1958—also gave way to more or less Caesarian regimes, we might legitimately wonder whether Bonapartism is not one of the stronger tendencies of French political life.

In the beginning, in 1799 (18 Brumaire) as in 1851 (2 December), a regime took shape on the ruins of a parliamentary republic demoralized by a coup d'état. The master architect had long since won the favor of popular opinion. Like Caesar about to cross the Rubicon, Napoleon Bonaparte used his military glory to take possession of the crowds. The Italian campaign of 1797 earned him the nickname "Our Lady of Victories" (Lodi, Arcole, Rivoli). He became a member of the Institut, banned at the Carnot siege. But the new leader knew how to forge his own image as national hero: with the wealth accumulated in Italy he financed the founding of newspapers that assailed the public with accounts of his prowess. From the outset, his political career relied on propaganda.

Louis-Napoleon Bonaparte would not have enjoyed a military reputation were it not for the fact that as Napoleon's nephew, he inherited the laurels received by his uncle. Politicians and literate, university-educated people considered the Napoleonic offshoot a "cretin"—easy to keep under their thumb. They were wrong: Louis-Napoleon was not eloquent but he had a scientific education and a knowledge of economics that was far above average. Above all, they underestimated the popular fervor the Napoleonic legend assured to the epigone of the victor of Austerlitz. Was he "Napoleon the Little," as Victor Hugo said? Perhaps, but he knew how to use his proximity to "Napoleon the Great" to attract the fascination emanating from the latter. The presidential election of 1848, which occurred after the February revolution by universal suffrage, gave concrete form to the magnetism exerted by the historic patronym. Instead of choosing among already known politicians, the people sent an obscure man—but one of brilliant lineage—to the Elysée Palace.

Thus there were two men judged to be out of the ordinary, one for the reputation of his exploits, the other for his name, now raised to the power of myth; one decided to take power illegally, the other to keep it illegally. They both succeeded because they were responding to an apparent need. The original coup d'état occurred at a time of crisis, in a republic in a state of decomposition. "Anarchy," said Napoleon. The Directory managed to sustain itself at all costs only through electoral manipulation and voided elections, sometimes against the Jacobins, sometimes against the royalists. The political system stemming from the failure of the constitutional monarchy desired by the 1789 Constituent Assembly could not find its equilibrium; the foreign war was expensive, finances were in shambles. Religious divisions remained deep: "When I placed myself at the head of affairs," explained Bonaparte, "France was in the same state as Rome when it declared that a dictator was necessary to save the republic."

The idea of a "savior" was even current in leftist ranks: before 18 Brumaire, the Jacobins had thought of concluding an alliance with the soldier of Italy and Egypt; barring that, they thought of Bernadotte, another general and a recent minister of war. The budding dictator, however, did not intend to have his hands tied by a single party: he was above them all. Yet he knew how to find support in the government leaders of the moment, beginning with Sieyès. In the end, it was Sieyès who reaped all the benefits: Bonaparte was unsure of himself before the Council of Five Hundred, which had moved to Saint-Cloud. He was showered with insults, threatened with being outlawed, and in the end, he owed his salvation only to the resolute intervention of his brother Lucien, chair of the assembly in revolt, and of his loyal soldiers, with Leclerc and Murat in the lead. The parliamentary coup d'état became a military coup d'état: the representatives of the people were dispersed by the saber.

The "coup of 2 December" in 1851 was completely different. A president of the Republic, ineligible for reelection, intended to remain at the head of the state by force. He succeeded, but through a bloody repression of sporadic uprisings—localized but not without intensity—triggered by his action. Far from being the result of a despotic caprice, however, the coup d'état came to a head as a replacement for a republican regime that had lost its soul. The Second Republic, in fact, emerged as a result of the cooperation of populist hopes and the apparent fraternization of different classes and philosophical convictions.

Between the two coups, the trees of Liberty, planted after the February Days in 1848, had been uprooted. During the bloody June Days, the fear of insurgent workers had established a conservative republic, within which out-and-out conservatives could not come to an agreement, in the first place about the necessary "dynastic fusion" (in other words, the reconciliation of the two branches of the royal family, the legitimist and the Orleanist), which would have allowed them to restore the monarchy as they wished. With the approaching electoral defeat, fear of the Reds impelled some of them to rally behind the Bonapartist solution. Only constitutional reform would have allowed Louis-Napoleon to be eligible for office once more, since he had originally been given a single mandate of four years.

They acted in vain: they failed in the face of a coalition between the right and the far left. Convinced that he represented the general sentiment in the face of resistance from a part of the political class, the president appealed to the people through posters and dissolved the Assembly with the help of the army. The bloodshed of the following days marked the regime with an indelible stain: the government had been born of a "crime," as Victor Hugo said. But the violence of the repression ought not to conceal the reality of the deep consensus among all strata of the nation: more workers were massacred by the Second Republic in June 1848 than opponents died during the coup d'état of December 1851. Nevertheless, that republic remained a danger even in the eyes of its leaders. Hence, the future Napoleon III could pride himself on offering the people revenge on the "burgraves" in power, and on offering the bourgeois the assurance of protection against revolutionaries. On one hand, he reestablished universal suffrage; on the other, he assured the restoration of order. Bonapartism defined itself as a joint guarantor of the values (or of certain values) of the left and the right, within a perspective of reconciliation and national union.

The Leader and the People

The use of force allowed the two emperors to govern a society in a state of endemic division. Beyond that, the regimes that resulted needed legitimacy. The two Napoleons sought it first in the principle of national sovereignty. Both could avail themselves of the support of the "masses" at the expense of castes and oligarchies. Both dictators, once their coups were accomplished, intended to have their power ratified by universal suffrage.

Three times, in year VIII (the Consulate), year X (the Consulate for life), and year XII (the hereditary empire), Napoleon Bonaparte presented the change in the constitution as a referendum, without going through the assemblies. The consultation of the people resembled a plebiscite: voters were to give, or not give, their confidence to one man. The measure took a democratic turn inasmuch as the defunct directorial regime had been established on the basis of suffrage of censitaires. The one-to-one relation between a leader and a people without intermediaries is one of the intrinsic marks of Bonapartism. In concrete terms, the first attempt was equivocal: the results of the first consultation were delayed for two months. Lucien Bonaparte, minister of the interior, made advantageous "errors" in computing: the popular base of the new regime had to be demonstrated. So it was as well with the nephew Napoleon. On the very night of the coup d'état, he began by proclaiming the reestablishment of universal suffrage, which had been noticeably mutilated at the poor's expense by the conservative assembly.[2] He proceeded to consult voters: first, in December 1851, to ratify the constitutional reform that awarded him a ten-year presidency; and again in 1852, to confirm the reestablishment of the Empire. In both cases, he enjoyed a victory.

Of course, neither the uncle nor the nephew overused the plebiscite: a negative or merely mediocre result at the outset might have cost either of them the legitimacy obtained from the ballot boxes. At the very least, it might have undermined that legitimacy. But the appeal to the people constituted a legal resource to be used as they wished; so it was for Napoleon I, when he returned from the island of Elba; and so it was for Napoleon III, who, challenged in the legislative elections of 1869, proposed a referendum on his reforms in 1870 and obtained a success that allowed him to patch up his authority. In 1844, Louis-Napoleon wrote: "Today, the reign of castes is over: the country can be governed only with the aid of the masses; they must therefore be organized so that they can formulate their will, and disciplined so that they can be led and enlightened about their own interests."[3]

Putting an end to "castes" also meant bringing the assemblies into line. Bonapartism is the opposite of parliamentarianism. Hatred and disdain for assemblies was "a characteristic and fundamental trait of its spirit," said Tocqueville, who refused to rally behind it. With universal suffrage in the place of divine right, the Bonapartist regime was a continuation of absolute monarchy: war on intermediate bodies! More liberty promised and less liberty offered! Increased centralization! And everywhere appointees rather than elected officials! In that area, Napoleon completed the work of the Bourbons: in 1800, he replaced the power of the intendants, suppressed by the revolution, with that of the prefects. They, as so many delegated departmental emperors, pieced together a network of influence, surveillance, and action throughout the country, for the purpose of unifying it under the leadership of the great man. "The chain of command," said Chaptal, "descended without interruption from the minister to the administration and transmitted the laws and orders of the government to the smallest branches of the social order with the speed of electric current."

Everything was organized to give absolute preponderance to the executive branch: the emperor had the initiative in making laws. Parliamentary opposition, if there was any, was reduced by every means possible, including "legal" means such as official candidacies. The regime also owed its modernity to its use of both the police and propaganda. Censorship and *images d'Epinal* happily coexisted in the Bonapartist regime. As for the university, from which objections could come, it also fell under the sway of the master, by means of a monopoly. "There can be no fixed political state," declared Napoleon, "if there is no teaching faculty with fixed principles."

University students were not the only targets: from childhood, French children had to learn obedience and gratitude. Thus Napoleon had a flattering question introduced into the catechism:

Are there not particular reasons that ought to attach us more strongly to Napoleon I, our emperor?—Yes, because he is the one God called forth in difficult circumstances to reestablish public worship of the holy religion of our fathers and to be its protector. He brought back and maintained public order through his profound and active wisdom. He defends the state with his powerful arm; he has become the Lord's anointed through the ordination he received from the Supreme Pontiff, head of the universal Church.

Nonetheless, Bonapartism was not merely a regime of demagoguery and law and order. Napoleon I and Napoleon III could not have created or restored the empire if they were not responding to a strong demand. In the eyes of the French people, Napoleon I had the merit of stabilizing political life after ten years of upheaval, civil war, and foreign wars. The Concordate of 1801, which laid the foundations for religious reconciliation, and the Treaty of Amiens, which in 1802 put an end to the foreign coalition, were the initial acts on which Napoleon could build his power. Both he and his nephew, placing themselves above parties, above classes, loudly declared they had only one goal: national greatness. In fact, the two Bonapartist regimes produced it in abundance.

That greatness implied economic dynamism and social peace. State voluntarism was notable in this area under the First Empire, and even more under the Second. From the creation of the Banque de France to the policy of public works projects (the draining of the Landes and the building of international highways and railway lines), from the treaty on free trade with England in 1860 to the construction of the Suez Canal, completed in 1869, there were abundant signs of the economic push coming from above. Success in all areas served as a corroboration of the plebiscite.

Among all the glorious achievements that fed Bonapartism's self-exaltation, the greatest remained its military power. In the beginning, the empire was peace.[4] But very quickly, whatever the extenuating circumstances, the name of the two Napoleons became synonymous with conquest. The very concept of empire implies war, since the essence of empire is ruling power. The same dream obsessed both men. Napoleon I imagined the creation of a French Europe, the "Great Empire": considered by other sovereigns to be a usurper stemming from the abhorred Revolution, he spent a good part of his reign and used up the greater part of his forces fighting the hydra of the coalitions. At the same time, he loosed the winds of revolutionary ideas over the whole continent, set the old monarchies in motion, awakened the sense of nationality, built roads and bridges, redrew the map of Europe ten times. "In Germany," wrote Engels, "Napoleon was the representative of the Revolution, the announcer of its principles, the destroyer of old feudal society." And Hegel wrote before him: "Such progress was possible only owing to an extraordinary man, whom it is impossible not to admire."

With reports on the great army, the great man spread his image as a legendary hero throughout the country. Once Napoleon was defeated and exiled, republicans and liberals saw him less as "the Corsican ogre" than as the valiant soldier of the Revolution challenging age-old dynasties, the remaining old regimes, the federation of tyrants. Napoleon the nephew, despite his vows, also found his way back to the battlefield after half a century of peace. Raised to his pinnacle by the names of victories whipping about him like banners, he could not survive defeat in war. Before the final fall of both emperors, lugubrious retreats prefigured the collapse of the empire: for Napoleon I, it was the retreat from Russia; for Napoleon III, the return from Mexico. Great dreams evaporated, Alexander had to go home. Then, the worst humiliation was inflicted on the strategist: the invasion of his own nation by foreign armies.

Two sides of the same coin: the trumpets of glory and the knell of defeat. The French people had been intoxicated by the extraordinary imperial epic; some still were. The nephew, as we know, could not begin again, but he cashed in the dividend of the capital accumulated by the founder. In *Les déracinés* (The uprooted), Maurice Barrès depicts five young people from Lorraine arriving in Paris and meeting at the Invalides:

For French persons of twenty, Napoleon's tomb is not a place of peace, a philosophical trench where a poor body that was once so active lay defeated; it is the crossroads of every sort of energy—audacity, will, appetite. For a hundred years, the imagination, dispersed everywhere else, is concentrated at that point. Fill with your thoughts that crypt where something sublime is laid to rest; raze history, eliminate Napoleon, and you annihilate the condensed imagination of the century. At this place, one hears not the silence of the dead, but a heroic murmur; this shaft under the dome is the epic bugle whose sound sets the hair of every young person to bristling.

We know the other side of the coin: hecatombs and other horrors of war, but also the need to conquer in order to remain in power. A colossus with feet of clay, the Bonapartist regime could not survive military defeat. No doubt that is the lot of new regimes; only old monarchies can allow themselves repeated defeats. But in the case of the Napoleons, it is as if the regime in place betrayed itself when it did not seek glory under cannon fire. It is as it were pushed toward Austerlitz or Magenta; and finally, toward Waterloo and Sedan.

Up to this point, we have considered Bonapartism as a unified bloc. In the interest of rigor, we must now introduce nuances. First, the term itself is more accurately applied to the regime created by Louis-Napoleon Bonaparte, even though the characteristics of the model were already well defined under Napoleon I. The two regimes, moreover, evolved in opposite directions. In the first case, a popular, plebiscitary dictatorship was transformed into an imperial monarchy. In the second, a presidency of the decade-old republic became an empire, but an empire that over the long term became noticeably more liberal, even allowing a significant role for Parliament in its last year. Despite these differences, both regimes suffered from a similar contradiction—the opposition between the principle of popular legitimacy and the principle of a new hereditary dynasty.

In the case of Napoleon I, the contradiction took the form of a caricatural evolution. His desire for dynastic legitimation was expressed in two acts, which again called his origins into question. The first phase was his marriage to the Austrian Marie-Louise after his divorce from Josephine. By forcing his way into the House of Hapsburg, the former Corsican general, the former Jacobin, the "Robespierre on horseback," as Madame de Staël called him, was transformed into a new version of the bourgeois gentleman, exchanging his revolutionary past for an ancien régime coat of arms. The second phase was the anointing of the emperor by the pope on 2 December 1804: thus, a legitimacy of divine right capped the transformation of the regime. As we saw above in the passage from the catechism, Napoleon wanted to be given the consideration awarded French royalty: he was "the Lord's anointed." The Bonapartist model was corrupted: Napoleon intentionally lost his originality, which had come from the compromise realized between revolutionary principles and the restoration of state authority.

In the case of Napoleon III, there was no inclination of that kind: until the end, universal suffrage remained the true source of his legitimacy. Yes, but he too intended to reestablish ties with a dynastic regime. As a result, how could the hereditary principle be reconciled with the plebiscitary principle? The former is an abstract notion referring to a function, while the latter is linked to a single individual and his position. If a no vote should happen to disavow the head of state, should he leave? Is it even imaginable that in such a case, an heir, whoever he might be, even a child, would take his place? We are touching here on the limits of Bonapartism. In its essence, it needs popular support to come about and to last; in its ambition, it dreams of perpetuating itself through its progeny. Therein lies the illegitimacy of the regime, torn between its declared sympathy for "the masses" and its monarchical aspirations.

To resolve the contradiction, Napoleon I, as we said, chose to return to divine right one way or another (at least until the Hundred Days); Napoleon III was condemned to appeal for universal suffrage. Universal suffrage was not invoked in plebiscites between 1852 and 1870, but was so regularly for legislative elections. At the same time, the regime had to take every precaution, use all the conditioning available at the time, imagine every sort of propaganda to keep the people's support. As an incomplete monarchy, the Bonapartist empire had to avoid the crisis of unpopularity. That was in great part the source of its voluntarism, but also, on the negative side, of its headlong rush forward.

Did Bonapartism rely on the privileged social classes? Was it a translation of class domination into political terms? In fact, contemporaries saw it as the guarantor of a bourgeois order against the danger of revolution:

the fear of the Jacobins in 1799, the fear of those advocating the division of property (the *partageux*) in 1851. The demand for state authority on the part of the propertied class has been pointed out many times. Writing after 2 December, which he considered "a true counterrevolution," Louis Veuillot used the dense language of a Catholic on the far right and did not mince words. For "men of order," he said, Louis-Napoleon is "the man with a whip who will give society back its solid grip on a duly mastered proletariat." Closer to our own time, Pierre Barberis, a literary historian of Marxist inspiration, presents Napoleon III as "the guard dog of French capitalism as it forged its future."

Marx's analysis was more subtle. For the author of *The Eighteenth Brumaire of Louis Bonaparte*, the 2 December coup responded to the need to put an end to the internal divisions of the bourgeoisie. That class was divided between its landed faction and its industrial faction. The only agreement possible between the two was the establishment of that neutral republic on the ashes of the defeated proletariat. To restore the monarchy would have entailed giving the advantage to one faction over the other. That was why dynastic fusion was impossible. That disagreement led one current of the law-and-order camp to rally behind the Napoleonic solution. Hence the coup d'état of 2 December arose from the incapacity of the bourgeois class to find a common language and a shared policy.

Nevertheless, that state-centered solution did not come out of nowhere. Louis-Napoleon Bonaparte was assured a social base, which was also a rock-hard electoral base: the peasantry of parceled-up land. In that profoundly rural France, Bonapartism signified the defense of small, conservative landed peasants, whose members, isolated from one another, found themselves unable to make their voices or class interests heard. With the Civil Code, Napoleon I had already consolidated the full-fledged right to own small pieces of property, newly acquired by the peasants; Napoleon III made himself their defender, both against the old masters and against the new notables living in the cities.

The successive elections never belied the small peasantry's attachment to the Bonapartist regime. Marx's adversary Proudhon confirmed his analysis. That said, Marx, faithful to his method, had a tendency to subordinate politics to the imperatives of the economy and of class struggle. The characters depicted onstage were always or almost always representatives of a class interest. But although Bonapartism is a political model applicable grosso modo to other times and other historical circumstances, its political specificity needs to be understood. Marx himself, in his famous book, noted the "particular interest" of one or another deputy, an interest that contradicted those of his class. He thus admitted that individuals and their peculiar passions can add at least a grain of salt to the political soup, changing the taste of the final dish. The actors on the political stage were not endlessly wondering what was better for the social group they came from. Even when that was the case, they could sometimes oppose colleagues belonging to the same group, not on the basis of the ends of their action, but on the basis of their means.

In short, I am not fully satisfied with Marx's brilliant analysis. The Napoleonic dictatorship, like every other political regime, did not come out of thin air, to cite Marx himself: it had to be rooted in society. Let us concede that the peasantry was its crucible for a long time. But we would not refer to the Napoleonic regime using a term ending in "ism" if we did not think that a certain type of political regime had been invented, some of whose traits belonged to the Caesarism of antiquity; and its fundamental characteristics can be found in other eras, when the majority of people were not peasants. The founding of the Fifth Republic is encouraging in that respect.

Of course, the differences between Gaullism and Bonapartism are obvious. De Gaulle did not destroy the reign of liberty (attacks against freedom of the press during the Algerian war had begun under the Fourth Republic). De Gaulle never installed a regime that gave a preponderant role to the army (his most resolute enemies were in fact senior officers). Above all, de Gaulle never wished to found either an empire or a dynasty. That said, the elements of Bonapartism are not lacking in the system he definitively set in place in 1962.

Originally, de Gaulle benefited not, perhaps, from a coup d'état but in any case from a show of force—that of 13 May—conducted on his behalf by the leading members of the Algerian army. Of course, the general was more skillful than Bonaparte at Saint-Cloud, and obtained the nomination of the National Assembly. But he returned to power under conditions that were at least as murky, in a country that believed it was on the brink of civil war. To be precise, de Gaulle placed himself above clans, challenging the "party system," which in his view had done so much harm to France, thus repeating in his own way Lucien Bonaparte's line: "The government no longer wishes, no longer knows of parties, and sees only French people in France."[5] The leitmotif of "rallying together" had its effect: to the end, part of the old electorate on the left remained faithful to him!

De Gaulle too was preceded by his "legend": that of the intransigent patriot, the man of 18 June, the liberator of the territory, the man who put France back within the ranks of the great nations after the terrible humiliation of 1940. He was heir to his own glory, a providential man welcomed as a savior by a country foundering in the contradictions of the moment and the struggle between factions. He adopted a constitution and established a system that included many characteristics of Bonapartism, especially after the constitutional reform of 1962: legitimation by referendum-plebiscite, weakening of the assemblies, strengthening of administrative centralization in a technocratic form, an affective relation maintained with "the masses." His travels in the provinces were one of the effective means he used to short-circuit the intermediary of assemblies: diving into the mob, shaking hands one after another, whispering words into ears that listened in wonderment. Let us add to all this the new art of propaganda. De Gaulle knew how to surround himself with famous writers—Malraux, Mauriac, and others—who gave the Gaullian epic color and style. The spread of television arrived just in time; he soon used it as an artist, all the while taking care to have its messages monitored.

When, today, we encounter young people making the pilgrimage to Colombey, we think again of the five young persons from Lorraine whom Barrès depicts in front of Napoleon's tomb. De Gaulle reawakened the desire for national glory: he had been the supreme resistance fighter; he remained the fierce guarantor of French independence. He may well have "abandoned" Algeria, that was part of the movement of history. But he compensated for colonial prestige with the new reputation of a great, modern, dynamic country resolved to forge weapons for its own defense: the perfecting of the A-bomb and then of the H-bomb, Gaullian diplomacy—which challenged the United States's imperial republic—the recognition of Communist China, the resignation from NATO. With each blow, the French, recovering their pride at such audaciousness, imagined they were reliving a heroic era. The economic development of the 1960s, the comeback of the franc, the progress in social legislation:[6] here again, there were many traits of resemblance, mutatis mutandis, with the Second Empire.

The Gaullist Synthesis: A Republican Monarchy

In the last three years of its existence, the Second Empire became more liberal. In the end, in view of the general evolution of Western industrial nations, one might imagine the imperial system evolving toward institutions and practices similar to those de Gaulle set in place. The major difference remained the dynastic choice. De Gaulle wanted to found, not a hereditary empire, but a republican—that is, an elective—monarchy. It is nonetheless true that both Napoleon III and de Gaulle gambled their legitimacy on a referendum-plebiscite every time any doubt insinuated itself between the leader and the nation. In the case of de Gaulle, the model was purified to rid itself of the contradiction mentioned above: the leader withdrew at the will of the people. The Gaullist synthesis demonstrated its validity through the general's departure following the referendum he lost

Table 2

Napoleon, Pétain, and de Gaulle

	NAPOLEON I	NAPOLEON III	PÉTAIN	DE GAULLE
Origin of regime	Coup d'état	Coup d'état	Military defeat	Show of force in Algiers
Prestigious personality	Miltary man (hero of Italy and Egypt)	Napoleon's nephew	Military man ("hero of Verdun")	Miltary man (former leader of Free French forces)
System of legitimation	Constitution ratified by universal suffrage	Constitution ratified by universal suffrage	Passage of special powers	Nomination by the Assembly Constitution ratified by universal suffrage
Referenda-plebiscites	4	3	0	3
Role of Parliament	Rubber-stamping	Rubber-stamping but progressive emancipation	Dismissed	Preeminence of executive power
Fate of personal freedoms	Under close surveillance	Under close surveillance Liberal evolution	Suspended	Respected after the Algerian war
The grand scheme	The Great Empire ("Europe–France")	French hegemony over the Europe of nations, Mexico	National revolution	French hegemony over the Europe of nations Military and diplomatic independence

Table 2, continued

	NAPOLEON I	NAPOLEON III	PÉTAIN	DE GAULLE
Positive references to 1789	Yes	Yes	No	Yes
Brutal end of regime	Miltary defeat	Military defeat	Liberation of territory from foreign occupation	Negative referendum

NOTE: This table suggests a certain number of shared traits between Bonapartism and Gaullism. It shows in contrast that the regime established by Marshal Pétain is quite clearly distant from the model—even though, like the others, it was founded on the failure of a parliamentary republic and on a "charismatic" leader.

in 1969. In that sense, his republican monarchy was also a democratic monarchy.

For a long time, the Revolution gave free rein to one of the major plot lines of French society: the struggle between the heirs of 1789 and those loyal to the Catholic monarchy. In fact, the dual failure of the Restoration and of the constitutional July monarchy gave way in the political field to a competition between two systems, both stemming from the Revolution: the parliamentary republic and the Bonapartist regime. Each of the four parliamentary republics, from the Directory to the Fourth Republic, ended to the advantage of a supreme savior, destroyer of the assembly government. After all, although the Vichy regime lies outside the category of Bonapartism, it did take on some of its characteristics (see Table 2), beginning with the hatred of parties and the scrapping of Parliament. On four occasions, a man radiating glory struck down the "party system" to the applause of the "masses." Each time, he was able—at least in the beginning—to count on a popular fervor that the defunct republics never attained.

The Third Republic, the most successful attempt at a parliamentary republic, was regularly the object of neo-Bonapartist assaults. Boulangism was its wildest episode: behind the panache of a general who electrified the crowds, "revisionists" indicted a regime they judged to be headless, without soul and without glory. The Boulangist Brumaire did not take place; at least, the demonstrators led by Boulanger's white horse could not piece together their passions after the defeat. In anti-Dreyfusard nationalism, as in the leagues of the 1930s, cries of hatred were again heard against parliamentarianism, a government of thieves, a government of shame, a government of impotence. The Fourth Republic had its constitution ratified by a minority of registered voters; since opinion polls are part of social mores, we may observe that the regime was dead in people's hearts long before 13 May.

For many French people, the plebiscitary republic so dear to Déroulède remained the regime they most desired. A great leader—extra- or anti-parliamentary—popular enthusiasm, a "grand scheme," an end to partisan quarrels, national communion. They found all that much more exciting than parliamentarianism, an English import, which was nothing but endless talk, shady deals, and weakness. For many, in fact, the political imagination had difficulty accommodating the formalities and slowness of the Assembly's work. Above all, the images of national representation were perceived as images of division. A deep-seated aspiration for order and union, particularly under circumstances of crisis, repeatedly impelled them to embrace the strongman, until the day when, unable to bear his tutelage any longer, they got rid of him.

Since the middle of the nineteenth century, our political history has seemed to waver between a parliamentary regime that functions poorly and a regime of the Bonapartist type that is appealing but ends in tragedy. Are we about to move beyond that history?

CHAPTER 12

Outlines of a French Fascism

WHAT IS THE seating capacity of the Salle Wagram in Paris? Three thousand, four thousand, five thousand? Opinions diverge in the reports. In any case, on 11 November 1925, it was full to the point of bursting with an attentive public made up of very proper people: engineers, business travelers, insurance employees. The date of the meeting was not chosen at random: the hall was decorated with the French flag and veterans were in the majority. One of them, Georges Gressent, who had long signed articles and books as "Georges Valois," dominated the stage, flanked by Jacques Arthuys—a former officer—and Philippe Barrès, son of a famous author who had recently died.

In the crowd, the informers for the police prefect conscientiously took down the themes of the speeches. The government in place, the Cartel des Gauches (Cartel of leftist parties), and the third Paul Painlevé ministry called down the wrath of the orators. Painlevé, though a mathematician, was as powerless as his predecessors to slow the fall of the franc. Scrap the parliamentary regime! Dump the old parties! They had betrayed the peace! They were dragging the country into monetary and economic ruin! It was time to react!

That day, the first French fascist party was founded amid enthusiasm and was welcomed with a rousing *Marseillaise*. It was called the Faisceau des Combattants et Producteurs (The cluster of soldiers and producers). It assigned itself a very simple goal: to create a true national state, beyond parties and beyond classes.

The French Origins of Fascism

The next day, one comment was unavoidable: Italian Fascism, in power since autumn 1922, had found a clientele for its ideological exports in

France. Was not the Valois movement calling itself the Faisceau? As for black shirts, the "legionnaires" exchanged them for blue shirts (like the blue line of the Vosges). In addition, Valois did not hide his admiration for Mussolini: "The honor will fall to Italy," he wrote on 3 December 1925, "for having given a name to the movement by which contemporary Europe moves toward the creation of the modern state."[1]

All the same, as Valois was to write a few years later: "There were a host of misunderstandings at the origin of the Faisceau in France."[2] Let us consider two of them.

1. The fascism Valois and his friends wanted to offer France was not just another movement on the far right, like Pierre Taitinger's Jeunesses Patriotes (Patriot youth), designed to protect the interests of the bourgeoisie against the Red Peril. Not only did Valois assert an "antiplutocratic" fascism, which could not harm anyone, but he proved to be the resolute advocate of an "absolutely free" trade unionism for workers and appealed to producers, without whom—he claimed—there was no hope.

2. Far from imitating Mussolini, Valois was intent on recalling on several occasions that on the contrary, the French precedents had inspired Italian Fascism. Mussolini had invented the word, but the idea originated in France before 1914. Georges Valois himself had contributed to its birth. "Our borrowings from Italian Fascism can be boiled down to the choice of the shirt as the characteristic item of the uniform and a conception of revolutionary operations inspired by the march on Rome. . . . That is all. As for the rest, the conception of the structure of the modern state, we are the inventors, and we were copied in Italy."[3]

In a book he published in 1927, Valois defined fascism as the fusion of two currents that had previously been contradictory: nationalism and socialism. The two currents would no longer wage war against each other; they would be reconciled. They had the same enemy, the triumphant individualism of the nineteenth century and its corollaries, liberalism and the parliamentary regime. That fusion might have been imaginable under French socialism—Blanquist or Proudhonian—except that, Valois said, "Marxism made it impossible." The desired synthesis had to come about in a new movement. That was the vocation of fascism.[4]

In other words, fascism was defined as "both on the left and on the right." It was on the left because its objective was to satisfy "the needs of the people" and to "defend them from the great and powerful"; and it was on the right, because it appealed to the authority of a restored state.

In the genesis of the fascist idea, Valois insisted on the debt he owed Maurice Barrès—the Boulangist Barrès, the "revisionist" deputy elected in 1889, and the freelance journalist: "His *Cocarde* [Cockade], made up of republicans, royalists, and socialists, was the prologue to our own work."[5]

The word "fascist" did not exist at the end of the nineteenth century, but the idea did. What is an idea, however, if it does not come from books, newspapers, or salons, where a few distinguished minds exchange it over a cup of tea or a petit four? And prefascism—let us give that name to the various movements before World War I that combined to bring together apparently heterogeneous forces, from the left and the right, against the regime in place—prefascism did not remain within the world of pure ideas; it took shape, was transformed, and in the end it failed, but not without leaving lasting traces and seeds that would grow out of the insecurities of war and of the postwar period. In a recent book,[6] Zeev Sternhell studies the French roots of fascism, where Boulangism, the leagues, strike-breaking unions, and even an unexpected convergence between the nationalists of Action Française and theorists of revolutionary unionism were intertwined, or perhaps followed one after the other.

Events generally provoked these unnatural alliances: they were favored by episodic crises that launched new attacks against the parliamentary republic and the bourgeois republic (it was all the same thing!). But they needed a catalyst, for otherwise the "fascist" formula (socialism + nationalism) remained inoperative. That was to be the lucky find of the *fin de siècle*, the secret password for the new right that took shape in the 1880s. A common enemy was needed for these bourgeois and proletarians whom fascism wanted to unite. In 1886, Edouard Drumont offered it to them in a large and frenzied book that its readers consumed voraciously: *La France juive*. On 20 October 1889, Henri Rochefort denounced "the triumph of Jewry." He was writing in *Le Courrier de l'Est*, Barrès's newspaper. A long and sinister history was beginning. Until 1914, all identifiably prefascist adventures in France resorted to anti-Semitism. Georges Valois was no exception to the rule.

He had learned the abc's of politics from anarchist papers, however. At twenty, he was a Dreyfusard. To be precise, he was part of that small cohort of Dreyfusard intellectuals who were soon disappointed by the achievements of the parliamentary left that acceded to power under the auspices of Combes and with Jaurès's support. According to Péguy, another of the disillusioned Dreyfusards, the Dreyfusard "mystique" had collapsed into mere "politics." Intrigues and sectarianism had come to occupy the seat of justice. All the same, beginning in 1906, a new situation turned the givens of politics on their head: the rising force of the revolutionary CGT, with Georges Sorel, another disabused Dreyfusard fighter, becoming its theorist, against "parliamentary socialism."

These two men, Georges Valois and Georges Sorel, certainly counted the most in the doctrinal genesis of fascism. Sorel, steeped in the ideas of Marx and Proudhon, a future admirer of Lenin and Mussolini, moved closer to the nationalists beginning in 1910. Valois, though a monarchist since 1906, felt he was in solidarity with the working class. He even formulated the idea of a "workers' monarchy," in which trade unionism, the authentic class organization, would defend "the working life" under the authority of the king, conservator of "national energy." Valois even said: "The intellectual father of fascism is Georges Sorel."[7]

In the end, the two men and their friends found common ground. All in all, that led merely to a few aborted projects and magazines (*L'Indépendance, Les Cahiers du Cercle Proudhon*), but the odd convergence of men and ideas so different from one another was potentially destructive to the established regime. Antidemocracy on the left and antidemocracy on the right, one inspired by the workers' revolt and the other by monarchist activism, such was the new explosive mixture—and let us not forget the anti-Semitic catalyst. Edouard Berth, Sorel's disciple, characterized that common ground as follows: "Two synchronic and converging movements, one on the far right, the other on the far left, have begun the siege and assault on democracy, for the salvation of the modern world and the greatness of our Latin humanity."[8]

Valois's Illusion

When Valois founded his Faisceau, the past was still alive, but the war had brought about a new configuration. Too many young men had died for the nation; the survivors did not have the right to betray their sacrifice. Victory carried with it obligations. But the regime in place, especially the Cartel des Gauches, revealed its powerlessness day by day. Valois remained in Action Française and took initiatives as an economist and organizer. In 1922, he launched the idea of an Estates General that would represent the interests of the nation as a whole. He was no longer speaking of monarchy. Yes, a responsible leader was needed, but one who could get different political communities to rally behind him. He wanted a state in which the bourgeoisie would retain its function as economic manager (contrary to what Lenin had done), but would be expelled from political leadership. He also wanted an organized working class and an adjudicating, responsible state standing above class. How to bring that national state into being? With the help of an elite that had proved itself, namely, soldiers, who had placed the nation above their own interests.

In February 1925, he launched a weekly, *Le Nouveau Siècle* (The new century). In it he published his "Appel aux combattants" (Appeal to soldiers). With the soldiers who answered the appeal, he created "legions" designed to militate against parliamentarianism. Caillaux and the banker Horace Finaly were his favorite targets during his campaigns on behalf of the franc. But anti-Semitism was no longer a part of his speeches, as if the suffering and memories of the soldiers of World War I had become the new uniting element.

The founding of the Faisceau provoked attacks from the Communist party. Valois, however, continued to make an appeal to its militant workers. Of the Communists, he said: "There is no very profound difference between them and us. Like us, they are revolting against the reign of money" (*Le Nouveau Siècle*, 19 March 1925). In March 1926, Valois was repaid for his efforts in a stunning manner: Delagrange, the Communist mayor of Périgueux, whom he had once confronted in a public meeting, joined the Faisceau.

The victory was more symbolic than substantial. Few workers joined the Faisceau, where the bourgeois component predominated.[9] Despite his desire to transcend the opposition between left and right, Valois's fascism remained bogged down on the right. It also received the harshest blows from that quarter, primarily from Action Française, which, after a few weeks of neutrality, moved to verbal offensives, then commando actions.

Nonetheless, during the first months following the founding of the Faisceau, Valois did achieve a few great successes. Inspired by the march on Rome, he put together a march on Paris, over several months and in several stages: first, Verdun, then Reims, Meaux, and so on. The first meetings attracted a large public. Special trains and buses brought in highly placed fascists. There were probably about twenty-five thousand of them at the time, but the movement weakened as it divided. The arrival of Delagrange, and Valois's speeches in favor of workers, displeased most members. Despite his intellectual abilities and his practical sense Georges Valois was not and did not want to be a "charismatic" leader, something that seems to be indispensable for the success of fascists. Finally, Poincaré brought the right back to power in 1926 and reestablished the franc's foundations in 1928. The same year, Valois was excluded from his own movement. His personal evolution toward the left began.

The Second Wind of the 1930s

The world, stabilized for a moment like Poincaré's franc, was again threatened by the chaos of the great economic crisis set off in the United States in 1929. In France, the electoral victory of the left in 1932 acted as a trigger: rightist leagues grew in number and new fascist-style organizations came into being. The victory of Hitler, who came to power in January 1933, elicited vicious comparisons between the parliamentary regime and the Radical-Socialist alliance, incapable of reestablishing order in the country's finances and the economy. A series of small reviews appeared during these first years of the decade: *Réaction, Esprit, Ordre Nouveau*, and so on. They were so many expressions of a new intellectual generation that despite its differences, shared an aversion toward the parliamentary and bourgeois republic.

On 6 February 1934, after a month of press campaigns and demonstrations provoked by Action Française and the rightist leagues, which used the Stavisky affair as a battering ram against the government and the regime in place, the Chamber of Deputies found itself besieged over the course of a day by a rather confused disturbance, whose clearest result was the resignation of Edouard Daladier as premier and the formation of a new National Union ministry under the leadership of Gaston Doumergue.

Commentators have often seen that famous day as an *aborted* attempt at a fascist putsch. In fact, it was a demonstration of *successful* intimidation of a leftist government by the leagues. The government finally gave way. Although some of the leaders of 6 February were hoping for a putsch, the total lack of coordination between the different demonstrating groups and the deliberate refusal of certain of them—for example, Colonel de La Rocque's Croix-de-Feu—to storm the fragile police roadblocks, indicate fairly well the classic character of that "day." As in 1926, the left, despite its electoral victory two years earlier, had to hand over the reins of power to the right, with the Radicals assuring that new majority by exchanging their Socialist allies of the past for new "moderate" allies, under cover of "national union."[10]

Far from perpetuating the right's power, however, the events of 6 February moved a flurry of organizations on the left to action. Despite their quarrels, they launched a counterattack and demonstrations that prefigured the Rassemblement Populaire and its victories in the elections of spring 1936. That victory of leftist forces, momentarily reconciled thanks to a tactical revision of the Communist Internationale, was achieved in the name of antifascism. The fascist threats from the outside were particularly visible: Mussolini's conquest of Ethiopia in 1935, the increasing strength of Hitler's dictatorship and Germany's remilitarization of the Rheinland in March 1936, the pronunciamento made in July of the same year against the Spanish republic and the beginning of the Spanish civil war, not to mention the electoral success of Léon Degrelle's rexism in Belgium in May, Metaxas's coup d'état in Greece in August, and that same summer, as an apotheosis, the Olympic Games in Berlin. For many on the right, one conclusion seemed obvious: while in France strikes and factory occupations led people to fear the Bolshevization of the country, foreign countries knew how to take the necessary authoritarian measures against "the specter of communism," which was again haunting Europe.

'Gringoire' and 'Je Suis Partout'

These fairly common class reflex reactions certainly encouraged the spread of a fascist state of mind in France. That social fear, however, though commonplace, is not enough to explain the kind of "fascist penetration," in Raoul Girardet's expression,[11] that occurred in France during those years. After all, part of the French right had been won over or contaminated not only by a group of organizations (we shall speak of them later) but also by an ideology of civil war, which the powerful rightist press of the time transmitted to the most remote departments.

A school advocating violence had long existed on the right: Action Française, and the daily newspaper of the same name. The newspaper was directed by Charles Maurras, who was canonized in 1936 as a result of his conviction to eight months in prison for his calls for murder. Action Française was not specifically fascist, but it had long constituted an extremist school of thought. In its disdain for liberal institutions and republican traditions, its exaltation of the "show of force" and authoritarian powers, and perhaps even more, its teaching of a certain style consisting of invectives, outrageous acts, slander, and ad hominem attacks, it largely contributed toward forming fascist "thinkers." These were the Maurrassians of the new generation, who behind their elder Pierre Gaxotte, animated *Je Suis Partout*: Robert Brasillach, Maurice Bardèche, Pierre-Antoine Cousteau, Lucien Rebatet, Georges Blond, and Alain Laubreaux. In addition to them, the large weeklies *Gringoire* and *Candide*, whose circulation exceeded several hundreds of thousands, exuded a violence that, if not fascist strictly speaking, was at least "anti-antifascist" in expression ("Fascism is for many a vital reaction, a sort of anti-antifascism,"[12] wrote Brasillach in 1938). *Gringoire* in particular, founded by Horace de Carbuccia, with contributions from Henri Béraud, Philippe Henriot, Jean-Pierre Maxence, and others, distinguished itself through the campaign it unleashed in 1936 against the Socialist minister of the interior, Roger Salengro, who was driven to suicide.

Their vehemence, combined with an old resurgent anti-Semitism, was directed especially against the leader of the Front Populaire, Léon Blum, whom Maurras called "human detritus" and whom Gaxotte characterized in these words: "He incarnates everything that turns our blood cold and gives us goose flesh. He is evil, he is death."[13]

That "breviary of hatred" composed day after day by the press and literature on the far right was complemented with praise for the great accomplishments of dictatorships. In fascist and fascistic speeches of the time, the France of the Front Populaire was depicted in the somber colors of decadence: demographic decline, alcoholism, "Jewish invasion," intellectualism. Céline's *Bagatelles pour un massacre*, and later Rebatet's *Les décombres* (The debris), expressed this physiological disgust for a vilified people. During the same period, the books of Drieu La Rochelle and Brasillach, which diagnosed the same physical and moral ruin of the country, appealed to the heroic ideal of the warrior, sang the praises of the body, fresh air, sports, action. That provided Brasillach with "antibourgeois" excerpts such as this: "Grave persons, loudly proclaiming their rights—'what-is-mine-is-mine'—protested against hitchhiking, which Germans and Americans have practiced for twenty years. They obviously did not have the fascist spirit."[14] For these intellectuals, fascism challenged communism—which claimed to incarnate "the youth of the world"—on its own terms.

Uniforms and Military Maneuvers

That fascist state of mind, which combined juvenile romanticism and aristocratic aesthetics with anti-Marxism, the most hateful anti-Semitism, and the exaltation of hierarchical power, thus spread in relatively strong doses among the right wing of the country. It is not accurate to say that people on the left were completely immune to it, as attested in the scission of the "neosocialists," who left the Section Française de l'Internationale Ouvrière (French Committee of the Workers' International, SFIO) with Marcel Déat in 1933. One of these neosocialists, Montagnon, declared at the Mutualité at the thirtieth congress of the Socialist party in July 1933: "The birth of fascism, the force of fascism, comes from the need that seems obvious everywhere for a strong state, a powerful state, a state of order." A full-scale pacifism and visceral anticommunism also led a certain number of unionists and leftist personalities to positions fairly close to fascist formulations. The failure of the Front Populaire, which disintegrated in 1938, only encouraged them. From this point of view, the evolution of Gaston Bergery and his weekly *La Flèche* is telling. In 1939, he expressed his anticapitalism as follows: "It is certain that Léon Blum, taking a break in 1937, achieved a gesture of submission that neither Mr. Hitler nor Mr. Mussolini could have achieved." Finally, it was a former Communist, Jacques Doriot, who created the most influential fascist organization: the Parti Populaire Français (French populist party).

Between 1933 and 1936, at least five fascist or fascist-style organizations were created:

1. Solidarité Française (SF, French solidarity), founded in 1933 by François Coty, a perfumer, who was the financial source for many newspapers and organizations on the right up until his death in 1934.

Bernanos said aptly of him: he was a Birotteau who took himself to be a Caesar. With the help of *L'Ami du Peuple* (The people's friend), a populist and xenophobic daily he launched in 1928, he acquired a following. At his death, Major Jean Renaud took over the leadership of Solidarité Française, whose members were among the most active on 6 February. The militia of SF wore the requisite blue shirt, boots, a military belt, and saluted "in the old manner." A panoply of ranks, badges, and armbands added even more to the martial appearance desired in these elite corps. Solidarité Française did not survive long after the measure of dissolution enacted against it and the other leagues in June 1936.

2. Francisme (Francism) was created in September 1933 by Marcel Bucard, a veteran wounded in the war, who had been part of Valois's Faisceau and had worked with Gustave Hervé at *La Victoire*. An admirer of Mussolini, Bucard was received by the Duce in Rome in September 1935. He brought together several thousand faithful, the most active of whom paraded around in blue shirts, sailor's bandannas, shoulder belts, and Basque berets. The party was dissolved in June 1936, but on 11 November 1938 Bucard, who in the meantime had spent time in prison, founded the Parti Unitaire Français d'Action Socialiste et Nationale (French unitary party of socialist and national action). Its manifesto announced the dual objective of the battle: "Against both the plutocratic reaction and Judeo-Marxism." In 1941, Bucard gave that party new life under the name Parti Franciste (Francist party).

3. Parti Populaire Français (French populist party). Jacques Doriot drifted away from communism and toward fascism in several stages.[15] An early member of the Front Populaire, he was excluded from the Communist party. Thanks to the popularity he had acquired in Saint-Denis, where he served as mayor, Doriot at first attempted to intervene between the Communists and the Socialists by means of the "Rayon Majoritaire de Saint-Denis" (Majority line of Saint-Denis). But the rapprochement and final agreement among Communists, Socialists, and then Radicals eventually excluded him from the unified group he had initially wanted. In the election of April 1936, he defeated the Front Populaire candidate. On 23 June, on the basis of his success, he founded the Parti Populaire Français, which over two years gained a certain following. The working-class base in Saint-Denis gave his party a proletarian foundation, while his eloquence as a public speaker singled him out as the new Mussolini. Intellectuals were captivated and joined with him: some, like Henri Barbé, had earlier been communists; others, like Paul Marion, had also spent time in the Socialist party; still others, like Claude Jeantet, came from Action Française. Alfred Fabre-Luce, Bertrand de Jouvenel, and Drieu La Rochelle are still the best known of the members. Thanks especially to

Pierre Pucheu, director of export services in France's iron and steel industry, Doriot received financial aid from industrialists and management associations, complemented by subsidies from Fascist Italy.

Unlike the two previous organizations mentioned, the PPF was successful in becoming a mass party. Its membership is usually estimated at 100,000, though the true militants were significantly fewer in number. They did not have to wear a uniform, but needed only a badge. In addition, their party did not declare itself fascist. All the same, they saluted "in the Roman manner"—a gesture in opposition to the raised fist of the Front Populaire. They had an anthem, *France, libère-toi* (France, liberate yourself) and they took an oath—not to mention the giant portrait of Doriot displayed at every meeting.

In 1938, the Munich accords and the discovery of the financial ties with Italy provoked dissension within the PPF. That was the beginning of a lasting crisis, which Doriot's party survived only with the help of the war and the collaboration.

4. CSAR, or La Cagoule (The Cowl). The Comité Secret d'Action Révolutionnaire (Secret committee for revolutionary action), founded in 1936, belongs more to the history of secret societies than to the history of fascism. Many of its members, however, embraced fascist ideas. After the victory of the Front Populaire, it was created by renegades from Action Française who were decided on action, in particular Eugène Deloncle and Jean Filliol. A company director, graduate of the Ecole Polytechnique, and a veteran who was decorated several times, Deloncle was particularly at ease in the world of conspiracies, oaths, and mysteries. For him, it was important to use clandestine action to fight the three designated enemies: Bolshevism, the Jew, and Freemasonry.[16]

La Cagoule, in possession of funds, weapons, and ammunition, turned to its own account a certain number of activities: sabotage of airplanes passing through France on their way to Republicans in Spain, and the execution of the Rosselli brothers, antifascist militants who were refugees in France. The ultimate goal, however, was a coup d'état. To that end, La Cagoule needed to draw in a part of the army. In March 1937, Marshal Franchet d'Esperey intervened to bring together Deloncle's plans and the activities of Major Loustanau-Lacau. The latter had created a "Corvignolles network," also called the "Cagoule Militaire," whose purpose was the surveillance and expulsion of communists in the army. But Loustanau refused to participate in any putschist movement. Without becoming discouraged, La Cagoule—after a few provocative attacks, against the headquarters of the Confédération Générale du Patronat Français (General confederation of French employers) on 11 September 1937, for example—decided on a show of force for the night of 15–16 November. Lacking the

support of the army, anticipated until the very end, the operation was finally canceled. The leaders of La Cagoule were arrested shortly thereafter.
The war set them free. One of these "Cagoulards" became particularly
well known under the Vichy regime: Joseph Darnard, head of the Milice.

5. Dorgères's Chemises Vertes (Greenshirts), a peasant fascism. Henri
d'Halluin, son of small tradespeople, journalist for the agricultural press
under the pseudonym "Henry Dorgères," became well known in March
1935 during an electoral campaign where he was barely defeated for the '
seat Camille Chautemps had just vacated after his election to the Senate.
Within a few months, he had become the eloquent leader of Défense
Paysanne (Peasant defense), where he was able to regroup regional peasant committees of defense, whose origins went back to 1929. At the time,
these groups were directed against the social security program. Propagan-
dizing a rural mythology against the "tyranny of cities," violently antista-
tist ("the government worker is the enemy"), anti-Marxist, and xenophobic, the Dorgères movement took on a fascist aspect with the creation of
Jeunesses Paysannes (Peasant youth). Dressed in green shirts decorated
with a badge (a pitchfork and scythe crossed against a bundle of wheat),
they sabotaged the meetings of adversaries and prepared to establish a
"peasant dictatorship," by means of which France would rediscover its ancient virtues.

The apogee of the movement was reached between 1936 and 1938.
The West, the North, the Paris region, the Nice region, and Algeria were
the most affected by Dorgérism, which could count on several tens of
thousands of members, of which about ten thousand were truly active. It
is to be noted that its influence reached beyond the world of notables and
small farmers; Dorgérism succeeding in integrating a good number of
salaried agricultural workers.[17]

Militarism and Corporatism

These movements, whether avowedly fascist or not, all turned to their
own account the Valois synthesis (fascism = nationalism + socialism),
varying the content but retaining fairly clear constants. These organizations emerged from the global crisis of the 1930s; they claimed they were
leading France out of decadence. Against external threats (the restoration
of Italy and Germany, the Soviet danger), they denounced the weakness
of the country: the parliamentary regime, class struggle, the communist
threat. The shared goal of their nationalism was to change the regime, put
in place a strong state capable of commanding respect from the outside
world, and reestablish and maintain order within the country. Sooner or
later, that nationalism turned the anti-Jewish panacea to its own account.

For Jean Renaud of Solidarité Française, the existence of an "Aryan race" rested only on "unverified hypotheses"; nonetheless, he denounced the "occult powers of the Jewish internationale, the Jew's control over the mind, thoughts, and work of the nation." "From pornographic literature to financial scandals to revolutionary meetings, there is always at least one Jew involved."[18] Although anti-Semitism appeared in Franciste propaganda only in 1938, Marcel Bucard quickly made up for the "delay": "hunting Jews" became an obsession with him. *Le Franciste* of 4 June 1936 declared that "the Front Populaire is a Jewish invention"; in 1938, Bucard published his declaration of war: *L'emprise juive* (Jewish ascendancy). Jacques Doriot professed no anti-Semitism in the early days of the PPF. With the advent of the Spanish civil war, however, his newspaper, *L'Emancipation Nationale* (National emancipation) began to speak of "Judeo-Bolsheviks." Imperceptibly, the organ of the PPF joined the anti-Semitic chorus, at first mezza voce, then fortissimo. On 23 July 1938, Drieu La Rochelle published an article in that newspaper entitled "A propos de l'anti-Sémitisme" (Regarding anti-Semitism), which said: "We cannot accept the fact, given the current inadequacy of mores and laws, that so many Jews hold the levers of command in the administration and politics." In the months that followed, the expressions "Judeo-Marxism" and "Jewish clan" became commonplace. Between *Le Droit de Vivre* (The right to life) directed by Bernard Lecache, president of the Ligue Internationale contre l'Anti-Sémitisme, and Doriot's *L'Emancipation Nationale*, the war was decidedly under way.[19] As for the writers of *Je Suis Partout*, who declared themselves openly fascist, they illustrated their age-old anti-Semitic virulence through the welcome they reserved for Céline's *Bagatelles pour un massacre*: "Democracy, everywhere and always, writes Céline in his dazzling [book], is never anything but a smoke screen for the Jewish dictatorship."[20] These journalists, direct heirs to Drumont, placed a wreath on the wall of the Federates for the anniversary of Bloody Week, even as they outdid one another in their verbal aggression against the Jews. It is as if, in France, the fascist current needs to wallow in the swamps of anti-Semitism at one time or another.

Every fascist organization proclaimed it was anticapitalist, but its "socialism" never went so far as to condemn private property. The social ideologies of the various fascisms were very clearly directed toward the middle classes: for Solidarité Française, the laborer had to "be facilitated as much as possible in acquiring property"; for its part, the PPF proposed "the maintenance and defense of all middle-class, peasant, artisanal, commercial, and industrial activities, which constitute the very essence of the nation." These preindustrial themes were often complemented by a nostalgia for the France of villages. Francism recommended the "return to the land," the "repopulation of the countryside," the "reorganization of rural life," while Dorgères made this return the great myth of his movement.

And what about socialism? For every group, the solution to social problems was corporatism. The class struggle, the confrontation between unions and employers, collectivist ideals had to come to an end. On the economic plane, corporatism was national unity realized through the harmonious collaboration between classes organized into professions. The state had to have the power of arbitration. It also had to take care of social programs in the general interest: social hygiene, sports, urbanism, housing—"in such a way," said the PPF, "as to engender a stronger, healthier race."

Diverse fascist organizations again recuperated the term "socialism," but this no longer had very much to do with the conceptions of Sorel and Valois. These men had defended the principles of trade unionism, which was supposed to remain free. For their part, the fascists of the 1930s dreamed of keeping the working class in line within corporatist institutions that would exclude workers' organizations proper. Italy and Germany became the models: "There are no more strikes over there!" The fascist equation—nationalism + socialism—was now just algebraic advertising.

What About the Croix-de-Feu?

We have not yet spoken of a movement that in the eyes of leftist militants of the 1930s, symbolized the fascist danger in France even more than the organizations already mentioned: the Croix-de-Feu (Cross of Fire). When this group, following its dissolution in June 1936, became the Parti Social Français (French social party), it was by far the largest of the new political organizations of the time, with as many as 700,000 members. But whatever the inclinations of one or another of its members—who, in fact, often moved on to groups with more "muscle"—La Rocque's party cannot be considered fascist, because it was careful to remain within strictly legal bounds and it defended a program more conservative than "revolutionary."

In the beginning, it was simply a veterans association like so many others. It was only when Comte François de La Rocque, son of General Raymond de La Rocque and himself a retired military man, became president of the Croix-de-Feu in 1931 that the association was gradually transformed into a mass movement. In 1933, it was opened to everyone through the creation of the Ligue des Volontaires Nationaux (League of national volunteers). After the events of 6 February, at which time the Croix-de-Feu refused to cross police roadblocks—La Rocque said he opposed "contagions of madness"—the movement attracted volunteers whose numbers continued to rise.

Some called the Croix-de-Feu "fascist" because it soon constituted the most powerful anticommunist organization; because it practiced the cult of the leader; because it also included shock groups—the Dispos—with a military organization, both a police force and a battalion for defense against Bolshevik subversion.

The PSF, established on 10 July with La Rocque as president and Jean Mermoz as vice president (Mermoz was killed shortly thereafter in a plane crash), retained the characteristics of the Croix-de-Feu movement, except that it now declared it was resolved to seize power through the ballot box, whereas the league had not put forward official candidates in the 1936 elections.

Virtually everything about the PSF tended to make it a French fascist party: its clientele from the middle classes, the financial support La Rocque may have obtained from big industry, the organization's militant anticommunism and antisocialism. But Colonel de La Rocque, brought up in a Christian socialist environment, left a mark more traditionalist than fascist on the ideology and practices of his party. His rejection of violence (even though, during certain demonstrations, for example in Clichy in March 1937, brawls broke out, leading to injuries and deaths), his rejection of anti-Semitism (even though, among the rank and file, many Croix-de-Feu shared the fascists' racism), his fervent Catholicism, and the themes of the conservative right, though steeped in the military spirit and the veteran mystique he lauded, made his organization what might be called a conservative mass party. Such was the novelty of the time in relation to the old right: the future of the country was not to be left to the general staff and the politicians; the people ought to be actively associated with it. Even better, they ought to be mobilized and to stand ever ready. Like Mermoz, La Rocque naively wanted to apply military solutions to political life, which led René Rémond to call the movement "political boy scouts."

La Rocque, however, played an appreciable role in the failure of fascism in France, in that, polarizing most of the Front Populaire's opponents on the right (and even the far right), he maintained complete autonomy and did his best to protect his flock from the contamination of fascist movements. This was clear in June 1937, when he refused to join the Front de la Liberté (Freedom front), which Doriot had created to curb the Communist party and the Front Populaire. At a meeting held at the time, La Rocque frankly declared: "Joining the Front de la Liberté would have meant closing our doors to popular recruitment. And we would have been classified as fascists—which we do not wish at any price."[21] Doriot had anticipated attracting the Croix-de-Feu in order to infiltrate them: the victory of fascism was undoubtedly depending on it. But La Rocque held firm and the PPF disintegrated.

Epilogue

Thus at the end of 1938, with the wave of social fear triggered by the Front Populaire subsiding, fascist movements were struggling to survive. On the eve of war, Daladier's France had reestablished a certain political stability. But is the break represented by the Front Populaire enough to explain the failure of fascism in France? That organization certainly contributed toward it but the example of Italy, which saw the rise and victory of fascism *after* and not *against* the revolutionary wave of 1920–21, ought to lead to a certain circumspection.

In fact, fascism was unable to take root in France because the French right was able to remain strong *within* republican legality. The usual clientele of various kinds of fascism—the middle classes, artisans, business people, employees, farmers—was quite large in France. But in large measure, these middle classes clung to republican traditions, still powerfully incarnated in the Radical party and in Marin's Fédération Républicaine (Republican federation). Economically, these social strata were affected by the crisis; socially, they were as opposed to the power of the "trusts" as they were to "collectivist" solutions. That dual rejection was expressed in a great diversity of political choices, however. Depending on the region and the cultural environment, members of these middle classes were either attracted to authoritarian solutions (but to La Rocque rather than Doriot) or faithful to a certain idea of the republic, that of their fathers or teachers.

The words of a respondent to a poll will illustrate this point. The man was a grocer from the outskirts of Paris, and he was reading Gustave Hervé's *La victoire* (written by the man who in 1936 published the premonitory brochure *C'est Pétain qu'il nous faut*); he held Blum up for public condemnation, and so on. He was asked if he was a Croix-de-Feu, like his neighbor the butcher. "Oh, no sir," he said, "I have always been *republican!*" The butcher in question, had he been present, would have sworn to high heaven that, for him as well, the republic was sacred.

Neither in Italy nor in Germany could those who were attracted to Fascism or National Socialism have had such reflexes. Although there were Marxist influences—circumscribed, however, within working-class and intellectual milieus—what we call democratic traditions did not exist. The Weimar Republic had been rejected from the beginning by a large proportion of public opinion, and was accused of being the product of a foreign diktat. As for Italy, universal suffrage had been established there only in 1919.

Since the 1890s, the French right, come what may, had accommodated itself to the parliamentary republic; it had in part colonized it. It was within that political framework that business people could prosper; that the petty bourgeoisie could protect its interests against the "big guys"; that workers could defend their class organizations; that employees could hope that their children would rise in social status, thanks to the virtues of secular schooling; and so on.

It is true that toward the end of the nineteenth century, the industrialization of the country, the boom in department stores, the rural exodus, and the progressivebookmark destructuration of village society began to call republican harmony into question. World War I, the Bolshevik revolution, and the crisis of the 1930s completed the upheaval, but not to the point of calling into question a political framework that, despite its weaknesses and corruption, at least allowed the different social strata the illusion that they were living in a free and peaceful country.

Fascism, however, entails imperialism. It entails war as a means of government, a collective ethic, and a national myth. A fascist nation is a militarized nation. French squads were hardly designed for war—as the Italian *squadristi*, German storm troops, and Spanish Falangists were. After 1918, France no longer had any conquests to make. French fascism might declare itself nationalist, but it was no use: it was pacifist, at least toward Germany, the source of danger. That was not the least of its contradictions.

Only war—imposed from the outside and lost—put fascism back in the saddle. Deloncle created the Mouvement Social-Révolutionaire, or MSR (Social revolutionary movement), which asserted it was "national," "socialist," and "racist," and declaimed against the Jews, "international bankers for whom the war is the main source of profits." Déat launched the Rassemblement National Populaire, or RNP (National populist rally), through a brief accord with Deloncle in January 1941; he took on the task of giving his movement a certain doctrinal coherence, which led to the publication of *Le parti unique* (The only party) in 1941. A graduate of the Ecole Normale, an *agrégé* in philosophy and former Socialist, he was now squarely in the camp of fascist anti-Semitism: "The problem, the sole problem, is thus to make the French people understand the need for a systematic and resolute defense against Jewish infiltration."[22] The French, he added, "will also make the very opportune reflection that our people, more than others, need to remake themselves biologically, that they are lacking in both quantity and quality, that the precautions taken by cattle raisers would be usefully applied to the raising of human young, French young, and that the purity of the race is the first condition for any demographic recovery."[23] For his part, Doriot relaunched the PPF and vied with Déat in the headlong rush toward collaboration, appropriating not only Hitler's ideas but even the German uniform. Bucard's Francism became unreservedly nazified. In the 27 December 1941 issue of his weekly, *Le Franciste*, we read: "In 1939, 300,000 Jews are living in French territory;

5,000 have already been deported. When will we decide to lock up and eliminate the 295,000 who remain?" That fanaticism was far from isolated; it was also that of the editorial staff at *Je Suis Partout*, of which Rebatet was a member. We read in *Les décombres*, which Rebatet published in 1942, at a time of round-ups and deportations: "Jewry offers the sole example in the history of humanity of a race for whom collective punishment is the only just punishment."[24]

These were now only imitative forms of fascism, venting their spleen and hatching their little plots under the protective wing of the German eagle.

Following the implacable logic of the situation, all these nationalists placed themselves in the service of a foreign nationalism, ironically enough, that of the "hereditary enemy." And Hitler preferred the collaboration of the marshal and patriarch, who was granted full powers in July 1940, to these incarnations of failed fascism. Pétain repeated the formula once launched by La Rocque: "Travail, Famille, Patrie" (Work, Family, Nation). The marshal's regime did not show the same prudence as the colonel's party, however. It made anti-Semitism law, an act that, along with other counterrevolutionary measures, instituted a break with 1789. In 1943, when La Rocque was deported to Germany after providing information to British intelligence, Pétain allowed the creation of the French Milice, whose future leader Darnand soon declared his "desire to see a national and socialist authoritarian regime installed in France, which will allow France to be integrated into the Europe of tomorrow."

I mentioned above what the "socialism" of French fascists had become; the ordeal of 1940–44 allows us to assess their "nationalism." Lucien Rebatet, trained in the school of full-scale nationalism, expressed its utter relativity in an article in *Je Suis Partout* on 28 July 1944: "I admire Hitler. We admire Hitler, and we have very serious reasons for doing so. . . . It is he who will go down in history for having liquidated democracy."

Decidedly, Valois's formula was no longer in season. But Valois himself, on the eve of his death in the Bergen-Belsen deportation camp, had long since ceased to be "fascist."

Fascism is intimately connected to World War I and the upheavals it caused, which led to the crisis of the 1930s. It is noteworthy, however, that the political, if not the linguistic, formulation of fascism was elaborated before 1914; that in France a certain number of attempts were made to ally a revolutionary working class with counterrevolutionary social strata and spiritual communities; and that anti-Semitism was used as the spark for the mixture. The fires set in France were only minor, and the violence usually remained verbal. The French political system remained solidly organized around ideological communities that had been set in place throughout the nineteenth century.

Although the fascist threat became more serious between the two world wars, and particularly in the 1930s, especially because of the real difficulties and vague apprehensions felt by the middle classes, the fact is that France successfully resisted it. In France, fascism was above all a state of mind among one section of public opinion; the organizations that more or less followed its model remained fairly weak.

Some have argued that the attenuated form taken by the economic crises in France spared it the fascist temptation. That is possible but only to a certain degree, since the examples of England and the United States, where the crisis was violent but did not threaten democratic institutions, show very well that other factors, belonging in particular to the heritage and cultural habits of the different nations, were at work. Socially speaking, the success of fascism rests on two groups of unskilled workers: the impoverished and frightened petty bourgeoisie, and unemployed or about-to-be unemployed workers in nations only recently unified and without deeply rooted democratic habits. There is no doubt that in France 150 years of "republican spirit" and periodic resistance to counterrevolutionary efforts immunized the social body to a great extent. In addition, bellicose enthusiasm, the spirit of conquest, and imperialist aggressiveness, which lie at the foundation of fascism, were no longer current in France. In the end, pacifism dominated public opinion on the left and right. Perversely, however, pacifism had the effect—against which it was ill equipped to fight—of finally facilitating war, defeat, and thus the fall of democracy. But that is another story.

All the same, even though *internal* fascism never seriously threatened French institutions (the Pétainist dictatorship owed its existence solely to the military defeat, and vanished as soon as France was liberated), we must note that in France almost every attempt that could be called "fascist" turned anti-Semitic ideology, which was not lacking in continuity, to its own account. Setting aside the Faisceau, which had a long life, we might note that all the other figures of French fascism reactivated Drumont's formulations in one way or another. For about sixty years, with the exception of a lull during World War I, anti-Semitism never set down its arms in France. Indeed, the defeat of fascism was needed to wrest its final pretensions to legitimacy from it.[25]

CHAPTER 13

French-Style Fascism, or Fascism Nowhere to Be Found?

THE HISTORIOGRAPHY of contemporary France has long diagnosed our national allergy to fascism. That import product may have had a few fans—but far fewer than the yo-yo or the Charleston. The word "fascism" has been used and misused, it was a handy insult to hurl against a conservative or reactionary adversary; but we have never really known more than an embryonic fascism, imitations at the small-group level, at worst a literary fascism without direct consequences for our political destiny. Yet for several years, a completely opposite impression has prevailed. Perhaps the nation of Jaurès and Clemenceau provided fascist ideas with their most fertile soil. It is in France that these ideas originated; from France that they reached Italy and the rest of Europe. Zeev Sternhell's writings have played a key role in calling upon us to dispel an illusion, probably the result of self-censorship.[1]

Thus Sternhell has called into question René Rémond's classic study, *Les droites en France* (The right wings in France).[2] That book showed the birth, the coexistence, and the continuity of three distinct right wings: legitimist (or traditionalist), Orleanist (or liberal), and Bonapartist—three currents that over the years might mingle together, but whose separate identities were always identifiable. For Sternhell, that schema, acceptable until the beginning of the Third Republic, no longer functioned after Boulangism. That is because, and this is undoubtedly what the Jerusalem historian has demonstrated most forcefully, in the next-to-last decade of the nineteenth century, a *new right* emerged, whose first manifestations were populist anti-Semitism, led by Drumont, and the plebiscitary movement, incarnated by Boulanger.

New conditions contributed to the germination of that new-style right, whose incarnations can be followed up to the 1914 war: the definitive victory of the republicans against the monarchists and clericals, the reign of public liberties, the real beginnings of the workers' movement, and the economic difficulties and existential worries of the petty bourgeoisie. The mass era was beginning. The political game was no longer confined to the society of notables and the vigilance of prefects. The daily newspaper became a product of popular consumption. Politics displayed itself, became impassioned, and moved out into the streets. Public opinion was there for the taking. "Decent people," as they were called during Thermidor, were in the minority; the "populace" had the right to vote. Thus, for Sternhell, René Rémond's three right wings merged into two at the end of the last century. A conservative, more or less liberal right remained, rallying behind parliamentary institutions, supported by traditional solidarities. But there was also a new right, with revolutionary aspirations, a right in bad company, antibourgeois, even proletarian, a right that dreamed of bringing down the parliamentary republic in the name of patriotic and plebeian virtues.

That new right had, not exactly its own theorist, but its poet, in the person of the young Barrès—not the conservative and member of the Académie Française during the Sacred Union, but the Boulangist deputy, the journalist of *La Cocarde* (founded in 1894), the man who declared to voters in Nancy: "We need a Republic concerned with the democratic interests of workers, of the unhappy, in the place of that bourgeois oligarchy."

That new right had its combat organizations: Déroulède's Ligue des Patriotes, far removed from its Gambettist origins; the "friends of Morès," La Villette butchers in uniform who disrupted leftist meetings; Jules Guérin's Ligue Antisémitique. It had its union organizations: Biétry's Jaunes, which for several years defended class cooperation from an authentic working-class base. It had its orators: Drumont, elected deputy in Algiers in the midst of the Dreyfus affair; and especially Rochefort, Badinguet's old foe, a former Communard who rallied behind anti-Semitic nationalism, satisfying undemanding anti-Dreyfusards of the lower classes with puns on the front page of *L'Intransigeant*.

If we add the collection of new ideas represented by racist determinism and the various stand-ins for Darwinism, illustrated by Vacher de la Pouge, Jules Soury, and Gustave Le Bon, as well as attacks against positivism and the vogue for Bergson, we discover the extent to which the panorama of popular ideas had been transformed since the Second Empire. The themes of blood, race, and instinct monopolized the political discourse on the right, which rejected all the "cosmopolitanism" of the ancien régime.

But—and it may be at this point that we grasp the real fertility of fascist ideology—that new right was not content to battle its populist public on the left; it also attempted a rapprochement, an unexpected union, which was to seal its alliance with what Sternhell calls a new left. It is more appropriate to call it an ultraleft, inasmuch as it rejected the distinction between left and right, which it looked down on as an electoral and parliamentary issue. It proclaimed it was a *revolutionary* unionism. Action Française, coming out of the Dreyfus affair, attempted a "takeover" of the CGT; its militants on strike confronted Clemenceau's troops on Draveil's work sites and near Villeneuve-Saint-Georges. That takeover failed but left a few traces behind. Sternhell is intent above all on following the operation that he believes is of the greatest importance: the connections and shared plans between Georges Sorel and Edouard Berth—theorists of heroic unionism—and Georges Valois, an AF economist, encouraged for a time by Maurras, who was seeking the workers' backing. The idea for *La Cité Française*, an "antidemocratic and anticapitalist" magazine produced together, did not get beyond its first drafts, but a Cercle Proudhon, led by Valois and Berth, held its first meeting in December 1911. It published *Cahiers*, and the first issue appeared in 1912. In 1927, Valois said of it: "It was the first fascist endeavor in France." In his 1914 publication, *Les méfaits des intellectuels* (The misdeeds of intellectuals), Berth wrote: "Two synchronic and converging movements, one on the far right, the other on the far left, have begun the siege and assault on democracy, for the salvation of the modern world and the greatness of our Latin humanity."[3]

In reading these *Cahiers* and a certain number of writings contemporary to Sorel and Berth, we can in fact identify what might be called a prefascism. There we find an exaltation of the virtues of war and nationalism, a condemnation of the philosophy of human rights, a disdain for parliamentarianism, an anticapitalism, an anti-Semitism, and especially, an ethical insurrection against decadence and a call for heroism. "Humanity," writes Berth, "all steeped in love and sweetness—such are the times of great corruption—will fall to the distaff side; then violence and war must call it back to a healthier and more virile sense of reality." And Berth explains the program: "Violence calls for order, just as the sublime calls for the beautiful: Apollo must complete the work of Dionysus."[4]

As Sternhell himself recognizes, these endeavors, which had their counterpart in Italy[5]—Sorel had numerous admirers there—remained at the stage of laboratory experiments in France. And yet whatever the later variations in Sorel (who celebrated Lenin before his death), in Berth (who returned to revolutionary unionism after embracing communism for a time), or in Valois (who died in a Nazi deportation camp), France experienced the real signs and formulated some of the first theories of a fascism before the fact. Thus when Georges Valois founded his Faisceau in 1925, he was more justified than anyone in saying that he was not imitating Mussolini, but that on the contrary, it was Mussolini who took the idea of "fascism"—if not the word—from France: "The intellectual father of fascism," Valois said, "is Georges Sorel."[6] And he added: "Long before the war, there was someone who foreshadowed fascism, who gave it its first expression, and that was Maurice Barrès."[7] Along the way, Valois defined "the great originality of fascism": "to realize the fusion of the two great tendencies, nationalism and socialism, which in the nineteenth century were the first anti-individualist creations of European nations."[8]

The Faisceau had a brief life: it did not survive Poincaré's return to power. In the excellent chapter he devotes to Valois's "naive fascism," Sternhell analyzes its principal cause: especially in France, where the conservative right had sufficient leverage, the new fascist right "could not get through."

The game was not over, however. On the contrary. Even though the parliamentary republic was able to resist the global crisis of the 1930s, during that time fascist ideas, though not designated as such, proliferated and penetrated deeply into all currents of thought in France. All the originality of Sternhell's book lies in passing quickly over vulgar fascism, that of the manuals—small packs of booted men, Doriot's PPF, the writers of *Je Suis Partout*, not to mention the Croix-de-Feu bugaboo—in order to pause at length on the ravages of unconscious fascism, of fascists-unbeknownst-to-themselves. By turns, the author sifts through the ideas of the Belgian socialist Henri de Man, which were introduced into France by André Philip; the development of the neosocialist current, with Marcel Déat at its head; the central planning ideology that took shape in the SFIO and especially in the CGT; and finally, one of the sources of fascism as vibrant as it was misunderstood, namely, revisionism. Not Bernstein's or Jaurès's revision of Marx, since that revisionism remained democratic, but the revision of Marxism, either by the left (the early Sorel), or by the right (de Man and Déat), which led to socialism without a proletariat and without democracy. In addition to that source on the left, there was a source on the right, the symmetrical revisions of conservative nationalism, undertaken by the dissidents of Action Française, which called for a spiritual revolution against bourgeois and decadent France. That move "beyond nationalism" was best elaborated and expressed in the review *Combat*, to which Thierry Maulnier, Maurice Blanchot, Pierre Andreu, and a few other intellectuals representative of the new right contributed. Here and there, the fascist ideology went forward masked: Sternhell tracks it and flushes it out even in reviews that profess antifascism, such as *Esprit*. Mounier's review, because of its attacks on parliamentary democracy, bourgeois liberalism, and simultaneously, on Stalinist

Marxism, finds itself accused of having undermined in advance the resistance to the monster.

Verification for the year 1940: revisionists on the left, neosocialists, plannists, and other defectors from socialism and radicalism (Déat, Marion, Marquet, Bergery, and so on) joined the neonationalists on the right to rally behind Vichy, and even the collaboration. Even more conclusive: Emmanuel Mounier asked the Pétainist censor for authorization to again publish his review—it was provisionally granted—and the personalist philosopher was so satisfied to see bourgeois parliamentarianism and liberal individualism run aground that he gave his backing to the National Revolution. In Sternhell's view, these lapses of 1940 are so many a posteriori proofs of the operation of the revolution/counterrevolution, which had been at work in French society and thought since the end of the nineteenth century. For lack of something better, the convergence between the revisionist left and the radical right eventually gave birth to the Vichy regime.

I have given only a broad outline of Sternhell's thesis. Let me add that his *Ni droite ni gauche* (Neither right nor left) represents a substantial piece of work on the part of a remarkable researcher, supported by vast reading and primary sources. I have no quarrel with him on the professional level: his information is meticulous. Certain readers, who once participated in the events, have registered indignant protests: "No! We were not fascists." The outburst is pointless, since Sternhell has proposed to demonstrate precisely that fascism was not or was only incidentally where it claimed to be; that it was primarily active in its unconscious forms. The fascist component remained unconceptualized. In addition, I do not believe the author's argument can be undermined on the basis of a quarrel about sources or the memories of veterans. I feel it is necessary to engage in debate on another level, that of method and interpretation.

A first remark on the question of proportion. There seems to be no doubt that "fascist ideas" circulated in France; exaggerating their importance is a more debatable matter. If the unifying principle of fascist ideology is, in Georges Valois's formulation, the synthesis of nationalism and socialism, it is only fitting to wonder what the concrete sites of that synthesis may have been. Sternhell rightly speaks of the Cercle Proudhon, Valois's Faisceau, the review *Combat*. All in all, these ventures had only a mediocre influence or a brief life. Does not that brevity itself or the private nature of the endeavors have *at least* as much meaning as their existence? All specialists have a natural tendency to privilege their own *part*, to amplify its importance by detaching it from the *whole*, within which it objectively occupies only a secondary place. Thus it is clear that anti-Semitism had a specific importance within our modern history, greater than that of fascism, inasmuch as *La France juive*, *La Libre Parole*, and *La Croix* spoke to millions of individuals, whereas the *Cahiers* of the Cercle Proudhon or Thierry Maulnier's *Combat* reached only a few hundred initiates. The question of proportion is also at issue when in the study of a particular author, Sternhell excessively privileges what supports his thesis at the expense of the rest of the oeuvre, which does not. On this subject, I do not doubt that the objections Raoul Girardet raised regarding Sternhell's treatment of Barrès[9] will be made by others regarding Sorel or Henri de Man. I will not insist on that point, but let us not underestimate that effect of optical enlargement of a subject, as a very consequence of the author's work and talent.

In the same way, I wonder whether Sternhell does not introduce too much coherence into a great deal of confusion. Enumerating the cases of revisionism on the right and the left, critics of every stripe of liberalism, the parliamentary system, and Marxism, he ends up formulating this conclusion: "Fascism . . . possesses a solid conceptual framework. . . . It constitutes a system of ideas organized to direct political action, to command certain choices, and to shape the world."[10] Yet the "solidity" of the conceptual framework is precisely what leaves the most to be desired in the case of fascism, even when it is channeled into a unified current, as it was in Italy. Fascism was as marked by its tendency to maintain and cultivate haziness as Nazi racism and Soviet Marxism were marked by their ideological vulgate. Addressing diverse clienteles, fascism used the most contradictory discourses. As Sergio Romano says: "We have a tendency to imagine fascism as a coherent system born rather like Athena from the head of Jupiter. . . . That is an error. It is a system conditioned by the events."[11] No doubt, once in power, Italian Fascism sought cultural legitimacy and granted itself ideological legitimacy. The works of Benedetto Croce, Giovanni Gentile, D'Annunzio, and the Frenchman Sorel, in their antipositivism and neo-idealism, were seen to have paved the way for the Duce's triumphal march. In the nation of Gramsci, it is undeniable that the movement of ideas plays an active role in the historical process, but the very eclectic character of that prefascist culture, which only assumes that meaning retrospectively, ought at least to be noted.

In reading Sternhell, we have the impression that every thought, every publication, every individual who rejected received ideas and inherited structures in the France of the 1930s contributed more or less to the penetration of fascism. In fact, we ought to wonder whether the antirevisionists in every camp, whether all the vestals of the republican temple and the Marxist temple, were not in their way equally responsible for the final tragedy. I shall return to that idea. For the moment, even though I know that the historian's role is to introduce rationality into the chaotic appearance of the past, I contest the coherence of French fascism, which can only be a construction after the fact from scattered and heterogeneous elements, which no political movement has ever been able to bring together and unify in a lasting manner.

Once he has crystallized a coherent fascism, Sternhell does not merely confer a structure upon it; he also has it remain fixed over time. It is as if the act of breaking ranks necessarily set individuals on the path to Vichyism or collaborationism. Hence, when Henri de Man pronounced the dissolution of the Parti Ouvrier Belge (Belgian workers' party) in 1940 and discovered the German Occupation as a sort of divine surprise, such an attitude could only be the *natural consequence* of his earlier theoretical positions. In short, the die was cast as early as 1927, the year of de Man's *Au-delà du marxisme* (Beyond Marxism); de Man was already in the fascist camp. The same is true for Marcel Déat: the fact that he founded the fascist RNP in January 1941 is only the logical endpoint of the propositions advanced in 1930 in his *Perspectives socialistes* (Socialist perspectives), and a fortiori during the "neosocialist" crisis of 1933.[12] And so on. That teleological interpretation is unfortunately crippled by all the exceptions that contradict it. On one hand, it neglects all the other itineraries that led from the various "revisionisms" to the Resistance—those of André Philip, Robert Lacoste, and even Mendès France, for example. Why do these individual cases not "change anything" in the author's view? They are all the more interesting and significant in that an entire part of Resistance ideology was steeped in the sources of that antiliberal and antiparliamentary critique.[13] Conversely, we would need proof to the contrary that fidelity to the principles of the parliamentary republic could have prevented its defenders from rallying behind the National Revolution in 1940–41, a period privileged by Sternhell. Historians of the 1940s have not provided us with that proof.[14]

The clearest objection to be made to Sternhell's book has to do with the historiographical genre to which it belongs. It is a pure history of ideas, a history that is assumed to follow its own consistent movement, beyond the reach of general evolution and without direct relation to the events. Events, however, are not to be taken as simple revelations or catalysts for potential ideas; they also produce changes and reshuffle the political and social issues. From this point of view, it is striking to note the tenuous place Sternhell attributes to World War I in the genesis of fascism. Yet it was these four and a half years of war that provoked one of the greatest upheavals in history. How are we to imagine the triumph of fascism in Italy without the war and the crisis it provoked within all quarters of civil society and the state? And in the same vein, the birth and rise of nazism? Are we to believe that everything was decided before the general conflagration of 1914–18? Before World War I, what was in place (in a still modest place) was a cultural contestation of Enlightenment philosophy, a few formulations that the fascist movements exploited. This was a small thing in comparison to the seismic shift represented by the funeral march of war and the "peace" that followed: the end of public freedoms, the first outlines of totalitarian dictatorships, the setting loose of the death drive, unheard-of suffering, hopes raised and then dashed, the collapse of currencies, the Bolshevik revolution, the revolutionary fire that set Europe ablaze in 1919, the fear of communism, the expanding counterrevolution, particularly in Old Regime countries where rootless liberal democracies had been installed. And, in the face of the mounting corpses, the growing doubt about Western reason, the worsening pessimism about the future of Europe, the rise of irrationality on the ruins of a suicidal continent. The continuity of certain currents of ideas can be observed; but they seem ridiculous when compared to the state violence that was unleashed and the social convulsions it provoked, particularly among the middle classes, which in Italy and Germany were the designated prey of Fascism and National Socialism.

Fascism is in league with war. Not only do its protagonists emerge permeated with a nationalist, irredentist, and imperialist aggressiveness, but fascism also borrows its style from war, taking its uniforms, its attitudes, and its words from it. "The true chance of fascism," wrote René de Lacharrière, "came from a perfect historical conjuncture created at the time, between the militarization of internal politics characteristic of it and the international war it was preparing to confront. That conjuncture implied the popularity of an aggressive foreign policy."[15] There is no pacifist fascism. What was most lacking in French fascism was precisely that martial aggressiveness. In the France depicted by Giraudoux, which had no territorial ambitions, which had paid the ultimate price to recover its lost provinces, and which was proud of its colonial empire, it was understood by everyone that "the Trojan War will not take place."

A pure history of ideas proves disappointing in that it follows the logic of words without penetrating the resistance of things or the force of individual and collective reactions to the event. Historical idealism is as powerless as Marxist materialism to account for the fascist phenomenon. Materialists reduce fascism to a mere by-product of the defensive strategy of big capital. Idealists wish to make fascism into a system of ideas that has its own life and mechanically follows its deductive destiny.

If the only events worthy of consideration in the case of France are those of 1940–41—the fall of the Third Republic, the installation of the Vichy regime, the proclamation of National Revolution—then we must wonder whether these events betrayed nothing but the fascism, real or supposed, that had undermined French society and the intelligentsia since Barrès and Sorel. In the first place, the massive adherence to Marshal Pétain lay less—once more—in the ideas he defended under the banner of National Revolution than in a situation of catastrophic events: defeat, exodus, armistice, recourse to a providential leader. Out of a legitimate concern to grant ideas their role, we also need to inventory them with no holds barred. The spirit of the armistice did stem in part from the currents of thought listed by Sternhell, and the new regime that followed was inspired by antidemocratic and antiliberal ideology; it did not take a resolutely "fascist" form, however, which the defeat and Occupation prohibited. Moreover, in that republican crisis of conscience, a role must be granted to other intellectual factors. The resistance to fascism during the 1930s cannot be confused with a mere resistance to the surreptitious *ideology* of internal fascism; it is also, it is perhaps above all, resistance to the conquests undertaken by fascist states. From this point of view, it seems surprising that Sternhell deals so little with foreign policy and the varying degree of vigilance demonstrated by the different French political groups facing the true rise of fascism, the fascism that had already been incarnated in a state apparatus and that aspired to bend others to its will.

From that angle, the previously defined positions are turned upside down. They are no longer as "fascist" as they appeared at first sight. Conversely, in the collapse of the parliamentary republic, we find entrepreneurs of destruction who can in no sense be called fascist. In other words, it seems to me there is good reason to believe that the defense policy against the Hitlerian danger had more effect than the critiques of liberalism and Marxism; that the resistance to nazism beginning in 1933 more effectively defended the republican regime than the resistance to various forms of revisionism.

Sternhell cites Gustave Hervé and Emmanuel Mounier as among the agents of fascist penetration. The two have nothing in common. But both were critics of, among other things, parliamentary democracy and Marxist socialism. Beginning in 1912, Hervé, a former champion of revolutionary antimilitarism, evolved toward what he himself called "national socialism." In his newspaper *La Victoire*, as well as in the small, short-lived parties he founded between the two wars, he railed against "the regime of political assemblies," preached cooperation between classes and the restoration of authority. In 1935, he launched an appeal in favor of Pétain, the natural hero "we need." Yet despite the high coefficient of profascism we are tempted to attribute to him, we must recognize the lucidity and firmness he displayed in relation to nazism. Hervé may have protested the inflexible policy Poincaré inflicted on the Weimar Republic, but he was also just as outspoken against the foreign ventures of Hitler and the racism of the Nazi state. In July 1940, Hervé rallied behind Pétain, whom he had called for, but apparently on the basis of a misunderstanding: in May 1941, he retreated to silence.[16]

Nothing is simple in that war of ideas. Take Mounier's review, *Esprit*. It contains many ambiguities, and it certainly contains a discourse hostile to (bourgeois) democracy and (Radical-Socialist) parliamentarianism. That hostility, let us admit, might have contributed to the destabilization of the regime, at least in the universe of symbols. But *despite* this discourse, it would be wise to note *Esprit*'s attitude toward the war in Ethiopia, the war in Spain, the Munich capitulation, and the wave of xenophobia and anti-Semitism that swept over France during those years of crisis. On all these concrete problems, Mounier's review took a position that committed it to the resistance to fascism. Of course, Mounier did not avoid the misstep of 1940; he believed a policy "of presence" within the National Revolution was useful, at a time when, like so many others, he believed the outcome of the war decided. Yet are we not also obliged to mention that *Esprit* was banned in July 1941, and its director incarcerated by the Vichy police? Are these insignificant details?

No, nothing is so simple. To complete the picture, we must address the lapses of faithful democrats, undisputed liberals, and orthodox Marxists in the face of fascism. We must examine the attitude of the liberal or conservative right, most of whom, facing Hitler during the time of the Front Populaire, preferred to safeguard their class interests rather than remain faithful to their national vocation. We must pause to consider the powerful pacifist currents that made for the Munich spirit of the noncommunist left. We must not forget to take the Communists into account as well: the incessant war they waged against the Socialists until June 1934, and then, after five years of resolute antifascism, the approval they gave to the German-Soviet pact and the denunciation of the war against Nazi Germany as an "imperialist war." Such words and acts hardly contributed to the "republican defense."

It was not Pareto or Croce, Mosca or D'Annunzio, who were the quartermasters of fascism in Italy. Certainly their works offered justifications for the Mussolini revolution/counterrevolution. But fascism did not develop from books; it emerged from the fallout left by the great revolutionary wave of 1919–20. In the end, it triumphed by filling the void left by a liberal government in a state of advanced decomposition, without legitimate guardians, without resolute defenders.

All in all, Sternhell displaces the central problem of fascism: its conquest of power and the nature of the state it set up. In his search for the Platonic idea of fascism, he does not allow himself to analyze the conditions for its possible advent in France. And for good reason, since the event never took place. The whole paradox in this historian of ideas is that he studies fascist ideology in a country where, precisely, it did not triumph, and thus where it could not be corrupted by the compromises of power. In France, fascism existed in a pure state because it did not govern. Such is the originality of his approach, and such are the limitations of his enterprise. After all, in the beginning of fascism was not the word but, as Mussolini said, "action." Sternhell reverses the perspective; that is his right. That may also be his illusion.

CHAPTER 14

Socialism and Fascism

ON 26 AND 27 November 1983, the Club de l'Horloge (Clock club) held a colloquium on a comparative theme: "Socialism and Fascism: The Same Family?"[1] The suggested kinship, even in the doubtful form given it, signaled the nature of the enterprise from the outset: to attack the ruling ideology in the area it believed itself the most secure. "Do not say you are antifascist, because you have many more points in common with fascism than we of the liberal right do." Q.E.D.

Let us leave aside the question of whether the Club de l'Horloge was as liberal as it wished to appear, and how long it had been so:[2] by definition, the club was timely, and the times, as we know, were those of triumphant liberalism. Let us confine ourselves to signaling the presence of the historians called upon to participate: François-Georges Dreyfus and Alain-Gérard Slama. They were not in agreement.

Dreyfus entitled his paper "Les sources socialistes du fascisme" (The socialist sources of fascism). It went straight to the point, without subtlety, but not without approximations. The polemical approach does not trouble itself with fine distinctions. For Dreyfus, "socialism" is not a polysemic term with referents as varied as Olaf Palme's Sweden and Stalin's Russia. In his view, it all amounts to the same thing; in particular, socialism amounts to national socialism. Since everything has been said within that socialist "family," he draws from one or another to suit the argument, draws so many proofs and so many elements as if from a sole source and a homogeneous philosophy. That modulated, differentiated, and appropriated use of socialist authors allows him to construct a crude genealogy of fascism, and his least contestable discovery is that socialism preceded it: the misdemeanor of paternity is thus confirmed. He has only to establish a short list of the components of fascism and to fish about within "socialist" culture for analogies, which are not lacking. Example: if you wish to demonstrate that fascism and socialism are both forms of superstatism, you will refrain from making reference to Proudhon. Take Déat instead. Conversely, the aforementioned Proudhon will be used in the chapter on anti-Semitism. And so on.

Alain-Gérard Slama's paper seems strangely out of place. For him, socialism is not a unified bloc: one need only examine the question of the state to measure the complexity of the responses given. We might add: the question of the party, the question of democracy, the question of revolution, and so many others. In addition, Slama underscores how fallacious it is to infer the socialist sources of fascism based on the individual itineraries of certain politicians, since they were by definition both defectors and marginals. He adds that in an apparent paradox, if socialism was part of the genesis of fascism, it came not from the "Marxist" family but from the "libertarian" family and its radical opposition to parliamentary democracy. In short, that paper raises doubts about the overly simplistic equations made by the other speakers.

If we try to forget all the underlying political motives and remain within the historian's field, the question of the relations between socialism and fascism may prove interesting, provided we do not mix everything together. From a macroscopic point of view, and within the realm of pure ideas far removed from any social and political practice, we can detect the seeds of totalitarianism within utopian thought. To live within the social perfection dreamed of by Morelly or Cabet does not correspond to our idea of freedom! In that sense, a certain intellectual voluntarism, the plan to revolutionize an imperfect society, to remodel it from top to bottom, in short, to create *the new man*, that project, both utopian and millenarian, is part of the totalitarian dream. Similarly, the regime we call "Soviet" by antiphrasis—which did not emerge fully armed from the head of Lenin (Is *The State and Revolution* a prefascist treatise?) but from a historical process that largely escaped the will of the founder—that regime, and particularly what it became under Stalin, displayed traits in common with what have been called totalitarian regimes. When the other states collapsed, it even became *the* totalitarian state if ever there was one, incontestable and long-lasting. There is a vast body of literature on that point, and reflections on it were only enriched throughout the 1970s. As far as I know, the colloquium at the Club de l'Horloge did not consider that homology. That is another matter. All the same, communism is something *different* from socialism, even if they have ancestors in common.

If we wish to return to socialism, to its *history*—and not merely to a few of its initial sources of inspiration—we must admit that, in France and elsewhere, it was an effective instrument for the democratization of political life. In France, socialism was made to fit the republican mold; Guesde as well as Jaurès accepted electoral competition. In fact, at a time when the danger of nationalism threatened the institutions of the parliamentary republic, party socialism made itself its guarantor, even when it had to ally itself with the representatives of the republican bourgeoisie against populist, anti-Semitic, and antiparliamentary demagoguery. I shall not go into detail about this well-known history, but let me say that democratic socialism, for which Jaurès was the privileged spokesperson, favored the integration of the working class into the system of liberal democracy. In other European countries, socialism did no less in this respect: it contributed decisively toward creating elementary democratic institutions, beginning with the establishment of universal suffrage, which had already taken place in France. In Austria, one of the very first objectives of the Social Democratic party, founded in 1888, was to establish universal suffrage, which was achieved following a long struggle, crowned by a general strike in 1905. That is only one example: in most European countries, socialist parties, whether or not they were Marxist in their ideology, worked for the installation of liberal democratic regimes, universal suffrage, and public and individual liberties. Subsequently, at the time of the Third Internationale, people got into the habit of calling these movements "social democratic" in a pejorative sense; they were more (in practice) or less (in theory) "revisionist" in relation to Marxist ideology. Granted! They were nonetheless socialist, in their formation as in their intentions. And in most European countries of the twentieth century, these socialist movements were the constant support of parliamentary regimes and the reign of freedom, against the rise of dictatorships—even if their effectiveness was sometimes doubtful. Generally speaking, socialism became one of the vital elements of the system in European democracies: it was the agent of compromise between social classes, facilitating an institutional balance between state interventionism and free enterprise. To suggest a filiation between that socialism and fascism because Déat or de Man became fascists, is the equivalent of making the Catholic Church one of the direct sources of Radical Socialism, on the pretext that Emile Combes had gone to a seminary. Let us move on.

The other socialism before 1914, libertarian, antiauthoritarian socialism, the unionism of direct action, socialism "from below," was in fact mentioned by Mussolini as part of the genesis of Italian Fascism. Especially in France, several convergences can be found between it and radicalism on the right before 1914. The "revolutionary right" and revolutionary unionism shared the tenet of *antidemocratism*. Their critique, however, did not have the same foundation: one denounced democracy in itself; the other, a pseudodemocratic system established to the advantage of the ruling class and at the expense of producers. But an alliance was imaginable. It was imagined against the common enemy: parliamentary democracy. This imaginable, imagined alliance (see Valois's efforts and those of the Cercle Proudhon) remained at the symbolic level, however. The vast majority of the troops and the vast majority of leaders of the CGT proved to be fundamentally faithful to the Third Republic, despite its "strike-breaking" governments.

Obviously, a great deal has been made of authors such as Sorel regarding the genesis of fascism: his antidemocratism, his anti-Semitism (but we know that Italian Fascism was not fundamentally anti-Semitic), his anti-intellectualism, which targeted the careers of socialist intellectuals, his Nietzschean exaltation of heroism, which had made him one of the champions of the general strike. Yes, no doubt, Sorel was one of the inspirations for the first Italian instance of Fascism, in the view of Mussolini himself. But what does Sorel represent within French socialism? Although Marxist in formation, he did not exert any real influence on the workers' movement; moreover, he broke with the plan for revolutionary unionism when he provisionally moved closer to Maurras.

The novelty of fascism was to assault liberal democracy with ideas taken from the left and the right. In fact, a certain number of anarchic unionists were the first combat *faisceaux*; and in fact, Mussolini was himself a former leftist socialist. Nonetheless, the filiation between revolutionary unionism and fascism is at the very least doubtful: a few "deviants" cannot implicate the whole of the CGT in the birth of fascism. Revolutionary unionism is the exact opposite of fascist corporatism. A shared group of adversaries (liberal democracy) does not constitute a shared political purpose. If socialism taken as a whole bears certain responsibilities for the installation of Italian Fascism, they lie in socialism's proven incapacity to oppose it: the maximalism and internecine divisions of the PSI weakened the defenses of a regime that liberal oligarchy and Catholic abstention had left defenseless.

We must therefore go back to the drawing board. The totalitarian nature of socialism—and communism is not simply a variant of it—remains to be demonstrated. In the French case, if we leave the marginals in their marginal place, it is clear that socialism was one of the forces that was gradually integrated into the democratic movement. Revolutionary unionism continued the critique of parliamentary democracy, but its kinship with the nascent Communist party (not beyond 1924) is better established than its relation to the incarnations of French fascism.

In conclusion, to state calmly, as François-Georges Dreyfus does, that "one might almost [*sic*] say that socialism is intellectually at the origin of fascism," is to indulge in the pleasure of ideological scrambling, since it suggests a common nature shared by two rigorously antagonistic systems. Of course, fascism—which constituted itself as a coherent doctrine gradually, and in a very eclectic manner—did not fail to borrow formulas and authors that may have belonged to socialist culture. But it was *against* that culture itself that it attempted to produce its own culture: authoritarianism, antiegalitarianism, nationalism, bellicosity. Above all, fascism wanted to resolve the contradictions of class through the construction of the "ethical state": "No individuals or groups (political parties, cultural associations, economic unions, social classes) outside the State. Fascism is therefore opposed to Socialism to which unity within the State (which amalgamates classes into a single economic and ethical reality) is unknown, and which sees in history nothing but class struggle. Fascism is likewise opposed to trade-unionism as a class weapon."[3] No one could state better than Mussolini the central opposition between fascism and socialism and the limits of the revolutionary unionist influence on the Duce's ideas. It is not merely a matter of ideas, however: Giacomo Matteoti's party has learned that painful lesson.

There is a crisis in socialist thought: it is not of recent date. The current "experiment" in government socialism has deepened that crisis. That is no justification for saying anything you like about socialism.

PART FOUR

Figures and Moments

CHAPTER 15

Boulanger, Providential Man

ONE HUNDRED years ago, in the aftermath of 14 July 1886, France as a whole became infatuated with a young general whose commoner's name became a symbol: Boulanger produced Boulangism, and since that time, Boulangism has been one of the categories of our political universe. It might be tempting to diagnose it as one of the shameful and endemic maladies of modern France, born of democratic mass culture. In the first place, it represents recourse to a providential man as the ultimate solution for a country too often torn apart, a country that irrationally relies on a Savior at hand. "*The soul of the mob,*" as Barrès said, is not entirely a dupe of its chimera, however, since Boulangism was also a movement demanding a new—more direct—democracy, in contrast to the republic of deputies. We must therefore examine this movement closely before labeling it, since its narrow meaning is ambiguous.

New Republic and Ancien Régime

On Sunday 27 January 1889, events were rising to a fever pitch in Paris. At stake was the legislative by-election in which, in accordance with the electoral law of the time, the entire department of Seine—the capital and its outlying areas—was participating. Except for one minor character, Citizen Boulé, nominated by a party of the socialist far left, the voters had to choose between General Boulanger and Jacques, chair of the regional council, who was also the Radical town councillor of Paris. If Boulanger were to win, who could answer for the immediate future of the parliamentary regime? On the other hand, if he were to be beaten, there would be some justification for predicting the decline and fall of that meteoric movement of public opinion called Boulangism. As citizens thronged to the ballot boxes, no one knew what the outcome would be: the city was so capricious, so nervous, and weighed down by so many living memories that anyone who could fathom its heart and mind must be very clever indeed!

Georges Boulanger, former minister of war, escaped the ordinary classifications of parliamentary politics. Since the arduous establishment of the Third Republic, two Frances had confronted each other: the proponents of the new republic and the partisans of the various ancien régime formulas; in short, the left and the right. But Boulanger was not part of that overly simple duality; he was on both the left and the right, or perhaps on neither the left nor the right. He wanted to place himself above the fray where the left and right exchanged blows; he intended to dissolve the distinction.

In that revolutionary city of legend, the paving stones beneath people's feet had been used in the construction of barricades not twenty years earlier. Voters equally hostile to Napoleon III and to MacMahon's Moral Order had installed Radicalism in the town hall. In that city, what could a general supported openly by the Bonapartist right and mezza voce by all the desires of conservative, monarchist, and Catholic communities hope for? Indeed, despite the favors coming from the right, who were a minority in the capital, Boulanger enjoyed the support of populist newspapers, including Rochefort's *Intransigeant*, which significantly broadened the horizon of his hopes. In addition, in other by-elections, in industrial departments such as Nord and agricultural departments such as Charente-Inférieure, votes that usually went to opposing candidates were now being united. Nonetheless, the Radical premier Floquet did not express a shadow of a doubt concerning the victory of Jacques, who was supported by both Radicals and moderate republicans, united in the resolution to fight Caesarism and deriving strength from a simultaneous defense of republican principles and public order. In Paris, Boulangism was in danger of coming to the limits of its success.

A Dazzling Career

During the long hours of waiting, Georges Boulanger was calm. Now that he had traded on so many hopes, he was no doubt assessing the path he had traveled since his birth in Rennes fifty-two years earlier. He had chosen a military career, and had been accepted to the Ecole de Saint-Cyr at seventeen. As a bright new second lieutenant, he had been sent to a baptism by fire in Algeria in 1857. There, Marshal Randon was undertaking the conquest of Great Kabylia, which was still in revolt. That campaign offered Boulanger a first occasion to display his bravery, in exchange for two slight wounds. Two years later, he participated in the Italian campaign against the Austrians; not far from Magenta, he received a bullet to the chest, which earned him the Legion of Honor and the rank of lieutenant. In 1861, Boulanger set off for Cochin China: he had hardly recovered from his Austrian wound when he took an Annamese bullet in the leg. Outcome: the rank of captain upon his return home in 1864.

The soldier temporarily yielded to the instructor: for half a dozen years, Boulanger exercised his talents as a leader of men with students at Saint-Cyr. According to testimony collected at the time of his later glory, the young captain distinguished himself from other leaders through his gusto and leniency. He soon became a major and was made a lieutenant-colonel of the 114th line during the Franco-Prussian War of 1870. In Champigny, he received another bullet wound, this time to the right shoulder: as a result, he was promoted to officer in the Legion of Honor in December 1870. Moreover, following battles he participated in outside Paris, he was made a colonel in January 1871. A few months later, at the end of the civil war against the Commune in Versailles, he received another wound, a bullet that struck his left elbow as he entered Paris with his men. That not only earned him another promotion in the Legion of Honor; it also meant he did not have to take part in the ruthless repression of Bloody Week. On Sunday 27 December 1889, many former Communards preparing to vote for him credited him for not having totally dirty hands. The man of multiple scars knew how to make the best of his wounds.

All the same, to be a colonel and a commander in the Legion of Honor at thirty-four is quite something, too much in fact. At least that was the view of the Commission de Révision des Grades (Commission on the review of rank), which, in late 1871, cleaning up after the excessively rapid promotions that occur during times of war and revolution, reduced Georges Boulanger to the rank of lieutenant-colonel. He was outraged to be demoted! He immediately sent his letter of resignation to General de Cissey, minister of war, who summoned the young officer, eased his resentment, and in the end got him to agree to withdraw his resignation. But the episode only revived the ambition of a man who believed he had been the victim of a terrible injustice.

Boulanger was not long in recovering his rank of colonel; it was granted in 1874. But by then, the adventure was over. Boulanger had to resign himself to garrison life, and under the reign of the Moral Order, though he had no religious feelings, he agreed to keep an aspergillum next to his saber. As part of the Seventh Corps, he did his utmost to obtain the favors of his leader, the Duc d'Aumale. Boulanger turned to him in January 1880, after the duke had become inspector of the army corps, to request a promotion to the rank of brigadier general. Even as he flattered the prince to gain his support, however, Boulanger also professed republican feelings and at times was savvy enough to crawl before Gambetta. Receiving the expected rank in May 1880, Boulanger expressed equal gratitude to both protectors.

Opportunism was never lacking in the ambitious Boulanger. In 1884, he was the youngest division general of his class. At that time, he was sent to command French troops in Tunisia, on which France had imposed its protectorate in 1881.

In Tunisia, Boulanger gave free rein to his unbridled inclination for ostentation, panache, and provocation. At every location, from one oasis to the next, he showed off, fraternizing with the kaids, inviting his junior officers to his table, forcing the admiration of the mob with his grand airs, his escort of spahis, and so on. That military power in full array could only annoy the civil resident, Paul Cambon. The conflict between the two men became obvious.

The presence in Tunisia of a large Italian colony was the source of endless friction between the Italians and the French military personnel. Following an incident at the Italian theater, Boulanger, ever a capitano, published orders urging his men to use their weapons in cases of aggression. A diplomatic incident was barely avoided. But the conflict between the two powers and between the two men brought Boulanger back to Paris while an inquiry was conducted. In January 1886, Boulanger learned he would not be returning to Tunisia: he was so to speak promoted to minister of war in the new Freycinet ministry. How are we to explain such a favor?

Ministerial Boulangism

For several years, the industrious Boulanger had already shown he could weave a network of relations within political circles. This had begun in earnest in 1882, when he was named to lead the infantry. In that post, as previously at Saint-Cyr, he had learned how to make his reformist zeal appreciated; at the same time, he never lost an opportunity to deliver heart-felt republican speeches, which he made every effort to have printed in the newspaper. That sense for publicity led to a familiarity with certain journalists. *La Lanterne, L'Evénement, La France,* and *La Nation* were Radical newspapers he could count on in the service of his glory. The parliamentary milieu had been opened to him; among others, Georges Clemenceau, his junior by three years and a fellow graduate of the Lycée de Nantes, and his friend Félix Granet, a Radical deputy, were sympathetic toward him.

As a result, it is not surprising that Boulanger obtained a minister's portfolio. After the 1885 elections, the Chamber contained only coalition majorities, over which the Radicals now exercised an arbitrating function. Clemenceau, anxious to republicanize the state apparatus, intended to obtain passage of military reform. Boulanger had the attribute, still unusual in the army, of displaying republican convictions. The Radical leader succeeded in convincing Freycinet to make him his minister of war.

A National Army

As a minister, Boulanger had two missions: first, to realize the reform in process, and in particular to create a true national army through compulsory service; and second, to purge the ranks of the army of the regime's enemies. Although the first part of the program was realized only after Boulanger's departure, upon his arrival the ministry did move toward several changes that elicited protests from conservatives. That was only the beginning.

In June 1886, after an excessively garish reception given by the Comte de Paris in the salons of the Hotel Galliéra, a law expelled heads of families who had reigned in France, as well as their direct heirs. An article of that law prohibited members of these families from joining the armies of land or sea. Boulanger interpreted that article in the most restrictive manner, dismissing Prince Murat, the Duc de Chartres, the Duc d'Alençon, the Duc de Nemours, and even the Duc d'Aumale, his former protector, from the army. The duke protested to the president of the Republic. Boulanger's reply was to proceed with the prince's expulsion. The royalists issued a challenge to the Chamber. Somewhat later, in August, *Le Figaro* published a letter that the fierce republican Boulanger had sent half a dozen years earlier to the Duc d'Aumale, whom he addressed as "His Grace" and in which he expressed his "profound gratitude" for the rank of general he had attained. Other letters followed in different newspapers, which at the very least nuanced the figure of that guardian of the republican temple. But by then, Boulanger had accumulated enough admiration to brave such revelations.

That fervor, which focused on his person, was brought about by a certain number of measures he had taken in favor of the army and the soldiers: improvement in the food, permission to wear beards, adoption of the Lebel rifle. But certain words and attitudes had had an even greater effect. Thus during the miners' strike in Decazeville, after an engineer named Watrin had been defenestrated, Boulanger was called to accounts by the Chamber on the army's role. Far from using the language of repression, he spoke in terms of civil peace: "Perhaps at the present time every soldier shares his soup and his ration of peace with a miner." The minister had held out his mess tin to the strikers, a gripping image that remained engraved in people's minds for a long time. "With those words," wrote Maurice Barrès, "the principles of humanity and fraternity, ordinarily so vague and entirely abstract, mere purple prose, made their way into real life."

"General Revenge"

General Boulanger became the darling of a people badly in need of a hero. The apotheosis took place on 14 July 1886. During the inspection organized at Longchamp, the soldier's histrionics were on full display. Wearing a cocked hat with plumes and white trousers and riding a black palfrey, he caused a sensation when he stood impeccably still in front of the presidential podium. On the way back to the Elysée from the racecourse, the president of the Republic was eclipsed by the glorious minister, who was met by an enormous ovation. That very evening, the cabaret singer Paulus created the song that was to do so much for the general's renown: "En revenant de la revue" (Returning from the inspection). Cheerful and contented, the people began to speak of "Boulangism."

Among whose who set to work to create excitement about Boulanger, Paul Déroulède played a major role. That martial poet had been at the head of the Ligue des Patriotes since 1882; a well-organized movement, it included many militants capable of rapid mobilization. The league was very republican in the beginning, setting for itself the goal of preparing minds and bodies for revenge against Germany in a Gambettist spirit, but it evolved along the way, as its leader became convinced of the need for a revision of the constitution. Revenge had to be subordinated to that revision. Ministerial instability, weakness of the executive power, and division among the French people were so many handicaps to the great cause. Déroulède conceived the plan for a plebiscitary republic able simultaneously to grant all its sovereignty to universal suffrage and all its power to state leadership. That was the idea, and Boulanger very opportunely became its incarnation. Radicals had called for him because of his republicanism; now he was acclaimed for his patriotism. The Schnaebelé affair was to cap the legend of "General Revenge," as he was called.

In early 1887, when Boulanger was still minister of war in the Goblet cabinet, which had been constituted in December 1886, tensions suddenly mounted between France and Germany. Bismarck, to defend his projected military budget before the Reichstag, evoked the danger represented by Boulanger. In April, Schnaebelé, a French supply officer, fell into a trap set by the Germans near the border, perhaps even on French territory. The French government demanded an explanation, which was not forthcoming. The press became excited; immediately, there was talk of a probable war. It was only ten days later, after an investigation, that Bismarck announced the liberation of the French government employee.

Boulanger had manifested a certain impatience, but he had no role in the chancellor's decision. Nonetheless, the decision was judged to be a retreat, caused entirely by the steadfastness of the minister of war. A cry went up: Boulanger had given Bismarck a fright. General Revenge was becoming General Victory, and hack poets did not hesitate to present their dreams as realities: "Look! He's all smiles as we watch him pass:/ He has just delivered Lorraine and Alsace."

The minister general began to be troubling. Jules Ferry became the spokesperson for the Opportunists—moderate republicans—and warned Jules Grévy, president of the Republic, that the braggart had to be gotten rid of. The idea of bringing about a change of ministry in order to have a change in the minister of war traveled the corridors of the National Assembly. Rochefort debated the matter in the columns of *L'Intransigeant*: "On the evening Boulanger is overthrown, twenty thousand men will roam the boulevards crying, 'Down with the traitors' and 'Long live Boulanger.' Is it so certain that the troops trying to bring them to their senses will not go over to their side?"

Nonetheless, on 18 May 1887, Goblet resigned his ministry. The procedure envisioned by Ferry was triggered. There were some misfires, however. Thus, since a by-election was planned in Paris for 23 May, Rochefort had the idea of recommending that his readers, unhappy with the new ministerial crisis, add Boulanger's name to the list of Radical candidates. The popular orator's call was an all-out success: almost 39,000 ballots were marked with Boulanger's name. Then certain of the general's friends, especially the Radical senator Alfred Naquet, recommended a show of force to Boulanger. He rejected the advice and never accepted the idea, but the Elysée was alarmed. Maurice Rouvier, responsible for a new cabinet that excluded the troublemaker, secretly reached an agreement with the conservative right that it would remain neutral, in exchange for which Rouvier agreed to halt the secularization under way. On 30 May, the new ministry came together, as the crowd chanted in the boulevards: "C'est Boulange, Boulange, Boulange / C'est Boulanger qu'il nous faut, / Oh! Oh! Oh!" (It's Boulange, Boulange, Boulange, / It's Boulanger we need, / Oh! Oh! Oh!)

The Syndic of Malcontents

Boulangism was now an opposition movement. Originating on the left, carried along for some time by the Radicals, supported by the populist press, extolled by the orator Rochefort, defended by Déroulède's leaguists, Boulangism was also one of the first successes of promotion methods that welcomed in the mass era. Barrès, who introduced Boulangism into literature, avidly used the term "masses": Boulanger had come from the "*desire of the masses*." But since that desire now counted, it had to be instigated, excited. To that end, every means of communication was put to use: posters, drawings, almanacs, songs, lithographs, pipes with the general's face on them, Boulanger playing cards, packets of Camembert cheese, bottles of aperitifs, ashtrays, and other knickknacks that spread his effigy everywhere, like so many holy medals. Everything became simple in the eyes of the defeated, the disappointed, the oppressed: a savior had been born among them. They became aware of that on 8 July 1887.

The government had decided to send Boulanger away from Paris before 14 July. Thus the general was named to the Thirteenth Corps in Clermont-Ferrand. It was a bullying tactic; Rochefort spoke of a *deportation*. Boulanger was to leave from the Gare de Lyon on 8 July. Answering the call of *L'Intransigeant*, and behind men Déroulède had mobilized, a host of Parisians invaded the train station singing Boulangist refrains. At the general's arrival, enthusiasm reached its height. They were shouting "To the Elysée!" singing *La Marseillaise*, rushing his train; some were lying on the rails, while others pasted posters on the locomotive. Owing only to a ruse conceived by police prefect Lépine's men, Boulanger finally managed to break free from the hands of his loyalists. Reaching a train waiting for him farther down the line, at the end of a platform, he scaled the locomotive while wearing his top hat and was able to get as far as Villeneuve-Saint-Georges, where he caught his train for Clermont.

Such scenes, destined to increase the number of Boulangism's advocates, triggered the break with the Radicals: these actions were not compatible with "*the republican doctrine*," said *La Justice*. In the Chamber two days later, Clemenceau confirmed that he had taken his distance from the new mob idol: "The popularity of General Boulanger came too soon, to someone who too much loved to raise a fuss."

That love kept Boulanger from allowing his retreat to Auvergne to stifle him. In autumn 1887, the decoration scandal broke publicly, bringing down Daniel Wilson, Grévy's son-in-law, who had trafficked in Legion of Honor awards to subsidize his newspaper ventures. Boulanger decided to give an interview to *Gil Blas* without asking for authorization. General Ferron, the minister of war, taken to task, had his subordinate locked up for thirty days without possibility of reprieve.

It quickly became clear that Grévy, as a result of his misfortune of having a son-in-law, would have to hand in his resignation; there was talk of a Jules Ferry candidacy. That name excited violent hatred, however. Ferry was the bête noire of Radicals, the incarnation of the Opportunist republic, which had starved the people and prostrated itself before Germany. He was equally odious to the conservatives because of his schooling policies, and he served as a reminder to Parisians of the bad days of the siege and the Commune. On 2 December, the day of Grévy's resignation, Séverine wrote:

Down with Ferry in the name of those who endured the suffering and misery of the siege . . . Down with Ferry the Famine! Down with Ferry, who misled Parisians on 31 October, who had them gunned down on 2 January! Down with Ferry the Killer of the People! Down with Ferry in the name of all the wives who have a poor, rotting, mutilated corpse at the bottom of a rice paddy in Tonkin. Down with Ferry the Defeat, Ferry the Lies, Ferry the Shame!

The next day, when Congress met in Versailles, an anti-Ferryist demonstration shook Paris. Finally, on Clemenceau's advice, deputies and senators named Sadi Carnot to be Grévy's successor. But the antiparliamentary wave again brought Boulanger to the fore.

The Clermont Exile

In January, Georges Thiébaud, a Bonapartist journalist, latched onto the gaiters of the Clermont exile and proposed that he use all the by-elections to get a foothold in public opinion. On 26 February 1888, there were to be elections in seven departments. Boulanger was not eligible, but Thiébaud distributed ballots with his name on them. Without even campaigning, the general obtained encouraging results everywhere. The ministry reacted by suspending Boulanger on 14 March. That decision led to a protest, orchestrated by the newspapers won over to the Boulangist cause. A "republican committee of national protest" was constituted around Rochefort. Believing he could cut the ground out from under protesters' feet, the minister stripped Boulanger of his duties on 26 March. Now that he had returned to civilian life, however, the general was suddenly eligible for office. As a result, the maneuver Thiébaud had envisioned became realizable. To be precise, a by-election was planned in Dordogne the following 8 April. Boulanger was still not officially a candidate, yet he won in a landslide, uniting conservative votes and far left votes. The following Sunday, there was another by-election, in Nord. This time, Boulanger was a candidate. His platform consisted of four words: "*Dissolution, Revision, Constituent Assembly.*" Triumph: Boulanger obtained 173,000 votes to his Opportunist adversary's 76,000, and the Radical candidate's 9,700. Two days before, Boulanger had handed in his resignation as deputy of Dordogne. The electoral "steeplechase"—Barrès's word—was launched: from one department to the next, Boulanger obtained a veritable national plebiscite, which should have opened the doors of power to him.

Who were these men around the general who now wore red carnations in their buttonholes as a sign of recognition? In the first place, there were the representatives of a far left that had broken free from Clemenceau: the Radical senator Naquet; the deputies Laguerre, Laisant, Francis Laur, and a few others. Then, there were newspaper editors such as Rochefort, Portalis, and Eugène Mayer. There was Paul Déroulède of course, and Thiébaud the Bonapartist. What did the Radicals want? Revision of the constitution, the elimination of the Senate, and a return to republican principles, which had been buried by the compromise of 1875. What did Déroulède want? To found a plebiscitary republic, return full prestige and power to a head of state supported by popular suffrage.

Although Boulanger was seated on the far left and was surrounded by militants of the same persuasion, it was no use. The monarchists soon realized that this adversary of the parliamentary regime might well be what MacMahon had refused to become: someone to aid them in restoring the monarchy, a French Monck.[1] One of them, Comte Dillon, acted as a go-between for Boulanger and offered him financial aid. Boulanger, who believed money had no odor, proved greedy. Dillon was able to overcome the hesitations of his friends, and the money began to flow into the movement's coffers, thanks to the kindness of the Comte de Paris. It was later learned that the Duchesse d'Uzès placed her entire fortune, which was considerable, in the service of the cause. In that royalist intrigue, which remained secret, Alfred de Mun was among those who went to dine with Boulanger sporting false beards, dreaming of making the general a high constable, opening the way for a king.

As for Thiébaud, he worked for Prince Napoleon. He hoped that, in case Boulanger was unable to "take advantage of the strength created around his name," that strength might be captured to the benefit of Prince Napoleon. Thiébaud organized a secret meeting between Napoleon and Boulanger, which took place in Switzerland on 1 January 1888. Without promising anything, Boulanger suggested to both parties that he was their man.

The socialist movement itself, still weak at the time but already divided into many tendencies, did not manage to escape completely the Boulangist attraction. The most revolutionary groups, the Guesdists and the Blanquists, hoped at least to seize hold of the movement and to divert it toward social revolution. In any case, they refused to help "the republicans" in the defense of a regime of exploiters. Only the possibilists (that is, the reformists of the time), with Brousse and Allemane as their leaders, were forthrightly anti-Boulangist. That attitude of a part of the socialists came from the fact that the parliamentary republic was proving incapable of solving the most urgent problems brought on by the economic crisis; and from the fact that given its liberal conceptions, it rejected any intervention by the state. Boulangism was thus the clumsy expression of a true workers' anger. It was not to be scorned; it could be used.

The Triumphal March

Thus the person of the general had become the locus for the most contradictory chimera and hopes. But all in all, these were only staff-level contradictions. The staff had put Boulanger center stage, but in the last instance, it was the people who would bring him to power. And the people had no platform; the people made fun of platforms: "What does his platform matter," said Barrès, "they have faith in his person. . . . They want to return him to power, because in every circumstance he will feel the same way as the nation."

On 19 August 1888, by-elections were to take place in Charente-Inférieure, Somme, and again in Nord. Meanwhile, Boulanger was defeated on 22 July in the department of Ardèche. Was this a consequence of his duel with Premier Floquet? After an exchange of insults in the Chamber, the lawyer and the soldier had met, swords in hand, on the Comte Dillon's property in Neuilly. The lawyer had the upper hand, skewering the general in the neck, which left him fighting for his life for several days. Barrès said of Ardèche: "That department turned away from a Messiah confined to bed." They were already burying, if not Boulanger, who recovered, then at least Boulangism, which was judged moribund. Prior to the vote, *La Croix*, fairly reserved until then, asked the general "if he would vote for freedom of religion, of association, of education, and if he would never persecute, as many feared he would"? Boulanger protested: "I answer without difficulty: I will never engage in religious persecution no matter what happens." Catholic backers of Boulanger took heart.

After a very active campaign, during which the Duchesse d'Uzès's millions came in very handy, Boulanger was reelected in all three departments. Workers, bourgeois, peasants, everyone seemed to find a reason to vote for him. What did the hero of that populist appeal do? The best-informed sources received this confidence from him: for nearly six weeks, Boulanger left his faithful to take a personal trip to Spain and Morocco. Boulanger was a bon vivant afflicted with a tedious wife, and he had continually accumulated so-called love affairs. But this time, he had found "true love" in the arms of Marguerite de Bonnemains. Thus while France was speaking of Boulanger in terms of national destiny, the general himself was working on his individual happiness. Such an escapade left Barrès indulgent: "Let us accept him with his so very French faults." His entourage was more harsh: "The weakest thing about Boulangism is Boulanger."

Upon his return, the intrigues surrounding him were worse than ever; the movement was in danger of falling apart. On 24 December, however, the death of a Paris deputy, the Radical Hude, was made known. It was a godsend: Boulanger would be able to reunite in a single stroke the different elements of Boulangism, all the while taking it to the top.

All Boulanger's adversaries—Radicals, Opportunists, and moderates of every stripe—campaigned for Jacques. He was supported by a battalion of newspapers: Clemenceau's *Justice*, but also the possibilist socialist *Parti Ouvrier*; *Le Temps*, which had sympathies for Jules Ferry; *Le Journal des Débats*, which was on good terms with the haute bourgeoisie of business people. Opposing them stood the same disparate groups, the same coalition of heteroclite interests: *L'Intransigeant*, but also *La Croix*; *Le Soleil*, which was monarchist; *L'Autorité*, which was Bonapartist; and even *Le Figaro*, where the staff as a whole could not agree.

On the evening of 27 January 1889, while waiting for the result, Boulanger in evening dress, with a red carnation in his buttonhole, dined in a private room of the Restaurant Durand. He was surrounded by the entire Boulangist staff. Hour by hour, election officials brought the results; hour by hour, the victory took shape. A crowd swelling around the restaurant began to chant: "Boulanger-in-the-Elysée!" His close friends, Laguerre, Déroulède, Rochefort, and others, urged him to take action. He had the people, universal suffrage, the army, and no doubt the police behind him. If he would just say the word, give the order: who could stop him in his triumphal march?

Boulanger would not hear of it, however. He was still filled with the conviction that a coup d'état ought not to be attempted. He slipped away for a moment. Some say he went to see Marguerite in an adjoining room, and that she strengthened him in his resolve not to attempt the adventure. At about eleven thirty, the final numbers were known: more than 245,000 votes for Boulanger, versus 162,000 for Jacques, and 17,000 for the Socialist Boulé. The resounding success encouraged Déroulède and other advocates to attempt a show of force; they again urged Boulanger. Whatever he would order, they were ready! To no avail: nothing could convince him.

"Five past midnight," declared Thiébaud. "Boulangism has been on the decline for five minutes!" In reply to the last supplications by Déroulède, who had grown more pale than ever, Boulanger reminded him of the Second Empire, "dying from its origins." His father had once recited Victor Hugo's curse against the man of 2 December. And then, what was the use? The general elections would take place in the fall. In a few months the movement would bring Boulanger to power lawfully.

The defenders of the regime had enough to worry about. All of a sudden, they were reduced to powerlessness. Floquet, always sure of himself, had predicted a crushing defeat for Boulanger: had not Paris been in the hands of Radicals since 1873? Floquet had not foreseen that so many former Communards, so many Radical voters, as well as the populist electorate and conservatives would elect Boulanger with such a large majority. This is clear in an analysis of the results: bourgeois neighborhoods, working-class arrondissements, and outlying regions all supported *"la Boulange."*

A Pyrrhic Victory

This time, assessing the danger, all the adversaries of the Caesarian movement joined forces and used every means, legal and illegal, to liquidate Boulangism before the elections of September and October. Minister of the Interior Constans, from the new Tirard ministry, undertook the task of digging defense trenches. He condemned the Ligue des Patriotes. He used blackmail. He got Boulanger drunk and sent him fleeing to Belgium and then England. He made the senate a high court of justice and convicted Boulanger in absentia. He reestablished constituency polls. He banned multiple candidacies. Everything was put to use, including the opening of the Paris International Exposition on 6 May 1889, under the protective watch of the brand-new Eiffel Tower.

In the elections of September and October, the Boulangists obtained only forty-four seats; Boulanger himself was elected in Clignacourt. A small minority of them were made up of conservatives; the rest—including Barrès, elected in Nancy—were to sit on the far left, beside the Socialists. Boulangism had subsided, it was becoming fragmented, but it had sown a new seed in political life and in French society: the seed of nationalism.

Boulanger himself, despite his wiliness, was not up to the role of providential man that public opinion had bestowed on him. He committed suicide on Marguerite de Bonnemains's grave in Ixelles, Belgium, on 30 September 1891. That led Clemenceau to say: "He died as he lived: as a second lieutenant." Another observer, Abbé Mugnier, had a different but just as lapidary comment, which he confided to his journal: "That revolver shot in the cemetery of Ixelles was another triumph for the republic."[2]

Boulangism resulted from three concomitant crises: economic, parliamentary, and nationalist. The economic depression had provoked a deep malaise in the countryside and in the cities since the beginning of the

1880s. The republican regime—dominated by the Opportunists—proved incapable of responding to the desires of voters, who had put so much hope in it. Convinced of the benefits of state nonintervention, the moderates did not envision social legislation. In addition, the parliamentary regime operated in a vacuum, following arcane rules and displaying apparent disorder, which provoked antiparliamentarianism. This was a result of a de facto separation between the political class—the men of the seraglio—and universal suffrage. The voters came to be disillusioned by the frequent elections. Nearly half of the French people were excluded, those whose representatives—Catholics, monarchists, Bonapartists—were deprived of republican legitimacy. The other half, finding it impossible to rally behind a dominant party, divided their votes between Radicals and Opportunists. These representatives, though standing in solidarity against the enemies of the regime, were incapable of governing together. Since the elections of 1885, both the forces of opposition on the right and the arbitrating forces among the Radicals had led to ministerial instability. The appearance of instability, even more than the reality, was intolerable.

For many republicans, however, the parliamentary system was merely an inheritance from Orleanism. The Boulangist crisis and its failure were precisely what would lead to the assimilation of the republic to the parliamentary regime. For many on the far left, there was rather an incompatibility between the two—a republic demanded the most direct democracy. But it was as if the founders of the Third Republic, shaped by the Second Empire, believed the people were a minority group who could be granted only strictly controlled freedom: anything close to direct legislation reeked of Bonapartist plebiscite. Popular sovereignty was revoked in favor of a "*governed democracy*" (Georges Burdeau), whose deputies were master wranglers.

The nationalist crisis appears to have been merely a spur. In fact, however, the exaltation of the patriotic ideal was just another way of contesting a political class judged byzantine, misappropriating, and powerless. Nascent nationalism touched the hearts of the mob; it offered them the share of poetry they had been deprived of by the system in place. This third element of the crisis allows us to better understand, in positive terms, the Boulangist fervor.

This was the beginning of the era of mass communication. Since 1881, there had been a free and inexpensive press. But when public opinion became massively involved in politics, frustrated citizens ran up against a complex system, which they found difficult to understand. In contrast to deputies who made and unmade cabinets without taking popular sentiment into account, while the president of the Republic played only a bit part, General Boulanger exerted great appeal, all the more so in that he represented a simplification of divided government. People no doubt exalted him because they hoped he would bring reform, but also because they expected him to transfer to the political field a system with direct bearing on daily life. They had confidence in his person, there was a direct relation between him and them. If he failed, they would know whom to attack. The fervor for the great man was in direct proportion to the disgust felt toward the opacity of the parliamentary regime, over which people had no control.

An Ancient Sediment of Idolatry

Let us add another factor. In a study in the 1888 *Revue Socialiste*, Eugène Fournière mentions "the mob, which retains an ancient sediment of idolatry." The history of the twentieth century suggests the depth of that sedimentation. In fact, democracy is a demanding, difficult, even ungrateful system. Montesquieu thought it impracticable because he believed it was based on virtue. As a result, what has been called "Wilsonism"—corruption, in other words—is much more intolerable in a democratic regime than in a monocratic or aristocratic one. But democracy also rests on a culture of rationality. It presupposes that citizens, equal among themselves, are capable of treating problems of the commonwealth with full knowledge of the facts. That can only be an ideal, an incentive no doubt, but beyond reach. That culture of rationalism must confront the culture of belief, which is much more widely shared. It offers incompetent people explanations and solutions for the misfortunes of the age. French society experienced the tragic antagonism between these two cultures during the Revolution. In principle, rational culture was the winner. In actuality, throughout the nineteenth century there was a resurgence of belief: superstitions of all kinds, the revival of Christian miracles, recurring apparitions of the Virgin, apocalyptic predictions, a profusion of portents, interest in the occult, and so on.

It is also through the prism of these attitudes that we must consider the Boulanger phenomenon. A miracle was expected from him because the history of France was understood as a sequence of miracles, beginning with Clovis and the battle of Tolbiacum.[3] That culture of belief extended beyond the Catholic community properly speaking and occupied a place even within the socialist far left. During those years, these socialists had the same state of mind as the first Christians awaiting imminent parousia. Democracy invited citizens to seek the solutions of collective life within themselves; providentialism promised them solutions imposed *from elsewhere*, and generally from on high.

Thus Boulangism may make its appearance as the conjunction of two contradictory movements: first, a demand for the rule of democracy, the desire for true popular sovereignty, the need for transparency in the political system; and second, an expectation on the part of the collective imagination, incarnated in a savior whose mission would be to expel the impostors in place (*dissolution*) and to assert, through his sacred person, the general will (*revision*). To varying degrees, these two tendencies were combined in every follower of Boulanger. Mass communication did the rest: the newborn democracy, in reforming itself, would have to answer the challenge of demagoguery, which is constantly being reborn.

Chronology

1882 19 Jan.	Crash of Union Générale
1885 30 Mar.	Fall of the Ferry cabinet
14–18 Oct.	Legislative elections
1886 7 Jan.	Boulanger named minister of war
13 Mar.	Boulanger questioned about the Decazeville strike
14 July	Longchamp inspection
11 Dec.	Boulanger minister of war for second time
1887 20–30 Apr.	Schnaebelé affair
30 May	Rouvier ministry without Boulanger
8 July	Demonstration at the Gare de Lyon
2 Dec.	Grévy resigns
3 Dec.	Anti-Ferry demonstration in Paris
	Carnot becomes president of the Republic
1888 4 Mar.	Boulanger suspended
8 Apr.	Boulanger elected deputy of Dordogne
15 Apr.	Boulanger elected deputy of Nord
22 July	Boulanger defeated in Ardèche
19 Aug.	Triple electoral victory for Boulanger
1889 27 Jan.	Boulanger elected in Paris
22 Feb.	Second Tirard ministry; Constans becomes minister of the interior
1 Apr.	Boulanger flees to Belgium
6 May	Inauguration of the Paris exposition
22 Sept.–6 Oct.	Legislative elections

CHAPTER 16

Jules Guérin of Fort Chabrol

There is one man whose characteristic silhouette reappears every time the public spirit is profoundly troubled, every time violent demonstrations occur. He takes pleasure in disorder the way certain sea fowl take pleasure in storms, or so they say.

His name is Jules Guérin.

Who will tell the life story of that strange man? Such a tale might take place on the ground floor of our newspapers, between *Les Pirates de Paris* (The pirates of Paris) and the *Mémoires de Mandrin* (Memoirs of Mandrin).

Jules Guérin could often be seen flanked by a few dozen "killers" and exercising a sort of dictatorship of the street.

SO IT WAS THAT on 9 October 1898, the newspaper *Voltaire* set great store in that curious political show-off, whose day of glory was near. The nation was in the midst of the Dreyfus affair. Since August, Guérin had provided the Ligue Antisémitique, of which he was the general delegate, with an official press organ bearing the candid and weighty title *L'Anti-Juif* (The Anti-Jew). The money for it came from the pretender to the crown, the Duc d'Orléans, who had publicly rallied behind the anti-Semitic cause and imagined that by subsidizing Guérin he would win the favor of the people.

Guérin congratulated himself for recruiting his faithful, not from among the bourgeois like Edouard Drumont, author of *La France juive* and editor of *La Libre Parole*, but from the ranks of workers and anarchists. In 1897, he reorganized the Ligue Antisémitique; there were now branches in every arrondissement of the capital and in the large cities of the provinces. Using his eloquence in every sort of forum, he defended small business against the great "Jewish bazaar," workers against "foreign" high finance; and he supported the "most violent revolutionary doctrines." In his own nineteenth arrondissement, he launched a local newspaper, then recruited a veritable praetorian guard from among the wholesale butchers, rendering plant workers, and butcher's boys from the slaughterhouses of La Villette, who tried to outdo one another wielding blackjacks in nationalist demonstrations.

Thus, in 1898 Guérin transformed his league into "the Grand Occident of France" (an anti-Jewish rite), and against the "scheming" of the "revisionists" and the "Dreyfusards," he made rowdiness the order of the day. During the legislative elections in June, he was so active in ensuring that Drumont would be elected in Algiers that he was sentenced to eight days in prison without possibility of reprieve. But he emerged, exhilarated, to the sound of Algiers hoorahs: "Long live Guérin! Long live Drumont! Down with the Jews!"

The man cut a striking figure, fluttering his lashes between his gray fedora and his musketeer's mustache. His chest thrust out, equipped with a leaded cane which he never abandoned, always with one or two pistols in his pockets, Guérin struck poses in front of the little people, who doted on the miles gloriosus. Sometimes, he went so far as to allow the butcher's boys to feel his biceps, which they appreciated as connoisseurs.

On 30 August, there was yet another duel with a journalist, Philibert Roger, whom Guérin wounded with a bullet to the jaw. Furious to see his victim writing more articles against him, however, he had him set upon a few days later by half a dozen thugs, chosen from his "marching brigades." Yet Guérin always went unpunished for his misdeeds. When he went to criminal court in October for striking a police superintendent during a scuffle, he made out superbly with one hundred francs in fines for "illegal possession of weapons." When he was tried for the Roger affair in January 1899, he was quite simply acquitted. The jury (made up of small property owners, merchants, and employees) were a fairly good representation of Paris public opinion, which was increasingly won over by nationalism: they liked Guérin.

L'Anti-Juif thus increased its imprecations against Zola, Picquart, and all the accomplices of the "traitor." In addition, it forthrightly called for a coup d'état. A savior, a decent and energetic man was needed, one who would cleanse the republic of Jews and Freemasons.

At that moment, Guérin became more than a mere "carnival strong man," as his adversaries depicted him. He had troops who could join with those of Déroulède and of the other leagues. The regime in place was threatened. And then, on 16 February 1899, the sudden death of the president of the Republic Félix Faure became known. The election of Emile Loubet two days later was a pretext for new street demonstrations. On 23

February, the day of the late president's funeral, Déroulède, seeking to make the best of the crowd, attempted to lead General Roget and his regiment to the Elysée; but it was no use, the coup d'état was brewing. And when Déroulède appeared before the Seine jury on 31 May, it acquitted the troublemaker. The temperature of public opinion rose again when it was learned on 3 June that the Cour de Cassation had just overturned the first judgment that had convicted Dreyfus, and that a new war council would have to be held. Within three days, indignation had replaced enthusiasm among anti-Dreyfusards. The next day, at the Auteuil racecourse, a poorly protected Loubet had his top hat flattened by the stroke of a cane. On 11 June, the Dreyfusard left replied, invading the streets from the Concorde to Longchamp; the Republic would show them it knew how to defend itself.

During these feverish days, the Dupuy ministry showed a lack of nerve. In its place, a republican defense ministry was entrusted to the direction of Waldeck-Rousseau on 22 June. He named Lépine to head the police prefecture; both were resolved to stamp out the seditious leagues, which had the upper hand and even had some sympathizers within the forces of law and order. Persuaded that a plot was being hatched against the state, Prefect Lépine proceeded with the preventive arrest of the leaders, including the most popular of them, Paul Déroulède. Jules Guérin was also on the list but he escaped Lépine's agents, who instead of going to his home, went to his mother's. While the other presumed conspirators were imprisoned at La Santé awaiting the Haute Cour, Guérin trumpeted the news: he would not surrender, he would shut himself up with his men at the headquarters of the Grand Occident of France and let the police lay siege if they dared. They would find someone to answer to.

Thus began the episode of "Fort Chabrol."

In April 1899, Guérin had installed the offices of the Grand Occident and the *Anti-Juif* at 51, Rue de Chabrol. There he had had considerable renovations done and was paying a tidy sum in rent. But Guérin had become accustomed to a lavish lifestyle, driving a carriage, entertaining his supporters in stylish spots, outdoing himself in elegance: the pretender's gold made its appearance in this ostentation. In that mansion on Rue de Chabrol, he had installed an assembly room, had use of a weapons room. In short, it was the lair of a magnificent condottiere.

On 12 August, that lair became "Fort Chabrol." Guérin and about fifteen of his leaguists barricaded themselves inside, after stocking up with a cartful of canned goods donated by a shop in the neighborhood. The first response from the government was to cut off the telephone. Then local and state police concentrated around the approaches to the place. But

Lépine did not attack. The hot-headed prefect pawed the ground. He wanted to force the rascal's door, but Waldeck-Rousseau forbade bloodshed. In the absence of a siege, therefore, there would be a blockade.

At first, Guérin was supported by a good part of public opinion. Gawkers applauded. On Sunday 20 August, Guérin's friends, including most notably the La Villette butchers, gathered in large numbers on Boulevard Magenta, not far from Rue Chabrol. Soon Lépine's agents were being assaulted with iron bolts; several collapsed on the sidewalk. Would the butchers deliver Guérin? Lépine's heart skipped a beat, as they say in penny novels. But the best thing to do is to let the heroic prefect, who wrote his memoirs, speak for himself:

My men were shaken, if not demoralized. . . . I called in my reserves and, leading everyone I could get my hands on, I charged on those savages, I burst through their ranks, and when the rout began, I pushed them back, sword drawn, first to the gate of the Gare de l'Est, then to the buildings, and then to the train platforms. And, with empty space in front of them, they dispersed and were not seen again.

From then on, it was simply a waiting game, as hunger and thirst did their work. The valiant besieged men tried every means of communication with the outside. Louis Guérin, brother of the braggart, armed with a pair of binoculars, read the instructions his brother wrote for him from an apartment located in the facing building. Provisions were passed across the roof. Some people even made holes in the walls of adjacent buildings.

Sympathizers tried to offer their help. The most dismal rumors circulated. Pistol shots were heard. But no! The men were well trained. A weeping mother finally obtained the right to enter to see her son, supposedly on his death bed. The brouhaha was unending on Rue de Chabrol, especially since street singers had taken the time to set the epic of the great Jules to rhyme, and they were now singing their couplets to the tune of *La Paimpolaise*, among others. One morning in September, a well-meaning person from Château-Gonthier sent the besieged a basket—of live geese. No doubt the farmer's wife had never heard of the sacred geese of the Capitol, but the police, more expert in Latin letters as we know, returned the fowl to the sender. Since tragedy had not erupted, comedy now occupied the stage.

After six weeks, when the excitement had died down and the public had lost interest, Lépine obtained authorization from Waldeck-Rousseau to force the door. Guérin's friends were alerted and negotiated the surrender of the slaughterhouse Vercingetorix. On 20 September 1899, Caesar Lépine triumphed; order reigned in the tenth arrondissement.

The hero of Chabrol was to have a less glorious end. Sentenced to prison, then to banishment, in 1902 he began a campaign against his previous allies, the Drumont group and *La Libre Parole*, whose competing anti-Semitism annoyed him. But one of his former compatriots from the siege of Rue Chabrol, a man named Spiard, published a book entitled *Les coulisses du fort Chabrol* (Behind the scenes at Fort Chabrol), in which he depicted Guérin as a swindler in the service of the government. Even worse, Gaston Méry, a friend of Drumont's, told the readers of *La Libre Parole* what was going on. For several weeks, he narrated the unedifying life of a certain M. Guérin, a bankrupt swindler, an incendiary, a trafficker in anti-Semitism, and finally, an agent provocateur for the police prefect.

Guérin sent his own witnesses, made threats, but it was no use. Méry, day after day without respite, continued to undermine Guérin and in the end convinced his readers that Fort Chabrol had been only a *"great profitable hoax."*

Jules Guérin remained in exile until 1905, living on the pension the Duc d'Orléans was still paying him. But he was in disrepute. Granted amnesty, he returned to France and allowed his name to be forgotten before his death in 1910 at the age of fifty. With Guérin, combat anti-Semitism had found a champion; in anti-Semitism, Jules Guérin, who had begun his career with gasoline, had found a blazing affair. But as Napoleon said, one can only give a first push to an affair; after that, it pulls you along.

CHAPTER 17

Huysmans and Decadence

FOR MANY generations of high school students, Joris-Karl Huysmans was simply one name among others that manuals of French literature coupled with the name of the "decadent" school. Well-read people knew more about him, but it was not until the 1960s and the reprint of *Là-bas* by Livre de Poche that Huysmans found a new public in keeping with his talent. Let us wager that his career is not over. We might in fact wonder whether, as we approach the end of the twentieth century, our attention will not be drawn to analogies from the end of the nineteenth: do we not hear the signs of a new "decadence" being denounced here and there? As a result, Huysmans might well become our contemporary once more.

Between Zola and Breton

Three books, almost equally famous, may provide a crude summary of Huysmans's itinerary. The first was *A rebours* (Against the grain) and dates from 1884; its author was thirty-six at the time. Without being completely aware of it, with this novel (but is it really a novel?) Huysmans signed the death warrant of naturalism. That is because, in the beginning, he was himself under the influence of Zola, and became a close friend of his. In these first books,[1] the most significant of which is *A vau-l'eau* (Downstream), Huysmans told seedy stories in which antiheroes gloomily killed time in sordid environments. But his style was not that of an ordinary hack: he borrowed some of his artistic tricks from the Goncourts, and if he depicted infamy, he did so with all the preciosity of a manuscript illuminator.

To have a change of air ("I was vaguely seeking to escape a cul-de-sac where I was suffocating"), he then imagined a character just as disgusted with life as his earlier marionettes, but who after the usual tribulations and through culture and wealth—placed in the service of an exuberant imagination—attempts to flee all the platitudes of existence by living the most extravagant of cloistered adventures. Barely budging from the villa to which he has retired on the outskirts of town, Duc Jean des Esseintes pursues his unbridled taste for the rare, the strange, the unusual of all sorts to a convulsive state of artifice. Fleeing the vulgarity of his century, he makes his days a rhapsody of exceptional sensations and his house a kaleidoscope of Baudelairean "correspondences," where sounds, colors, smells, flavors, and emotions correspond in luxuriant harmony.

"Nature" was no longer in season. The modest government employee of Sûreté Générale (Huysmans was decorated with the Legion of Honor as deputy chief clerk of his bureau) fed his fantasies with obsessive images of lust and blood, images painted by Gustave Moreau that haunted his contemporaries. A new art was bursting forth at the limits of the imagination and from within the confines of neurosis. The drunken excesses of Zola's *L'assomoir* (The dram-shop) had become nauseating; the Surrealist revolution could be glimpsed on the horizon.

The second great book by Huysmans was *Là-bas*, which appeared in 1891. Durtal, the central character, is doing historical research on Gilles de Rais, the former companion to Joan of Arc who became the legendary Bluebeard; along the way, he becomes involved with occultism and satanism, and frequents excommunicated priests who celebrate black masses. He manages to maintain his composure thanks to the utterly sensible conversation of Carhaix, the bell-ringer for the church of Saint-Sulpice, in whose residence (located in one of the church towers) Durtal savors both peace of mind and the culinary delights of the bell-ringer's wife. Everything is permeated with an astonishing odor of sulfur and pot roast, the sacred and the profane, religion and eroticism. Huysmans told one of his friends that like a number of his fellow citizens, he was looking to occult science for "compensation for the displeasures of daily life, for the everyday filth, the purulence of a loathsome age." But Huysmans had truly diabolical obsessions: his extreme sensitivity exposed him to supernatural terrors, which some in his rather loony entourage reinforced.

If Huysmans embraced Catholicism, as he claimed in *En route* (On the way), 1895, he did so by several of the strange paths announced in *Là-bas*. In particular, the influence exerted by Joseph-Antoine Boullan, an unfrocked priest, a healer and member of a cult obsessed with sexual problems, is today well known. In fact, Huysmans's conversion was long taken for suspect. *En route*, which is largely autobiographical, tells of Durtal's return to the Catholic faith and describes the monastic life in detail. It did not have the good fortune to convince everyone. Certain critics expressed their doubts about Huysmans's sincerity, claiming that for him, religion was only a pretext for literature. Numerous priests reacted sharply to attacks contained in the book against the mediocrity of the lay clergy: "Such a book," wrote a Jesuit, "cannot be placed in the hands of girls or young men or respectable women."

In any case, Huysmans remained Catholic until his death in 1907. At a time when the Church seemed incapable of overcoming its internal crises, its intellectual mediocrity, and the blows that republican laws had dealt it, a series of startling conversions within the literary world announced the Catholic revival of the early twentieth century. In addition to Huysmans, Paul Claudel, Francis Jammes, then Jacques and Raïssa Maritain (godchildren of Léon Bloy), Charles Péguy, Ernest Psichari, and Henri Massis were among the best known of these converts; there were lesser but no less famous talents as well, such as Emile Baumann, whose novels were extremely successful. The anti-intellectualist reaction of the time, one of whose currents later blended with nationalism, had its repercussions on literature. Richard Griffiths, an English historian, has even written that for the first time in two centuries, writers combined profound religious convictions with real literary talent.[2]

"Modern Man Is Blasé"

It was not as a Catholic writer that Huysmans secured his posthumous glory. His most powerful works undoubtedly preceded his conversion: almost all readers who discover *Là-bas* in the Livre de Poche edition and then begin to read *La cathédrale* (The cathedral), published shortly thereafter in the same collection, face the same disappointment. It is the decadent who has maintained his prestige up to our own time. But what precisely is decadence?

In the interest of clarity, let us distinguish decadence from decline (of a people, a society, a civilization). Decline can be assessed in objective terms—with statistics, graphs, weights and measures—since decline is proper to the economy, demography, cultural production. In that last case, the objective criteria are less sure: one might very well establish that a particular country has not received the Nobel Prize for x number of years, but it is more difficult to assert that it has no more poets. Imperceptibly, we arrive at the notion of decadence, a more subjective, more impressionistic notion, which may rest on certain signs of decline, but which may just as well rest only on prejudices or illusions. Decadence refers to the state of mores, the "ethics of the nation"; the most visible aspects of economic, political, social, and psychological changes are interpreted in negative terms. Decadence may in certain cases designate simply change leading to anxiety: the reference points of my childhood are crumbling away, what will become of me?

There are nearly always people in our society who despise decadence. Sometimes, however, they can reach sufficient numbers and can be gifted enough to be heard, especially if there are some elements of decline to be criticized. Reactionary movements denounce decadence in the name of a golden age that has been lost.

At the end of the nineteenth century, was France in decline? That subject could lead to lengthy discussions. What is certain is that a reactionary movement developed against political innovations (the reign of freedom), philosophical innovations (the process of separating Church and state), economic innovations (industrialization), and social innovations (urbanization and the threat it represented to patriarchal society). People can always find new verses to put to the tune of "decadence."

For their part, writers and artists who proclaimed themselves "decadent" denounced the "flatness," "triviality," and "boredom" of an age when "Americanization" was already lying in wait.[3] The aristocracy was dead, epic times were past, the era of democracy was beginning with its funeral procession of egalitarian horrors, journalism, and soon cinema. Hence decadents vituperated against the style and mores of their age, characterized by a standardized tastelessness. At the same time, however, they defiantly assumed that decadence and embraced it, by setting off on aesthetic paths that the common people found morbid: the search for the bizarre, the precious, the artificial, but also the corrupt, the deleterious, the perverse. Decadents warped their writing, used a host of neologisms, carried the exotic to an extreme, took an oath to astonish in every detail, all against the banality of their time. Everything had to work toward the creation of an artistic world separated from the common herd. But in one of those paradoxes with which life abounds, these artists, by dint of fleeing their age, in the end gave it a style. It was only one step from literature and painting to the decorative arts, a step soon taken. And now in the capital, the Paris metro—as living proof of a disparaged modernity—proliferated with the cast-iron elegance of decadence, which was immediately rebaptized "art nouveau." In his final days, Huysmans found it astonishing that there might be a relation between des Esseintes's avowed disgust and the cast-iron flora in metro stations, built about twenty years after the publication of *A rebours.*

The decadents thus maintained ambiguous relations with decadence, a complicity that was denounced by the new champions of national energy. The Dreyfus affair, then the German danger beginning in 1905, plunged France back into political passions: the decadent movement did not survive them. Nationalism, among other things, dealt it a lethal blow. In the

name of classical harmony and the Latin race, Maurras denounced Huysmans as the "barbarian": "Violence for the sake of violence, vulgar howling for the pleasure of howling, childish crudeness, foolishness: nothing is
more repugnant to pure French genius." Léon Daudet, another writer for
Action Française, criticized "the stupid nineteenth century" (the title of
his book) as a century of raw numbers, quantities, where "audacity lay on
the side of the destroyers." And, he added, "we need to make sure that it
shall now be on the side of the reconstructors, those who possess good
sense and an awakened and active reason."

In fact, the twentieth century called on artists to commit themselves:
the nationalist, fascist, socialist, and communist movements appealed to
them to build a new world, a new order, a shining city. And now, at the
end of our own century, all these political commitments seem to many
people like so much "useless service"; the future, shining or not, escapes
us. New "decadent" tendencies might well blossom on the graves of dead
hopes, reinforced by new evidence of a decline of the West, but also by
new spiritual aspirations. In his own time, J.-K. Huysmans, ill at ease with
himself and his century, already tried to live that way—against the grain.

CHAPTER 18

Georges Sorel: A 'Fascist' on the Left?

THERE HAS BEEN a great deal of talk recently about Georges Sorel. The debate on "French fascism," launched anew by Zeev Sternhell, has placed the name of that political theorist back in the public eye. Sorel had a prominent influence in Italy, with Mussolini declaring his debt to him. For Zeev Sternhell, Sorel represents the prototype of certain leftist intellectuals in France itself. Without calling themselves fascists, these individuals broadly contributed to the phenomenon of fascist penetration during the interwar period. Was not Sorel both a revisionist of Marxism and a resolute antidemocrat? In addition, Sorel not only supplied Italian Fascism with some of its leading ideas—indirectly, unbeknownst to him; in about 1910, he himself moved toward the far right, going so far as to collaborate with Georges Valois and other Maurrassians. He, a former Dreyfusard, even came to offer sacrifices to the demon of anti-Semitism.

Fine connoisseurs of Sorel have reacted emotionally to that reductionism. Although it is true that the political variability of the author of *Réflexions sur la violence* (Reflections on violence) still leaves his readers perplexed, one ought not to neglect the imposing theoretical work to which he devoted his entire life. Among other originalities, he was one of the leading experts in France on Marx's philosophy. Gramsci said of him: "He is complicated, disjointed, incoherent, superficial, and cryptic, but he provides or suggests original points of view, finds links one never would have thought of, but which are nonetheless true. He obliges us to think and examine things more thoroughly." Hence Sorel's defenders have attempted a counterattack. The magazine *Esprit* was its first instrument, publishing a critique of Zeev Sternhell's *Ni droite ni gauche* written by another Israeli academic, Shlomo Sand, one of the leading experts on Georges Sorel's thought.[1] In a less polemical vein, Jacques Julliard cautioned Sternhell in *Annales* against the confusion, common in his writings, between Georges Sorel and the old CGT's "unionism of direct action."[2]

It is within that context of intellectual controversy (though that controversy was not its cause) that new research on Sorel has come to enrich the knowledge of what one is tempted to call the chameleon of social thought. Jacques Julliard, director of studies at the Ecole des Hautes Etudes en Sciences Sociales, and editorial writer for the *Nouvel Observateur*, launched the *Cahiers Georges-Sorel* in 1983, with Shlomo Sand and a few others; its second annual issue has just been published.[3] This is a scholarly venture, to be complemented by the gradual publication of Sorel's complete works; the dispersed state of those writings now makes interpretation of them all the more difficult. Shlomo Sand has also just published a scholarly study, *L'illusion du politique: Georges Sorel et le débat intellectuel 1900* (The illusion of the political: Georges Sorel and the 1900 intellectual debate).[4] In short, the fog is lifting from around that hippogriff of political thought.

Born in 1847, a graduate of the Ecole Polytechnique, Georges Sorel first worked as a state engineer, until the age of forty-four. After that, he devoted himself to his writing, producing many articles and books. There is little to be said of that first "life," except that Sorel's origins, we may surmise, set him apart from the usual intellectual networks, in particular from the university environment, which he hated with a passion throughout his life. In addition, that son of Norman bourgeois (he was born in Cherbourg) fell in love with the daughter of poor peasants, Marie-Euphrasie David. At first a manual worker, she was employed by a hotel in Lyon. It is there he met her, when he was twenty-eight: she took care of him while he was sick. They were never separated again, until Marie's death in 1897. Sorel wrote to Benedetto Croce at the time: "I lost my dear and devoted wife, who had been my companion for twenty-two years of work and to whom I was attached *per la forza del primo amore*. Her memory, I hope, will remain the best part of myself and the true soul of my life."[5]

Yet that beloved woman was never Sorel's legitimate wife, which is surprising in a man of extremely scrupulous morals, who was always quick to denounce moral decadence. It seems that Sorel, respectful of his parents, never wanted to go against their wishes, not even after their death. Nevertheless, the presence at his side of a nearly illiterate woman from the lower classes had the effect of marginalizing Sorel in his own social circle and allowed him to know the working class better than he would have through books alone.

In 1893, he began his career as a socialist thinker. Casting the scornful gaze of a moralist on his age and on the bourgeois republican regime (this was the era of the Panama scandal), passionate about absolutism, he thought he had found the scientific tools for a social philosophy in Marx's writings. For five years, as Shlomo Sand says, he became "a kind of fellow traveler of the Guesdist party." With Lafargue, Deville, and other intellectuals close to the Parti Ouvrier Français, he collaborated on the first two Marxist reviews in France, *L'Ere Nouvelle* and then *Le Devenir Social*. In 1898, however, he veered to the right for the first time. Following Edouard Bernstein, Sorel began a revision of Marxism, leaving his Guesdist friends in the lurch. When the Dreyfus affair broke in January, he became a militant for that other sort of revisionism, equally abhorred by the Guesdists: the revision of the trial that had sent the Jewish captain to Devil's Island.

During that "Dreyfusard" phase, Sorel, who had always felt the greatest disdain for democratic socialism, praised Jaurès to the skies and even supported Millerand's participation in Waldeck-Rousseau's bourgeois government: "Jaurès's admirable conduct is the best proof that there is a socialist ethic." Against the reaction, which had again become extremely dangerous, socialists had to assume their responsibilities and not hesitate to support the left. But in 1902, Sorel veered to the left, and farewell Jaurès! After the elections that made Emile Combes head of the government, the spectacle of a Radical republic—Jaurès even gave socialist backing to its pettiness—distanced him from the Dreyfusards and other socialist intellectuals, who had gone for the "kill" between 1903 and 1908. Sorel became a fellow traveler of another group, revolutionary unionism, a new opportunity for "proletarian socialism," of which the Marxist parties and the parliamentary practices of the reformists had proved to be such wretched interpreters.

During that new five-year sequence (it is Sand who points out this five-year pattern in Sorel's evolution), Sorel expressed the views of disappointed Dreyfusards, including the most eloquent of them, Charles Péguy. Moreover, Sorel and Péguy had traveled part of the road together. Sorel was a regular at Péguy's *Cahiers*, and Péguy paid this homage to his elder: "*Our good master M. Sorel*." Another coterie also made its critique of political Dreyfusism: *Le Mouvement Socialiste*, a journal edited by Hubert Lagardelle, with whom Sorel momentarily found himself in agreement. It was during that period in 1906 that he published the book that would remain his most famous, *Réflexions sur la violence*, reputed to be a kind of unofficial theory of revolutionary unionism.

The CGT's unionism appealed to Sorel, in that it remained at the level of class struggle, unlike democracy, which "mixed classes together." Aspiring to an ideal of heroism, Sorel found nothing so repugnant as the scenes of compromise—for which the Chamber served as theater—between the bourgeoisie and parliamentary socialists. Proletarian violence ought to remind "the bourgeois of their class identity"; there was no adversary more desirable for revolutionary unionism than combative capitalism! Sorel did not envision improving workers' lives through legal reforms, which he called "a management of appetites under the auspices of lawyer-politicians." His Corneillian soul aspired to the "sublime." He was not interested in "future society"—he despised utopias—but rather in the moral greatness achieved in and through struggle. That was how he justified the general strike, the generating myth of the fighting spirit and the road to glory: "In the total ruin of institutions and mores, there is still something powerful, new, and intact, namely, the soul of the revolutionary proletariat strictly speaking; and it will not be dragged into the general downfall of moral values, if the workers have enough energy to bar the way to bourgeois corrupters, by responding loud and clear to their advances—with brutality."[6]

During that Red period, Sorel also began to exude anti-Semitism, all the more curious in that he had previously denounced it as a way to dupe the working class and had praised Jewish culture and history. In an excellent summary, published in the last volume of *Cahiers Georges-Sorel* (proof that the journal was not simply celebratory), Shlomo Sand carefully follows that astonishing slippage in Sorel's thought. It was not the only one of its kind. In July 1906, *Le Mouvement Socialiste* published an article by Robert Louzon entitled "La faillite du dreyfusisme ou le triomphe du parti juif" (The bankruptcy of Dreyfusism, or the triumph of the Jewish party). Sorel agreed with it, to the point, Sand tells us, of suggesting to Lagardelle that he send the article to Drumont himself.

In 1909, after the events at Villeneuve-Saint-Georges,[7] Sorel diagnosed the bankruptcy of revolutionary unionism, and once more veered to the right. This time, however, it was very much to the right, infinitely more to the right than Jaurès's or even Millerand's socialism. He now sought to apply his visceral antidemocratism to the currents of the far right, under the influence of Maurras. He made several small steps toward an agreement: in September 1909, Sorel gave an interview to *Action Française*; in 1910, Maurras devoted an article to Sorel; in April of the same year, Sorel contributed an article to the monarchist newspaper. Sorel engaged in an exchange of ideas with Georges Valois, who, in publications dealing with "full-scale nationalism," recommended bringing together the working class and the monarchy. The two men conceived of the plan for *La Cité Française* (The French commonwealth), "an antidemocratic and anticapitalist review." The plan was aborted but Sorel had the free time to develop his new positions for the review *L'Indépendance*, while his friend Edouard Berth solidified the link with Valois by creating the *Cahiers du Cercle*

Proudhon in 1912. Valois later said of it: "It was the first fascist undertaking in France." During that White period, Sorel indulged in an anti-Semitism "more simple-minded than theoretical" (Shlomo Sand), which he never abandoned until the end of his life.

Did he therefore sound the call for patriotism in 1914? No, not at all! The previous year, he had broken with far right circles and now, at a time of great heroism, something he had so desired, he turned his back on the Sacred Union. Here is something that is not easy to understand. Some believe Georges Sorel was a moralist above all, a social philosopher made anxious by what he considered the decadence of civilization, seeking the historical agent of regeneration. That would explain the contradiction between his ethical coherence and his political incoherence; but then, why did he retreat to the Aventine Hill just as force of circumstance thrust millions of men into the heroic life, in Verdun and the daily trenches? Did Sorel, who saw violence as an instrument for moral greatness, find the violence of war too foreign? In any case, in his correspondence he condemned the "thirst for carnage" among political leaders and "the servility" of peoples.

This was Sorel's latest and last veer to the left, confirmed in the enthusiasm he showed in the last years of his life for Lenin and the Bolshevik revolution. His hatred of "haughty bourgeois democracies" was reconciled with his demand for the sublime, which found satisfaction in the heroic tale of the Russian revolution. Life had been a Feydeau novel, and now Corneille had come back from the dead! On that point, Sorel did not change his mind, since he died before Lenin, in a state of poverty he had known all his life.

And what about Mussolini, you might ask. Haven't some people claimed that at the end of his life, Sorel admired Mussolini as much as Lenin? On this point, Shlomo Sand is categorical: that was a tall tale, something he supposedly confided to Variot, a dubious character, with whom he had broken all ties in the meantime. But must we follow Sand on this point? There are a few sentences in Sorel's correspondence that show us he was receptive to the actions of the Fascists. Thus he wrote to Benedetto Croce on 26 August 1921: "At the present moment, the adventures of Fascism may be the most original social phenomenon in Italy: they seem to me to go far beyond the schemes of politicians."[8] In saying that, Sorel remained true to his antidemocratism. To admire both the future Duce and the creator of the Bolshevik party was only a *political* contradiction, and it is not in that domain, as we said, that one must seek the coherence of Sorel's thinking.

"An awakener of ideas," "one of a kind," as Boris Souvarine said,[9] Sorel sowed seeds in every direction. Italian Fascists and French fascists (true and false) claimed his ideas; supporters of workers' socialism, opponents of state socialism, of the socialism "of intellectuals," and of parliamentary socialism could all take lessons from it. Others, reaching the end of their journey, tired of veering this way and that, might confess, more prosaically, that they are slightly seasick.

CHAPTER 19

Péguy: Prefascist or Insurgent?

CHARLES PÉGUY, French poet, was born 7 January 1873 in Orléans; he died at the front from a blow to the forehead on 5 September 1914. Since then, he has incited a battle of experts of every kind—in literature, socialism, Catholicism, and nationalism, among other things—over his life and work. That is because Péguy, like other "sacred monsters" in France—Proudhon and Sorel, for example—belongs to a class of men and authors whose unity is difficult if not impossible to grasp. Opposing parties claim him, both the Vichy regime and the Resistance. He is loved on the left and the right; he is hated by both. Very few can boast they have read his complete works, which have never been published in their entirety. All parties have formed their own idea of him, good or bad; and most often, they believe passionately in it. In 1973, Jean Bastaire published *Péguy tel qu'on l'ignore* (Péguy as we do not know him).[1] This is a wholly remarkable anthology representing a certain point of view, "Péguyism on the left," let us say. The author alerts us to this: "Péguy is a dangerous author because he disrupts received ideas, threatens conformism. . . . The right reduced him to the dimensions of a little soldier in dark red pants, dying for his country with crucifix in hand. The left did even better: it made him vanish." The collection that follows, without forgetting Péguy the patriot and Christian, restores the "revolutionary," "socialist," and "anarchist" Péguy. Two years later, Jean Bastaire repeated the offense in his essay *Péguy l'insurgé* (Péguy the insurgent).[2]

That title attracted the mocking laughter of Henri Guillemin, who after research spanning about "twenty years," in 1981 published his *Charles Péguy*.[3] In it he recalls with wicked pleasure that in 1942 Brasillach called Péguy "a very great sociologist worthy of being the inspiration of the new France, in short, a French national socialist." Well before him, Mussolini had written: "In the great river of fascism, you will find the currents. . . . of Sorel, Péguy, and Lagardelle."[4] Bernard-Henri Lévy, in his stunning *Idéologie française* (French ideology), maintains that the question of "Péguy the nationalist or Péguy the socialist?" was of little interest, inasmuch as, like Barrès, he announced "a *French-style national socialism*," no less![5]

Fortunately for the good health of French letters, all these passions at odds with each other have not discouraged patient criticism and research, from which the tragic figure of Péguy has gradually taken shape, wrested simultaneously from his unconditional "fans" and from his posthumous attackers. Let us therefore signal the work of Simone Fraisse, particularly her excellent *Péguy*, in the "Ecrivains de toujours" collection. It is designed for anyone wanting to learn something of the life and work of the founder of *Cahiers de la Quinzaine*.[6] Above all, I must recommend the book Géraldi Leroy devotes to Péguy's political philosophy and itinerary: *Péguy entre l'ordre et la révolution* (Péguy, between order and revolution).[7] In sober and precise language, drawing from the best sources—in particular, those possessed by the Centre Charles-Péguy in Orléans—Leroy displays the two qualities required of the historian: empathy and a critical mind.

Immutable or changing, loyalist or renegade? Was Péguy a timeless prophet or a weathercock shifting from anticlerical socialism to Catholic nationalism? One of the great merits of Leroy's book is that it organizes and analyzes Péguy's writings chronologically. Regardless of what the man himself may have said in his time to prove his invariability (retrospectively attributing his youthful Dreyfusism to his recently acquired Catholic faith, for example), Géraldi Leroy distinguishes the stages of his political evolution. The son of an upholsterer, the Orléans scholarship student was first a republican and a patriot. Between 1891 and 1898, he "converted" to an essentially moral socialism, under the influence of the trinity from the Ecole Normale: Jaurès, Andler, and Herr. In 1898, he became one of the sublime agitators of the Dreyfus affair, kindling the passions of the indifferent, leading along the prudent, badgering all the socialist bigwigs to engage in the battle for justice. A Latin Quarter strategist, he mobilized his troops between Rue d'Ulm and the Sorbonne to counter nationalist gangs. He became disillusioned in 1899 at the socialist congress at the Salle Japy, when he discovered that Jaurès, the great Jaurès he admired, was sacrificing some of his convictions on the altar of unity with the Guesdists. The libertarian part of him rejected the dogmatism and sectarianism threatening the party as a result of Marxist domination: "I found Guesdism in socialism just as I found Jesuitism in Catholicism." He published his *Cahiers de la Quinzaine* under heroic conditions of perseverance and poverty; between 1900 and 1914, that journal recorded the marks of his progressive break with official socialism, his sympathy for revolutionary unionism, then his break with it. It also recorded the decisive shock he received from the "Tangier coup" in 1905, when he began to believe that everything had to be subordinated to the defense of the threatened nation. As a result, he marginalized himself from the workers' movement, remaining silent in the face of violent class confrontations in 1906–1909. In the last years of his life, he became a Catholic apart, a nationalist apart, a man alone, breaking with his friends one after another, filling his *Cahiers* with blind anger against the "modern world" and nasty furor against the men who incarnated it—Lavisse or Seignobos at the Sorbonne, Marc Sangnier within Catholicism, Jaurès within socialism. Despite all the ad hominem attacks, which have done such a disservice to his memory (those launched against Jaurès are the most famous), he has remained one of our great writers on poverty. In 1913, he wrote in *L'Argent Suite*:

I do not want anything to do with a Christian charity that would be a constant capitulation to princes, to the rich, to the power of money. I do not want anything to do with a Christian charity that would be a constant abandonment of the poor and oppressed. I recognize only one kind of Christian charity, my young comrade, and that is the charity that proceeds directly from Jesus (the Gospels, *passim*, or rather *ubique*): it is constant communion, both spiritual *and temporal*, with the poor, the weak, the oppressed.

Péguy rallied behind Poincaré, but he made an odd sort of Poincarist, repeating: "I am an old revolutionary" and glorifying the memory of the Paris Commune.

Géraldi Leroy tells us:

The circumstances made him a leftist who marched on the right. He now juxtaposed a flowery language of revolution with conservative practice. That contradiction, those oscillations between an obstructed and conservative present, which, in spite of everything, he could not reach, and a militant past, from which he could not and did not wish to detach himself altogether, explains the uneasiness of his prose, which tries to bridge the gap with unilateral excesses, forced antitheses, assertions as peremptory as they are disputable.

Despite Péguy's indisputable political evolution, the man and the work conserve a secret unity. A socialist, he did not join the class struggle; close to revolutionary unionists, he never said a word in favor of the general strike; when he became a nationalist, he remained firmly and definitively opposed to any form of anti-Semitism and asserted his constant admiration for Israel. "There is a Jewish resonance in Péguy," writes Edmond-Maurice Lévy, "that is absolutely unique in French literature." Péguy was never a party man. In Dreyfusism, he espoused a holy cause that combined people of all classes in a battle that was moral in its essence. For him, what followed Dreyfusism was a betrayal, because Dreyfusism lost its "mystique" and became "politics." His disgust with parliamentarianism, his moralism, and his distrust of the class struggle finally revealed a repugnance for politics, which must have its explanation somewhere. For Géraldi Leroy, the key to Péguy must be sought in his childhood, in the education he received; he was "too good a student" of the republican school, a son who respected the taboos of an authoritarian mother. He "internalized the imperatives of the social and familial ethic far too much to be able to liquidate them completely, even at the price of spectacular manifestations. Thus he obeyed them in disguised form."

In any case, Péguy was not only a moralist in the political life of France, he was one of the country's best prose writers as well. One must seek not "doctrinal coherence" in him, but cries of splendid fervor and indignation; the finest hymns to justice, truth, and poverty, next to the most unfair polemical digs; a sense for the lapidary expression within a plodding prose style. That is why he is still spoken of today. It remains to be seen whether he is destined to remain an author known only for selected excerpts—the best and the worst of legacies.

CHAPTER 20

Gustave Hervé: From Social War to War

GUSTAVE HERVÉ was not much to look at. But his looks were like no one else's. Short and plump with cropped hair, he carelessly let a few whiskers sprout on his chin; his myopic eyes peered out from pince-nez. One might easily have taken his flaccidity for that of a character from a Courteline novel, if he had not had the idea of squeezing his flab into a tight jacket with a military collar, which he had had tailored into an old officer's tunic. It was no doubt that martial attire that accounted for his nickname, "the General."

He was a general, in fact, but of a peculiar army: the army of antimilitarists and antipatriots. In about 1910, when he was editing the weekly *Guerre Sociale* (Social war), he could boast he had thousands of "good fellows" at his command, who awaited only his signal to cause an insurrection. For a feverish minority of the Socialist party and a good number of anarchists, then, Gustave Hervé was a true revolutionary. He did not seek a career in the Chamber, like the "blabbers" and "bourgeois" of the party. Some called him the "modern Blanqui": he believed in the show of force more than in the ballot box and spent a good part of his time in prison— just like Blanqui.

The department of Yonne was the district where his first armed exploits took place. Hervé was a true Breton, however: he was from Brest. After receiving a scholarship, he was able to study in Paris. And then, by dint of obstinacy, sacrifice, and solitary work, he was transformed from a school prefect into a professor. He obtained his *agrégation* in history in 1897. He settled in Sens in the midst of the Dreyfus affair; it was there his public career began.

His career as a professor was short-lived, for he was dismissed fairly quickly by the Conseil Supérieur de l'Instruction Publique (Higher council of public education). It seems that despite the debonair impression he left of himself, Hervé was a violent man. A socialist of the extremist stripe, he took the lines of *L'Internationale* literally. An explosive article published on 6 July 1900 in *Le Travailleur Socialiste* of Yonne was the beginning of his glory. In it, Hervé celebrated the anniversary of the battle of Wagram in his own way: "Wagram, day of shame and mourning!" The conclusion of the piece attracted particular attention:

As long as there are barracks for the edification and moralization of the soldiers of our democracy, I should like, in order to dishonor militarism and wars of conquest in their eyes, to have all the garbage and sewage from the barracks assembled in the main yard of their quarters; and solemnly, in the presence of all the troops in dress uniform, the colonel with his plume, to the sound of military music, should come plant the regiment flag in it.

The article was signed "Man without a Country," but given the reaction it caused, little time was lost finding the true author. General André, minister of war, lodged a complaint. Prosecuted in Auxerre in November 1901, Hervé was defended by Aristide Briand. The jury, apparently unmoved by the opprobrium heaped on the French flag, or charmed by the soothing voice of a lawyer who would go on to seduce others, acquitted Hervé of the sacrilege. In the eyes of the vigilant patriots of public education, however, no one consigns the flag to the dung heap with impunity: on 6 December 1901, Gustave was kicked out of his teaching job.

But no matter, the pedagogue in Hervé was not to lie dormant. He gave free rein to his vocation as a teacher throughout his life, and not only in the newspapers. He wrote history books and manuals in civic instruction, unofficial ones of course, which he proudly signed: "Gustave Hervé, *agregé* of the university, dismissed professor." These manuals were not to the liking of his alma mater. In them, Hervé professed his socialist faith with strong images and simple words: "The socialists maintain that beyond borders, all exploited workers have the same interests; that they must come together to prevent the ruling classes from setting them upon one another in international fratricidal wars."

You can imagine the scandal these manuals caused, at a time when all little French children were weaned on the patriotic ideas of Ernest Lavisse, and where grownups, even those on the left, still considered the army an "Ark of the Covenant."

Gustave Hervé had few ideas of his own. He was merely repeating the doctrine of the socialist left on the question of the army and the nation. But he had character. As a born instigator, he knew the art of concentrating these ideas into formulations designed to shock. His infamous *Histoire populaire* (Popular history) was the subject for a debate in the Chamber, which earned him Jaurès's solidarity and an overwhelming vote against him.

A fallen professor, Hervé earned his *licence* in law and became a lawyer. Another career quickly cut short! Hardly had he joined the Paris bar in 1905 than he was struck from the list of the Conseil de l'Ordre (Council of Order) before he could save the hide of the most inconsequential apple thief. Concession, it seems, was not his style, and he continued his antimilitarist campaign, distinguishing himself one more time in 1905, with his signature on the Red placard "to the conscripts," which raised protests even in socialist ranks.

Clearly, there was now only one forum in which he could continue to throw his firecrackers in full independence: the newspaper. With several friends, he launched a revolutionary weekly, *La Guerre Sociale*, in December 1906. It was the newspaper, he would say, of antiparliamentary and antireformist socialists; of unionists of direct action; of libertarian communists who were preparing to lead the masses toward future insurrection; in short, "an organ with a revolutionary focus."

Success eluded them. The newspaper was sharp and well written. Almeyreda, the assistant editor, had a knack for making up titles that were right on target. The articles and caricatures delighted an entire faction of the far left, which made fun of "pinko socialists." Hervé and his companions fed the insurrectional, antimilitarist, and anticolonialist spirit with rounds of thundering declarations and reporting used for effect. The Moroccan crisis gave them the opportunity to rail against the "thievery" of conquest and to take the side of the Moroccans. Indictments rained down, convictions accumulated, La Santé and the Conciergerie became Hervé's secondary residences. Nothing seemed able to stop him. Yet apart from his articles, the extremist journalist gave all the appearances of a quiet man. He did not "go out," despised restaurants, slept like a baby, did not have a mistress as far as anyone knew. He had only one weakness— for little ready-cooked dishes and, from time to time, good bottles of burgundy, which he had learned to appreciate in his adopted province. He went to prison and left prison with the peacefulness of a government worker going to the office. This vociferator did not like swear words or bad manners. Behind his heated rhetoric a soul at peace looked on.

Between two stints at La Santé, he led protests at socialist congresses and was followed by an "insurrectionist" faction. His specialty was to demolish parliamentary action. He could boast that Hervéism was gaining ground, and not only through words. In October 1909, he was the one who organized the demonstration in front of the Spanish embassy following the execution of Francisco Ferrer, one full night of pitched battle, during which the unavoidable police prefect Lépine was nearly killed. Even better, in 1910 Hervé sent his troops to save another condemned man from the guillotine; the man, named Libeauf, was said to be innocent. Naturally, after that battle, Hervé found himself once more in prison.

But in the end, prison mellowed him.

When Gustave Hervé was once more released from the Conciergerie in July 1912, he published the result of his prison meditations in *La Guerre Sociale*. He was still the same Hervé—he said, he proclaimed—still the revolutionary socialist they had always known. But he had done some reflecting. Tactics had to change on three points. First, there would be no more attacking parliamentary activity, because that was weakening the party. Second, a "disarmament of hatred" was needed, in the face of the danger of Caesarism and war; only a unified bloc made up of the Socialist party and the CGT stood in the way of a new Boulangism. Third, and this was the most novel point, Hervé asked his friends to reconsider the military problem. If they were to make revolution, they had to count on the support of the army, or a part of the army; thus antimilitarism was dead, long live "revolutionary militarism." Now he needed to get his socialist ideas into the barracks, transform the Blues into Reds, and even win over the underpaid noncommissioned officers and even the officers, most of whom were impoverished intellectuals.

The ordinary reader of *La Guerre Sociale* was left stunned. The "General," who clearly deserved that nickname, tried to explain himself at a large meeting at the Salle Wagram (the name "Wagram" pursued him!) on 25 September 1912. There was a crowd, but the orator was heckled by the anarchists of the Communist Federation. Fists and gunshots vied for attention. Hervé, protected by his young muscle-bound guards, retained his control over the hall. He was able to shout out his new watchword, which he borrowed from Napoleon: "A revolution is an idea backed up by bayonets."

When the war broke out in 1914, Hervé wanted to join up, but the minister of war maintained that, as head of his newspaper, he was too precious. Of course! Since Hervé always made too much of everything, he now went all out in his patriotism. On 9 August, *La Guerre Sociale* reproduced Déroulède's *Le clairon* (The bugle) on the front page, with a photograph of the leaguist poet as a bonus.

Neo-Hervéism antagonized the authorities of the SFIO just as much as early Hervéism had done. On 1 January 1916, Hervé the poilu exchanged his *Guerre Sociale* for a daily, whose name—*La Victoire* (Victory)—was more appropriate for the circumstances. In his editorials, he developed the idea of a "national socialism," which he opposed to the class struggle and internationalism. On 22 October 1916, Hervé was expelled from the Socialist party.

The war completed the metamorphosis of the ex-insurgent. In the 1920s and 1930s, he kept the same passion, but he changed his faith. Yesterday, revolution; today, the nation. For another twenty years, he would expend all his energy in support of his "national socialism," as founder of short-lived groups, and as the always disinterested and always vehement editorialist at *La Victoire*. In 1935, he called for an authoritarian and plebiscitary republic. After the left's victory in 1936, he published a pamphlet with the sadly premonitory title: *C'est Pétain qu'il nous faut* (It's Pétain we need). Hervé, however, ceased all political activity when, with France lying in defeat, the marshal dictator whom he had so desired was installed.

Gustave Hervé's life is both touching and ridiculous, the history of a renegade, of a shifting weathercock. The twentieth century is crammed full of them. Similar itineraries have been known to turn in a more dangerous direction. Mussolini was also a champion of antimilitarism. One must always beware of champions.

CHAPTER 21

A Fascist Parable: Drieu La Rochelle's 'Gilles'

DESPITE THEIR political failure in France, fascist ideas were able to find fertile ground: a spiritual community that formed around the works of Drumont, Barrès, and Maurras naturally leaned in that direction. Is it not in France that the clearest signs—at least in terms of doctrine—of proto-fascism before 1914 were visible? Drumont's and Morès's activities, Barrès's "socialism," the convergence of Valois and Sorel: these were so many steps in the genesis of fascism, that is, in the theoretical alliance between nationalism and socialism against liberal and parliamentary democracy. Whatever might have come out of it, fascism was long thought by its French intellectual followers to be the result of a voluntary synthesis of the left wing of Action Française (Valois) with the defectors from revolutionary unionism (Berth, Sorel), a synthesis that occurred before 1914: "They are two movements that seem to be, and in fact are, at opposite ends of the spectrum; and yet it is from the free opposition between them that the new social equilibrium will surge forth."[1] As in Italy during the same period—the meeting of a far left and a nationalist far right around *Lupa*, a journal edited by Paolo Orano[2]—there was a melting pot in France, described by Drieu La Rochelle:

When we turn to that era, we undoubtedly find that several elements of the fascist atmosphere came together in France in 1913, before they existed elsewhere. There were young people from various classes of society who were motivated by the love of heroism and violence and who dreamed of doing battle with what they called evil on two fronts: capitalism and parliamentary socialism, and of taking the best part from both. There were people in Lyon, I believe, who called themselves royalist socialists or something like that. The marriage of nationalism and socialism was already being planned. Yes, in France, around Action Française and Péguy, there was the nebula of a kind of fascism.[3]

Let us set aside the approximate nature of such an evocation: the important thing is the definition of fascism, as it was believed in (and not as it was realized), as that explosive alliance between two "absolutes"—as Berth also said—on which Georges Valois attempted to impose a structure by founding the Faisceau in 1925 on the Mussolini model.

"The opposition between nationalism and socialism," he wrote, "appeared irreducible in the parliamentary regime. The rescue operation of fascism consisted in negating the irreducible character of that opposition."[4]

The Faisceau enjoyed a long life, as we know, but the idea underlying it—that famous operative synthesis—did not. The common denominator of what has sometimes been called "the spirit of the 1930s"[5] was the rejection of bourgeois and parliamentary democracy, and the desire to unite the energies of the right and left against the lifeless republic of integration, so as to build a "new order." After February 1934, the "nonconformists of the 1930s"[6] had to choose their camp: some chose the right, others the left. It was clearly difficult to change the rules of the political game in France. It was at that moment, however, that Pierre Drieu La Rochelle was overwhelmed with new hope: at the demonstration of 6 February, could not communist workers be seen marching in step with nationalist bourgeois? Shortly thereafter, he declared himself a fascist and published a series of articles, which were soon collected under the title *Socialisme fasciste* (Fascist socialism).[7] In 1936, Drieu thought he had found the political expression of his ideas in the PPF and its leader, Doriot, the finally discovered master of fascist synthesis. For two years, Drieu stood as one of the most prominent spokespersons for *L'Emancipation Nationale*, the PPF newspaper, until his break with Doriot in October 1938.

During the same period, another fascist writer, Robert Brasillach, followed a parallel if not identical itinerary. For him as well, the "great quest" was to realize "the fascist or national socialist idea," that is, "the union between a strong social doctrine and a national intellect."[8]

If such was the originality of fascism in its beginnings, its failure can be legitimately surmised: in the Mussolini and Hitler regimes, taken as an example by French fascist writers,[9] we know the extent to which nationalism completely suffocated "socialism." But even if we remain within the scope of the French fascists, we can assess the poverty of their own socialism: although Valois remained close to Sorelian conceptions, Drieu and especially Brasillach did not take the most common founding principles of socialism seriously. The word "socialism" was handy, and it was misused. In Drieu's case, we might even wonder how far his nationalism went: was it not the tragedy of French fascists to believe they saw "the dawn of fascism breaking over France"[10] after 6 February, and to then have to suffer the victory of the Front Populaire two years later? Doubts about France ("Will they really make us believe that henceforth noble feelings are incomprehensible to France?")[11] led to hope in Europe, a Europe that in many places was already escaping liberal decadence. Drieu's nationalism, impracticable within the French framework, led logically to a "European nationalism" that already anticipated the "collaborationist" impasse of the Occupation years.

If Drieu's socialism is more than suspect, if his nationalism is unreliable, what remains of the fascist synthesis and the novelty of fascism? Very little, in truth, as attested in *Gilles*, that final balance sheet of a novel, the autobiographical novel Drieu wrote on the eve of war.

The novel is indispensable for the historian of political ideas. In the apparent disorder of the plot but in accordance with a logic proper to the author's ideology—Drieu was the key thinker for the PPF for two years—it presents, better than most theoretical writings, a rich catalog of fascist ideas as they were expressed within the French framework.

Gilles was published in October 1939, and the war censor suppressed many passages from the novel at that time; the complete version appeared in 1942, augmented by a preface written by the author in July of the same year.

Let us recall the main lines of this story, which retraces in its own manner about twenty years of history, from World War I to the Spanish civil war.

The first part of the novel, "La permission" (The leave) narrates the return to Paris of a young soldier, Gilles Gambier, who has just been wounded at the front. With no family except an impecunious guardian retired to Normandy, the young man, without money but wanting to enjoy to the maximum the delights available away from the front, manages to live in comfort with the help of women, on whom he exerts universal appeal. One of them, Myriam Falkenberg, the sister of two comrades in arms "who died on the battlefield," succeeds in holding onto him. She is pretty, intelligent; above all, she is rich. This "good match" decides him in favor of marriage, despite his prejudices, while at the same time he obtains a post at the Quai d'Orsay through the favor of his future wife's family. Following this profitable but immoral marriage, an attack of dignity sends Gilles back to the front, where new love affairs serve to complete the breakup with a wife he never loved.

The second part, "L'Elysée" (The Elysée) is set in the 1920s. Gilles leads a frivolous and inattentive life in Paris; he is devoid of ambition, despite his duties at the ministry. After divorcing Myriam, he seems finally to be successful in love, with Dora, a young American woman, mother of two children—until the day when, as both he and Dora are faced with a decisive choice, he feels the sorrow of losing his mistress and the conviction that he is being punished for his mediocrity. That mediocrity is bigger than he, it is a characteristically French mediocrity that also afflicts his entourage. He frequents a group of revolutionary literary writers, led by a man named Caël, and he places his hope in these new friends. He wants to destroy or help to destroy the bourgeois society that horrifies him. He soon notices, however, the pusillanimity of these café revolutionaries: the plot they are contemplating against the honor of the president of the Republic ends in the most piteous and shameful manner for them.

The third part, "L'apocalypse" (The apocalypse), transports us to the 1930s and especially to 1934. Leaving the Quai d'Orsay, deliberately choosing poverty—a poverty he had always feared—Gilles retires to the Algerian desert. He later returns to Paris with Pauline (whom he later marries) and male resolutions. In Paris he founds *L'Apocalypse*, a journal of opinion, which allows him to earn a modest living for himself and Pauline. The journal is a satire of Radical Socialist France: it is also, he says, a "prayer." Having now entered the political arena, Gilles for some time awaits salvation from a fruitful alliance of the powerful forces remaining in France: the far right and the far left. For a moment, he believes the occasion has arrived when he senses intentions similar to his own in Clérences, a radical Young Turk. But 6 February carries him from the greatest exaltation to the most profound depression, all within a few hours. Pursued by the mad hope that everything is becoming possible, Gilles urges Clérences to act, but the notably indecisive character of his friend confirms his feeling, which was challenged during the uprising, of the irremediable decadence of France. It is on the occasion of these tragic days, the last chance for insurrection finally ruined, that he declares himself openly "fascist."

The Spanish civil war is the setting for the "epilogue." Gilles participates on the side of Franco. The harsh discipline of war saves him in his own eyes from the fall his country has been led into. Military asceticism, the taste for action, the ethics of risk, prepare him for a heroic death at the very least, which he awaits rifle in hand.

Let us note in passing the indisputably autobiographical nature of this novel. Gilles has more than one of Drieu's character traits. If we confine ourselves to the factual resemblance between the novelist's life and the character's, we also note obvious coincidences. The novelist who published *Gilles* in 1939 was forty-six years old, roughly the same age as his hero, like him a veteran, and like him wounded in battle. Both had a first marriage to a Jewish woman; both divorced. Drieu frequented the Dadaists and then the Surrealists, just as Gilles became part of the Caël group— Caël is a recognizable caricature of André Breton. There are many other traits in common as well. We know that Gilles's despair after Dora left him is an episode actually lived by his literary father in 1925; that Drieu was an associate of Bergery just as Gilles was the friend of Clérences; that he finally acknowledged his fascism in 1934, just like his hero. These examples are sufficient: under the mask of artistic creation, a writer and political man admits a fascist "vocation" and at the same time gives us an assessment of it.

In the first place, *Gilles* is no doubt the analysis, or self-analysis, of a particular case, that of Pierre Drieu La Rochelle. In a study that appeared recently, Dr. Robert Soucy shows us that Drieu's political and ideological choices can be explained on the basis of what might be called his "inferiority complex."[12] That is not my purpose here; on the contrary, I would like to point out the more universal content of *Gilles*, the part that transcends Drieu. How are the ideas, images, and myths conveyed by this novel linked to an ideology that, while properly Drieu's, was also shared in many respects by the entire intelligentsia on the right of his time? The fact that psychoanalysis, or any other school of psychology, allows us to better understand Drieu's path appears indisputable, but in my view it cannot explain the ultimately fascist choice he makes. His predisposition toward neurosis, acquired in early childhood, his efforts to conquer his fear, his desire to overcome his anxiety, might have dictated completely different choices. In other words, the analysis of "political ideas" does not seem superficial to me; these "ideas" may not exist by themselves, but that does not mean they emerge from the mere fantasies of an isolated individual; they are part of a culture and a time. By that very fact, they transcend the person who propagates them. It is the specific character of this novel by Drieu that I want to hold onto, and at times the least personal aspects of what it conveys: how it bears witness to French fascism as a whole. Fascism as it appears in this book is a violent rejection of contemporary France, an avowed nostalgia for a bygone golden age and a less precise dream of a new order. It is within that secret structure that the lesson of *Gilles* is revealed; it is that lesson I shall pursue.

A final remark on method is indispensable from the outset. Drieu's discourse can be understood on three levels: first, there is direct discourse, the author setting out his thoughts in an explicit manner; second, there is indirect discourse, symbolic or parabolic, with the author consciously attempting to complement his lesson with an example or an image, leaving the reader the responsibility to draw conclusions; and finally, there are unconscious confessions in the narrative that the author makes in spite of himself. In my discussion, I will combine these three registers out of concern for synthesis. That will lead me simultaneously to give an ideological transcription of the novel as Drieu might have plausibly accepted it and to risk a personal interpretation—which may obviously include a critique.

Decadence

In the preface to *Gilles*, Drieu situates his novel—and all his writings, in fact—on the dung heap of French decadence: "Like every other contemporary writer, I found myself faced with an overwhelming fact: decadence."[13] The word (or the idea) is the leitmotif of *Gilles*: there is no event or character that does not take it into account in a certain manner. In addition, that decadence appears "irremediable" (94), at least in the eyes of Carentan, Gilles's old guardian. Drieu presents Carentan to us as a kind of seer, retired to his Norman property, someone who is consulted from time to time like Pythia of Delphi: "Behold," says the oracle, "the last days of that infamous 'civilization.' The Europe that did not crumble in 1918 is slowly headed for its ruin" (179).

"France is dying" of multiple incurable maladies. One has only to visit the Norman village to assess the ravages of depopulation and alcoholism. There were the dead of World War I, the wounded, the disabled, survivors without progeny, or those who had children "who all died at an early age; alcoholism and syphilis" (342); then there were all those who left for the city. The description turns the stomach. France has not recovered from its great blood-letting, and those who have survived it are afflicted with dipsomania and infertility. If decadence has corrupted even the village, you can imagine the depravity eating away at the city. "Cinemas, cafés, brothels, newspapers, stock markets, political parties, and barracks" (340) are all so many ignominious attributes of the modern world. The nadir is Paris, which has become a concentration of slovenly intellectuals (they have lost "the dignity of ancient mores" [384]), revelers, homosexuals ("They are everywhere. Along with drugs, that is the malady most responsible for tearing Paris's heart out" [455]), Picasso's paintings, cabarets, Catholic novelists, Jews, "wily Freemason radicals" (ibid.). One gauges the depth of the evil.

The so-called elites make a degrading spectacle of themselves; Gilles, whether turning toward the men in power, incarnated by the Radicals, or toward those representing revolt, such as the young people gathered around Caël (i.e., the Surrealists), feels the same nausea. In Drieu's caustic writing, Radicalism is rent to pieces. Herriot, paragon of parliamentarianism, pillar of the bourgeois republic, easily recognizable behind the caricature Chanteau, expresses all the moral and physical obesity of declining Radicalism. He is nothing but a tub of lard (391, a noun repeated with delight as a key word), incapable of a forceful outburst, but cunning and self-satisfied, entrenched in this republican regime whose staff "is truly a world of heirs, of descendants, of degenerates, a world of stand-ins" (386). The fascist style of satire showed a particular fondness for sexual images and vocabulary, and Drieu is no exception to the rule. Hence, between the Radical speaker and his public, "in the place of a healthy and fertile sexual encounter, two instances of onanism come together, brush against each other, then go their separate ways" (390). Such men could be in power only because "there is a virulent syphilis in France" (343). Against the Radicals, the petty bourgeois of the journal *Révolte* contested bourgeois France, but to no avail: they were its parasites. The portrait Drieu draws of them is often of dubious intellectual honesty: by combining true, notorious acts (certain public pronouncement by Breton, for example) so that there can be no mistake, with fictional inventions that depict the figure in an ignoble light, the author indulges in the pleasure of railing against his enemies in public view but within the shelter of fiction. The Surrealists (who are never called by that name) are rebels who tremble before the police; when they fight, they use nasty little kicks, and not "great swipes of the tiger's paw" (211), as heroes do, before calmly filling their pipes. Caël, alias Breton, is merely a "café Grand Inquisitor" (330); around him is a crowd of feeble bourgeois, women, impotents, who despite their blustering words against the well-off, in the end join with the previously criticized Radicals out of political opportunism. Things come full circle, the young bourgeois eventually back up their flatulent progenitors. Professional politicians and Montparnasse rebels belong to the same family.

Two figures in the novel personify French decadence. First, there is Gilles himself, the early Gilles, the one who marries for money, who agrees with Carentan, his old master, when he argues for the suppression of brothels but cannot resolve to stop going to them; the idle Gilles, the nihilist, frequenting the Caël gang, participating in its mascarades for the sheer pleasure of destruction, the only force remaining within him; the childless Gilles, guilty of the sin of "avarice." Second, there is the symbolic figure of Pauline, a former "tart" who has become Gilles's lady companion. Like France, she is not lacking in virtue, but like it she is mortally wounded: "He moved toward her now as toward a dilapidated temple struck by lightning, where a troubling atmosphere of disaster, ruin, and sterility reigned" (400). Since Gilles has lost faith in France, "he no longer believed in Pauline, sterile, marked by death, but above all bourgeois" (408). And he adds further on, so that the allegory will be clear: "France was dying while Pauline was dying" (425).

What is the secret of that decomposition? Looking closely, we must seek the most profound explanation in a sort of "physiological determinism":[14] France is dying as a race. Apart from the increased presence of foreigners in France—"wogs," Czechs, Poles—the glaring proof of French decadence is the omnipresence and occult power of the Jews. According to Robert Soucy, who refers to an article by Drieu on "the Jewish question," in 1938 Drieu "was not yet converted to racism": "It was only after the defeat of France, and after Drieu had rallied behind collaboration" that that conversion supposedly occurred.[15] The text of *Gilles* does not confirm that conclusion: Drieu's racism is asserted throughout. Not only are the Jews denounced as products of culture but—already as a race biologically distinct from the others—as factors of natural degeneration.

The Jew, according to Drieu, is the modern world made flesh: "As for me, I cannot bear the Jews," says Carentan, "because they are the modern world par excellence."[16] And he adds, "the Jew is horrible as a student at the Ecole Polytechnique or the Ecole Normale" (100). And again: "The most frivolous of Jewesses rams the stock market and the Sorbonne down your throat" (ibid.). Drieu does not fail to recall the explanation for that Jewish modernity, which is found in the anti-Semitic tradition on the right: "The Jews remain aridly faithful to 1789, which got them out of the ghetto" (401). A rootless nomad, the Jew is the parasitic insect in the belly of the nation. When a country has lost the wisdom to seek inspiration from its own traditions, to drink from the spring of its age-old virtues, the Jew, product of the Revolution, of capitalism, and of scientism, springs up from the guarded perimeter where our ancestors had the wisdom to contain him. Through cunning and money, he insinuates himself into the weakened social body: "There must be a biological necessity to the Jews' role, for the saliva of decadence always contains their words" (387). That allusion to biology is still merely a figure of speech, but it is only a short step from the image to the "scientific" explanation.

The Jews are antiphysical, disincarnated mind; for them, fiduciary value takes the place of metal coins. In short, they are a personification of the abstract. Drieu provides this key to the Myriam character: "In her milieu, there was no knowledge of physical experience, whether in sports, love, or war" (29). This is not a family defect, but a racial one, since it is also found among other Jews, for example, Cohen, whom Gilles meets in Spain in a tragic case of mistaken identity. While together in the same airplane in distress, "Cohen was abominably exasperated not to be able to do anything to alter their chances. He had run up against necessity and the simplicity of physical action. . . . He would have liked to communicate his cunning [to the pilot], his art of landing on his feet in life. But how could he change that paper money into the gold of a man's work?" (447) The stock market and the Sorbonne become inoperative as soon as physical action is required: revenge of the old race, of peasant civilization. When ruse becomes powerless, the "voice of the blood" speaks.

That is because the Jews' faults are not exclusively cultural phenomena: they are congenital, hereditary, and unavoidable. Although *Gilles* depicts a gallery of Jews, the existence of each one is subordinated to a higher essence: they are consubstantially part of Jewry, so many hypostases of a pure idea. Whatever they say, whatever they do, they belong to the ac-cursed race. Gilles/Drieu explicitly believes in the theory of races: "Oh! Races, races. There are races, I have a race" (91). And that race must guard against intermixing if it wishes to safeguard its intrinsic qualities: on that point, instinct tells no lies. Gilles marries the Jewish Myriam because he needs her money, but, despite his good intentions, it takes enormous effort for him to successfully fulfill what is here strictly speaking his conjugal duty, so much so that the day of his wedding he goes to see a prostitute of his acquaintance to build up his courage. He is never cured of his reflex-ive disgust, and as a result, he finally seeks a divorce. Drieu thus illustrates the so-called law of repulsion imagined by Gobineau, which postulates the instinctive opposition to racial mixing.[17] To purify himself of sexual intercourse with a representative of the forbidden race, Gilles, once his di-vorce is granted, "rushed to Scandinavia."[18] The allusion is clear. Drieu La Rochelle is already lending credit to the Aryan myth. Just as Myriam re-pels Gilles physically in spite of himself, Dora (that is, the Doric, the Indo-European woman, the Aryan) attracts him and triumphantly holds onto him. "That American woman, with her mix of Scottish, Irish, and Saxon blood, combined and multiplied several characteristics of Nordic peoples. And that was where all Gilles's emotions were concentrated."[19] For Gilles/Drieu, to have married a Jewish woman is "the ineffaceable stain";[20] the "terrible silence of the flesh"[21] established between Gilles and Myriam is in the nature of things, one cannot with impunity infringe upon "blood affinity." Without appealing to Büchner's *Blutsverwandtschaft*, which became a dogma of the Hitler regime, Drieu expresses ideas drawn from French culture—especially and primarily from Barrès, whom he fervently admired.[22]

In that description of "the winter of the people,"[23] it is not difficult to detect the recurrent influence of Barrès. As a novel of decomposition, *Gilles* abounds in images of death, the void, decay. France is described as a moribund prostitute; around her bed "feeble and perverted old men,"[24] "petty intellectuals, the last drops of sperm squeezed out of them,"[25] and Jewish charlatans move in a grotesque danse macabre. Barrès's funereal romanticism, his "dread of the mutable,"[26] his obsession with death, are picked up by Drieu in these passages. Drieu is even more persuaded than his master of the incurable malady from which France is suffering. If we find the same lugubrious images of French decadence in Barrès that later proliferated in Drieu's writings, we also read the same disappointment in not being able to count on a French race, a "pure" race that would assure national recovery: "Alas!" wrote Barrès, "there is no French race, but only a French people, a French nation, that is, a collectivity that is political in its formation."[27] And considering with the same uneasiness the gravely significant difference between Dora's Aryan "purity" and the random characteristics of his "Latin race," Gilles/Drieu wonders: "What did he know about his race?"[28] He is a bastard of unknown origin, a product of unknown mixing, like the French nation. This is certainly one of the reasons for Drieu's Europeanism: from a France of mixed blood, a "Jewified" France sinking "to the level of death,"[29] he appeals for a Europe where the Nordic element would have preeminence—as a guarantor of strength and resistance to "petrification."

The Myth of the Golden Age

The contemporary world is a universe plucked bare in which the fascist hero finds only the morbid flavor of the void, since he is nostalgic for the bygone time before decadence. The first bittersweet fruits of decline may have been gathered in the springtime of more or less distant times. Some miss "the century of Louis XIV," others "the golden age of nobility," situated between the Hundred Years' War and the early seventeenth century; in general, such nostalgic people are agreed in thinking that decadence was definitively in place with the triumph of democracy. For Drieu, the luminous era was the Middle Ages. The myth of a golden age is part of every place and every time. Even Homeric poems describe the past in a captivating manner: it was the age when all mortals lived as gods, "their heart free from worry," writes Hesiod, "safe from weariness and misfortune." "And comparing present misery to the happy colors of the past as he has imagined it, the poet in despair contrasts the dark days of the iron age to the sunny days of the golden age."[30] That notion of the Middle Ages varied across time: scorned by Boileau's contemporaries and later by those of Emile Combes, the Middle Ages progressively became a constant reference point in the ideology of the French right (and among great Catholic writers, if we think of Bloy and Bernanos). Drieu turns the myth to his own account: in *Gilles*, the modern world, against which he cannot launch too many barbs, has as its radiant contrary the time of the Capetians, an era of an authenticity of land, as opposed to the falsity of chattel in the contemporary world. True France is not the product of dubious values—the stock market, the Sorbonne, the Ecole Normale, the Ecole Polytechnique, Freemasonry, Jewry, and so on—but rather of "mountains and rivers, trees and monuments. . . . Stone constructions touched and captivated him, for they were still so close to the stone lying in the gangue of the earth."[31] What follows is even more reminiscent of Barrès: "He had heard his steps echoing alone in all the churches of France, great and small. . . . The French people had made churches and they would never again make anything like them: the whole life adventure lay in that fact, the terrible necessity of death."[32] Periodically, Gilles returns to the forest, the village, the provinces, to rediscover "the value of gold . . . primitive value before any deterioration."[33] Fascist religion has clearly chthonian aspects: it worships *Terra Mater* and through her rediscovers the lost source of wisdom and of the race.

The ancient symbol par excellence of that ancient religion is the tree. A symbol of a prodigious fecundity in traditionalist French literature, it assumed major significance with M. Taine's plane tree. And as his disciple Barrès demonstrates, woe be to men wrested from their natural environment, uprooted. "As child of the earth, the tree is order, fidelity, tradition. Not liberty, but biological necessity. Not progress, but timelessness."[34] When Gilles takes Dora out for a walk, it is "always toward the forest,"[35] yet "he had never before dared take a woman among the great trees."[36] That last observation is rife with meaning: Drieu's hero sees very well the communication spontaneously established between the sacred forest and Dora, the representative of the great "Nordic" virtues; for she too "feels [her] roots."[37] When Gilles comes to seek counsel from his old Norman guardian, the latter quite naturally points out a beech tree as the seat of eternity: "What this beech tree says will always be said again, in one form or another, forever."[38] And when in the forest with Dora, Gilles places his hands on the trunk of a beech tree (yet another one!),[39] he finds it "odd to see such hands [long, white, slender] on that bark."[40] The city has made him effeminate and perverted. Dora, who understands the meaning of his reflection, rushes to reassure him: "You might have had another life" (ibid.), she says. The life of a rooted man.

In *Gilles*, the lament of a nostalgic man standing on the "ruins of the last medieval pillars" (402), Drieu sings melancholically of the time of epics, cathedrals, illuminations, crusades. When his hero devotes himself to journalism, he does so to declaim, in an even-tempered voice, against the modern world and, in his own expression, to sing "the ecstatic praise of truths lying forgotten in their graves" (364). Once upon a time, virtue preferred to wear mud-caked clogs; naïveté and spontaneity won out over the quibbles of pedants. That virile world was guided by feeling, one of the secrets of the Middle Ages. "The French were soldiers, monks, architects, painters, poets, husbands, and fathers. They had children, built things, killed, got themselves killed" (393). Such were the true heroes of

"French reason," the exact opposite of rationalism: "Yes, there was a French reason; but so vibrant, so hard, so naive, and so broad, embracing all the elements of being. Not only rational thought but the leap of faith" (392). Obviously, the Sorbonne so despised by the author was not part of that imagined Middle Ages: Thomas Aquinas counts for little compared to a single crusader. Catholicism was "male" (463), probably in contrast to a female Christianity of Semitic origin; it was the Catholicism of Simon de Montfort rather than Poverello. Drieu's Catholics were more likely to extend the sword than the other cheek.

Gilles/Drieu does not get his idea of the Middle Ages from the historians, but from the "devotees of antimodernism, from de Maistre to Péguy" (364). It was in their books that he sought the divine rule of lost wisdom and order. And if by chance the vicissitudes of life offered him a touching reincarnation of the ancient world, where everyone had a place (in the provinces, under the roof of the august Carentan), he waxed sentimental: "As she left, the servant girl closed the door, casting a long look of pride at them: *she was proud to serve*" (102). Such was the founding principle of the Middle Ages: it was an aristocracy, a hierarchized world, built on the strength and heritage of virile virtues. To believe Drieu, the Middle Ages had nothing but charm. Violence, famine, epidemics, superstitions, and wars were all mere trifles. One land, one king, one faith, one people: that is the lost and lamented paradise.

In *Gilles*, Carentan is obviously the one who incarnates medieval values. He is a sort of spirit, the specter of a rough-hewn thirteenth-century man, lost in the France of M. Doumergue. He spends his time studying the history of religion: he moves from one faith to another like an alchemist seeking eternal wisdom in every subsequent distillation. In France, he is the only Frenchman left—or almost. Sometimes, Drieu still bestows ancestral virtues on the peasants he meets, but they seem to him "the cantankerous rear guard of a routed army" (339). For a time, he believes he can sniff out "healthy and vigorous men" (402) in communist ranks—they have gone astray of course, but they are the descendants of the ancient common people in revolt. All things considered, the true French have already crossed the Atlantic: in Canada there are "French people for whom 1789 did not happen, nor the eighteenth century, nor even the seventeenth when all is said and done, nor the Renaissance and the Reformation. They are French people in their raw and naked state" (101). Rome is no longer at Rome; France follows on the heels of Quebec.

An artificial representation of the French past is characteristic of all ideologies. In Drieu's vision, the Middle Ages attest to the perfection of France's origins, that early time of harmony before the flood. Quite logically, Gilles/Drieu, its poet, aspires to restore a "New Middle Ages" (340).

A New Order

Gilles is a novel about grace, the story of the moral path taken by one man who, born at a time of decadence and nourished on its bitter fruits, attempts to transcend the era he disdains. In that attempt to escape contemporary mediocrity and to rediscover the traces of paradise lost, women are the first to be asked to play the mediating role. But on closer inspection, women prove to be artificial paradises: Gilles, who uses a large number of women, does not manage to emerge from decadence through their intercession, despite the time, affection, and love he sometimes lavishes on them. In fact, like Pauline, women are too often the living symbols of the Fall. The definitive salvation for Gilles, a man of the quest, a nostalgic knight errant, is politics. There, Gilles/Drieu finally discovers the means to transcend himself, his tangible hope for wresting himself from decline, and above all, his religion: "It would be his way of praying" (358).

Gilles's political maturation is slow. By birth and education, he says he is part of the right. But the French right, immoderately moderate and self-righteous, has no more appeal for an absolutist than Radicalism. Gilles has imperatives other than the defense of the prosperity of notables. He is sympathetic toward everything that, in a senile country such as France, has the ardor of youth; toward those who, whatever their banner, spit in the face of the old world of decadence. That is what sends him to the Surrealists, whose verbal aggressiveness and nihilism seduce him with their suicidal energy. He takes leave of them when he discerns the same shameful face of the feeble (another key word) bourgeois behind their mask. In the same way, Gilles, who has no fondness for Marxism, nonetheless declares his respect for communist militants, as we have seen. They have been deceived by theorists but are capable of violence against the modern world, which he also desires. All in all, Gilles wonders at one stage in his evolution, "Why not take the leap into communism?" (398) Let France be swept clean by destruction. Hastening death's destruction is one way of living. "He saw communism not as a force, but as a weakness that might coincide with France's weakness" (ibid.). It is not only that worst-case policy that links Gilles/Drieu to the communists; in reality, he has always dreamed of the union of all valiant people, of all rebels, of all agents of destruction. That dream to overthrow "the Freemason dictatorship . . . through a coalition of young bourgeois and young workers" (422) was not new: Drumont, Morès, and Barrès had already conceived of such a project in their time. The birth of that radical conservatism appealing to workers and Catholics against the "Jewish republic" occurred in the last decade of the nineteenth century. But that uniting of powerful forces—arbitrarily separated by ideologies until that time—was also, in another way, one of the illusions of that "spirit of the 1930s," which it would be wrong to assimilate to fascism. These diverse aspirations to transcend the traditional oppositions between the left and the right, to incite neo-Marxism in some, neo-nationalism in others, are found broadly expressed in *Gilles*. Traditionalists wanted to break with the capitalist compromises, while other factions wanted "to found a new Marxism in France that [is] neither obedient to Russia nor within the parliamentary routine of the Socialists" (378). Gilles brings together these factions—coming from every direction—who wish to wipe the slate clean. They have their heart set on a politician who might become their leader. This politician still belongs to the Radical party, but he also wants to get out of the cesspool: this is Clérences (a caricatural composite of Bertrand de Jouvenel, Bergery, and other Radicals with new ideas). Gilles feeds Clérences's energy, participates in the activities of his group, before finally becoming discouraged: "All these men belonged to the legal profession, clerics as they say, completely sterile. It was clear that life was not in France" (408).

But on his road to Damascus, Gilles is suddenly thrown off his horse by the thunderbolt of 6 February 1934. Until then, the storms so desired had all risen on the other side of the Rhine or of the Alps; the French skies remained drab. But joy! On 6 February, the revolt finally drenched Paris: "France was finally receiving the thoughts of all Europe, of the entire world in movement" (418). Every pillar of the old Palais-Bourbon was trembling. Gilles cries out to Clérences: "If a man stands up and throws his entire destiny into the balance, he can do what he likes. He will catch Action Française and the communists, Jeunesses Patriotiques and the Croix-de-Feu, and many others in the same net" (420). Gilles/ Drieu thus provides a perfect description of the genesis of the fascist movement, the first elements of a tactical coup d'état:

Attack Daladier or defend him, but in actions that are altogether concrete. Invade a newspaper on the right and a newspaper on the left, one after the other. Have someone on each side beaten at home. At all cost, leave behind the old parties, demonstrations, meetings, articles, and speeches. And you will immediately have a formidable binding power. The walls between the left and the right will be forever rent asunder, and the flood of life will rush out in every direction. Do you not sense the rising tide? The flood is there before us: we can channel it in the direction we wish, but we must channel it immediately, at all cost. (421)

A Mussolini was also needed, according to Malaparte, who draws this portrait of the Mussolini of October 1922: "A modern, cold, audacious, violent, and calculating man."[41] Alas! France does not find its leader and 6 February is only a day of fools. The old rascal quickly regains the upper hand, and Gilles "is sorry he came out of his prophetic disbelief for a moment on 6 February. After this last spasm leading nowhere, France could only sink to the level of death."[42] From then on, Gilles/Drieu's fascism assumed its clearest form: it entailed rediscovering, come what may, what his generation had learned from the war, in spite of the "people of France with hardened arteries":[43] namely, "the moving idea of a life of force."[44]

The worship of physical force, the obsession with virility, the disdain for intellectuals, are the many expressions of a defense of instinct. There again, Drieu invented nothing but simply illustrated the lesson of his masters, especially Barrès. Hence, in Drieu's fascism, the nostalgia for war, for the front, for danger, flourishes: war is man's ordeal; everything is simple in war, the exercise is never fake. Faced with danger, man is stripped bare, clothed only in his fears and his strengths: nerves, heart, and muscles. "The war is my nation,"[45] says Gilles. Did not Jules Soury, who taught Barrès so much, say: "War, happy or unhappy, eternal war, source of all higher life, the cause of all progress on earth."[46] The force that war reveals is above all the force of the body, since the body is the tabernacle of the most essential principles, those of instinct and race. The proof is that when a Jew, even an intelligent and clever one, finds himself in the grip of physical danger (for example, Cohen, whom we saw in the skies above Spain), he is obliged to confess his powerlessness.

The first governing idea, that of health, is linked to that of bodily force. "He knew he was the only one in his milieu who represented health."[47] Even when he is not climbing mountains, the fascist is a healthy man with bright eyes, the direct opposite of library men, who are doddering and myopic: "That whole little world of bourgeois intellectuals, shivering and quivering, made the agents grimace in disdain."[48] This is the same opposition found in Barrès, between the people and intellectuals. "The people," he says, "revealed the human substance to me and, more than that, creative energy, the vitality of the world, the unconscious."[49] In contrast, intellectuals, spoiled by Kantism and all other forms of abstraction, are characteristically disincarnated, they no longer even have a body. Burdeau-Bouteiller's indictment continues in Drieu: the cult of energy and action must replace the cult of reason. In the 1930s, Drieu felt as Barrès had in the 1890s. Barrès, disdaining doctrines, cried out: "It is vitality I savor."[50] And Drieu, dreaming of dissolving ideas into the purity of action, spitefully exclaims before an inert France: "Only one thing is missing: vitality."[51]

The corollary of Drieu's anti-intellectualism is the incessant glorification of virility. Intellectuals are "impotent"; on several occasions, Drieu puts dresses on them ("miserable little clerks, little monks in dresses" [338]). As with the ancient nobility, these men in robes are contrasted to men of the sword: "In the end, to think was to deal or receive a sword blow" (339). And he later adds something that leaves no doubt about the phallic symbolism: "Yes," thinks Gilles, entering a brothel, "they are men without swords" (ibid.). Hence it is clear that what separates the intellectual on the left from the fascist is first of all virility: "All those boys begrudge me," says Gilles, "because women like me" (337).

A second governing idea is to remake the aristocracy. The source of decadence is democracy. A hierarchized world must be recreated, a world where leaders—knights and not knaves—can command. "Gilles never believed for a second that it would be possible to believe in equality, in progress" (367). Those pernicious ideas were widespread in the eighteenth century: "One had to get rid of all those absurd claims to rationalism, to Enlightenment philosophy" (368). Gilles has more faith in obscure forces, mysterious gifts that ordain a leader. "I want to destroy capitalist society," he says, "in order to restore the notion of aristocracy" (102). The best man, the leader, is not the wealthiest or the most intelligent (the intellectual is good for nothing except being president), he is the man of action, the anti-Jew par excellence—since the Jew is the man of the transaction, the deal. How can we fail to mention once more the master Barrès: "A people and a country that lack an aristocracy have no model, no direction for perfecting themselves."[52]

The third governing idea is that "nationalism is outdated."[53] After 6 February, when the Café du Commerce and the lodges liquidated the revolt, Gilles understood there was nothing more to be hoped from "France by itself." Gilles admires Maurras, but he now judges him "small and powerless for the time being" (398). The new order had to be European or nothing at all. Drieu moves beyond the Barrésian perspective at this point: the new order will rise up from international fascism. In that new order, the Church has its role to play; it must again become the medieval Church. Virile Catholicism will have to consolidate the new Europe. "For myself, I have withdrawn from nationhood. I belong to a new military and religious order that was founded somewhere in the world and pursues the reconciliation of the Church and fascism, toward and against everything, and their dual triumph as one nation over other nations" (475). Whatever his political attitude after the German invasion, in 1929 Drieu clearly envisioned a fascist war against fascist Germany and Italy—did he not break with Doriot after the capitulation in Munich? But looking ahead, he predicted "the invasion of Europe by the Russian army"; against Russia, Germany would have to form a federation of nations (not dissolve them) and bring about "a European spirit of patriotism" (ibid.). Germany's vocation was thus clearly established: "By virtue of its force and the tradition of the Holy Roman–Germanic Empire, it is up to Germany to lead the European line of tomorrow" (476).

All in all, Drieu's fascism appears to be a desire to rebuild a united and aristocratic Europe, where true men and leaders will again rule clerks, women, Jews, and louts. To restore faith in the place of rationalism, revalue instinct over intellect and force over money, inundate mechanization and scientism with agrarian virtues: that was the program.

The later Gilles—Gilles the convert—is a symbol of that new order. He abandons Paris to serve Franco and European fascism, finds his bearings within war's simplicity, far away from women and from illusions, a fighter once more, and this time a soldier/monk. The last image in the book is particularly suggestive: Gilles is alone in an arena, and he fires on the approaching Republicans. The setting for that ending is not chosen at random: "The home of the bulls had to be defended," writes Drieu (484).

In *Gilles*, an astonishing catalog of fascist ideas, there are in fact few novelties. I have noted one central influence on Drieu, namely, Barrès. Nearly all Barrès's fundamental themes are transcribed in only slightly different terms: the keen sense of France's decadence, the racist explanation given for it, the nostalgia for ancestral values, aristocratic aspirations, the cult of instinct, anti-intellectualism. The filiation is clear. Other influences are apparent, already converging in Barrès. I am thinking in particular of Nietzsche, mentioned on several occasions in *Gilles*: Drieu's hostility toward "slave morality," which is "essentially a morality of utility";[54] his fondness for an aristocracy of force and the will to power; the aspiration, beyond nationalism, to see "future Europeans" come into being.[55] But more than these influences, what I find distinctive about fascist discourse in *Gilles* is its mythological character. With Drieu, we are far removed from the positivist claims made by Maurras and from Greco-Roman moderation. He finds his inspiration in Nordic peoples and praises excess. An intellectual, he deliberately prefers mythos to logos, since the critique of modern France goes hand in hand with a critique of rationalism, from which it stemmed. No doubt Drieu is not wrong to denounce the contempt for force, widespread among his contemporaries, and the primacy of intellectual values in the French educational system; no doubt he has arguments enough for his indictment of the France of the interwar period. In a review of *Gilles*, Emmanuel Mounier himself notes "that prewar France needed muscle and a little savagery."[56] But Drieu based his judgment of French decline as much on nonsense as on the realities: to prove decadence, he cited willy-nilly the falling birth rate and the rural exodus, that is, a trait of decline and a trait of modernism; cited alcoholism and Picasso's paintings, drugs and Catholic writers, and so on, all in the same breath. Refusing to give a serious analysis of the real and profound ills afflicting France, Drieu magically summed up all its misfortunes in the parabolic personality of the Jew, who represented at once the antiwarrior, the city-dweller, the banker, the quibbler, the Sorbonne pedant, and the Marxist, in short, a working model of everything he abhorred. More than a symbol of decadence, the Jew was decadence itself, its very incarnation: he was the modern man, just as for Maurras, Dreyfus was the republic. That willful mutilation of intelligence, that inclination for the irrational, that rejection of the real world, in short—a world whose complexity surely required intellectual rigor and humility more than hasty explanations—led Drieu into the dream world. His conception of the Middle Ages was nothing more than a gilded dream, the rejection, once more, of reality (historical reality this time). In the absence of science, the fascist preferred to abandon himself to a delirium about restoring a so-called golden age (which, by the way, varied from author to author), rather than taking the world as it was and attempting to transform it one step at a time. This was an eschatological vision of the world: the present had to be obliterated so that the perfection of origins could be rediscovered, recreated, by means of a return to the source. "Anything at all, provided that piece of junk over there at the edge of the water falls apart,"[57] says Gilles of the Palais-Bourbon. The important thing, the necessary thing, was to "destroy today's society" by any means.[58] The blank slate would then serve to prepare for the birth of a new world. As in archaic ways of thinking described by Mircea Eliade, "in the end, it is always a matter of obliterating the time that has elapsed," of "returning to the past," and "beginning existence over again with all its virtualities restored intact."[59] To complete that analogy between Gilles's behavior and archaic thought, we might be tempted to define fascism as ritual more than politics. Is not the hero's worship of the tree such a "return to the origin"—"the only means that archaic thought believes effective in nullifying the work of time"?[60]

Action is glorified less as action in view of something than as action for its own sake: defend Daladier or not, what does it matter! But act with furor, do your thinking with an automatic pistol, "give free rein to your force, as Nietzsche would say." That is the way to rediscover the very principle of life.

The doctrinal incoherence and mythological nature of fascist ideas were so many assets working for the success of their defenders in societies in crisis. Where fascism could not take root, it remained in large measure—as was the case in France—an aesthetics, a way of living, a way of not being able to live here and now, and finally, as we know, a way of dying. In *Gilles*, living in "prophetic disbelief," struggling for a "lost cause," choosing one's own death, seems to be the fascist hero's proud destiny. What he believes he is doing for an external cause, Gilles is in reality doing only for himself.[61] The "ego" remains the sacred object of the "cult."

CHAPTER 22

The Céline Scandal

IN DECEMBER 1937, Denoël published Céline's *Bagatelles pour un massacre*. That anti-Semitic pamphlet was so outrageous that André Gide interpreted it as a farce, an ironic outburst written "in-the-manner-of." For example, in the manner of Jonathan Swift's "Modest Proposal." "He does his best," writes Gide, "not to be taken seriously." One need only observe that for the Jews in his "massacre," Céline brings in every famous name that does not elude him: Cézanne, Picasso, Maupassant, Racine, Stendhal, Zola. Thus it is a joke—in bad taste no doubt!—but a joke all the same. Unless it is the work of a lunatic. André Gide himself maintained that if *Bagatelles* was not a game, then Céline must have been "completely nuts." Pierre Loewel, who also expressed some doubts about the author's mental faculties, also wrote in *L'Ordre*: "It is also exactly the sort of book to make an intelligent anti-Semite wonder whether, at bottom, it was not paid for by the Jews."[1]

Among anti-Semites, however—even "intelligent" ones—the uneasiness experienced was altogether tolerable. Lucien Rebatet even told of his race with Robert Brasillach to publish the first article on *Bagatelles pour un massacre*. Of course, the sensitive Brasillach only half appreciated Céline's curse words, but he nonetheless concluded: "Have whatever opinions you wish about the Jews and M. Céline. We do not agree with him on every point, far from it. But I tell you: this enormous book, this magnificent book, is the first signal of 'the revolt of the indigenous people.'"[2] Céline expressed in his own manner—unique, excessive, torrential—a good number of fears and fantasies current in the France of the Front Populaire. The surprise for many was that this umpteenth incarnation of Edouard Drumont's *La France juive* (1886) had taken shape in the hands of a nonconformist writer, whose first books apparently gave no hint of what was to come.

Nonetheless, Céline had already astonished and appalled, provoking as much anger as admiration. In 1932, he published *Voyage au bout de la nuit*, fragments of an autobiography transposed into an apocalyptic fantasy, which in a single stroke eclipsed the French novel as it had existed until then. His relative market success was due primarily to the public conflict tearing apart the Académie Goncourt. Lucien Descaves, a leftist, and Léon Daudet, polemicist for Action Française, both championed that fearsome book, which denounced willy-nilly the butchery of World War I, French colonialism in Africa, the robotization of workers in American Taylorized industry, and the atrocious poverty of the Paris outskirts, where the hero of the epic, Bardamu/Céline, had been unsuccessful as a doctor to the poor. Declared the winner of the Prix Goncourt a week before the awards at Drouant, when the big day arrived Céline found himself passed over for a likable drudge from the Gallimard stable, strongly supported by the distributor Hachette. *Voyage* received as consolation the Prix Renaudot, but Céline, feeling he had been wronged, found the shell game hard to stomach. Lucien Descaves swore never again to set foot in the Goncourt lair. All that racket finally served the best interests of the book.

The critics for their part, despite a few discordant voices, made no mistake about the masterpiece: a great writer had been born, someone who had a *style* (savage), a vision of the world (gloomy), and inspiration (from the storm). At the time, Céline received his strongest support from the left. In particular, he was a big hit in libertarian and antimilitarist circles. In *Le Canard Enchaîné*, Pierre Scize was not sparing in his enthusiasm for the rebellious newborn: "We read it and liked it immediately. We? That is to say, all who have kept some rage in the belly, some gall in the heart. We who accept neither the world as it is, nor the society we are part of, nor men as they are" (14 December 1932). The communists—especially Paul Nizan and Henri Lefebvre—were less favorable. In *Le Monde*, however, the review edited by Henri Barbusse, Georges Altman conferred a true leftist's certificate on Céline: "Understand," he said, "that Louis-Ferdinand Céline is one of us."

That favor coming from the left rested on a misunderstanding. On this point, Trotsky proved to be more shrewd. He praised *Voyage* but pointed out its "limitations": "Céline shows things as they are. And that is why he seems like a revolutionary. But he is not a revolutionary and does not wish to be. . . . 'Célinism' is a moral and artistic antipatriotism. Therein lies its force, but also its limitations."[3] That observation appeared even more pertinent when *Mort à crédit* (Death on the installment plan) was published in May 1936. That novel—again very broadly autobiographical and melodramatic in the extreme—today passes for Céline's masterpiece. At the time, it caused a true scandal, so much so that many of the defenders of *Voyage*—

beginning with Léon Daudet and Lucien Descaves—maintained a prudent silence after the eruption of this new literary volcano. As the slang-laden lava poured down the peaceful hillsides of the literary Hexagon, it provoked stupor and anger in the ranks of critics, who were resolved to defend beautiful language and lofty sentiments to their last breath.

They did not find the "little music" in Céline's writings that the author had made every effort to compose; they did not feel its breathless rhythm; they did not understand its inventiveness. They thought they saw only the intromission of the crudest spoken language into literature. In reality, this was a total misinterpretation: in real life, who speaks the way Céline writes, or the way Céline has his characters speak? No! André Rousseaux of *Le Figaro* and other licensed critics on the left and right denounced its *abject, monstrous, ignoble* character, and almost all called for the denunciation of that "garbage." Not only did the vocabulary used come from the *"sewer,"* but the French language and its syntax were torn to shreds by this odd agent of destruction. Paul Nizan at *L'Humanité* echoed Rousseaux at *Le Figaro*. Nizan, however, was sensitive to the content. Following Trotsky, he emphasized Céline's radical pessimism, his nihilism, his lack of solidarity with the masses. Céline was no longer depicting the class struggle, as he had with the character Ford in *Voyage au bout de la nuit*. The poor themselves were brutes and bastards. Here was a vision destined to despair all proletarians! In Céline's eyes, contradiction lay not within the human *condition*, but within the *nature* of man, the most vile of animals. Simone de Beauvoir later asserted that she and Sartre changed their ideas about Céline at that time, moving from admiration to distrust: *"Mort à crédit* opened our eyes. There is a certain hateful disdain of the common people, which is a prefascist attitude."[4]

Céline was a marginal, a solitary man, a writer who did not sign petitions, who was not part of a clique, who earned his living as a free clinic doctor, an eccentric, a kind of mad anarchist, down in the dumps, vociferating, irredeemable by any side whatever. In the divided France of the 1930s, no one knew what camp Céline belonged to. To none, no doubt. To his own, solely to his own! Vandal or genius, he would not fall in line; in the ideological war, he was unbowed; in political combat, he was the one who boasted of never voting, never signing, never applauding. A rebel, yes! Unclassifiable! He had admirers and nay-sayers in every camp. Then *Bagatelles pour un massacre* came out. This time, doubt was no longer permitted. At a time of anti-Jewish persecution in Germany and the Front Populaire in France, Céline wrote: "I say it straight out as I believe it to be, that I would prefer twelve Hitlers to one omnipotent Blum. Hitler I could even understand, whereas Blum is useless, will always be the worst enemy, absolute hatred to my last breath."[5]

It would be inaccurate to say that the Céline of *Bagatelles* caused a true scandal. In a sense, *Mort à crédit* caused a much more violent jolt. Today, the anti-Semitic pamphlet of 1937 seems to have branded Céline, thrown a cartload of filth on his literary accomplishments, so new and powerful nonetheless. But we must concede the retrospective nature of that shame. After the war, Céline himself, prosecuted by the courts of the Purge, protested against that anachronism of which he was the victim. They wanted his hide because of *Bagatelles*, dating from 1937, not for acts of collaboration, which he judged nonexistent (we will return to this). Of course, the Ligue Internationale contre l'Antisémitisme protested and the press on the left repudiated the man it had once believed one of its own. But what is more surprising today is the moderation of the criticism at the time Céline's firebrand was published. Why? Because in the France of the 1930s, anti-Semitism enjoyed real respectability; it belonged to a cultural and political tradition that was dictatorial; it was a commonplace passion. In his unbridled book, Céline was original only in one respect: he was a writer who had perfectly mastered his art, the art of rhythmic vociferation, of an unleashed imagination, the art of delirium.[6]

The banality of anti-Semitism can be seen in the sources Céline used. The review *Esprit* already noted the absence of all personal observation and the plagiarizing of a work by De Vriès, *Israël, son passé, son avenir* (Israel, its past, its future), and of two little propaganda brochures, *Le règne des Juifs* (The reign of the Jews) and *La prochaine révolution des travailleurs* (The coming workers' revolution). "The way he reproduced statistics, skewing them to enhance the effect, is in this regard symptomatic." Emmanuel Mounier's review gave a few enlightening examples. Fifty years later, an American scholar, Alice Yaeger Kaplan, setting out to decipher the sources of *Bagatelles*, demonstrated that Céline's unacknowledged borrowings were in fact innumerable. The little Célinian bomb was in reality only a big skyrocket in a fireworks display already tolerably well stocked at the end of the nineteenth century. Above all, Céline used the freshest literature on the subject, in terms of its ink if not its inspiration, writings from the years 1936–37.

Céline's anti-Semitism first elicited a sociological interpretation. The author of *Mort à crédit* was making fun of the accusatory discourse of his father, a modest office worker, husband of a no less modest shopkeeper in Passage Choiseul in Paris. To believe him, his parents, working like mules, were always one step from bankruptcy. Within the gale of his failing business, his father held the Jews and Freemasons responsible, just like Drumont's readers, Rochefort's loyalists, and those (Céline's father was one of them) who applauded Jules Guérin when he was holed up in "Fort Chabrol" during the Dreyfus affair. The Jew was designated the universal agent of their misfortunes, the owner of cannibalistic banks, vampirish department stores, the man in charge of the stock market and the Chamber, the press and the theater. The whole of the worried petty bourgeoisie reassured itself by *understanding* the source of its troubles. In reality, not all petty bourgeois sank into poverty or ended their days at the factory. Céline's biographers have shown the gap that existed between the version given by Céline of his parents' tribulations and the reality as it was lived by them. There is a noticeable discrepancy; the omnipresent bankruptcy as Céline remembered it was a mere shadow. To put it simply, the origin of the anti-Semitic denunciations on the part of the author's father, Fernand Destouches, lay less in the objective reality of a worsening social condition than in a hallucination created by fear of the future. Repeatedly, Céline heard there was an enemy within the walls relentlessly pursuing the ruin of good people: this was the Jew and his Freemason allies. Dozens and dozens of books since *La France juive* had claimed to make that demonstration.[7]

The anti-Semitism of *Bagatelles pour un massacre* does not date from the Front Populaire. Those familiar with Céline's writings know that even before *Voyage*, its author had composed a play, *L'église* (The church), which included an act indicting the League of Nations, depicted as a Jewish association with universal pretensions. Céline did not reject the old anti-Jewish legacy of his family environment, though he sometimes smiled at it. New elements contributed toward consolidating his prejudices, however, toward bringing them out of their latent state. And once more, Céline proved to be much better at *expressing* a social malady than at producing an original way of thinking: "I did not discover anything," he wrote in *L'école des cadavres* (The school of cadavers). "No pretensions. Merely virulent and stylized vulgarization."

Let us pass quickly over certain personal explanations: for example, that Céline became an anti-Semite late in life because he was the *victim* of a certain number of Jews (his failure to be awarded the Goncourt prize, the poor reception of *Mort à crédit* by the critics, his antipathy toward Grégoire Ichok, the Jewish doctor of Lithuanian origin who directed the Clichy clinic). Given the excellent relations he had with other Jews throughout his life,[8] the tendency to generalize might have led him more surely toward philo-Semitism. It is possible that some event in his personal life served as the trigger for writing *Bagatelles pour un massacre*, but that is not the important thing. What is certain is that Céline wrote a malicious book at a time when France was experiencing an anti-Jewish outbreak: this time, far from going against the current, he was on the side of those who were setting the tone.

The electoral victory of the Front Populaire and the wave of strikes that followed revived two passions, which were often combined: anticommunism and anti-Semitism ("Jews and communists are synonymous for me," wrote Céline). *Voyage au bout de la nuit* was translated in the USSR, and Céline, like Gide, went to spend time there in 1936. Or rather, like Gide (on his second trip), he brought back a negative view, which he expressed in a published text, *Mea culpa*. But unlike Gide and so many other intellectuals invited and coddled by Stalinist masters at the cost of the proletariat in power, Céline arrived without a reception committee. He funded his stay with the unexportable rubles he had received in royalties. From that visit, Céline drew a conclusion in dissonance with the hymns to popular unity: it was not class exploitation that made man brutish and unhappy; the source of man's unhappiness was man. It was an antihumanist, radically pessimistic, and catastrophist vision: to trust man, the animal closest to filth, to allow him to glimpse the possibility of happiness, was to sugarcoat the pill for everyone and at the same time to prepare for the worst. And who was in charge of this market in illusions? The Jews! They were the ones—just look at the names—who caused the Bolshevik revolution. In France, the communists had helped set up a government that for the first time had a Jew as premier. Let us note, however, that Céline's hatred was not the most virulent directed at Léon Blum: at the time, a good part of the "old Gallo-Roman country" (as Xavier Vallat called it) consigned the Socialist leader to hell, often with filthy language.

The Front Populaire did not provoke only social fear. In the view of anti-Semites, it represented another sort of danger, to which Céline was particularly sensitive: that of a new international conflict, which the war in Spain prefigured beginning 18 July 1936. Later, when accounts were being settled after the war, Céline returned twenty times to his explanation for *Bagatelles*: it was an act of peace, a desire to stop new carnage, the cry of a war veteran who wanted to spare his fellow citizens. In fact, Céline's pacifism had become visceral. He had been a young cuirassier of the class of 1914, who volunteered in 1912; he had become an antimilitarist only after the fact. But that was the case for most of the soldiers: their patriotism in World War I had been transformed into pacifism.[9] In his hero Bardamu, Céline's hyperbolic exaltation had only exaggerated a widespread feeling. Who wanted war in 1937? Who, in other words, wanted to teach Hitler a lesson? The answer was obvious in the minds of those who had always denounced the occult power of Jews: those the Führer was then bringing into line in the restored Germany, those who were leaving their ghettoes and coming to invade democracies in order to turn them against Hitler! "A war for the delight of the Jews," wrote Céline. The same reasoning is found in the vast press on the far right, from newspapers with a wide circulation such as *Gringoire* to the intellectual and doctrinal reviews such as *Combat*.

In the latter publication, one reads in April 1936, following the remilitarization of the Rheinland: "In the world outside Germany, there is a clan that wants war and that insidiously propagates the case for war under cover of prestige and international morality. This is the clan of the former pacifists, revolutionaries, and immigrant Jews, who are ready to do anything to bring down Hitler and put an end to dictatorships." Farther on, the author mentions the "raging Jews whose theological furor required every sanction against Hitler immediately." Céline invented nothing.

There was another ingredient in the composition of Célinian anti-Semitism: the defense of the race. Dr. Louis-Ferdinand Destouches was a hygienist. He did not smoke, he did not drink. Practicing on the outskirts of the city, he could observe workers' poverty at his leisure, in particular the ravages of alcoholism. In the paranoid interpretations of anti-Semitism, analogistic reasoning made the Jew the microbe that had attacked the healthy body and was gradually undermining it. "King Bistro" was only a vassal of Jewish power. The proof? It was the Blum government that had voted in the forty-hour work week. And what did the workers do with their new leisure time? They drank a bit more in one of the 350,000 bars that "handed the people over to the Jews." That reflection on the degeneration of the race (alcoholism, but also Malthusianism, a lack of athletic habits, venereal diseases, and so on), belonged to a part of the French intelligentsia, who in their observations did not hesitate to combine a certain number of allusions, or even arguments, that were straightforwardly racist. Of course, we know of Brasillach's admiration for Hitler's Germany, which wanted "a pure nation, a pure history, a pure race," and Drieu La Rochelle's biological obsession (see his novel *Gilles*). They at least proclaimed themselves "fascist." It is more surprising to find these ideas in Giraudoux, a moderate and liberal author, soon used by a republican government in the service of propaganda. What did he write in *Pleins pouvoirs* (Full powers) on the eve of war? That people needed to protect themselves from "the curious and greedy mob of central and eastern Europe," in other words, to "suppress every element that might corrupt a race that owes its value to selection and refinement over twenty centuries."

It is clear, then, that *Bagatelles pour un massacre* was in no respect a book brilliant for its novelty. It was inspired by all the anti-Jewish imaginings known since Edouard Drumont. It adapted the mythology of *The Protocols of the Elders of Zion*, that famous hoax which now has its own historian,[10] and which presented false evidence of a Jewish conspiracy designed to subjugate the entire world, finding the hidden hand of the children of the

Talmud in every misfortune. Céline's pamphlet added its own incantatory effects to those of a vast racist body of writing, revived by the international circumstances. Nevertheless, Céline paid an enormous tribute to the anti-Semitic cause: he offered it his rare talent as a writer, that is, a creator of language. *Bagatelles* represents the marriage between the most advanced literature and the most reactionary prejudices. In the end, that is the real scandal: the content of the book stemmed from ordinary racism, but its style was that of a great writer.

Moreover, and more seriously, in a country he claimed to serve, and which was gathering its energy to face the Nazi imperialist ventures, Céline, who said he belonged to no party, became what is called an agent of influence for Hitler's Germany. It is not that Céline, as Sartre later asserted, became anti-Semitic for money. He was not and never would be "bought." He even made it a point of honor never to depend on anyone, not on a party or on a state. But set in motion by his anti-Semitic obsession, he was soon to find himself in the most indefensible position on the political chessboard.

To begin with, for the purposes of writing *Bagatelles*, he made wide use of the many brochures of National Socialist propaganda. As already mentioned, Alice Kaplan has shed light on the influence of the *Welt-Dienst*, the propaganda service subsidized by the Nazis, and its bulletin *Service mondial* (World service), published in France beginning in 1933. In February 1937, this bulletin recommended the book by the Belgian De Vriès, *Israël, son passé, son avenir*, one of the principal sources, as mentioned above, for Céline's pamphlet. In addition, that German agency supported and subsidized a certain number of very French anti-Semitic hotbeds, as well as their publications: Henry Coston's *Le Siècle Nouveau* (The new century), which had published *La conspiration juive* (The Jewish conspiracy) in 1937; Lucien Pemjean's *Le Grand Occident* (The Grand Occident; Pemjean was a former Boulangist and an associate of Drumont at *La Libre Parole*); Jean Boissel's *Le Réveil du Peuple* (The people awaken), interrupted during the summer of 1937 but soon resumed under the more explicit title *L'Anti-Juif* (The Anti-Jew; Jules Guérin's newspaper had the same title during the Dreyfus affair). In addition to the names cited, Henry-Robert Petit and Darquier de Pellepoix complete the picture. Petit, Darquier de Pellepoix's secretary and author of several books, contributed to the Centre de Documentation and to Coston's *La Libre Parole*. Under various titles, this little group peddled the fundamentals of anti-Jewish and anti-Masonic propaganda with the Germans' blessings. Céline, who until then had never participated in their activities, was led to make contact with certain of these propagandists. Hence, in a letter to Henry-Robert Petit, Céline makes this confessions: "Of course I do not hide the fact that I consulted your work, chewed on it, haphazardly copied off you."[11] On 3 December 1938, the apolitical author, highly allergic to meetings, petitions, and other forms of public agitation, actually went to a meeting organized by *La France Enchaînée*, the newspaper that replaced *L'Anti-Juif*, the official organ of the "Rassemblement Anti-Juif" (Anti-Jewish rally) in France. Céline was no longer afraid to be seen with the vanguard militants of the National Socialist cause in France. It is tempting to conclude from this that Céline himself had become a Nazi. H.-E. Kaminski took that step, also in 1938, in a book with an unequivocal title: *Céline en chemise brune* (Céline in brownshirt). "To make Céline harmless," he writes, "we need only unmask him. What is inadmissible is that he should sell his Nazi rubbish as original literature. What we need to do is shed light on the fact that this is neither art nor psychology, but Hitlerian propaganda." In fact, Céline appears to have been a prisoner of the pacifist system. To avoid war at all cost was the proclaimed goal. And since war would be a "Jewish" war against Hitler, he saw salvation only in the denunciation of Judeo-Communism and in the alliance with Germany.

The Munich pact was supposed to reassure nations. A thousand-year peace: that was the refrain of autumn 1938. The following spring, they had to change their tune. Cheerfully trampling accords from the famous conference, Hitler swallowed up everything that remained of Bohemia and seized control of Slovakia. This time, the Treaty of Versailles and its iniquities were no longer at issue: Hitler was proving to be an insatiable conqueror. If he continued, war was inevitable. The most ardent neopacifists on the right reconsidered the question: in their long-myopic eyes, Germany was on the verge of once more becoming the principal enemy. In November 1938, Céline, tormented by the terrible mechanism to which he had devoted his pen and his life, decided to publish *L'école des cadavres*—another pamphlet, entirely devoted to glorifying an accord with Hitler's Germany. He stood by his words:

I am not a great advocate of veiled allusions, half-tones. One must say everything or nothing at all. A Franco-German union. A Franco-German alliance. A Franco-German army. It is the army that makes alliances, solid alliances. Without a Franco-German army, the accords remain Platonic, academic, changeable, indecisive . . . Enough of the slaughterhouses! A Franco-German army first of all! The rest will come on its own. Italy and Spain will quite naturally join the Confederation in the bargain. A Confederation of the Aryan states of Europe.

Undoubtedly, Céline was not a Nazi strictly speaking. But at the very least, in the months preceding the war he was one of the very first collaborationists before the fact. Even Rebatet felt some discomfort about that: "Céline was always going too far."[12] In fact, Céline was following the logic of full-scale pacifism. It was no longer very opportune to proclaim such a view in the spring of 1939, but again, that pacifism pushed many publicists and true writers into German arms. Since 1935, they had denounced the danger of war as the fruit of a Judeo-Masonic plot, intent on crushing the German leader who had resolved to "clean up" his country. Céline remained a loner. In that he was not a true Nazi. But that anarchist spirit despairing of humanity had suddenly been struck, he said, by a glimmer of hope: he was supposed to play a role in sparing men a new world war, a new "*massacre*." Having "understood" where the evil was coming from, he began to *vulgarize* his knowledge in his own way: "I might have put it into science, into biology, of which I am an expert. I might have given in to the temptation to be authoritatively right, but I did not want to. I was keen on fooling around a little, a lot, to remain at a popular level."[13] Céline, who doubted everything, had begun to preach. Years later, he would be annoyed with himself for that fleeting return of optimism!

Obviously, the 1940 defeat convinced him he had been right. Unfit for service because of his World War I wounds, Céline wanted to offer his services as a doctor. That led to several pilgrimages as dangerous as they were picturesque during the "phony war" and exodus—which he made in a surgeon's gown in the company of his future wife, Lucette, a makeshift nurse, and with two newborns and their grandmother, all in the municipal ambulance of Sartrouville that had been entrusted to him. Here was a new chapter in the misadventures of Bardamu in the human jungle.

When the Occupation took place, Céline did not become one of its cutting-edge collaborationists. He did not join any of the fascist parties and spent even less time in the vicinity of Vichy. The style of the National Revolution was too boy-scoutish for it to put the author of *Mort à crédit* on the list of recommended writers. All the same, Céline, as usual, was hardly inspired by prudence. Although a modest eater, he was haunted by the fear of going without, so much so that he spent a good part of his time begging for butter and bacon from his Breton and Norman relations. In contrast, he certainly had no awareness of the risks he was taking when he emerged from silence and left his medical duties behind. These duties, moreover, had changed. He was now responsible for the free clinic in Bezons—again on the Paris outskirts! But to obtain that post, he did not hesitate to wave about his rights as an "Aryan" against the overcrowding of French medicine by Jews. Certain convictions can sometimes prove very opportune. In May 1941, he published his last pamphlet, *Les beaux draps* (A fine mess). The book was published by Nouvelles Editions Françaises, which was simply a subsidiary of Denoël, and a very specialized branch: Dr. Montandon's *Comment reconnaître un Juif* (How to rec-

ognize a Jew), Dr. Querrioux's *La médecine et les Juifs* (Medicine and the
Jews), Lucien Pemjean's *La presse* (The press; meaning the Jewish press),
and Lucien Rebatet's *Les tribus du cinéma et du théâtre* (The tribes of cinema and theater) were also published there. In his new lampoon, Céline
recounted France's military defeat but—contrary to the official Vichy discourse—without making the slightest concession to army leaders: "Perhaps we ought first to understand each other . . . Who should defend
France? Civilians or soldiers? Twenty-ton tanks or old men? Crackpots,
babies, snotty kids, prudent draftees, or machine gun regiments? Oh! Intentions are not so clear . . . we don't understand each other very well.
There's confusion, equivocation, they're not telling the whole truth."

Nevertheless, that fit of good sense is not the crux of the book. In German France, in the France of the *statut des Juifs*, Céline had not given up
his anti-Semitic obsessions. To those who had difficulty tolerating the
German presence, he replied: "And what about the presence of the Jews?"
He saw them everywhere: in the press, in bar associations, at the Sorbonne,
in medicine, at the theater, at the opera, in industry, in banks. It was obvious: "France is Jewish and Masonic, once and for all." True, for Céline,
this was also a metaphorical way of expressing his resentment, his shame,
his disgust with a French people he judged flabby, basely materialistic, al-
coholic to the core. Yet when someone personifies all the negativity in the
world in a very precise ethnic group, a group that is moreover the object
of the systematic hatred of the conquering power, "metaphor" becomes a
call for murder. Nonetheless, the tone of the book was so far from the official discourse that the Vichy censor had *Les beaux draps* banned in the
unoccupied zone. Here, for example, is the author's judgment of the Marshal's capital city: "Vichy . . . that chief rabbit warren of the Jewish bog."
It always came back to that. A Molièresque doctor, Céline kept repeating:
"The lungs! The lungs I tell you," though using a different word.

Although he remained independent of all political groups and newspapers, of all administrations and missions, Céline did not hesitate to allow
letters he had sent to journalists to be published. These carry great weight
in the assessment of his record. For example, he wrote to Jean Lestandi of
Le Pilori on 2 October 1941: "To recreate France would have required re-
building it entirely on racist-communitarian foundations. We are moving
away from that ideal every day." Anti-American, anti-Soviet, anti-Gaullist,
and more anti-Semitic than ever, Céline ought indisputably to be classified on the side of the moral forces that supported Nazi Germany. And
yet he maintained his autonomy and his contradictions. Dr. Destouches
never hesitated to sign unwarranted medical certificates to spare young
men from the Service du Travail Obligatoire (Obligatory work service);
even Jews benefited. In addition, it never crossed his mind to denounce

his neighbors below him on Rue Girardon, Robert Champfleury and Simone Mabille, whose Resistance activities were perfectly well known to him.[14] When he went to Berlin in 1942, he did not do so at the invitation of the National Socialist government, but rather to take care of his assets, invested in Holland and Denmark. When he was invited to deliver a few words at the Foyer des Ouvriers Français (French workers' residence) in Berlin, he took revenge on the Germans who had stolen his savings by declaring coldly: "French workers, I am going to tell you one good thing. I know you well, I am one of you, a worker like you, they [the Germans] are *ugly*. They say they are going to win the war, I don't know about that. The other ones, the Russians on the other side, are no better. They may be worse! It comes down to choosing between cholera and the plague! It's not funny! So long!" The unpredictable Céline.

He rightly felt he was too compromised to remain in France after the Allied landing, however. A few days after the liberation of Paris, he fled with his wife, Lucette, and his cat, Bébert, for Baden-Baden. Thus began the long, bumpy, burlesque, tragic period of drifting, which finally led Céline to Denmark via Sigmaringen, where he came near the court of King Pétain. Then came Danish prison, exile, conviction in absentia, amnesty, the return to France in 1951, the definitive move to Meudon. From this second exodus, Céline drew other "novels," of which the best known is *D'un château l'autre* (Castle to castle) and, perhaps the most accomplished, *Nord* (North). Through the intermediary of his lawyers, Albert Naud (a Resistance fighter) and Jean-Louis Tixier-Vignancour (a Vichyist), whom he skillfully played against each other, Céline made every effort to limit his responsibility:

Do not forget that I never belonged to any Franco-German medical, literary, or political society, to any party—and that I never wrote an article in my life. Under the Occupation, I wrote *PRIVATE* letters of protest to editors of newspapers, which did not publish them—or which completely tampered with them—deformed them—I was harassed throughout the Occupation by the BBC (for no reason), was perpetually threatened—clandestine newspapers, coffins, etc., you will not find me either in *Signal*—or in *Cahiers Franco-allemands* [Franco-German notes]—or at the "visits of French literary writers in Germany," or as ambassador to Pétain—NOTHING AT ALL—I did not derive any benefit—I did not take any revenge on anyone, I LOST EVERYTHING—I did not bet on Hitler—I was hated at the embassy—I am a pacifist patriot—I did not want war—That is all—Nothing nothing nothing ELSE.[15]

In that *pro domo* defense, Céline's anti-Semitism was gone, vanished without a trace! During the time when the Vel' d'Hiv' round-up was being planned, however, Céline had allowed *Bagatelles pour un massacre* to be reissued and continued to vituperate against the designated victims of the

Nazis as architects of France's misfortune. Oh no, he had simply been a pacifist; he stuck to his guns! The *"racist-communitarian"* tirades were forgotten! Céline was only a writer, concerned with his art above all, with his music; Dr. Destouches was a doctor who had moved heaven and earth for his poor patients in Bezons. Irresponsibility of literature and impartiality of medicine!

Céline's history, beginning with *Bagatelles pour un massacre*, is first of all a collective history: that of French anti-Semitism, which soon ran into the blind alley of Collaboration. Like all the other champions of anti-Judaism, Céline wanted to denounce the "decadence" of his country. The symptoms of that "decadence" were sometimes depicted accurately, sometimes fantasized. Mere regret for what had been and what was no longer gave free rein to every sort of denunciation. In the search for a global explanation, that hatred of the present and that fear of the future led to the "discovery" of the principle of decline. A sole and unique principle, which had an answer for everything. A diabolical crew had sworn the ruin of old France, of the Gallic race, of the nation's cardinal virtues. Another nation—parasitic, corrupting—was working in an occult manner for its advent on the ruins of the race. The Jews—since they were the guilty parties—operated at both ends of the spectrum: they were Capital (Rothschild) and they were Revolution (Trotsky). "France," wrote Céline, after a dozen, a hundred others, "France is a colony of international Jewish power."[16] France's recovery necessarily entailed anti-Semitism, just as in 1789 it had entailed the abolition of privilege.

Yet these good French people, haunted by the decomposition of their nation, were led by the logic of "diabolical causality" to make their country a vassal of the foreign conqueror. This was not the least of the paradoxes. For Pierre Drieu La Rochelle, that infernal impasse led to suicide; for Robert Brasillach, to the firing squad. These are painful cases and still elicit reverent reflection. Céline was less compromised and more prudent, and so escaped these bloody epilogues. But his case appears all the more scandalous. His final refuge in literature, his denials, his petty bourgeois ruses to survive on the move, from castle to castle, hardly do a great service to belles-lettres. And that is what troubles us: the books of Brasillach and Drieu, whatever the authors' talents, are second-rate; one can do without them. In contrast, Céline's writings are those of one of the great writers of this century: they cannot be trashed. The fact that the author of *Voyage au bout de la nuit*, *Mort à crédit*, and *Nord* could have been in league with the greatest venture of extermination in this century, or even in the history of humanity, remains strictly intolerable.

From this fact, one may draw all the reflections one wishes, and all the interpretations. That Céline was paranoid; that he never recovered from his World War I wounds (he wrote between migraine headaches); that he was merely a sensitive soul, an imaginative man incapable of political reasoning; that he was a solitary man, an autodidact, having never existed within the framework or sphere of influence of any environment whatever, since he was rejected by both the medical establishment and the literary elite; that he had never ceased to elaborate a vision of the world at its darkest, haunted by apocalyptic hallucinations, despairing of human nature; that as the child of his parents, he was also the product of a social stratum that was dying, secreting a deadly pre-Poujadism. What do I know? None of that is false. But none of that can attenuate the extent of the scandal: that an artist of that stature participated in genocide through his howling and his legendary use of ellipses.

That perplexity, no doubt, is itself naïve. It rests on a most contestable postulate: that the best writers are politically the most clear-sighted. The Céline case should disabuse us of that illusion once and for all.

Chronology

1894 27 May	Ferdinand Destouches is born in Courbevoie, son of Fernand Destouches, employee at the Phénix Insurance Company, and Marguerite Guillou Destouches, shopkeeper in fashions and lingerie.
1899	The Destouches move to the Passage Choiseul (the "Passage des Bérésinas" depicted in *Mort à crédit*).
1907	Louis-Ferdinand completes secondary school. During the next two years, he spends time in Germany and England to learn the languages.
1910	Apprenticeship in commerce (hosiery and jewelry).
1912	Louis-Ferdinand enlists in the armed forces before he can be drafted and joins the cavalry for a three-year term.
1914 27 Oct.	Wounded in his right arm during a volunteer mission. Receives the Médaille Militaire a month later. Another wound in the head condemns him to ceaseless neuralgia.
1915 May	Assigned to the French consulate in London.
1915 Dec.	Obtains deferment.
1916–17	Employed by Franco-English condominium in the Cameroons.

Chronology, continued

1917–18	Returns to France. Works at the review *Eurêka* with Raoul Marquis (the model for Courtial des Péreires in *Mort à crédit*). Becomes propaganda lecturer for the Rockefeller Foundation, against tuberculosis.
1919–23	Resumes studies thanks to the special terms offered veterans. Receives his bachelor's degree, then studies medicine in Rennes. On 10 August 1919 Destouches marries Edith Follet, daughter of the director of the school of medicine in Rennes. Colette born 15 June 1920.
1924 1 May	Defends his thesis in medicine, dedicated to the life and work of the Hungarian doctor Semmelweis (1818–64). This is his first literary work (a Hungarian critic reproaches him for his approximations and exaggerations).
1924 27 June	Placed on the hygiene committee of the League of Nations in Geneva, under the direction of Father Rajchman.
1924–27	Various trips to the United States, Cuba, Canada, Great Britain, Africa. Divorce, for which he is judged at fault (June 1926). Begins an affair with Elisabeth Craig. Writes the beginning of a play, *L'église*, which will contain an indictment of the Jews in the League of Nations. The play will be published in 1933, after the success of his first novel.
1927 Nov.	Opens medical office as general practitioner in Clichy.
1928–32	Doctor for the outlying regions of the city, he supplements his income in a pharmaceutical laboratory. Closes his office in 1929 to take a position in the new Clichy free clinic.
1932 14 Mar.	Father dies.
1932 15 Oct.	Louis-Ferdinand Destouches, under the pseudonym "Céline"—the first name of his maternal grandmother— publishes *Voyage au bout de la nuit* with the publisher Denoël. Receives Prix Renaudot.
1936 May	Second novel, *Mort à crédit*, with Denoël.
1936 Aug.	Trip to USSR ("All bluff and tyranny").
1937	Two pamphlets: *Mea culpa* and *Bagatelles pour un massacre*.
	Meets the dancer Lucette Almanzor, whom he will marry in 1943. Leaves the Clichy clinic.

Chronology, continued

1938	Publication, again with Denoël, of *L'école des cadavres*.
1939–40	Resumes service as a doctor in the merchant marine. Exodus with Lucette in the Sartrouville ambulance.
1941 28 Feb.	*Beaux draps* goes on sale.
1941–44	Doctor in Bezons. Writes *Guignol's Band* (the first part is published by Denoël in 1944). Allows his anti-Semitic pamphlets to be reissued and has compromising letters written by him published in collaborationist newspapers.
1944 17 June	Flees to Germany with Lucette and cat, Bébert. Beginning of a long tour, from Baden-Baden to Copenhagen, via Sigmaringen. Eleven months of imprisonment in the Danish capital. Freed on 24 June 1947. Authorized to remain in Denmark.
1950 Feb.	Sentenced in absentia to a year in prison.
1951	Granted amnesty, he returns to France. Settles definitively in Meudon.
1952–60	Gallimard reprints the novels published by Denoël, and publishes new titles—especially *D'un château l'autre* in 1957 and *Nord* in 1960.
1961 July	Céline dies, just after the second draft of *Rigodon*, which will be published in 1969. In 1964, the second part of *Guignol's Band* will appear under the title *Le pont de Londres* (London Bridge).

CHAPTER 23

The Bernanos Case

On His Own Two Feet
I am an average man who has remained free, I am an
average man whom propaganda has not yet taught to leap
through all the hoops presented him. . . . I stand on my
own two feet!

MORE THAN twenty years after Georges Bernanos's death, one does not
enter his political writings as one would a French garden; they were not
traced along the straight lines of political positivism, and in any case, his
spirit of freedom would have quickly toppled whatever the spirit of
geometry might have strived to organize. In relation to Bernanos, simplifying labels are less justified than ever.

Seen from afar, he might be called a reactionary. Did he not consistently opt for monarchism, up until his death? Was he not the belated admirer of Drumont, to whom he devoted one of his most famous books?[1]
And did he not preserve the ineffaceable imprint of the anti-Semitism
learned from *La Libre Parole*? After World War II, was he not one of the
most eloquent champions of anticommunism? These few traits might well
earn him the sympathy of rightists, but how could those among them who
did not have too short a memory forgive him for denouncing the
Ethiopian campaign at a time when the French intellectual "elite" was defending the Duce; for publishing—he, a Catholic writer—one of the
most virulent pamphlets against Franco and his bishops;[2] for standing up,
despite the professional patriots, to the Munich capitulation; for writing
his harshest pages against neopacifism on the right; for criticizing the odd
genuflection to Hitler by those who only a few years earlier, were appalled
at the "generosity" of the Treaty of Versailles toward a disarmed Germany
and at the "humanitarian pacifism" of the Socialists; for challenging the
armistice of 1940 without hesitation, calling it an act "in strict conformity
with the spirit of Munich"; for calling for resistance against Nazi totali-

tarianism and for revolution against the "Vichy acrobats"? Once the war was over, however, that did not prevent him from turning his weapons on the leftist parties who founded the Fourth Republic.

Some have judged that he fluctuated a bit too much, have wished that he had chosen his camp once and for all. But although Bernanos was unclassifiable, that does not mean he was frivolous. The truth is he was a lonely man, a poor man, without social conventions, religious obligations, or professional courtesy to constrain him. That was his strength. "People have tried in vain to pull me to the right or the left, the path I have forged for myself is too familiar for me not to be able to take care of myself, I know my way."

In fact, throughout his life Bernanos remained faithful to values inspired by a fervent Christianity—including the dual requirement for honor and freedom. His political works attest to a tireless battle against everything that in his view threatened individuals and peoples with the dishonor of submission and servitude.

If to our astonishment he believed monarchy to be the best kind of regime, the idealized and largely untheorized conception he had of it stands at the opposite extreme from monarchy according to Maurras. Where Maurras, a disciple of Auguste Comte, saw a body of institutions and a hierarchical order, Bernanos defended a form of government that had "a word of honor," that is, in his view, the exact opposite of the modern state, which was the government of public servants and police officers. His membership in Action Française appears to have been the result of a misunderstanding; for the young Bernanos, becoming a Camelot du Roi was the only way he saw before 1914 to rebel against self-righteous people. As soon as the Maurrassian school appeared to be one of the pillars of the party of law and order, he did not linger—though he took up the defense of the AF when it was censured by Rome in 1926. The rise of dictatorships clearly brought relations between Bernanos and Maurras to a head; they no longer had any language in common. Bernanos had always belonged to the king's party; Maurras had always been solely in the league's party.

All the same, Bernanos shared Maurras's condemnation of "democracy," but he warned his readers on several occasions about the word: the democracy he condemned was not the freedom of peoples, but rather institutionalized democracy. Both within the framework of bourgeois parliamentarianism and under Soviet Communism, instead of guaranteeing that freedom, institutionalized democracy tended rather to abolish it. Bernanos warned against the myth of equality, on which democracy rested. Freedom and equality, he said, are not compatible. In the name of the principle of equality, every coercive method used by every tyranny is possible. The Reign of Terror was instituted in the name of equality, as was a state religion, that is, in the end, the apotheosis of bureaucrats and slave drivers. There was only a difference of degree between Western democracy and communism: servitude began with compulsory military service and ended in Siberian camps.

According to Bernanos, freedom has nothing to do with liberalism. He was always convinced that "in a society dominated by money, freedom is only an illusion." He reserved his harshest blows for law-and-order men, self-righteous profiteers of the capitalist regime sheltered by the Church and the banner of anticommunism. Denouncing the social fear of so many Catholics under the Front Populaire, he accused the official church of giving its backing to the bourgeoisie and its masters: "All the same, it is disagreeable to hear hale and hearty canons speaking of the Sermon on the Mount as a conservative manifesto." The mission of the Church was to form free men, not law-and-order men.

The most redoubtable sort of law-and-order men, Bernanos tells us, are finally not those who have a rifle on their shoulder, but the masses who follow like sheep, the "silent majority," or, as he says, the respectful, the circumspect, the moderate, those so obsessed with security that they are willing to abdicate anything, beginning with their own freedom. "The most imprudent thing you can do is to disregard the mediocre. Mediocrity is a colorless, odorless gas; if you calmly let it accumulate, it suddenly explodes with incredible force." Bernanos was always immoderate: moderation and mediocrity led to the Munich pact and served as godparents to the old Marshal, Munich's illegitimate son.

After Hiroshima, Bernanos devoted much of his remaining strength to sounding the alarm against the despotism of uncontrolled technology. From this point of view, the two great regimes in competition, capitalism and communism, were only two faces of the same anticivilization. Its most intolerable aspect would be, already was, the reduction of man to the state of a robot. It was not that Bernanos recommended a return to the land and the spinning wheel; he did not denounce machines, which would have been absurd, but rather the mechanical, speculative, and productivist spirit, which necessarily led to man's subjection to economics and, as a result, to the monster modern state.

Bernanos repudiated ideologies, on the right and on the left: "In the name of 'social justice,' as once upon a time in the name of 'social order,' millions of people are killed, deported, tortured, entire peoples subjugated, displaced from one location to another like herds of cattle." But confronted with the joined forces of mechanical, state, and political tyrannies, whose advance often led him to despair, Bernanos was far from preaching some vague "liberal" resignation. He believed to the end that

France, which been so disappointing but which harbored within itself such age-old reserves for recovery, would sound "the signal for the insurrection of the Spirit."

"*My Old Master*"

Bernanos's attitude toward totalitarian states, particularly after the conquest of Abyssinia, most often placed him in direct conflict with his former politics. At the same time, he acquired a new public and a new reputation for himself. Christians on the left, who became numerous in the postwar years, were grateful to him because he had allowed a great Catholic voice to be heard, against all the recent dishonors of the nation: Munich, the armistice, the Collaboration, Vichy given the bishops' blessing. It was only too rare that a writer of that force was also a man of that caliber. Who in the world of letters and in the Catholic world could boast of having held firm in the face of advances from the Nazi dictatorship and imperialism? And in his case, it was not from a residual Maurrassian Germanophobia, since he had also risen up—and with what vehemence—against Italian Fascism and General Franco's so-called crusade. Of course, it was well known that Bernanos always called himself a monarchist, but perhaps that was just a harmless old mania, an oddity of no consequence? But what about his anti-Semitism? Might it not also be true that in the same context, people also minimized it, dismissed it as a sin of his youth, long since forgiven? All admirers of Bernanos ought to consider themselves obligated to raise that doubt.

The first unavoidable fact on this matter, which continues to be troubling, is the constant admiration Bernanos showed toward Edouard Drumont, whom he called his "old master." When the author of *La grande peur des bien-pensants* (The great fear of the self-righteous) called *La France juive* a "magical" book—it is that, in fact, but not in the flattering sense Bernanos meant it—was this really the case, as Jean Bastaire has said, of "an aberrant Bernanos,"[3] that is, a Bernanos momentarily led astray? This is a difficult hypothesis to sustain, since until the end of his life, Bernanos applied himself to defending the memory of Drumont and embraced his ideas. No doubt it could be claimed that Bernanos did not see what is glaringly obvious to us in the work of the most famous French anti-Semite: the call for pogroms. There is no doubt that he took only what he wanted to take from Drumont: "the indictment of a heartless society."[4] And although the Jew had something to do with that, it was not as the privileged or exclusive agent of decadence, but rather as a symptom of it. You will say that is still anti-Semitism. Let us make no mistake about that. All the same, the nuance is noteworthy.

Bernanos's anti-Semitism (he still accepted the word in 1936: "I shall explain *my anti-Semitism* wherever you like")[5] can be found even in his first articles for *L'Avant-Garde de Normandie*[6] and up through *La grande peur*, which is its climax. But there are still many expressions of it— though now attenuated—in his later writings. He combined the Christian anti-Judaism and the social anti-Semitism once put forward by Drumont, picked up by the Assumptionists of *La Croix*, and widespread in Catholics circles before 1914. The first charge: the antagonism between Christian civilization and the Jewish mentality. "I hold the Jew to be the enemy of Christianity," he said, though he added: "I do not despise him."[7] Second charge: Jewish gold, Jewish usury, the Jewish bank.

Let us confine ourselves to a summary of what they had done, as formulated in the conclusion of *La grande peur*:

Once they have become masters of gold, [the Jews] soon make certain that, in a fully egalitarian democracy, they can also be masters of public opinion, that is, of mores. . . . Beginning in the mid-nineteenth century, in the key positions of the administration, banking, the magistrature, the railroads, and the mines, everywhere in short, the heir to the haute bourgeoisie, the Polytechnique student in his pince-nez, became accustomed to finding these strange fellows who talk with their hands like apes . . . so different from the dear old hosier or notary, as if they had landed here from another planet, with their black hair, their features chiseled by the anguish of many millennia, the fierce pruritus in their marrow, exhausted since the reign of Solomon and squandered in all the beds of shameless Asia.[8]

I want to believe Bernanos when he says he is not a racist because racism is the belief in a hierarchy of races and he does not distinguish between superior and inferior races.[9] We must concede, however, that the passage just cited did slip out.

Whether speaking of "Jewish lords" or "crafty little yids from Moscow,"[10] Bernanos believed in an "age-old instinct"[11] belonging to the Jew, which leads him, either through capitalism or communism, to prosper in modern society, which is incapable of defending itself because of its laziness and mediocrity.

All in all, in the early 1930s, Bernanos was still expressing the anti-Semitic prejudices, if not the stereotypes, characteristic of his Catholic and anti-Dreyfusard family of origin—except in one respect, which is not insignificant. He loathed the conservatives and the self-righteous, precisely those who comprised the majority in anti-Dreyfusard Catholic circles. He was certainly an anti-Semite, but in the name of a popular monarchy that had nothing to do with the compromises of the conservative right, and would soon have nothing more to do with the calculating and positivist monarchism of the Maurrassians.

In the years following his break with Maurras and Action Française, even as Bernanos stood apart from anti-Semites on the right, who admired the new law-and-order regimes set up beyond the French borders, he continued to evoke the "Jewish problem." In 1939, in a variant from *Scandale de la vérité* (The scandal of truth), he declared he had *repudiated nothing* in Drumont's *anti-Semitism*. He conceded that the "word" was "unfortunate," but attacked Jacques Maritain, who had just spoken of "impossible anti-Semitism." One ought not to "hate or despise the Jews," he said, but noted that their presence within the national community posed a problem that had to be settled peacefully and legally. "I am not anti-Jewish, I believe only that every Christian state ought to deal with its Jews in accordance with the rules of equity. . . . Why should the states not deal with them the way they deal with the Church?"[12] And Bernanos then gave a few details of his *treaty* (not some "status" imposed or granted). He wished to reserve a "large number of places in the administration of finances, or even in the serious press" for Jews, but wanted to "keep [them] away from politics" and "the education of French young people."[13]

Nonetheless, Hitler's coming to power, the persecution of the Jews in Germany, the new wave of anti-Semitism spurred by the powerful far right newspapers in France, the end of the 1930s and the war that followed, necessarily modified first the expression and then the content of Bernanos's ideas on the "Jewish question."

Before the war broke out, denouncing "the hideous anti-Semitic reign of terror,"[14] he cried out that he would rather "be whipped by the rabbi of Algiers than make a Jewish woman or child suffer."[15] During the war, he made numerous accusations against Nazism and Vichy: "Do you understand that the victory itself would not be enough to efface the stain made on our history, if only for handing over the anti-Nazi Jewish refugees among us to Germany and the Spanish Republicans to Franco?"[16] When Georges Mandel—former associate of Clemenceau, former minister to Daladier and Reynaud—was deported to Germany, Georges Bernanos wrote:

As for Mandel, you may say to yourself that, having never shown any fondness for the Jews, I will not speak of that one? Open your eyes! He's the one you hate the most, you and your masters. In that respect, he is a thousand times more sacred to me than the others. If your masters do not return Mandel to us alive, you will have to pay for that Jewish blood in a way that will stun history—understand that, dogs that you are—every drop of Jewish blood shed in hatred of our old victory is much more precious to us than all the purple of a Fascist cardinal's robe—do you understand what I mean, Admirals, Marshals, Excellencies, Eminences, and Reverends?[17]

From his distant Brazilian exile, Bernanos was infinitely sensitive to the tragedy of the Jewish community; he did not in any way take the view his reading of Drumont might have encouraged him to take—that the "Holocaust" should be ascribed to "justice" finally carried out. In the tribute he paid to the memory of Georges Torrès, his attitude toward the Jews had definitively changed: "The charnel houses slowly grow cold, the martyrs' remains return to the earth, sparse grass and brambles cover over the tainted soil where so many of the dying sweated their last sweat, the crematoria themselves stand gaping and empty in the morning and evening, but the seed of the heroes of the Warsaw ghetto now rises up far from Germany, on the banks of the Jordan."[18]

The evolution was obvious. All the same, his old ideas had not been totally eradicated. "I am neither anti-Jewish nor anti-Semitic," he now said, but a "problem" remained in his view:

I am neither anti-Jewish nor anti-Semitic, but I have always believed there is a Jewish problem, the solution to which matters a great deal to the world of tomorrow. I have always believed and I still believe that the obstinacy of Jews—admirable though it is in many respects—in not blending in completely with the various national environments is a great misfortune for everyone. But I am also too Christian to wish to see them deny their beliefs out of self-interest or even patriotism, and their religion is based precisely on a racial privilege, granted by God to the Jewish race, Jewish flesh and blood. Hence the problem is almost insoluble, but it would be a step toward a future solution if we all consented to raise the problem without bias instead of denying it.[19]

Beginning during these years of Hitler's terror, Bernanos was horrified by the word "anti-Semitism," but only because it now referred to state racism, against which he protested with all his might. Hitler kept him from being an anti-Semite. Bernanos uttered this astounding phrase: Hitler "dishonored anti-Semitism."[20] The German dictator "used anti-Semitism and anticommunism to corrupt European public opinion, divide it, separate it out, provide the people with their future victims, the themes for civil war." That led him to declare: "I have never believed in the sincerity of Hitler's anti-Semitism."[21] He now challenged the "word 'mob'" the "word 'masses,'" since "the destiny of such words, sooner or later, is to spill innocent blood."[22] Moreover, Bernanos did not intend to repudiate Drumont in any way, since in his view there was no similarity, no filiation, between Drumont and Hitler.

It is not only his abandonment of certain terms of his old vocabulary that is noteworthy in Bernanos's evolution. On the origins of the "Jewish question," there is no doubt that he revised and corrected his first interpretations. The proof is in this passage, taken from the tribute to Georges

Torrès, cited above, where he explains the *exclusion* of Jews from the medieval Christian community not only in terms of what he once called "Jewish racism" but in terms of the blindness of Christianity

> to the real causes of the survival of the Jewish people throughout history, its fidelity to itself and to its laws and ancestors, a fidelity that nonetheless has something to move the soul. Since that fidelity was not a military fidelity, military in tradition or in spirit, it kept the Jew outside a military fraternity, from which even the Infidel was not excluded. And the Jew *necessarily* [my emphasis] had to accommodate himself to such an exclusion, settle into it, profit by it. Hence the misunderstanding has continued to worsen over time.[23]

Such words, it is clear, are certainly not those of a stubborn disciple of *La France juive*. Between 1931 and 1948 (the date of his death), it is clear that Bernanos's discourse on the Jews evolved. Bernanos continued to honor Drumont's name to the end, but only because in his view, he said, and contrary to that of the "imbeciles," the work of his old master could not be reduced to anti-Semitism. This can be put another way: in this now impossible word "anti-Semitism," Drumont had a vision of the world and of history that remained fundamentally Bernanos's own.[24]

A Man of Old France

In Bernanos's view, the term "anti-Semitism" had undergone a shift in meaning. For an attentive reader of Drumont, this semantic slippage is not obvious: *Mein Kampf* follows close on the heels of *La France juive*. Why could Bernanos not resign himself to accept that continuity? There are both historical and personal reasons. He did not read Drumont as we do, with Auschwitz in mind. Bernanos felt a debt toward him. In the historical context and the environment in which Bernanos was raised, Drumont was the one who first incited him to rebel, not against the Jews—he tells us this explicitly—but against contemporary society. Drumont revealed social injustice to him, the betrayal by conservatives and the hypocrisy of the self-righteous. Bernanos's entire polemical oeuvre flowed from that initiatory reading of Drumont. In addition, behind the author, Drumont the man appeared to Bernanos as the representative of that old society in whose name he was fighting. Drumont stood as the affective reference point of his struggles: how could he repudiate him?

Obviously, Bernanos's reading of Drumont was selective. He saw neither his racism nor his paranoia. Not once does the author of *La grande peur* lend the slightest credence to the "Aryan myth,"[25] so in vogue at the end of the nineteenth century, and again in the 1930s. Similarly, he rarely embraced explanations based on "diabolical causality,"[26] which filled Drumont's books and articles. On the contrary, Bernanos recognized that his master sometimes took the effect for the cause. Bernanos did not see the Jews, as Drumont did, as the principle of all evil, the cause of decadence, the occult force undermining Christianity from within, the obsessive conspiracy whose aim was world domination. Bernanos took no notice of these hallucinations.

Two correlative aspects of Drumont's oeuvre filled Bernanos with enthusiasm: the rejection of capitalist society and the reference to Old France.

To paraphrase Bebel's formulation that "anti-Semitism is the socialism of imbeciles," we might say that, at the end of the nineteenth century, anti-Semitism was the socialism of Catholics. In their attacks, Catholics socialists and early Christian democrats combined capitalist society and Jewish banking, money and the Jews. We know that confusion was not exclusive to Catholics, and that many socialists fell into it. Catholics, however, had additional reasons to embrace it. The old anti-Jewish tradition was still alive in a religious community imputing the crucifixion of its Messiah to the Jews (through the intermediary of their ancestors). Since the definitive victory of the republicans, moreover, Catholics had been excluded from the state and their institutions had been under siege.

Bernanos's college years date from that time, when the Catholics most concerned with the "social question" easily assimilated it to the "Jewish question." *La Croix*, monitor of Catholic anti-Semitism, thus sympathetically echoed the ideas in a book by Abbé Féret entitled *Le capitalisme, voilà l'ennemi* (Capitalism is the enemy). A Christian weekly was saluted jointly by Drumont and Abbé Lemire for defining its objective as the simultaneous struggle against Jews, Freemasons, and "Panamites." A Catholic workers' committee, constituted in Brest in 1894, proclaimed in a manifesto: "Long live the French and Christian republic. Down with the Jewish and Freemason republic!"[27]

It was from Drumont that Bernanos learned about social protest, because he could not learn it from Guesde or Jaurès. As a member of a Catholic community, he made no allowances for those of his well-off coreligionists who were always ready to go along with the Freemason and atheist bourgeoisie and to crush the strikers or Communards. Hence, in 1947, during the general strikes, he told François Mauriac, who was reminding the Catholic bourgeoisie of its "social duty," that Drumont had been one of the rare people in the 1880s to speak to the bourgeoisie of that duty, altogether forgotten in the teachings of religious institutions.[28] The Drumont from whom Bernanos sought inspiration and to whom he always remained faithful was the Drumont who asserted in *La Libre Parole* on 19 March 1898: "Anti-Semites are the true avengers of the Commune"; the Drumont who denounced societies through actions "more collectivist than collectivism itself";[29] the Drumont who braved the power of money.

That fidelity to Drumont had another source. Drumont did not indict capitalist society in order to imagine a socialist utopia, something that would be incompatible with the Christian ideal. Above all else, Drumont was a "prophet of Old France." Bernanos's critique of capitalism was embedded within a broader critique, that of modern society, industrial and democratic society, which had forgotten old virtues and old rhythms of life and where the Jew was entirely in his element. Old France and Jewish prosperity were incompatible; conversely, there was an equivalence between modern society and Jewish conquest. Drumont said: "As long as Christianity was faithful to the doctrine of the Fathers of the Church, who prohibited usury and borrowing with interest, the Jew was a wanderer."[30] The collapse of Christian doctrine, the beginning of modern times, led the West to a race for profits, and step by step, to the construction of a society where plowmen and cobblers were replaced by bankers and stockbrokers. The industrial revolution that followed the capitalist revolution transformed the people into a "proletariat definitively cut off from their national, political, and social roots."[31]

In *La France contre les robots*, which he wrote in the last years of his life, Bernanos demonstrated a continuity with his first intuitions: "I am a man of Old France, I have freedom in the blood. You will tell me that Old France was not kind to the Jews. I do not approve of those injustices, but one must understand them. The Jews have always been precursors. In the eleventh century, they endeavored to constitute a capitalist society by any means possible within the Christian city."[32] The "Jewish question," according to him, was a product of the modern world. It was not that the Jew had created that world, but he was its most demonstrative expression. Medieval Christianity, with a brutality condemned by Bernanos, knew how to keep its Jews in their place; modern times liberated their energies, which had been kept under the yoke for centuries.

Bernanos's anti-Semitism rested on that equivalence between the Jew and modern man. In his vision, the Jew was less the age-old image of the usurer than the polyvalent myth of modernity. That was not incompatible with the increasingly widespread representation made of America, the paragon of technocratic excess. It was no accident that 3 million Jews lived in the single city of New York, the head of that "giant with the baby's brain." Hence this obvious fact for Bernanos: "A Frenchman is much closer to an Englishman and more capable of understanding him than he is to an American."[33]

La France contre les robots, a denunciation of mechanization and productivism, a declaration of war against industrial society, was still inspired by a vision of the world that was already implicit in Drumont's book, and which attested to a nostalgia and an anxiety discernible within the anti-Semitic movement.

"Nostalgia" is no doubt not the word Bernanos would have chosen. Let us use it nonetheless to express the conviction that there was once a model of society that if not perfect, was at least in harmony with human nature and the Christian conscience. That society, founded on honor and freedom, was replaced by modern society, founded on money and technological hubris. "The ardent Jewish minority," writes Bernanos in *La grande peur*, "quite naturally became the nucleus of a new France that gradually grew at the expense of the old."[34]

That nostalgia for a lost world is another way of formulating anxiety. It is particularly manifest in the middle strata of society, threatened or ruined by the consequences of the industrial revolution. From this point of view, Bernanos, like Drumont, was sociologically representative of this world of artisans and small business people, which the factory and the department store had sent into a decline beginning with the Second Empire. Anti-Semitism gave an identity to the obscure threat burdening their existence. They clung to it like the paranoid to his interpretive fantasy.

The threat was not only economic—it was also spiritual and moral. The industrial revolution was shattering not only old ways of life but a group psychology, an age-old philosophy of life itself. The Jews brought with them "a new mystique, admirably in agreement with the mystique of progress, the modern form of messianism that expects from man only the revelation of the future god."[35]

In *La petite peur du XXᵉ siècle* (The little fear of the twentieth century) Emmanuel Mounier writes that "around the dawn of modern times, European man achieved a kind of uterine life, which he led within a universe closed upon him like an egg upon its germ, within a Church that directly guided his first steps."[36] The nostalgia for this old world, whose protective image is reconstructed for the needs of the cause, reflects the uneasiness felt by modern man in the face of an indecipherable future. Truly, the acceleration of material transformations and the loss of old beliefs combined to create "civilization and its discontents."

This was one of the strongest motivations for modern anti-Semitism—in any case as it is expressed by Drumont and his disciples. For them, the image of the Jew was linked to wandering, instability, change. "What are those wanderers doing among us?" asks Bernanos. "Let them become fixed in place or let them suffer the imposition of our laws on their wandering."[37] He looked upon these "eternal vagabonds" as a man of the land threatened by nomads. The duality between Christian and Jew leads to the polarities between stable and changing, immobility and evolution, stone construction and canvas tent. Péguy wrote that Israel had a *great vice* that was also a *great secret virtue*, a "great vocation": to be "a people whose real property will never be more than tents." But in citing this text, Bernanos deliberately forgets "the great virtue" and speaks only of the "vice." "In the end, this vice became that of the modern world. Is that merely a coincidence?"[38] Bernanos was intent on defending "races such as our own, so closely tied to the soil, the hearth, the stone at their doorstep," against the aggressions of modern mobility.

Since antiquity, many authors, with Plato in the lead, have interpreted change as a synonym for evil; immobility was a reassuring ideal. Immobility became land and stone, real property. Banking and industrial technology shattered the old stable world, the "closed society" Karl Popper speaks of,[39] which for millennia was the "natural" framework for humanity. This was a society where everyone had a place, where children continued the work of their parents, where the future resembled the past. That old order was shattered. "The transition from the closed to the open society," writes Popper, "can be described as one of the deepest revolutions through which mankind has passed."[40] The end of rural society and of the patriarchal family, the development of cities, the individualization of society, the personal responsibilities that the most modest individuals—wrested from their "tribe"—had to assume, the formidable mutation that began slowly at the end of the Middle Ages and accelerated until the nineteenth and twentieth centuries, was a leap into the unknown and the uncertain (Popper).

Like Drumont, Bernanos certainly expressed that anxiety about the modern world, an anxiety that was the result of rootlessness. But the ambivalence in his work, which sets him apart from ordinary reactionaries, was that in his eyes Old France was the exact opposite of a "closed society," the sort of society that the fascist and communist movements dreamed of reconstructing on new foundations. "Nothing less resembles totalitarianism, in fact, than our old French order with its almost inextricable accumulation of services and privileges stemming from one another and balancing one another out."[41]

That idealization of preindustrial society converges with anti-Semitism. In Bernanos, however, anti-Semitism is the erroneous expression of *moral* values (honor and freedom). These values were so firmly rooted in Bernanos that he turned away from the *political* logic that ordinarily motivated anti-Semites between 1933 and 1945. Hence the strictly unclassifiable situation of Bernanos, a renegade who always remained faithful to himself.

When *Les grands cimetières sous la lune* (The great cemeteries under the moon) was published, André Thérive expressed his surprise in *Le Temps* at Bernanos's incoherence. After all, *La grande peur des bien-pensants* was an antiliberal, antibourgeois, and antidemocratic pamphlet that anticipated fascism, and now, "that student of Drumont seems to have become a Dreyfusard."[42] In fact, however, for anyone who reads the conclusion to *La grande peur* carefully, Bernanos necessarily appears as the most resolute adversary of every form of totalitarianism. Even that is not saying enough: all his work is tensed, standing ready against the many incarnations of modern tyranny, and opposes to them not a strategy (is there one?) but "a certain strictly religious conception of the human person." What is lying in wait for us, threatening us, and will soon exclude us if we refuse to walk in lock step is "the universal factory, the full-scale factory," which the engineer, flanked by the banker and the people's representative, is in the process of building. That society without a goal—"except perhaps that of lasting as long as possible"—will have "the total subjugation of the individual, his crushing defeat" as its finality. The last sentences of the book sound like an alarm signal: "Our lungs will be gasping for air. No more air." The enemy is neither on the left nor on the right; it is everywhere that human freedom is in danger.

There is no question that his points of reference may appear chimerical today: the poet's imagination played its part in his depiction of Christianity. But when Bernanos asserts, "The history of my country was made by people who believed in the supernatural vocation of France,"[43] we are back to a historical reality. The drafters of the Rights of Man, the revolutionaries of 1848, a good number of Communards and Dreyfusards[44] did not call it "supernatural," but they certainly had an unshakable belief in France's "mission."

The important thing, it seems to me, is not so much the Christian medieval reference as the mind that made something of it. The dream of a lost society can inspire law-and-order men just as well as libertarian spirits. Bernanos imagined an archetype of the Frenchman, a strong and free man, who was incarnated in "the man of the ancien régime." He "had a Catholic conscience, a monarchist's heart and mind, and a republican's temperament."[45] He did not invent that portrait of robots in order to keep people in line, but rather to contrast it to the slave of modern tyrannies.

· Similarly, the anti-Semitism that surfaces in Bernanos's works is not central, as it is in the work of his "dear old Drumont." He used it at times, as bad rhetoric; he never recited a "breviary of hatred." It would be a misrepresentation of truth and an injustice to leave the impression that there is any comparison between the writings of Bernanos and the anti-Semitic influences of which they bear the marks.

CHAPTER 24

De Gaulle, the Last Nationalist

"I ACT ONLY ON the nation's imagination; when that means fails me, I shall be nothing." A century and a half after Napoleon uttered those lines, Charles de Gaulle could have turned them to his own account. He had reigned for about ten years, and first in the French imagination. Then the French people distanced themselves from him because he was short on inspiration or because they no longer wanted to dream.

General de Gaulle's return to power in 1958, however, was primarily the result of circumstances. In 1947, the former leader of the Free French forces already had a fixed idea of the constitution he wished to bestow on the French people. In addition, he possessed a powerful mass organization, the Rassemblement du Peuple Français (RPF, Rally of the French people), founded in April; the municipal elections of October 1947 had given an indication of his following in the country. De Gaulle, however, did not obtain the hoped-for dissolution of the Assembly that had been elected in 1946. Without real support in Parliament, he had to champ on the bit, condemned to powerlessness, before resigning himself to the "desert." There he might have been condemned to live out the rest of his days, between his memories and his mirages.

The crisis that emerged out of the Algerian conflict, however, finally designated him and no other as the final recourse in 1958. Abandoned by his compatriots in previous years, he became the arbitrator of the game under the sudden threat of civil war, in exchange for a few public declarations, a few more or less secret meetings, and a few minimal concessions of form. The qualities of the tactician and the contradictions of the French left converged in this unprecedented comeback. Once installed in power and until the end of the Algerian war, de Gaulle was to have at his disposal the massive support of metropolitan public opinion, as attested in the referenda of 1958, 1961, and 1962. What did that popular backing depend on?

First, the French people recognized Charles de Gaulle as a historical figure. He did not fail to brandish from time to time the invisible scepter conferred upon him by the appeal of 18 June 1940 and by his actions at the head of the Free French forces. Hence, in the course of the famous "week of barricades" in Algiers, in late January 1960, he went on television to invoke not only the people's mandate but also "the national legitimacy [he had] incarnated for twenty years." It was as if the period between January 1946, when he left his position as premier, and May–June 1958, the date when he got back "to business," had been only an insignificant parenthesis. Since the humiliation of France in 1940, he had been and remained the voice of the nation in resistance and finally in victory. That coincidence between his person and the person of France led him to extraordinary claims that coming from anyone else, would have been buffoonish. For example, he exclaimed during a council of ministers: "I've been saying that for a thousand years." He was the Gaullian mystery of the incarnation, the French holy trinity under one kepi: the mother country, the son Charles, and the Holy Spirit, who began to inspire all persons of good will from a London microphone, when all seemed lost.

The legendary episode of 18 June was reinforced by what was learned—too late—about the general's military prescience. The defeated officer had done everything to prevent the defeat. In *L'armée du métier* (The army of the future) in May 1934, then a lieutenant-colonel, he published a justification for mobile warfare based on the use of tanks, against the thesis of the general staff, which had been won over to the war of position. That resurrection of the "great cavalries of the past" would make it possible to eliminate trench-digging: six divisions and 100,000 men, experts and technicians were the means drawn up. Complementary "air squadrons" were to "play a key role in the war of the future." That vision of the future had encountered star-studded opposition, notably that of the glorious Marshal Pétain. In 1938, in a preface to a book by General Chauvineau, Pétain reasserted the defensive doctrine. In addition, responding to an interlocutor questioning him on the fact that the Maginot line stopped west of the Ardennes, the "hero of Verdun" superbly declared: "The forest of Ardennes is impenetrable, and if the Germans were to be imprudent enough to set out into it, we would catch them when they came out."[1] The French campaign of 1940 assured the general's military prestige. Not only did he save French honor—which Pétain betrayed by bowing to Hitler—but he demonstrated his intellectual superiority over the old marshal.

Charles de Gaulle's legitimacy also lay in the unity he imposed on the

Resistance, in the unified, or apparently unified combat sorties that operated despite the power of the communists. He had succeeded in maintaining discipline among the communists, and he soon succeeded in disarming them. The image of the extraordinary parade down the Champs-Elysées on 26 August 1944, which photographers imprinted in the minds of the French people, was again recalled in the rough days of May 1958. That human ocean surrounding the liberator, after the dark night of Occupation, inspired one of the most beautiful passages in his *Mémoires de guerre* (War memoirs).

And it was up to this liberator, who had intuited the kind of war to conduct, who had reestablished France among the victors and, as a result, among the great powers, to give an accurate view of the constitutional weaknesses of the Fourth Republic. In 1958, the defenders of that republic were lacking in ardor; antiparliamentarianism had been nourished by ministerial instability and the inability to govern on the part of so many cabinets without a lasting majority. All the polls showed how disparaged the regime was. For his part, de Gaulle had predicted its misfortunes when it was installed. Full of contempt for the "reign of parties," he finally took advantage of his wager: had he not been right from the outset? From then on, the misadventure of the RPF tended to be forgotten. The fact that François Mauriac rallied behind him says a great deal about the evolution in public opinion, given that de Gaulle had not varied since the postwar constitutional debates.

In addition to national, military, and political legitimacy, there was also republican legitimacy. In fact, despite criticism on the left that made comparisons with Italy in the grip of Mussolini, de Gaulle always respected universal suffrage. Nothing in his past put him in the category of a seditious general. During the episode of 1947, when he was in a position of strength, he opposed all illegal ventures. Even though his return to power occurred under conditions that were at the least ambiguous, he did not hesitate to have it ratified, first by Parliament, then by referendum. Of course, his idea of the republic had few points in common with that of the Freemason and positivist republicans who had gradually fixed it in the minds of the French people after the 1871 defeat. But precisely, he was able to revise its principles and make it everyone's regime.

Thus the general's past was a certificate of guarantee. His cause was the French cause, and not the cause of a faction: he had given adequate proof of that. But as strong as that legitimacy may have been, did the French like *him*?

Less strong than the "Napoleonic legend," which pervaded the Restoration and the July monarchy, the Gaullian legend existed nonetheless. That is, there was a kind of laudatory hum working on his behalf: primary school images; half-price books on the French Free forces and other friends of the Liberation. Even in leftist circles, which did not favor him, there was always Roger Stéphane to recall the great man's merits.[2] De Gaulle himself had taken to glorifying his past actions. The first volume of *Mémoires de guerre*, that "masterpiece of Latin literature in the French language," as it was so nicely called, came out in 1954, the second volume in 1956, and the third and last in 1959. In a sovereign style, the general, speaking of himself in the third person like Caesar, retraced the epic of France in combat, with himself at its head, obliged to struggle not only against Germany, not only against Vichy, but also against the Allies—Roosevelt in particular—who balked at hearing "the voice of France" coming from his mouth. The success of the first two volumes disposed many readers in favor of that intransigent leader, who treated heads of state as equals when he was only an obscure and even recently promoted brigadier general; who stood up to the president of the United States without concern for the meager material forces he possessed; who brought everything back around to the interests of the nation.

The war films, superabundant after the Liberation, periodically reminded the forgetful of the role of the sublime exile. "This is London, Frenchmen speaking to Frenchmen." The capital accumulated by the Free French forces earned de Gaulle all sorts of dividends, which took the form of stories of all kinds. Even when no one was thinking about him in terms of his forming a government, he remained within the popular memory.

De Gaulle also benefited from what Max Weber has called "charismatic power." His physical presence was imposing. Perhaps we need not insist on his size: Napoleon proved once and for all that history does not forbid temporal greatness to the small of stature. Nonetheless, that tall figure added even more to his exceptional character. Working the huge crowds he valued so much, he stood above everyone. He could be seen from afar, and one wonders how the assassins on his heels could have missed him. I remember as a child—it must have been about 1945—that I was fascinated watching him go along a Paris avenue in a covered car. I watched open-mouthed as his long arms unfolded above his kepi, like a semaphore signal tirelessly repeating the letter V. In 1958, the French people, naturally comparing his bearing, his gestures, and his words to those of President René Coty or other of his colleagues, were filled with the obscure feeling that they were dealing with a "somebody."

Words in particular were one of his best weapons. Radio, now portable thanks to transistors, and television, which was becoming widespread at a rapid rate, were effective aids for an orator. Yet one still needed talent and the art of adapting to the new communication technology. Many made jokes about the general's style: Jean-François Revel even wrote a spicy lit-tle pamphlet[3] in which he makes fun of the tautological turns of phrase characteristic of Gaullian discourse: "The situation being what it is," "French people being what they are," and so on. Next to this ease of communication, which was not insignificant (it reminds us that the man of action must also allow for "things," gravity, natural laws), de Gaulle knew how to use his art to produce purple passages, which were admired all the more in that they were thought up in the midst of the storm.

During times of crisis, he was almost always at his best; in the face of danger, he found that mixture of banter and classicism that made his ap-peals to reason moving, satisfying, sometimes grandiose. He did not im-provise: he learned by heart the formulations he had constructed, honed, and repeated, and which he then thrust on hypnotized journalists or tele-vision viewers. The reiterated demands he made for the French people's support regularly brought him closer to them: "Well then, my dear old country, here we are, together again, facing a severe ordeal"; "French men and women, help me!" How could the children remain indifferent to the voice of the father who had become so friendly, so affectionate? In 1958, the general's speeches, complemented if need be by those of André Mal-raux, placed the birth of the Fifth Republic within the legend of the ages.

The general had been formed by the army: nowhere did he feel hap-pier than in an officers' mess; his cabinet was filled with "Colonel Blimps" (*culottes de peau*); he did not rest until France had recovered its military greatness (the atomic bomb was one condition for that). And yet he avoided all the shortcomings of his caste. It would be tempting to see the two little stars that adorned his kepi as a sign of modesty, an amuse-ment at soldiers' vanities. In fact, however, they were more a sign of his pride. In deliberately remaining at the bottom of the hierarchy of general officers, his tunic or jacket free of decorations, he was indicating that his destiny went beyond the advancement structure, and though he belonged to the army, that it was to remain an instrument, nothing but an instru-ment. Political power took precedence. The French people saw that this man, military to the core, would never let his conduct be imposed by the "colonels." The adventure of the Free French forces, which earned him a death sentence in absentia and the hatred of so many officers, elevated de Gaulle far above his professional milieu of origin.

I do not know if people loved him in 1958, but at least they respected him. That was true even of his adversaries, as illustrated by Pierre Mendès France's speech to the Assembly, in which he argued against the general's return by a show of force, but retained his admiration for the man of 18 June. Among politicians, de Gaulle took on an aspect that calmed hostility, and he also knew how to elicit enthusiasm, unconditional loyalty, heroic devotion among those he had forever converted to his person. The fact that personalities as different as Michel Debré, André Malraux, and Edmont Michelet stood beside him in an unassailable manner despite all their disappointments (I am thinking of Michel Debré, defender of "French Algeria") suggests the magnetism de Gaulle could exert.

That attachment included a good dose of irrationality. All his merits can be laid out, all his titles to glory verified, but it is no use: they are not enough to fully explain the spontaneous confidence the majority of French people had in him at the time. In the crisis situation, he possessed all the attributes of the providential man. His legend, his solitude, his career as a misunderstood prophet, everything designated him as the savior that the country on the edge of the abyss needed. The power granted was all the greater inasmuch as professional politicians had failed to exercise it. In the chaos, people no longer believed in ordinary statutory procedures; the solution had to be commensurate with the danger. It could not come from mere mortals, divided among themselves and powerless. In this country where incredulity had become a political system, people had never stopped believing in miracles. When the churches emptied, astrologers made a fortune. Emerging as a demigod from his solitude in Colombey, de Gaulle satisfied the need to believe that surges forth from despair, the need for order felt in times of upheaval, the demand for a state that is fed by parliamentary incompetence.

What did he say? We still do not know very well. His speeches were often logographs to be deciphered, which everyone interpreted as he or she wished. To foster unanimity, it was important to be ambiguous. He did not always know the side he would take. The main thing was for people to follow him, grant him every confidence, know once and for all that he was heart set on serving France and nothing more.

Communication between the French people and de Gaulle had to be direct. On this point, the general was explicit. For example, announcing the referendum on Algerian self-determination, he declared on 6 January 1961: "French men and women, as you know, you will be replying to me. . . . I turn to you, over the heads of all intermediaries. In truth—who does not know this?—the matter is between each of you and myself." One could not be clearer about the political short-circuit.

De Gaulle wanted to have a physical sensation of these privileged relations with his people. Hence the Gaullian ritual included frequent trips through the provinces. Once there, he uttered banalities to the dignitaries. The serious matter was elsewhere, outside prefectoral buildings and official monuments, in the streets, where the crowd could barely be held back behind metal fences. De Gaulle wanted to hear their cheers, feel their trembling, welcome their enthusiasm and attachment. Leaving the procession, and to the great distress of his bodyguards, he plunged his immense arms into the ocean of hands moving toward him; he shook as many as he could; he immersed himself in popular enthusiasm as if to receive a new baptism. In the crowd, the great man's "outing" revived feelings of filiation. People would return home, overcome at having touched the hand or a piece of fabric belonging to the sovereign. Even when he good-naturedly "worked the crowd," the sacred character of the exchange between de Gaulle and the assembled people escaped no one. In Gaullism, direct democracy began with that direct theophany on the cobblestones of cities bedecked in banners.

The referendum became the institution par excellence. In each case, whatever the question asked, the purpose was to renew the confidence the French people had given their guide. Democrats, adversaries, and jurists sometimes protested the disguised plebiscite. In fact, nothing was more clear for de Gaulle and his voters. He repeated: If you do not give me your backing, I will withdraw. They did not base their vote on anything else, did not read the texts proposed for their sagacity, did not try to complicate matters: they reasserted (or failed to reassert) their profession of faith. De Gaulle may have been king, but his monarchy was neither hereditary nor for life: it hinged on the credit granted him by universal suffrage. That was what backed him up, guaranteed him, supported him against the maneuvers of his adversaries. It was the supreme arbitrator, which might one day or another reverse its decision. There was no clause regarding "renewal by tacit agreement": the lease had to be renewed on a regular basis.

After the triumphal vote of 28 September 1958, in which 80 percent of voters approved the new constitution (the constitution of the Fourth Republic had obtained only a relative majority in 1946), de Gaulle organized two decisive referenda: one on 8 January 1961 on the self-determination of the Algerian people, and the other on 8 April 1962 on the independence of Algeria. The first took place at a time when the president of the Republic had already been won over to the idea of Algerian independence. But apart from the difficulties remaining on the means for an accord with the Front de Libération Nationale, he had to impose his view on the French Algerians, and especially on the army, most of whose officers had not given up on "integration." Some even envisioned another "13 May" to reverse the policy of self-determination set in place in Paris. Against both the leaders of Algerian nationalism and senior officers in the French army, de Gaulle needed broad support from the country. He confided to his entourage that he would abandon everything if 50 percent of registered voters did not say yes. In the end, he obtained 56 percent, that is, 75 percent of those who actually voted. Since the Communist party, which favored Algerian independence, had recommended a no vote, the head of state could boast he had demonstrated that the adversaries of negotiations were a small minority.

His electoral campaign on television, however, had only hardened the opposing camp. General Challe confessed that the speech given by de Gaulle two days before the vote—a speech judged unworthy of him—resolved him to act. He took part in the April putsch, the same month that the Organisation Armée Secrète (Secret Army Organization) showed its first signs of life. In the face of the crushing political power of the president of the Republic, supported by the metropolis, the partisans of French Algeria had to resign themselves to illegal, clandestine, and violent action. De Gaulle masterfully used television against them. Another instrument of direct monocracy, these "strange windows," to use the expression of *Le Canard Enchaîné*, offered the general the means to bring down the adversary by securing unanimity in the metropolis. We know how he railed against the perpetrators of the putsch and how effectively his words were among soldiers in the contingent, who heard them on their "transistors" via RMC. The IFOP polls, another means for the resident of the Elysée to relate to the French people, revealed record popularity achieved by de Gaulle in April 1961, breaking the previous record achieved during the Algiers "barricades" in January 1960. To most French people—those who lived between Dunkerque and Perpignan—the general appeared to be the protector of civil peace.

The referendum of 8 April 1962 on Algerian independence procured the general his greatest success, nearly 91 percent of the vote. The interminable conflict had convinced people of the inevitability of decolonization. The problem that had cost so much—in human lives even more than in billions of francs—was finally settled. There was immense relief; de Gaulle, who knew how to overcome all resistance—first that of the army, then that of the Organisation Armée Secrète—reaped the fruits of his actions. The murderous violence of the desperadoes in the OAS elicited the general's indignation and reinforced his power, which was at its apogee.

At the same time, the independence of Algeria earned him the lasting hatred of those who had dedicated themselves to the defense of the lost "province." In one of those paradoxes that continues to astonish, the most nationalist head of state France had ever had counted as his most implacable adversaries the nationalists themselves. A hard little kernel, recruited among doomed soldiers and politicians in exile, polarized the bitterness of a portion of the "repatriated." In the history of the relations between the French people and General de Gaulle, no party, no group focused more execration on him than the disabled soldiers from French Algeria. While the general received the gratitude of the vast majority, that little minority never got over its resentment. Sometimes, the bitterness combined with more ancient resentments: this camp included many faithful to Marshal Pétain, those purged in 1944, the survivors of the Collaboration. In that fierce minority, blind to the march of time and disdaining the over-whelming majority that disavowed them, despair and anger eventually led to attempted murder.

In fact, the episode of Petit-Clamart, where, on 22 August 1962, the president of the Republic's car was machine-gunned (de Gaulle was un-harmed), completed the magical power of an uncommon man who kept his Olympian head in every circumstance, a man armor-plated against all adversities and impregnable to conspirators.

In addition, the attempt on his life once again raised the question of the president's succession. De Gaulle had already thought of the solution: give the person who would occupy his post, but without his charismatic power, a surplus of legitimacy through an election by universal suffrage. This was a delicate matter. De Gaulle had the majority of the political class against him: now that the Algerian war was over, they dreamed of sending the general back to small-town life in Colombey. They were also again becoming steeped in republican principles. Not since Napoleon III had the president of the Republic been elected by universal suffrage; in fact, the Third and Fourth Republics made universal suffrage an impre-scriptible rule. De Gaulle did not take any notice. Once more, he ap-pealed to the people; he proposed a referendum. The jurists of the consti-tutional council gave an unfavorable opinion: the procedure chosen to change the constitution was not constitutional. The president of the sen-ate, Gaston Monnerville, spoke of "abuse of power." But never mind, de Gaulle would disregard him. On 28 October 1962, nearly 62 percent of voters approved the plan. The institution that would become the most popular of the Fifth Republic was established against the views of profes-sional politicians and lawyers.

The method was questionable. The result was conclusive. "Alone against everyone," de Gaulle had convinced the French people that democracy could not be destroyed by turning directly to them to designate their president. For too long, under previous republics, they had been swindled out of their vote: the "party system" formed a screen between their will and government decisions. In spite of discouraging historical memories, the French very quickly adopted that new instrument of direct democ-racy. The simplification of the game gave them the feeling that they were finally participating in the choice of an executive power, until then aban-doned to political arcana. The direct relation between the leader and his troops was institutionalized. It no longer lay in a fortuitous encounter be-tween an exceptional man and the voters; it became a law of the republic.

The Surprise Runoff Election of 1965

Although the Algerian war definitively earned the general his maximum popularity, it also remained a painful tragedy that left a stain on his memory. Posterity was grateful to him for having cleansed France of the fruitless wars of colonial defense. But the means often did damage to the victims, and some never forgave him for what they associated with contempt, indifference, or an inhumane conception of the state.

"Nothing heightens authority better than silence" (*Le fil de l'épée*; The edge of the sword): so wrote a man gifted at breaking the silence at the opportune moment. Although prompt to make public pronouncements, however, de Gaulle sometimes sought refuge in a hurtful silence. On 17 and 18 October 1961, approximately one hundred Algerian workers, peaceful demonstrators from the Paris region, were killed by police. That "night of horror," in the words of the centrist deputy Claudius-Petit, did not wrest a word of condolence from de Gaulle. The "deaths in the Caronne metro"—a demonstration against the OAS in December 1961, which ended in terror under police repression—did not get him to open his mouth either.

The Algerian repatriates, or, as some preferred to say, expatriates, could not forget the contempt he showed toward them. No doubt many of them now admit the inevitability of Algerian independence, but they still believe they were "ill used" by de Gaulle. After the false hope he fostered about their lives, they reproach him for failing even to pass the important indemnity law in their favor, which they quite justifiably expected. Similarly, the fate reserved for those other victims of independence, the Muslim auxiliary or "harkis" (they were sometimes exposed to a settling of accounts in Algeria or were received in France with a lack of hospitality) did not shed a favorable light on Gaullist generosity. "Everything but de Gaulle," said French Algerian associations during the 1965 electoral campaign. In hatred as in fervor, de Gaulle stood apart. For him, character could abrogate personal commitments: "The passion to act on one's own," he wrote in *Le fil de l'épée*, "is obviously accompanied by a certain roughness in the means. The man of character incorporates into his person the rigor appropriate to the effort. Subordinates feel it and sometimes complain about it." Of course. Still it would have to be demonstrated that such "roughness" was justified in all cases.

The first round of the first presidential election by universal suffrage within the framework of the Fifth Republic took place on 5 December 1965. All the commentators noted only one striking result: de Gaulle would have to take part in the runoff election; he had received support from only 43.7 percent of voters (36.78 percent of registered voters). Behind the general was François Mitterrand, who received 32.2 percent, Jean Lecanuet, with a full 15.9 percent, and Jean-Louis Tixier-Vignancour, whose share was made up of unyielding opponents on the far right and those nostalgic for French Algeria (5.3 percent), with the balance going to Senator Pierre Marchilhacy (1.7 percent) and the unexpected Marcel Barbu (1.2 percent). We may be surprised by the stupor felt by the general's loyalists, and the disappointment felt by de Gaulle himself, since in the meantime we have experienced other presidential elections and we know how small the final victor's margin can be. But in 1965 there was no basis for comparison. People remembered only the triumphal referenda of the Algerian years. Above all, they still believed de Gaulle untouchable.

The president of the Republic, moreover, had neglected to campaign, remaining within the empyrean of his grand politics, while his socialist and centrist adversaries scored points every week owing to the dynamism of their speeches. The French people were discovering that there were replacement solutions, reserve troops opposing the eternal general. For the first time, they heard on the airwaves scathing judgments of his management and his choices. This was a good opportunity to make known to the president the grievances that had sometimes piled up against him. The theme of Europe, eloquently defended by Jean Lecanuet, was hardly well suited to call Gaullist foreign policy into question, since de Gaulle's international prestige flattered the pride of the French people; but that was not the case for the criticism, made especially by the leftist candidate, of his economic and social policy.

In this area, de Gaulle was vulnerable. Preoccupied, first, with making peace in Algeria, then with returning France to the ranks of a mid-level power with a competent military policy and diplomacy, he seemed to be neglecting what he rather carelessly called "money matters" (*l'intendance*). It was not that he had contempt for the economy, but it was to be put in the service of national greatness rather than promoting the material satisfaction of the French people. The polls showed that during his entire tenure, de Gaulle had the majority of public opinion against him in this area. The lowest level of his popularity was reached in 1963 during the miners' strike; beyond that event, however, Jean Charlot, a specialist in Gaullism and political analysis, speaks of an "endemic discontent" on these economic and social questions.[4] Hence, in July 1964, three-quarters of the French people believed that the stabilization plan decided the preceding year was a failure. The glorious 1960s, swept away by the race for growth, created more dissatisfied people than happy ones. It is only with hindsight that we can appreciate the progress accomplished; at the time, people felt only their own frustrations, the inequalities in gains in the standard of living, the personal impression that they were being granted only the crumbs of expansion.

The truth is that de Gaulle was now less necessary to the life of the country, and people sensed this more or less consciously. The stormy times were over. The policy of greatness and neutrality against the two antagonistic blocs on the international stage may well have seduced certain intellectuals on the left; de Gaulle's anti-Americanism in particular may have satisfied the Soviet embassy and been appreciated by the communist press. But it was no use: these realities were distant from the immediate worries. The great industrial shift under way was uprooting some and worrying others; even the end of inflation had consequences on people's notion of their income. This time the choice was no longer between a reassuring yes vote and a risky no vote, but among competing men and policies.

In the second round, de Gaulle won with 55 percent of the vote, to François Mitterrand's 45 percent. It was a clear majority, which returned the general to power but limited his influence. In terms of registered voters, de Gaulle had obtained only 45 percent. Desacralization was under way. Unlike the unanimous crowds who had shouted their fervor, the profane slogans of social protest now rose from the demonstrations: *"Charlot, des sous!"* ("Charlie, money!"). Once the disappointment of the first round had passed, de Gaulle fully assumed his role as candidate, neglecting nothing, especially not the television cameras. That was how the game was now played. Once more, adversity elevated him to his highest art; he masterfully regained lost ground, at least in appearance. In fact, however, everything had changed. The hero had fallen from his pedestal. Direct democracy contradicted direct monocracy. In that battle, the colossus discovered his feet of clay.

The two years that followed forced that dual reality on the general: success, at least apparent—and sometimes insolent—in his foreign policy; and growing protests domestically. The great Gaullian scheme, that France should become the champion of the mid-sized nations against the policy of the two blocs, was asserted with enthusiasm. In March 1966, de Gaulle signaled his resolution to President Johnson to withdraw French forces from NATO. In September in Phnom Penh, before Prince Sihanouk, 200,000 Cambodians, and the international press, he audaciously denounced American intervention in Vietnam, shortly before finding himself again in Mururoa, where he witnessed the explosion of a French atomic bomb. The general proclaimed the need for a fierce will to strategic and diplomatic independence for all nations, up to and including those he called the "French in Canada," during a resounding speech delivered in Montreal on 24 July 1967, on the theme of "Free Quebec." The symbolic fulfillment of that policy was the choice of Paris as the negotiating site between the warring Americans and the Vietnamese. Even the sports gods seemed to be joining in: the Winter Olympics, which took place in Grenoble in February 1968, were an apotheosis for French skiers, both male and female.

Grumbling threatened the domestic scene, however. The first warning lights of unemployment were blinking; fairly severe strikes erupted in 1967. The legislative elections that same year confirmed the fragility of Gaullist power, which required the support of deputies overseas to assure a bare majority in the Assembly. Even in foreign policy, de Gaulle was disavowed after the Six-Day War: the polls showed the opposition of a majority of French people favoring Israel to his decision of neutrality toward the Near East. More generally, France's independence policy became illusory. Jean Charlot, analyzing these polls, speaks of "the broken spell." The crisis of May 1968 completed the hobbling of the republican monarch's Olympian figure.

In the weeks between the student revolt (beginning of May) and the last round of legislative elections (30 June), de Gaulle was caught between two profound tendencies of society, neither of which he could satisfy. We might, if not summarize, then at least schematize the crises by resorting to the dialectic of liberation and security. On one hand, society, led by a new generation and spearheaded by university students, was expressing a desire for autonomy against all constraining, authoritarian, and hierarchical institutions. On the other hand, it was manifesting, first with prudence and then with growing conviction, its need for protection. The dual movement sometimes existed within the same individuals: in May the strike, in June the truce! Most often, the tension set two camps against each other, camps defined sometimes by their age cohort, sometimes by their income or some other factor. And de Gaulle seemed powerless against that contradiction.

In the heat of events, he struggled to make sense of it all. This became clear when he left for an official visit to Romania on 14 May, that is, the day after the large demonstration that combined students and salaried employees and announced a social crisis. His departure was a caricature of the imbalance in Gaullian policy. The primacy of foreign policy was being reaffirmed during a full-scale domestic crisis. The Hercules of the Elysée had not given any thought to what Pascal called "the power of flies: they win battles, prevent our souls from acting, eat up our bodies." These "flies," these French people, had got it into their heads that they existed! On 14 May, de Gaulle had not yet conceded as much: France preoccupied him more than its residents. In the eyes of his fellow citizens, the trip to Romania confirmed the psychological as well as the geographical distance between the general and their daily problems.

The students' social revolt expected nothing from Gaullian power. His presence even fed it: "Ten years is enough!" The old man, lost in anachronistic dreams of national greatness, was not exactly antipathetic: he was outdated. He had done his time; he symbolized the hierarchical, military school, military-industrial, technostructural, bureaucratic, national-productivist (and so on) state, precisely what the students wanted to get rid of. The "flies" wanted to live their fly lives and not serve as a halo to the solitary knight fighting windmills. The most noble flies, the most disinterested, the least needy, preferred freedom to "greatness."

As the days went by, the opposing camp became more worried at the sight of the barricades and burning cars, in the discomfort of the general strike, and began to wonder when the chaos would end. The general was no longer in their good graces either. At other times, de Gaulle had been able to reestablish calm with one appearance on TV, two or three words, and a few injunctions. And now here he was, even after he had become aware of the gravity of the crisis, powerless to impose order. The fiasco of his televised outing on 24 May presaged increasing unrest. People were upset, alarmed, and gradually got used to the idea of finding a replacement for de Gaulle. Soon a single cry could be heard from the law-and-order camp: Pompidou was the one needed. A replacement was at hand, and de Gaulle himself had prepared him for the job. Heaven knows we must be leery of the legend of a deliquescent de Gaulle and a radiant Pompidou, the latter absorbing the substance of the former as in communicating vessels. Rightly or wrongly, however, in these days of unrest the straightforward man from Cajarc, the sly Auvergnat, the Sancho Panza of the regime, offered the reassuring image of a calm realist, whereas de Gaulle was now only a disoriented dreamer.

I shall not give a final accounting of the two courses of action, the two men, the two allies who unintentionally became rivals. Let us simply note the now widespread idea that it was owing to Pompidou that de Gaulle rallied. Old age is a shipwreck, the general had said of Pétain. In his turn, de Gaulle had aged; he was no longer master of events. He disappointed the frightened: property owners, heads of families badly in need of authority, mandarins who could not even suffer in their posts since they were being forced to step down, motorists in search of gasoline, and all those who were in the movement and getting tired. In that mess, in that "uncontrollable" situation (the term used by the general himself), the demand for a state grew stronger and stronger. And day after day, de Gaulle led people to believe he was no longer the state, that there was no longer any state.

Let us pay heed to François Mauriac, a Gaullist on the left: "I feel entirely and passionately on the side of the state, not at all because I was born bourgeois, but because I do not doubt that the greatest misfortune for a people is that there should no longer be any state."[5]

When the May crisis and the June reprieve had passed, de Gaulle recovered, and not only in the area of political maneuvering. The counteroffensive had been accomplished in a few weeks: the trip to Baden-Baden, plus the short speech transmitted over the radio on 30 May, plus the massive demonstration in support of him on the Champs-Elysées, plus the elections of a Chamber nowhere to be found. The pendulum swung back and returned power—for a moment threatened—to the great strategist of the Elysée. More than that, de Gaulle had assimilated the two imperatives born of the crisis: he reasserted his legitimacy and responded to the aspirations of the social movement. The referendum was again used to this dual effect. More profoundly, having heeded the widespread needs of a society desiring more autonomy, he attempted to bring about the synthesis of liberation and authority, to resolve the contradiction by personally offering the instruments for participation and regionalization that broke the restraints of a hidebound France, even while maintaining the state's solidity. Auguste Comte called that the alliance between order and progress. Such was the entire meaning of the referendum of 27 April 1969.

Everyone Becomes a Gaullist

Fifty-three percent responded to him with a no vote. Some voters demanded the murder of the Father: society no longer needed a guardian; it had to become an adult; it had to take the risk of its emancipation. Others decided to change fathers: de Gaulle was dead, long live Pompidou! Advocates of law and order and progressives both rejected him. De Gaulle fell simultaneously on the right and on the left. Rejected by the spirit of youth that had risen up in May and by the spirit of old age badly in need of assurance, de Gaulle was no longer up to the task of inventing the future for his people or of assuring the future of the patrimony.

With de Gaulle's death on 9 November 1970, everyone became, or became again, a Gaullist. Or almost everyone. And the more time passed the more the new party recruited, on the left and on the right. With the exception of the last wardroom of old Pétainists going gray under the marshal's photo, and the last company of condemned men who, despite the amnesty, remained stuck in their "Algerian" bitterness, everyone sang his praises. Some embraced him for legitimating their political party, others for stigmatizing the betrayal of epigones. People vied with one another to put his memory to immediate and inglorious ends. More profoundly, the French people, who in the meantime had experienced unemployment and had returned to the flatness of ordinary days and ordinary politicians, waxed sentimental over the image of the last of the great men.

And what years were the 1960s! People forgot the dissatisfactions of the times, the negative opinion polls, "*the ill temper, the crossness, the grumbling*" (*la hargne, la rogne, et la grogne*). It had been a time of growth, the years when the average citizen had bought a television, a first car, a washing machine. In the grayness of economic difficulties, people became wistful about those years of expansion. "Money matters will follow," de Gaulle said. They had followed, they had crowned that Gaullian tenure with plenty.

We must probe deeper into that posthumous love for de Gaulle, however. Now that we sense, more or less clearly, that we are living through the end—or the beginning of the end—of the nation-state and that Europe is becoming the only way out of our mediocrity, we may be grateful to de Gaulle for having been the man, the ultimate prophet, who "wanted to resuscitate France."[6] However fragile his diplomatic achievement, however illusory his grand scheme, the French people under de Gaulle regained a national pride that is no longer in season. "*I too was a myth,*" Malraux has him say. We sense that the end of that myth might be the end of national history as well. From the soldiers of Valmy to the ragtag soldiers in the maquis, from the appeal of 18 June to the speech in Phnom Penh, national history had—if only by proxy—given the French people the sense that they were a great nation. De Gaulle was the last credible nationalist.

The curtain has fallen. Cyrano will not return. We have returned home, our heads filled with alexandrines whipping about like banners. The heroic age is over. And so we are disenchanted.

Reference Matter

*Two in One Blow: Drumont Proposes to Settle the Jewish
Question and the Social Question Jointly*

"Who bears the greatest burden under the current regime? The revolutionary
worker and the Christian conservative. One is attacked in his vital interests; the
other is wounded in his dearest beliefs.

"For the worker, social revolution is an absolute necessity. . . . For my part, I
am convinced they will not succeed; they will very easily get their hands on Paris,
but they will be unable to seize France. . . .

"Might not that goal, which the workers pursue and which they are not wrong
to pursue from their perspective, be achieved peacefully? Why would a Christian
prince, a leader of solid and generous ideas, who, instead of seeing the questions
in terms of commonplaces, instead faces up to them—why would he not confis-
cate the wealth of the Jews?" (*La France juive*, 1: 517ff.).

Drumont fixed the total of that Jewish capital to be confiscated at 5 billion
francs. As a candidate for the municipal elections in Paris in 1890, in the Gros-
Caillou neighborhood of the seventh arrondissement, he declared in his platform
statement: "With 5 billion tomorrow, we will take on the task of solving the social
question without upheaval or violence."

The majority of voters remained skeptical. To avenge his failure, Drumont
forthwith compiled his *Testament d'un antisémite* (Testament of an anti-Semite), in
which he said: "The conservatives have not had the courage to unite with us and
attempt to reconstitute French society on the foundations of justice; they have
preferred to link their cause to that of moribund Jewry; they will collapse with
it."

As we know, however, the idea had a future.

A Problem Solved: The Secret of Fourmies

STATEMENT OF PROBLEM

On 1 May 1891, Fourmies, a small textile city in Nord, was the scene of a bloody confrontation between the army and striking workers. Outcome: ten dead and dozens of wounded. Among the victims, the city mourns a child of twelve. That painful tragedy necessarily has a hidden cause, since in Fourmies, everyone is kind. "A population of weavers and spinners . . . docile as the lambs whose wool they comb and work"; "very cordial relations between workers and employers"; "a humble priest" with "a heroic soul"; a "good pastor" watching over his flock. In short, a little town of Christian France, where there may be squabbles from time to time, but nothing serious. How are we to explain that our brave soldiers could have fired on those good people?

SOLUTION

Socialists spoke of the responsibility of the mayor, a wool merchant who, pushed by industrialists—his clients—called in the troops. But no! Drumont immediately grasped the source of the tragedy. On 4 May, he sent this telegram to Deputy Albert de Mun: "The Jewish subprefect Isaac, son of a citizen naturalized by the Crémieux law, had the Lebel rifle tried out on French workers. Those who love you hope you will be the one to pronounce the avenging words to castigate the murderer. The prefect Vel-Durand is also Jewish, they are all Jewish in there" (AN F7 12527, intercepted telegram).

Having laid siege, Drumont had only to go conduct his investigation. He published the results in his book, *Le secret de Fourmies* (The secret of Fourmies) in 1892. It was a Jewish story, in fact. "Perhaps Isaac simply wanted to celebrate in his own way the centennial of the emancipation of the Jews in 1791, which certain newspapers had the nerve to recall shamelessly as a glorious date."

MORAL AND POLITICAL CONCLUSION

"The Jew, who has become our master by leading Frenchmen to fight among themselves, will one day see all Frenchmen reconciled over his hide."

Q.E.D.

Notes

INTRODUCTION

1. Of the twenty-four chapters in the present book, six are from *Edouard Drumont et Cie*.

Part One

CHAPTER 1

L'Histoire 73 (December 1984).

1. Charles Péguy, "Les élections," in *Oeuvres en prose, 1898–1908* (Gallimard, "Bibliothèque de la Pléiade," 1959), p. 1311. Throughout this book, place of publication is noted only when it is not Paris. [Unless otherwise noted, quoted passages are my translation.—Trans.]

2. See Raoul Girardet, *Le nationalisme français, 1871–1914* (Seuil, "Points Histoire," 1983), pp. 8 and 9.

3. Cited by Jacques Godechot, *La pensée révolutionnaire, 1780–1799* (Colin, 1964), p. 122, my emphasis.

4. Jules Michelet, *Le Peuple* (1846), pp. 276–78.

5. "We cannot repeat often enough that the Paris revolution was only the counterstrike to the false combat engaged by the men of 4 September against the national enemy." Jules Andrieu, *Notes pour servir à l'histoire de la Commune de Paris en 1871* (Payot, 1971), p. 107.

6. Cited by Pierre Barral, *Les fondateurs de la Troisième République* (Colin, 1968), p. 206.

7. Paul Déroulède, *Qui vive? France! "Quand même": Notes et discours, 1883–1910* (1910), p. 254.

8. See Michel Winock, *La fièvre hexagonale: Les grandes crises politiques, 1871–1968* (Seuil, "Points Histoire," 1987).

9. See Philippe Levillain, *Boulanger, fossoyeur de la monarchie* (Flammarion, 1982).

10. On 23 February 1899, on the occasion of President Félix Faure's funeral, Paul Déroulède attempted to lead General Roget on a march to the Elysée

Palace. Despite his acquittal by the jury of the Seine, Déroulède, again arrested, was sentenced by the Haute Cour to ten years of banishment.

11. See Zeev Sternhell, *La droite révolutionnaire* (Seuil, "Points Histoire," 1984). [The term *juiverie* is pejorative.—Trans.]

12. See Jean-Pierre Rioux, *Nationalisme et conservatisme, la Ligue de la patrie française, 1899–1904* (Beauchesne, 1977).

13. Zeev Sternhell's *Maurice Barrès et le nationalisme français* (Presses de la Fondation nationale des sciences politiques, 1972) might be criticized for overly systematizing a way of thinking that was not systematic.

14. Maurice Barrès, *Scènes et doctrines du nationalisme* (1902), p. 8.

15. Maurice Barrès, *Mes cahiers* (Plon, 1929), 1: 114.

16. Cited by Jacques Paugam, *L'âge d'or du maurrassisme* (Denoël, 1971), p. 117.

17. Cited by Girardet, *Le nationalisme français*, p. 224.

18. Charles Péguy, *L'Argent Suite*, in *Oeuvres en prose, 1909–1914* (Gallimard, "Bibliothèque de la Pléiade," 1961), p. 1239.

19. Quotations taken from Eric Cahm, "Péguy et le nationalisme français," *Cahiers de l'Amitié Charles-Péguy* 25 (1972): 116–18.

20. See Michel Winock, "Socialisme et patriotisme en France 1891–1894," *Revue d'Histoire Moderne et Contemporaine* 20 (July–September 1973).

21. Jean Jaurès, *L'armée nouvelle* (1911; new ed. Editions sociales, 1977), p. 326.

22. See Winock, "Socialisme et patriotisme en France."

23. Antoine Prost's *Les anciens combattants et la société française 1914–1939* (Presses de la Fondation nationale des sciences politiques, 1977), 3 vols., demonstrates the dominant pacifism of the veterans organizations in France between the two world wars.

24. See Frédérick Vitoux, *La vie de Céline* (Grasset, 1988), and Jacqueline Morand, *Les idées politiques de Louis-Ferdinand Céline* (Librairie générale de droit et de jurisprudence, Pichon et Durand Auzias, 1972), p. 192.

25. See Michel Winock, "L'esprit de Munich," in *Les années trente* (Seuil, "Points Histoire," 1990).

26. Charles de Gaulle, *Lettres, notes, et carnets, 1919–juin 1940* (Plon, 1980), pp. 474–76.

27. Cited by Eugen Weber, *L'Action française* (Stock, 1964).

28. Jean Touchard, *Le Gaullisme, 1940–1969* (Seuil, "Points Histoire," 1978), p. 299.

29. On the New Right, see especially Pierre-André Taguieff, "La stratégie culturelle de la Nouvelle Droite en France, 1968–1983," in *Vous avez dit fascismes?* (Arthaud-Montalba, 1984).

30. Jean-Marie Le Pen, "Le Front national"; Jean Cau, "Réflexions sur la décadence," in Jean-Pierre Apparu, *La Droite aujourd'hui* (Albin Michel, 1979).

CHAPTER 2

Le Monde, 11 June 1987.

1. The term "national populism" was introduced into France in 1984 by Pierre-André Taguieff.

CHAPTER 3

L'Histoire 50 (November 1982); and as "La guerre froide" in *L'Amérique dans les têtes: Un siècle de fascinations et d'aversions*, edited by Marie-France Toinet, Denis Lacorne, and Jacques Rupnik (Hachette, 1986).

1. René Rémond, *Les Etats-Unis devant l'opinion française, 1815–1852* (Colin, 1962).
2. François Furet, *L'atelier de l'histoire* (Flammarion, 1982), p. 209.
3. Simon Jeune, *De F. T. Graindorge à A. O. Barnabooth: Les types américains dans le roman et le théâtre français (1861–1917)* (Didier, 1963).
4. Hippolyte Taine, *Notes sur Paris: Vie et opinions de M. Frédéric-Thomas Graindorge* (1867).
5. André Siegfried, *Les Etats-Unis d'aujourd'hui* (Colin, 1930).
6. Georges Duhamel, *Scènes de la vie future* (Mercure de France, 1930).
7. Robert Aron and Arnaud Dandieu, *Le cancer américain* (Rieder, 1931).
8. See Maurice Vaïsse, "Les aspects monétaires du *New Deal* vus en France," *Revue d'Histoire Moderne et Contemporaine* 16 (July–September 1969).
9. Roger Lambelin, *Le règne d'Israël chez les Anglo-Saxons* (Grasset, 1921). The following appeared during the war: Pierre-Antoine Cousteau, *L'Amérique juive* (Ed. de France, 1942); H. Petit, *Rothschild, roi d'Israël* (1941); H. Bordat, *Les Etats-Unis contre l'Europe* (1943).
10. Jean-Baptiste Duroselle, *La France et les Etats-Unis, des origines à nos jours* (Seuil, 1976).
11. Philippe de Saint-Robert, *Le jeu de la France* (Julliard, 1967), pp. 173 and 182.
12. Jean Baby, "L'impérialisme américain et la France," *Cahiers du Communisme* (January 1948).
13. Claude Aveline, "L'engagement et le choix," *Les Lettres Françaises*, 29 April 1948.
14. François Jarraud, *Les Américains à Châteauroux 1951–1967* (Les Cassons-Arthon, 36330 Le Poinçonnet: by the author, 1981).
15. Pierre Daix, "France, pays occupé," *Les Lettres Françaises*, 28 October 1948.
16. Simone de Beauvoir, *Les mandarins*, pp. 254 and 515.
17. Cited by Raymond Aron, *L'opium des intellectuels* (Gallimard, "Idées," 1948), p. 310.
18. Cited by Jean-Noël Jenneney and Jacques Julliard, *Le monde de Beuve-Méry ou le métier d'Alceste* (Seuil, 1979), p. 104.
19. Vladimir Pozner, "Lettre à un ami américain," *Les Lettres Françaises*, 29 April 1948.
20. Armand Salacrou, "Le pays de la solitude," *Les Lettres Françaises*, 25 November 1948.
21. Pierre Abraham, "Littérature américaine," *Les Lettres Françaises*, 14 April 1949.
22. Henri Malherbe, "Les Français n'achètent plus les romans américains," *Les Lettres Françaises*, 24 March 1949.
23. *L'Avant-Garde*, 25 February–2 March 1948.

24. François Mauriac, *L'Express*, 29 August 1959; and *Nouveau Bloc-Notes, 1958–1960*, p. 238.

25. See Duroselle, *La France et les Etats-Unis*.

26. See "L'homme standard," *Esprit* 271 (March 1959). Sidney Lens writes in particular: "A standard man is slowly developing in the United States. He is immunized against radicalism in spite of his social needs and his horizon is limited to the closest realities. . . . Hundreds of thousands of young people are becoming delinquents rather than socialists. They are the ones Robert Linder has called 'rebels without a cause.'"

27. Cf. Alain de Benoist, *Elements*, April–May 1980: "The torch of American freedom has for too long dazzled the world, handing over peoples and cultures to the most profound and the most dangerous oppression. To rediscover their identity and their independence, the nations subjected to American hegemony will have to be done with Western civilization and with its racist [*sic*] and leveling egalitarianism."

28. The United States and American civilization have sometimes had unexpected advocates among their numerous defenders in the French language. Let us cite in particular the case of Jacques Maritain, who published, among other things, *Anti-moderne* (1922) and *Primauté du spirituel* (1936). Such interests should have predisposed him against American "technicism," "mechanization," or "materialism." Yet the Christian philosopher, familiar with the United States after living and teaching there for many years, wrote an apologia for the United States, *Réflexions sur l'Amérique* (Fayard, 1958), on the basis of his own system of values.

Part Two

CHAPTER 4

Edouard Drumont et Cie (Seuil, coll. "XXe Siècle," 1982).

1. This chapter is based primarily on a voluminous press file, conserved in the Archives de la Préfecture de Police (Ba/1313 and Ba/1314). On the literature of the time, a particularly evocative book is Mario Praz's *La chair, la mort et le diable dans la littérature du XIXe siècle: Le romantisme noir* (Denoël, 1977).

2. The term *franc-fileur* is borrowed from the history of the siege of Paris (1870–71): at the time, it applied to those, generally rich, who had been able to flee Paris before the blockade imposed by the Prussians. The newspaper *L'Intransigeant* belonged to Rochefort, a former Communard who had moved on to national socialism.

3. [A play on "Golgotha" and *Almanach de Gotha*, the registry of the peerage and the diplomatic corps.—Trans.]

CHAPTER 5

Lignes 4 (October 1988).

1. Julien Freund, *La Décadence* (Sircy, 1984). This scholarly work covers three

millennia of textual "decadence." In his conclusion, the author decides that this time, we (Western Europe) have truly attained it.

2. Edouard Drumont, *La France juive* (Librairie Victor Palmé, reed. 1890), preface, p. xxxv.

3. Pierre Drieu La Rochelle, *Gilles* (reed. Livre de Poche, 1962), p. 204.

4. Maurice Barrès, *Mes cahiers* 11; cited in André Gide, *Journal I* (Gallimard, "Bibliothèque de la Pléiade," 1951), p. 1064.

5. Colette Capitan-Peter, *Charles Maurras et l'idéologie d'Action française* (Seuil, 1972), esp. pp. 107–8.

6. Cited in André Harris and Alain de Sédouy, *Qui n'est pas de droite?* (Seuil, 1978), pp. 90–91.

7. Drieu La Rochelle, *Gilles*, p. 341.

8. Louis de Bonald, *Théorie du pouvoir politique et religieux* (reed. "10/18," 1966), p. 21.

9. Ernest Renan, *La réforme morale et intellectuelle de la France* ("10/18," 1967), p. 46.

10. François Brigneau, in Harris and de Sédouy, *Qui n'est pas de droite?* p. 80.

11. Louis Veuillot, *L'Univers*, 13 April and 17 May 1871.

12. Charles Péguy, *Lettres et entretiens* (L'Artisan du Livre, 1927), p. 196.

13. Maurice Bardèche, *Qu'est-ce que le fascisme?* (Les Sept Couleurs, 1960), p. 184.

14. Jean Cau, "Réflexions sur la décadence," in Apparu, *La Droite aujourd'hui*, p. 142.

15. See Patrick Lasowski, *Syphilis: Essai sur la littérature française du XIXᵉ siècle* (Gallimard, 1982).

16. Drieu La Rochelle, *Gilles*, p. 343.

17. Ernest Renan, *La réforme morale et intellectuelle*, p. 91.

18. Jean Jaélic, *La Droite, cette inconnue* (Les Sept Couleurs, 1963), p. 61.

19. Cited in Stanley Hoffmann et al., *Le mouvement Poujade,* Cahiers de la Fondation nationale des sciences politiques (Colin, 1956), p. 184.

20. Cited in *L'Express*, 18 March 1955.

21. Maurice Barrès, *Les déracinés* (Fasquelle, 1897), p. 318.

22. Gustave Le Bon, *Psychologie des foules* (reed. PUF, "Quardrige," 1933), p. 57.

23. Jean-Marie Le Pen, cited in Apparu, *La Droite aujourd'hui*, p. 181.

24. Karl Popper, *The Open Society and Its Enemies* (Princeton: Princeton University Press, 1950); Erich Fromm, *Escape from Freedom* (New York: Rinehart, 1991). [The French title of Fromm's book is *La peur de la liberté*, that is, "The fear of freedom."—Trans.]

25. Mircea Eliade, *Aspects du mythe* (Gallimard, "Idées," 1963), p. 106.

CHAPTER 6

L'Histoire 32 (March 1981).

1. Léon Poliakov, *La causalité diabolique: Essai sur l'origine des persécutions* (Calmann-Lévy, 1980).

2. *La Première Internationale*, collective work published by the CNRS, 1968.

3. Poliakov, *La causalité diabolique*, p. 66.

4. Edouard Drumont, *Les héros et les pitres*, p. 192.

5. Eugen Weber, *Satan franc-maçon* (Juillard, "Archives," 1964).

6. Cited in Eberhard Jäckel, *Hitler idéologique* (Calmann-Lévy, 1973).

7. Norman Cohn, *Histoire d'un mythe: La "conspiration" juive et les "Protocoles des Sages de Sion"* (Gallimard, 1967).

8. Poliakov, *La causalité diabolique*, p. 235.

CHAPTER 7

Edouard Drumont et Cie.

1. See Pierre Sorlin, *L'Antisémitisme allemand* (Flammarion, 1969).

2. Jeannine Verdès-Leroux, *Scandale financier et antisémitisme catholique: Le krach de l'Union générale* (Centurion, 1969).

3. Pierre Pierrard, *Juifs et Catholiques français* (Fayard, 1970).

4. See Jules Isaac, *Genèse de l'antisémitisme* (Calmann-Lévy, 1956).

5. See Cohn, *Histoire d'un mythe*.

6. Pierre Sorlin, *"La Croix" et les Juifs* (Grasset, 1967).

7. Cited in Pierrard, *Juifs et Catholiques français*.

8. Drumont, *La France juive*, 2: 443.

9. Ibid., p. 418.

10. See Léon Poliakov, *Histoire de l'antisémitisme* (Calmann-Lévy, 1968), vol. 3.

11. Ernest Renan, *Histoire générale et système comparé des langues sémitiques* (1855).

12. Drumont, *La France juive*, 1: 7.

13. "Guerre de races," *La Libre Parole*, 7 December 1898.

14. Ibid., 27 September 1900.

15. Ibid., 2 November 1897.

16. Drumont, *La France juive*, 1: 9.

17. Edouard Drumont, *De l'or, de la boue, du sang* (1896).

18. V.-E. Michelet, *Les compagnons de la hiérophanie* (1937), p. 31.

19. Edouard Drumont, *La dernière bataille* (1890), p. 512.

20. Letter to Jules Mery, cited in Robert F. Byrnes, *Antisemitism in Modern France* (New Brunswick: Rutgers University Press, 1950).

21. Drumont, *La dernière bataille*, p. 513.

22. Ibid., p. 517.

23. *La Libre Parole*, 10 May 1894.

24. Ibid., 4 May 1893, cited in Stéphane Khémis, *Les Juifs selon Edouard Drumont* (Université de Paris-VIII, 1972, master's thesis).

25. On Drumont's "sincerity" and personality, see Jean Bastaire, "Drumont et l'antisémitisme," *Esprit* (March 1964). In this article, Bastaire wants to "take stock" of the Drumont case, positioning himself "at equal distance between praise and invective." My purpose here is not to "understand" the man Drumont, but rather the place he occupied in political history, not his profound intentions (the "implacable denunciation of the reign of money," according to Bastaire) but the

effects of his writings. Jean Bastaire's article thus provides the reader with a useful counterpoint to this account. As the author says very well, in Drumont one finds both "sincere indignation" and "an execrable analysis."

26. *L'Action Française*, 28 March 1911. Cited in Capitan-Peter, *Charles Maurras et l'idéologie.*

27. On Maurice Barrès, see Sternhell, *Maurice Barrès et le nationalisme français.* Among other claims, Sternhell writes the following: "In modern anti-Semitism Barrès discovered the ideal means for integrating the proletariat into the national community."

28. Ernst Nolte, *The Three Faces of Fascism: Action Française, Italian Fascism, National Socialism* (New York: Holt, Rinehart and Winston, 1966), p. 75.

29. Robert F. Byrnes, "Morès, The First National Socialist," *Review of Politics* (1950). The article was in fact one of the chapters of Byrnes's *Antisemitism in Modern France.*

30. Drumont, *Les héros et les pitres.*

31. Nolte, *The Three Faces of Fascism*, p. 583n.

32. Cohn, *Histoire d'un mythe.*

33. Consider that other renegade aristocrat Henri Rochefort, braggart of the opposition at the end of the Second Empire, who was by turns a Communard, a Boulangist, an anti-Semite, and an anti-Dreyfusard, and who, at the time of his death in 1913, displayed the posthumous talent of uniting around his remains representatives of the far left and the far right. A book has been devoted to that other marquis: Roger L. Williams's *Henri Rochefort: Prince of the Gutter Press* (New York: Scribner's, 1966). Alas! Despite references to serious sources, it is an insipid study that teaches us nothing truly new about this figure, who was more often "clown" than "hero." His anti-Semitism, mentioned only in passing, does not elicit any attempt at interpretation. In addition, the author appears quite unfamiliar with the history of socialism in France, seeing "Marxists" everywhere, even in the person of Lissagaray, which is wrong, and in Benoît Malon, which is grotesque. Writing about the Commune, he uses a tone I thought had been banned from university historiography (example: the elected representatives of the Commune are a gang [*sic*] of *old* [*sic*] revolutionaries and journalists on the left). He makes flagrant errors (for example, he has the Comité Central de la Garde Nationale [Central committee of the national guard] operating several months before its actual birth and misspells the name "Chaudey" on several occasions as "Chaundey"). In the section on the following period, things get even worse. He confuses the *Société* des Droits de l'Homme with the *Ligue* des Droits de l'Homme; cites many minor works on Boulangism but ignores Jacques Néré's work, which is key; makes Barrès a member of Action Française, and so on. As for the translation (*Le prince des polémistes: Henri Rochefort* [Trévise, 1971]), it is nothing less than scandalous. The translator, categorically ignoring the original French texts, transposes very famous formulations from the English, which sometimes leads the reader to laugh outright. Everyone knows, for example, the word Gaston Crémieux shouted at the Bordeaux Assembly: "*Ruraux!*" Everyone knows about the Assembly of *ruraux*, except the translator who, applying himself with zeal, gives us *péquenots*, and repeats the word—with quotations marks, if you please—as if he were not inventing a

thing! [*Ruraux*, generally translated as "country bumpkins" in this context, is in fact closer to "country people." *Péquenots* is more pejorative in French.—Trans.] Worst of all, he cites the French reference accurately (Maurice Reclus), and then does not even take the trouble to consult it.

34. Another farce, but not an insignificant one, is the story of that other circus anti-Semite, Jules Guérin. See Chapter 16, "Jules Guérin of Fort Chabrol."

35. See Claude Willard, *Les Guesdistes* (Editions sociales, 1966), who shows the ambiguities in the Guesdists' relation to anti-Semitism.

36. See Chapter 10, "The Left and the Jews."

37. Among the recent works on anti-Semitism published in France since this article, let us note Yves Chevalier, *L'Anti-Sémitisme*, preface by François Bourricaud (Cerf, 1988).

CHAPTER 8

Edouard Drumont et Cie.

1. See Michael R. Marrus, *Les Juifs de France à l'époque de l'affaire Dreyfus* (Calmann-Lévy, "Diaspora," 1972), pp. 142–43.

2. On that entire episode, see Rosemonde Sanson, "La fête de Jeanne d'Arc en 1894: Controverse et célébration," *Revue d'Histoire Moderne et Contemporaine* 20 (July–September 1973).

3. Anonymous brochure, *Jeanne d'Arc, sa mission, son exemple* (1942).

4. H. de Sarrau, *La leçon de Jeanne d'Arc* (1941).

5. Robert Brasillach, "Devant l'avenir," *Je Suis Partout*, 12 May 1941.

6. Georges Valois, *Le fascisme* (1927), p. 82.

7. J.-J. Brousson, "Rétablissez l'Edit de Nantes en faveur des chrétiens," *Je Suis Partout*, 20 November 1937.

8. J.-J. Brousson, "La fête nationale de Jeanne d'Arc, de Voltaire à Léon Blum," *Je Suis Partout*, 15 May 1937.

9. Abbé J. Ygouf, *Panégyrique de Jeanne d'Arc*, 21 May 1905.

10. Sarrau, *La leçon de Jeanne d'Arc*.

11. Ibid.

12. Henri Rochefort, "La non-pucelle d'Orléans," *L'Intransigeant*, 27 November 1904.

13. Edouard Schuré, *L'âme celtique et le génie de la France* (1921).

14. Jean-Baptiste Ayroles, *M. Thalamas contre Jeanne d'Arc* (1905), regarding the rehabilitation trial.

15. Abbé J. Lémann, *Jeanne d'Arc et les héroïnes juives* (1873).

16. Agathon, "Béatification de Jeanne d'Arc," *La Revue*, 15 April 1894.

17. Robert Brasillach, "Pour une méditation sur la raison de Jeanne d'Arc," *Je Suis Partout*, 13 May 1938.

18. Drumont, *La France juive*, 1: 427.

19. Rochefort, "La non-pucelle d'Orléans."

20. Brasillach, "Pour une méditation sur la raison de Jeanne d'Arc."

21. Brousson, "Rétablissez l'Edit de Nantes."

22. Drumont, *La France juive*, 2: 16.

23. Ibid., 1: 2.

24. Lucien Rebatet, "Le fait juif," *Je Suis Partout,* 14 January 1944.

25. Ygouf, *Panégyriqe de Jeanne d'Arc.*

26. Drumont, *La France juive,* 1: 104.

27. Drieu La Rochelle, *Gilles.*

28. Drumont, *La Libre Parole,* 7 March 1892, and preface to Octave Tauxier, *De l'inaptitude des Français à concevoir la question juive* (1900).

29. Jules Soury, *Campagne nationaliste, 1899–1901,* cited in *L'Action Française,* 1 January 1904.

30. Léon Daudet, *L'Action Française,* 6 March 1908.

31. Drumont, preface to Tauxier, *De l'inaptitude des Français.*

32. Drumont, letter cited in *L'Action Française,* 15 December 1904.

33. Dorsay, "Toute la France derrière Pétain contre l'Anglais," *Je Suis Partout,* 13 May 1944.

34. P. Bellet, "L'invasion juive," *Revue du Monde Catholique* 9 (1 January 1887).

35. Drumont, *La France juive,* 1: 9.

36. Ibid., p. 90.

37. Renan, *Histoire générale et système comparé,* p. 4, cited by Jules Soury and Maurice Barrès. See Sternhell, *Maurice Barrès et le nationalisme français.*

38. Drumont, *La Libre Parole,* 2 August 1893.

39. Rebatet, "Le fait juif."

40. Raoul Bergot, *L'Algérie telle qu'elle est* (1890), cited by Verdès-Leroux, *Scandale financier et antisémitisme catholique.*

41. Agathon, "Béatification de Jeanne d'Arc."

CHAPTER 9

Vingtième Siècle, Revue d'Histoire 5 (January–March 1985).

1. André Figueras, *Ce canaille de D . . . reyfus* (Publications André Figueras, 1982), p. 19.

2. François Mitterrand, "Politique et littérature," *Les Cahiers Naturalistes,* Société littéraire des amis d'Emile Zola, 51 (1977); cited in Marc Knobel, *La réhabilitation du capitqine Dreyfus, 1898–1945* (master's thesis for the Université de Paris, I, 1982).

3. Benoît Malon, *La troisième défaite du prolétariat français* (Neuchâtel: G. Guillaume fils, 1871).

4. See General Appert's *Rapport d'ensemble* on military justice procedures relating to the 1871 insurrection (National Assembly, 1874).

5. See Christophe Charle, "La lutte des classes en littérature," in *Les écrivains et l'Affaire Dreyfus,* papers from the colloquium organized at the Université d'Orléans and the Centre Péguy, 29–31 October 1981, texts collected by Géraldi Leroy (PUF, 1983); and especially, Christophe Charle, "Champ littéraire et champ du pouvoir: Les écrivains et l'affaire Dreyfus," *Annales ESC,* March-April 1977.

6. See Michel Winock, "Les intellectuels dans le siècle," *Vingtième Siècle, Revue d'Histoire* 2 (April 1984).

7. Pierre Quillard, *Le Monument Henry* (1899); and Raoul Girardet, *Le nationalism français,* in *Anthologie, 1871–1914* (Seuil, "Points Histoire," 1984).

8. See especially Sternhell, *La droite révolutionnaire.*

9. I pointed out that "drifting" in *Edouard Drumont et Cie*; and in "La Commune 1871–1971," *Esprit* (December 1971).

10. Maurice Barrès, *Mes cahiers*, 1: 263.

11. See, among others, Jacques Paugam, *L'âge d'or du maurrassisme* (Denoël, 1971); Weber, *L'Action française*; Capitan-Peter, *Charles Maurras et l'idéologie d'Action française*.

12. Figueras, *Ce canaille de D . . . reyfus*, p. 200.

13. See Knobel, *La réhabilitation du capitaine Dreyfus*, pp. 232ff.

14. Jean Renaud, *La solidarité française attaque* (Les Oeuvres françaises, 1936).

15. Pierre-Antoine Cousteau, *Je Suis Partout*, 7 April 1939.

16. Henri Béraud, "Le pauvre homme," *Gringoire*, 12 October 1938.

17. Laurent Viguier, *Les Juifs à travers Léon Blum* (Baudinière, 1938), p. 122.

18. On the xenophobic currents in France during the 1930s, see Ralph Schor, *L'opinion française et les étrangers en France, 1919–1939* (Marseilles: Université d'Aix-Marseille, 1980), vol. 1 of 5 vols.

19. *L'Action Française*, 14 July 1935.

20. Jean Guéhenno, *Entre le passé et l'avenir* (Grasset, 1979), p. 275.

21. Cited by Pascal Ory, *Les collaborateurs, 1940–1945* (Seuil, "Points Histoire," 1980), p. 158.

22. Robert Valléry-Radot, *Sources d'une doctrine nationale, de Joseph de Maistre à Charles Péguy* (Sequana, 1942).

23. Cited by Henri Michel, *Le procès de Riom* (Albin Michel, 1979), pp. 316–17.

24. Ibid., p. 324.

25. Cited by Ory, *Les collaborateurs*, p. 164.

26. *Au Pilori*, 21 February 1941, cited by Ory, *Les collaborateurs*, p. 158.

27. See Weber, *L'Action française*, p. 513.

28. Ibid.

29. *De la Résistance à la Révolution, Anthologie de la presse clandestine française* (Neuchâtel: Baconnière, 1945), pp. 82–83.

30. Ibid., p. 219.

31. In a sense, given the importance of Christians in the battle against torture and for peace in Algeria, anticlericalism changed camps. For example, in March 1958, at a congress of Radical dissidents (against Mendès France), Vincent Badi protested against "the agents of imposture and mystification, such as those doctors in religious faith, always ready under cover of Scripture to judge France at fault." For his part, André Marie railed against readers of "those papers sold under certain Gothic portals." Still another writer denounced "the work of disintegration that undermines Catholic and Protestant circles." In contrast, the denunciation of the intelligentsia, "whose naïveté is at the same level as its culture," remained within the anti-Dreyfusard tradition.

32. See Pierre Vidal-Naquet, *La torture dans la République* (Maspero, "Petite collection Maspero," 1983 edition).

33. Christian Pineau, minister of foreign affairs, declared before the United Nations, regarding the torture scandal: "Those are inventions of *France-Observateur*" (February 1957).

34. See *Le Monde*, 2 April 1957. On the parliamentary hostility to Pierre Mendès France, see the debate on the outline law, defended by M. Bourgès-Mamoury in late November 1957.

35. When the session of the Assembly was suspended during the debate of 15 April 1958, I overheard this comment at the refreshment bar: "The French people are not aware, and they need to be, that would be a way of alerting them. In the first place, newspapers ought to publish large headlines every day to make readers understand their national interests. You know, for my part, I believe in advertising: when they have read that Tunisia, the United States, and England have betrayed us, the French will believe it—and then things will change."

36. Henri Marrou, in *La question algérienne* (Minuit, 1958), p. 28.

37. After the European elections of 17 June 1984, *Le Matin* printed a report on the success of the Le Pen slate and the way the winners celebrated the event of the "siege of the National Front." One person, referring to Olivier Stirn, one of Jean-Marie Le Pen's opponents, remarked: "You know he's the great-grandson of Dreyfus!" (Jean Darriulat).

38. See René Girard, *La violence et le sacré* (Grasset, 1971), particularly chap. 3, "Oedipe et la victime émissaire."

39. I could not conclude this chapter without paying tribute to the last—successful—overview of the Dreyfus affair, Jean-Denis Bredin, *L'Affaire* (Julliard, 1983); and, more recently, after the publication of this article, Pierre Birnbaum, *Un mythe politique: "La République juive," de Léon Blum à Pierre Mendès France* (Fayard, 1988).

CHAPTER 10

Edouard Drumont et Cie.

1. At issue was the emancipation of the Jews of Alsace and Lorraine, who by themselves represented nine-tenths of the Jews of France; the rest—Jews of Bordeaux, of Bayonne, and of Comtat—had been granted French citizenship in 1789.

2. Bernard Lazare, *L'antisémitisme, son histoire et ses causes* (1894), p. 195.

3. See Pierre Pierrard, *Juifs et Catholiques français.*

4. On Voltaire, Diderot, and the Encyclopédistes, see Poliakov, *Histoire de l'antisémitisme*, vol. 3.

5. Albert Regnard, *Aryens et Sémites* (1890). The book was first published in seven installments of *La Revue Socialiste*, June 1887 to October 1889.

6. Lazare, *L'antisémitisme, son histoire et ses causes.*

7. See Jean Bouvier, *Les Rothschild* (Fayard, 1967).

8. Marrus, *Les Juifs de France à l'époque de l'affaire Dreyfus*, p. 137.

9. Pierre Vidal-Naquet, preface to Marrus, *Les Juifs.*

10. See J. Psichari, at the general assembly of the Ligue Française pour la Défense des Droits de l'Homme et du Citoyen, 4 June 1898.

11. See Claude Willard, *Les Guesdites* (Editions sociales, 1965), esp. chap. 21, pp. 410ff.

12. Anatole Leroy-Beaulieu, *L'Antisémitisme* (1897), p. 61. Leroy-Beaulieu's re-

markable book, *Israël chez les nations* (1893, preface by René Rémond, notes by Roger Errera), was reprinted by Calmann-Lévy in 1982.

13. Article "Jaurès" in *Dictionnaire biographique du mouvement ouvrier français, 1871–1914*, vol. 13.

14. On Jaurès's hesitations, see especially Madeleine Rebérioux, "Zola, Jaurès et France: Trois intellectuels devant l'Affaire," *Cahiers Naturalistes* 54 (1980); and Erik Cahm, "Le mouvement socialiste face au nationalisme au temps de l'affaire Dreyfus," *Bulletin de la Société d'Etudes Jaurésiennes* 79 (October-December 1980).

15. Julien Benda, *La jeunesse d'un clerc* (Gallimard, 1968), p. 120.

16. *La Petite République*, 9 June 1898.

17. Charles Péguy, "Le 'Triomphe de la République'" in *Oeuvres en prose, 1898–1908*, pp. 103–22.

18. Wladimir Rabi, *Anatomie du judaisme français* (Minuit, 1962).

19. See Schor, *L'opinion française et les étrangers en France.*

20. Ibid.

21. Ibid., p. 102.

22. Ralph Schor notes that contrary to the accusation launched by the right, in the years 1936–37 the Front Populaire did not noticeably increase the number of naturalizations.

23. The communist resistance before the USSR entered the war is a subject of controversy that has been raised a thousand times. Let us simply recall here the communist attacks of that period against Léon Blum, in particular the article signed by Maurice Thorez, published in the Swedish German-language newspaper *Die Welt* in 1940, whose anti-Semitic character has been noted several times. See Annie Kriegel, *Le pain et les roses*, ("10/18"), pp. 391ff. On the general attitude of the PCF during the war toward the Jewish question, see idem, "Résistants communistes et Juifs persécutés," in *H/Histoire* 3 (November 1979); and idem, "Vérité historique et mensonges politiques," *Commentaire* 12 (Winter 1980–81).

24. *L'Humanité*, 29 November 1952; and Artur London, *L'aveu* (Gallimard, 1969).

25. See Thomas Frejka's letter to the tribunal, *Le Monde*, 27 November 1952.

26. François Furet, "Entre Israël et la gauche française: Trente ans de malentendus," *Nouvel Observateur* 705 (16 May 1978).

27. One should not confuse the anti-Zionism of the members of the Diaspora who refuse to recognize Israel as the center of the Jewish world, the religious anti-Zionism of ultraorthodox Jews, the anti-Zionism of Communists, which does not officially call into question Israel's right to exist, and the anti-Zionism of the PLO, which fixes as its objective the disappearance of the Jewish state, etc.

28. See especially, Jacques Givet, *La Gauche contre Israël* (Pauvert, 1968); and Léon Poliakov, *De l'antisémitisme à l'antisionisme* (Calmann-Lévy, 1969).

29. On the theory and practice of German terrorism, see in particular Alain Geismar, *L'engrenage terroriste* (Fayard, 1981); and Hans-Joachim Klein, *La mort mercenaire* (Seuil, 1980). In terms of France, the observer concerned with accuracy ought to refrain from lumping together the different leftist currents of the 1970s. One of my readers in *L'Histoire*, when this chapter first appeared as an article, criticized me for not having sufficiently nuanced my thesis—in particular, for not

having distinguished clearly between *L'Humanité Rouge,* "orthodox Maoists," who "openly asserted the heritage of the 'ingenius Stalin,' not leaving out the slightest purge" from the organ of the Ligue Communiste, *Rouge,* which "in contrast, exalts the Jewish revolutionary past, the Warsaw ghetto, etc." I am happy to concede this to my correspondent. In an article embracing almost two centuries of history, I was not concerned with delving into the sociology of political groups or subgroups. That is also the reason I did not wish to mention the Faurisson affair. Faurisson denies the existence of the gas chambers and is supported by the sympathizers of the Old Mole, libertarian or "anarcho-Marxist" communists. That would merit an in-depth study in itself (on this matter, see especially Pierre Vidal-Naquet, "Un Eichmann de papier," *Esprit,* September 1980). I simply wanted to mention how anti-Zionism could be a factor in neo-anti-Semitism, making it clear that there is no necessary slippage from one to the other.

30. Alain Finkielkraut, *Le Juif imaginaire* (Seuil, 1980).

31. See Jean-Marie Meyeur, "Les catholiques dreyfusards," *Revue Historique* 261, 2.

32. See the IFOP poll published in *Le Nouvel Adam* 5 (1966). It indicates that anti-Semitic prejudices are still tenacious in public opinion on the left.

33. That tract was published in extenso in the collection *La presse antiraciste sous l'occupation hitlérienne, 1940–1944* (Centre de Documentation de l'UJRE, 1950).

34. Edouard Drumont, *La fin d'un monde,* p. 530.

35. Cited in Harris and Sédouy, *Qui n'est pas de droite?* p. 90.

36. Since the first publication of this text, Pierre-André Taguieff has given a remarkable analysis of the double life of racism: see his *La force du préjugé* (La Découverte, 1987). In addition, let us note two studies likely to stimulate a reflection on the theme discussed here: Michael Graetz, *Les Juifs en France au XIXe siècle: De la révolution française à l'Alliance israélite universelle* (Seuil, 1989); and Pierre Birnbaum, "Sur l'étatisation révolutionnaire: L'abbé Grégoire et le destin de l'identité juive," *Le Débat* 53 (January–February 1989).

Part Three

1. Raymond Aron, *Mémoires* (Julliard, 1983), p. 185.

2. See Nicos Poulantzas, *Fascisme et dictature* (Maspero, 1970).

3. Philippe Burrin, "La France dans le champ magnétique des fascismes," *Le Débat* 32 (November 1984).

4. Zeev Sternhell, *Ni droite ni gauche* (Brussells: Complexe, 1986).

5. Since these polemics, an excellent guide has become available—finally!—on the question of fascism in France. See Pierre Milza, *Le fascisme français* (Flammarion, 1988).

CHAPTER 11

L'Histoire 124 (July–August 1989).

1. Louis-Napoleon Bonaparte, *Des idées napoléoniennes* (Plon and Amyot, 1860).

2. The electoral law of 31 May 1850, introduced by Thiers and passed by the majority of the Assembly, required electors to reside for three years in their districts before having the right to vote, which disqualified a good part of "the vile multitude" (about a third at least of electors).

3. Cited by Alain Plessis, "Napoléon III, un dictateur?" in *Dictatures et légitimité*, edited by Maurice Duverger (PUF, 1982).

4. Allusion to the line delivered in Bordeaux by Prince Louis-Napoleon Bonaparte in spring 1852: "Some people say, the empire is war; I say, the empire is peace."

5. Cited by Jean Tulard, "Les dictatures de l'époque libérale: Napoléon 1er," in Duverger, *Dictatures et légitimité*.

6. That social legislation, however, fell short of the inclinations de Gaulle displayed, especially in his theory linking capital and labor. The theme of "participation" might have become the axis of a social policy, but de Gaulle realized this only too late: worldwide greatness was a priority. The crisis of May 1968 revealed his error. Bonapartism wants to be populist but does not give itself the means for being so to the end.

CHAPTER 12

"Le fascisme en France," in *Edouard Drumont et Cie*.

1. Cited by Pierre Milza, *L'Italie fasciste devant l'opinion française 1920–1940* (Colin, "Kiosque," 1967).

2. Georges Valois, *L'homme contre l'argent* (Librairie Valois, 1928), p. 179.

3. Ibid., pp. 264–65.

4. Georges Valois, *Le fascisme* (1927).

5. Georges Valois, *L'homme contre l'argent*, p. 184.

6. Sternhell, *La droite révolutionnaire*.

7. Valois, *Le fascisme*, p. 5.

8. Emmanuel Berth, *Les méfaits des intellectuels* (Rivière, 1914).

9. See Zeev Sternhell, "Anatomie d'un mouvement fasciste en France, Le Faisceau de Georges Valois," *Revue Française de Science Politique* (February 1976).

10. Serge Berstein, *Le 6 Février 1934* (Gallimard, "Archives," 1975).

11. Raoul Girardet, "Notes sur l'esprit d'un fascisme français, 1934–1940," *Revue Française de Science Politique* (July–September 1955).

12. Cited by Pierre-Marie Dioudonnat, *Je suis partout, 1930–1944: Les maurrassiens devant la tentation fasciste* (La Table Ronde, 1973), p. 418.

13. Pierre Gazotte, "L'homme maudit," *Candide*, 7 April 1938.

14. Robert Brasillach, *Notre avant-guerre* (Grasset, 1941), p. 193.

15. See Jean-Paul Brunet, "Doriot, du communisme au fascisme," *L'Histoire* 21 (March 1980); Dieter Wolf, *Doriot, du communisme à la collaboration* (Fayard, 1970); and more recently, Philippe Burrin, *La dérive fasciste, Doriot, Déat, Bergery, 1933–1945* (Seuil, 1986).

16. See Philippe Bourdrel, *La Cagoule* (Albin Michel, 1970).

17. See Pascal Ory, "Le dorgérisme," *Revue d'Histoire Moderne et Contemporaine* (April–June 1975).

18. Renaud, *La Solidarité française attaque.*

19. See Patrice Hollemart, *L'idéologie de "L'Emancipation Nationale,"* 1936–1939, *mémoire de DEA* for the Institut d'études politiques in Paris, 1980.

20. Pierre-Antoine Cousteau, cited in Dioudonnat, *Je suis partout 1930–1944*, p. 224.

21. Cited by Philippe Machefer, "L'union des droites, le PSF et le Front de la Liberté, 1936–1937," *Revue d'Histoire Moderne et Contemporaine* (January–March 1970).

22. Marcel Déat, *Le parti unique* (1943), p. 129 (collection of articles published in *L'Oeuvre* from 18 July to 4 September 1942).

23. Ibid., p. 131.

24. Lucien Rebatet, *Les décombres* (Denoël, 1942), p. 566.

25. See the excellent summary by Pierre Milza, *Fascisme français, passé et présent* (Flammarion, 1987).

CHAPTER 13

Le Débat 25 (May 1983).

1. See especially Sternhell, *Maurice Barrès et le fascisme français*; idem, *La droite révolutionnaire*; and idem, *Ni droite ni gauche.*

2. René Rémond, *Les droites en France* (Aubier, 1982), most recent edition.

3. Berth, *Les méfaits des intellectuels*, p. 325.

4. Ibid., p. 329.

5. See E. Santarelli, "Le socialisme national en Italie: Précédents et origines," *Le Mouvement Social* 50 (January–March 1965).

6. Georges Valois, *Le fascisme* (Nouvelle Librairie Nationale, 1927), p. 5.

7. Ibid., p. 6.

8. Ibid., p. 24.

9. Raoul Girardet's preface to Sternhell's *Maurice Barrès et le fascisme français.*

10. Sternhell, *Ni droite ni gauche*, p. 297.

11. Sergio Romano, "Le fascisme," in Duverger, *Dictatures et légitimité.*

12. See Georges Lefranc, "Une scission malencontreuse: La scission 'néo-socialiste' de 1933," in Georges Lefranc, *Visages du movement ouvrier français* (PUF, 1982), pp. 117–38.

13. Even without mentioning de Gaulle, we know that Léon Blum himself wrote in *A l'échelle humaine* in 1941: "What will probably not survive the bourgeois experiment, continued for more than a century, is the representative regime properly speaking, that is, the full-scale delegation of popular sovereignty to the elected Chamber and its concentration in legislative assemblies." See other texts in Henri Michel and Boris Mirkine-Guetzévitch, *Les idées politiques et sociales de la Résistance* (PUF, 1954).

14. See especially the remarks of Yves Durand on certain secular teachers and the National Revolution in *Vichy 1940–1944* (Bordas, 1972), pp. 89–90.

15. René de Lacharrière, *La divagation de la pensée politique* (PUF, 1972), p. 261.

16. See Catherine Grumblatt's *mémoire de DEA*, *Le socialisme de Gustave Hervé et de "La Victoire" 1916–1940* (Institut des études politiques de Paris, 1982).

CHAPTER 14

Unpublished paper, December 1983.

1. Club de l'Horloge, *Socialisme et fascisme: Une même famille?* (Albin Michel, 1984).

2. On the relations between the Club de l'Horloge and the New Right, see Pierre-André Taguieff, "La stratégie culturelle de la Nouvelle Droite en France (1968–1983)," in *Vous avez dit fascisme?*.

3. Benito Mussolini, *Fascism: Doctrine and Institutions* (New York: H. Fertig), p. 11.

Part Four

CHAPTER 15

L'Histoire 92 (September 1986).

1. Monck was an English general who became leader of the country after Cromwell's death, assuring the restoration of the Stuarts in 1660.

2. *Journal de l'abbé Mugnier (1879–1939)* (Mercure de France, 1985), p. 63.

3. See especially Jacqueline Freyssinet-Dominjon, *Les manuels d'histoire de l'Ecole libre 1882–1959* (Colin, 1969).

CHAPTER 16

Le Matin Magazine, 21 November 1981.

CHAPTER 17

L'Histoire 13 (June 1979).

1. *Marthe, Les soeurs Vatard, En ménage*, and *A vau-l'eau*, among other titles, were reissued in 1975 in the excellent collection "Fins de siècles," edited by Hubert Juin (Editions UGE/10/18). Works by Hugues Rebell and Marcel Schwob were published in the same collection; books by the brothers Goncourt, Jean Lorrain, and Joséphin Péladan will soon follow.

2. Robert Griffiths, *Révolution à rebours: Le renouveau catholique dans la littérature de France de 1870 à 1914* (Desclée De Brouwer, 1971).

3. "Society is disintegrating under the corrosive action of a deteriorating civilization. Modern man is blasé. Refinements of appetites, of sensations, of tastes, of luxury, of pleasure, neurosis, hysteria, hypnotism, morphine addiction, scientific charlatanism, extreme Schopenhauerism, such are the premonitory symptoms of social evolution." *Le Décadent*, 10 April 1886.

CHAPTER 18

L'Histoire 78 (May 1985).

1. *Esprit*, August–September and December 1983.

2. Jacques Julliard, "Sur un fascisme imaginaire," *Annales ESC* (July–August 1984).

3. *Cahiers Georges-Sorel* 2 (Société d'études soréliennes, 1984).

4. Shlomo Sand, *L'illusion du politique: Georges Sorel et le débat intellectuel 1900* (La Découverte, 1984).

5. Cited by Pierre Andreu, *Notre maître M. Sorel* (Grasset, 1953).

6. Georges Sorel, *Réflexions sur la violence*, 10th edition (Rivière, 1946).

7. See Jacques Julliard, *Clemenceau briseur de grèves* (Julliard, "Archives," 1965).

8. Cited by Andreu, *Notre maître M. Sorel.*

9. Letter from Boris Souvarine published in *Cahiers Georges-Sorel* 2:187–98.

CHAPTER 19

L'Histoire 52 (January 1983).

1. Jean Bastaire, *Péguy tel qu'on l'ignore*, texts selected and presented by Jean Bastaire (Gallimard, "Idées," 1973).

2. Jean Bastaire, *Péguy l'insurgé* (Payot, 1975).

3. Henri Guillemin, *Charles Péguy* (Seuil, 1981).

4. Quoted in ibid.

5. Bernard-Henri Lévy, *L'idéologie française* (Grasset, 1981).

6. Simone Fraisse, *Péguy* (Seuil, "Ecrivains de toujours," 1979).

7. Géraldi Leroy, *Péguy entre l'ordre et la révolution* (Presses de la Fondation nationale des sciences politiques, 1981).

CHAPTER 20

Le Matin Magazine, 19 December 1989.

CHAPTER 21

Edouard Drumont et Cie.

1. Emmanuel Berth, cited by Andreu, *Notre maître, M. Sorel*, p. 88.

2. See Santarelli, "Le socialisme national en Italie." The author mentions the influence of Sorel in this rapprochement.

3. *Les Nouvelles Littéraires*, 2 February 1934.

4. *Le Nouveau Siècle*, 25 January 1926.

5. See Jean Touchard, "L'esprit des années 1930," in *Tendances politiques dans la vie française depuis 1789* (Hachette, 1960).

6. Jean-Louis Loubet Del Bayle, *Les non-conformistes des années trente* (Seuil-Gallimard, 1969).

7. Pierre Drieu La Rochelle, *Socialisme fasciste* (1934).

8. Brasillach, *Notre avant-guerre*, p. 30.

9. See Paul Sérant, *Le romantisme fasciste . . . ou l'oeuvre politique de quelques écrivains français* (Fasquelle, 1960).

10. Henri Béraud in *Gringoire*, cited in Brasillach, *Notre avant-guerre*, p. 151.

11. Ibid., p. 271.

12. Dr. Robert Soucy, "Le fascisme de Drieu La Rochelle," *Revue d'Histoire de la Deuxième Guerre Mondiale* (April 1967), pp. 61–84.

13. Drieu La Rochelle, *Gilles*, p. 111. I refer to the complete edition of 1949.

14. I borrow this expression from Sternhell, *Maurice Barrès et le nationalisme français.*

15. Soucy, "Le fascisme de Drieu La Rochelle," p. 68.

16. Drieu La Rochelle, *Gilles,* p. 99.

17. See Gobineau, *Essai sur l'inégalité des races humaines* (1867), p. 208.

18. Drieu La Rochelle, *Gilles,* p. 182.

19. Ibid.

20. Ibid., p. 38.

21. Ibid., p. 64.

22. "Barrès is obviously the prince of contemporary literature and every year I reread a series of his books." Pierre Drieu La Rochelle, cited by Jean-Pierre Maxence, *Histoire de dix ans, 1927–1937* (Gallimard, 1939), p. 41. On Barrès's racism and Jules Soury's influence on it, see Sternhell, *Maurice Barrès et le nationalisme français.*

23. Drieu La Rochelle, *Gilles,* p. 340.

24. Ibid., p. 403.

25. Ibid., p. 338.

26. Jean-Marie Domenach, *Barrès par lui-même* (Seuil, 1954), p. 74.

27. Maurice Barrès, *Scènes et doctrines du nationalisme* (Plon, 1925), p. 74.

28. Drieu La Rochelle, *Gilles,* p. 89. Or again: "I am very Latin, combining sentimentality and filth. And I, who pretended to be Nordic with her" (p. 276).

29. Ibid., p. 426.

30. Gustaze Glotz, *Histoire grecque* (PUF, 1938), 1: 152.

31. Drieu La Rochelle, *Gilles,* p. 393.

32. Ibid.

33. Ibid., p. 204.

34. Louis Bodin and Jean-Marie Royer, "Vocabulaire de la France," *Esprit,* December 1957.

35. *Gilles,* p. 200.   36. Ibid.

37. Ibid., p. 203.   38. Ibid., p. 341.

39. It is not insignificant that the beech tree [*hêtre*] is the homonym of the verb "to be" [*être*]: the play on words is no doubt intentional. It is telling that in a single sentence by Carentan, within three lines, he evokes by turns this *hêtre* and *l'être* (p. 341). The value of the ontological symbol of the beech tree is thus mirrored in phonetics.

40. Drieu La Rochelle, *Gilles,* p. 201.

41. Curzio Malaparte, *Technique du coup d'Etat* (10/18, 1964), p. 158.

42. Drieu La Rochelle, *Gilles,* p. 426.

43. Ibid., p. 340.

44. Ibid., p. 423.

45. Ibid., p. 76.

46. Jules Soury, *Campagne nationaliste,* p. 185; cited by Sternhell, *Maurice Barrès et le nationalisme français,* 2: 49.

47. Drieu La Rochelle, *Gilles,* p. 241.

48. Ibid., p. 322.

49. Maurice Barrès, *Le jardin de Bérénice* (Plon, 1891), p. 183.

50. Idem, *Du sang, de la volupté et de la mort* (Plon, 1959), p. 49.

51. Drieu La Rochelle, *Gilles*, p. 422.

52. Barrès, *Mes cahiers*, 10: 74.

53. Drieu La Rochelle, *Gilles*, p. 475.

54. Nietzsche, *Beyond Good and Evil*, trans. Walter Kaufmann (New York: Random House, 1966), p. 207.

55. Ibid., p. 176.

56. *Esprit*, April 1940.

57. Drieu La Rochelle, *Gilles*, p. 417.

58. Ibid., p. 365.

59. Eliade, *Aspects du mythe*, p. 106. Maurice Bardèche, a "fascist" writer, writes: "All fascism is a reaction in relation to the present, and all fascist reaction is resurrection." Bardèche, *Qu'est-ce que le fascisme?*, p. 175.

60. Eliade, *Aspects du mythe*.

61. I borrow a line from Montherlant, who in *Solstice de juin* (NRF, Gallimard, 1943), illustrates a "morality of order" (p. 424) similar to the morality of *Gilles*.

CHAPTER 22

L'Histoire 16 (November 1988).

1. François Gibault, *Céline* (Mercure de France, 1985), 2: 169.

2. Vitoux, *La vie de Céline*, p. 320.

3. Céline's works are cited from the "La Pléiade" edition, Gallimard, 1: 1266.

4. Cited in ibid., 1: 1409.

5. Céline, *Bagatelles pour un massacre*, p. 192 (1942 edition).

6. It is difficult on this point to follow Philippe Muray, *Céline* (Seuil), who writes: "With *Bagatelles* in December 1937, then with *L'école* in November 1938, Céline was ahead of French ignominy. These racist torrents can be read as a collossal anticipation of Pétainism" (p. 131).

7. The reference to Drumont, the main vulgarizer of anti-Semitism in France, is obligatory. But—and Philippe Muray rightly insists on this point—while Drumont's anti-Jewishness is still marked by his Christian origins, Céline's was radically anti-Christian, contrasting Aryan polytheism and Judeo-Christian monotheism.

8. Especially with his boss at the League of Nations, Ludwig Rajchman, of Polish Jewish origin.

9. See Prost, *Les anciens combattants et la société française*.

10. Cohn, *Histoire d'un mythe*.

11. A. Yaeger Kaplan, *Relevé des sources et citations dans "Bagatelles pour un massacre"* (Tusson [Charente], Du Lérot, 1987), p. 33.

12. Vitoux, *La vie de Céline*, p. 329.

13. Kaplan, *Relevé des sources*, p. 36.

14. Vitoux, *La vie de Céline*, p. 390.

15. Ibid., p. 503.

16. Céline, *Bagatelles*, p. 85.

CHAPTER 23

Edouard Drumont et Cie.

1. Georges Bernanos, *La grande peur des biens-pensants* (Grasset, 1931).
2. Georges Bernanos, *Les grands cimetières sous la lune* (Plon, 1938).
3. Jean Bastaire, "Drumont et l'antisémitisme," *Esprit*, March 1964.
4. Georges Bernanos, "Edouard Drumont," lecture given to L'Institut d'Action Française, 28 May 1929, in *Ecrits de combat I* (Gallimard, "Bibliothèque de la Pléiade"), p. 1169.
5. *Sept*, 31 July 1936, in *Bulletin de la Société des Amis de Georges Bernanos* 28–29, Christmas 1956.
6. See especially his campaign against "M. Alexandre," a Jewish businessman from Rouen, in *Ecrits de combat I*, pp. 930, 952.
7. Letter to Henry Coston, director of *La Libre Parole*, 29 April 1935, in *Courrier Georges-Bernanos* 8 (June 1972).
8. Georges Bernanos, *La grande peur des bien-pensants* in *Oeuvres de combat I*, pp. 328–29.
9. Georges Bernanos, "Encore la question juive," May 1944, reprinted in *Le chemin de la croix des âmes* (Gallimard), pp. 421–24.
10. Georges Bernanos, "Primauté de la peur," *L'Action Française*, 5 December 1929, in *Oeuvres de combat I*, p. 1183.
11. Georges Bernanos, *L'avant-garde de Normandie*, in *Oeuvres de combat I*, p. 966.
12. Variant of *Scandale*, in *La grande peur des bien-pensants* (Livre de Poche, 1969), p. 436.
13. Ibid.
14. *Bulletin de la Société des Amis de Georges-Bernanos* 47 (September-December 1962).
15. Georges Bernanos, *Nous autres Français*, in *Oeuvres de combat I*, p. 735.
16. Georges Bernanos, "Réflexions sur le cas de conscience français," 15 October 1943, in *Le chemin de la croix des âmes*, p. 91.
17. Georges Bernanos, article of February 1943, in *Le chemin de la croix des âmes*, pp. 148–49.
18. Georges Bernanos, "L'honneur est ce qui nous rassemble," *Français si vous saviez* (Gallimard, 1961), pp. 322–27.
19. Georges Bernanos, letter to Jean Hauser, *Correspondance* (Plon), 2: 546.
20. Bernanos, "Encore la question juive."
21. Georges Bernanos, *Lettre aux Anglais* (Gallimard, 1946), pp. 161–62.
22. Bernanos, "L'honneur est ce qui nous rassemble."
23. Ibid.
24. See Georges Bernanos, "Encyclique aux Français" (Winter 1947), in *La vocation spirituelle de la France*, unpublished writings presented and collected by Jean-Loup Bernanos (1975), p. 208.
25. See Léon Poliakov, *Le mythe aryen* (Calmann-Lévy, 1971).
26. See Léon Poliakov, *La causalité diabolique*.
27. See Maurice Montuclard, *Conscience religieuse et démocratie* (Seuil, 1965).

28. Bernanos, "Encyclique aux Français."

29. Edouard Drumont, *La fin d'un monde,* p. 171.

30. Edouard Drumont, *La Libre Parole,* 15 April 1895.

31. Bernanos, "Edouard Drumont."

32. Georges Bernanos, *La France contre les robots* (Livre de Poche, 1973), p. 228.

33. Bernanos, *Les chemins de la croix des âmes,* pp. 476–77.

34. Georges Bernanos, *La grande peur des biens-pensants,* in *Oeuvres de combat I,* pp. 133–34.

35. Ibid., p. 329.

36. Emmanuel Mounier, *Oeuvres* (Seuil, 1962), 3: 354.

37. Georges Bernanos, "A propos de l'antisémitisme de Drumont," variant of *Scandale.*

38. Ibid.

39. Popper, *The Open Society.*

40. Ibid., 1: 175.

41. Bernanos, *Le chemin de la croix des âmes,* p. 419.

42. Cited by Joseph Jurt, "*Les grands cimetières sous la lune* devant la presse non catholique en 1938," *Etudes Bernanosiennes* 13 (*La Revue des Lettres Modernes,* 1972, vol. 2).

43. Bernanos, *Scandale de la vérité,* in *Oeuvres de combat I,* p. 581.

44. I intentionally refer here only to the republican tradition, though I do not believe I am doing an injustice to Bernanos. As unsympathetic as he was toward the Dreyfusards, he nevertheless asserted: "There are thousands of French people who were Dreyfusians because they believed in the innocence of Dreyfus, refused to sacrifice an innocent man to *raison d'état.* For which I could not blame them." Georges Bernanos, *Nous autres Français,* in *Oeuvres de combat I,* p. 666.

45. Bernanos, *Scandale de la vérité,* p. 588.

CHAPTER 24

L'Histoire 102 (July–August 1987).

1. Cited by Jean Lacouture, *De Gaulle,* vol. 1: *Le rebelle* (Seuil, 1984), p. 258.

2. In particular, Roger Stéphane defended Gaullist theses in *France-Observateur,* where Claude Bourdet and Gilles Martinet expressed a leftist anti-Gaullism. Several articles published in that weekly in the months before 13 May reveal these divergences.

3. Jean-François Revel, *Le style du Général* (Julliard, 1960).

4. See Jean Charlot, *Les Français et de Gaulle,* presentation and comments on the IFOP polls (Plon, 1971).

5. François Mauriac, *Le dernier Bloc—Notes, 1968–1970* (Flammarion, 1971), dated 22 June 1968.

6. André Malraux, *Les chênes qu'on abat* (Gallimard, 1971), p. 175.

Index

In this index an "f" after a number indicates a separate reference on the next page, and an "ff" indicates separate references on the next two pages. A continuous discussion over two or more pages is indicated by a span of page numbers, e.g., "57–59." *Passim* is used for a cluster of references in close but not consecutive sequence.

Library of Congress Cataloging-in-Publication Data

Winock, Michel.
  [Nationalisme, antisémitisme et fascisme en France. English]
  Nationalism, anti-semitism, and fascism in France / Michel Winock ;
translated by Jane Marie Todd.
    p. cm.
  Includes bibliographical references and index.
  ISBN 0-8047-3286-8 (cloth : alk. paper). — ISBN 0-8047-3287-6
(pbk. : alk. paper)
    1. France—Politics and government—20th century. 2. Nationalism—
France. 3. Antisemitism—France. 4. Nationalists—France—Biography.
I. Title.
  DC369.W5613   1998
  944.081—dc21   98-11298
                                                          CIP

∞ This book is printed on acid-free, recycled paper.

Original printing 1998
Last figure below indicates year of this printing:
07 06 05 04 03 02 01 00 99 98